Automobile
Year

Automobile
year

No. 38   1990/91

Body. Style.

ASC — the international design, prototyping, engineering, manufacturing and marketing resource.

Europe • North America • Asia.

CONTENTS

Editor-in-chief: Jean-Rodolphe Piccard

Editor: David Hodges

Translator: Paul Treuthardt □ Layout: Lucette Boillat

Automobile Year is published in French under the title *l'année automobile* and in German under the title *Auto-Jahr*.

Published by EDITIONS JR, J.-R. PICCARD
Boulevard de Grancy 12
Tel. 41 21 617 88 00 Fax 41 21 617 88 54

Copyright © 1990 by EDITIONS JR, J.-R. PICCARD, Lausanne
Printed in Italy
ISBN 2-88324-012-4

Advertising sales: Pragmatic S.A.
Avenue de Saint-Paul 9
CH-1208 Genève
Tél. 41 22 736 68 06 Fax: 41 22 786 04 23

The Piston.

6

ACKNOWLEDGMENTS

The Publisher is grateful to the following photographers and organizations for the illustrations in this edition of *Automobile Year*:

2-3: P. Nygård — 23-25: M. Pfundner/General Motors Austria — 26-27: Romilly Lockyer/The Image Bank — 28-29: VAG UK Ltd — 30: P. Vann — 31: P. Vann — 32: J. Farenc — 33: W. Eisele — 34: Ford UK — 34-35: J. Lamm — 35: J. Lamm — 36: Renault — 36-37: P. Vann — 37: J. Farenc — 38-39: J. Lamm — 39: Fiat, Alfa-Lancia, Alfa-Lancia — 40: J. Lamm — 41: Ford France — 42-43: BMW, Volvo — 43. J. Farenc — 44: Audi, Italdesign — 45: PSA — 46: PSA, J.-P. Gosselin, PSA — 47: PSA, J.-P. Gosselin — 48: PSA — 49: PSA — 50: J.-P. Gosselin — 51: J.-P. Gosselin — 52: PSA, BMW, BMW, BMW, BMW, BMW — 53: PSA, Mercedes-Benz — 54: J.-P. Gosselin, Saab — 55: J.-R. Piccard — 56: J.-R. Piccard, J.-R. Piccard, J.-R. Piccard, J.-R. Piccard, Toyota Australia — 57-59: J.-R. Piccard — 60-61: GM Design Staff — 62: GM Design Staff — 62-63: GM Design Staff — 63: GM Design Staff — 64: GM Design Staff — 65: GM Design Staff — 66: Ford Motor Co. — 67: Ford Motor Co. — 68: Chrysler, Chrysler, General Motors, GM Design Staff — 69: Ford Motor Co. — 70: Chrysler — 71: Chrysler — 72-73: GM Design Staff — 73: GM Design Staff — 74: GM Design Staff — 74-75: GM Design Staff — 75: GM Design Staff — 76-77: Nissan — 78: P. Nunn — 78-79: P. Nunn — 79: P. Nunn — 80: P. Nunn — 81: P. Nunn — 82: P. Nunn — 83: Car Graphic — 84: P. Nunn, Suzuki — 85: P. Nunn — 86: Suzuki, Nissan — 86-87: J.-R. Piccard — 87: Mitsubishi — 88: Toyota, Honda — 89: Dentsu Inc. — 90-96: Dentsu Inc. — 97: *Automobile Year* archives — 98: Automotive News Service — 99: Automotive News Service — 100: Automotive News Service — 100-101: Automotive News Service — 101: Automotive News Service — 102: *Automobile Year* archives, Automotive News Service, *Automobile Year* archives, *Automobile Year* archives, *Automobile Year* archives — 102-103: *Automobile Year* archives — 103: *Automobile Year* archives, Automotive News Service — 104: J.-M. Pierret — 104-105: J.-M. Pierret — 106: Ford Australia — 107: GM-Holden, GM-Holden, Ford Australia, GM-Holden, GM-Holden, GM-Holden — 108: Toyota Australia, Toyota Australia, Mitsubishi Australia — 109: Nissan Australia — 110: P. Vann — 112: P. Vann — 113. P. Vann — 114-115: P. Vann — 115: P. Vann — 116: Mercedes-Benz, J.-P. Gosselin — 117: PSA, Stern/Dr. Gebhardt — 118: General Motors, J.-P. Gosselin — 119: General Motors — 120: General Motors — 121: I.DE.A. — 122: J. Farenc — 123: I.DE.A. — 124: I.DE.A. — 125: I.DE.A. — 126: I.DE.A., J. Farenc, J. Farenc, J. Farenc, I.DE.A. — 126-127: J. Farenc — 127: J. Farenc, I.DE.A. — 128: Fiat — 129-135: N. Bruce Photographic — 136: P. Vann — 137: P. Vann — 138: P. Vann — 139: Italdesign — 140: N. Bruce Photographic — 141: PSA, Rover, Honda — 142: VW, Porsche, Audi, General Motors Europe, Daimler-Benz, Mercedes-Benz — 143: BMW, Citroën, Renault, Fiat, Fiat — 144-145: S. Domenjoz — 146-147: F. Kräling — 147: G. Berthoud, F. Kräling — 148: F. Kräling, P. Nygård — 148-149: Photo 4 — 149: Photo 4 — 150: P. Nygård, D. Reinhard — 151: S. Domenjoz, Photo 4 — 152-153: D. Reinhard — 153: Photo 4, D. Reinhard, D. Reinhard — 154: Photo 4, Photo 4, Vandystadt — 155: S. Domenjoz, G. Dawkins — 156: ARC, ARC — 156-157: G. Berthoud — 157: E. Strähle — 158: ARC, ARC, ARC, ARC, ARC — 158-159: ARC, ARC — 158: K. Kräling — 159: P. Nygård, ARC — 160: S. Domenjoz, ARC — 161: ARC, D. Reinhard, S. Domenjoz — 162: ARC, Photo 4, P. Nygård — 162-163: Photo 4 — 163: ARC — 164: ARC, F. Kräling — 164-165: F. Kräling, D. Reinhard — 165: Berthoud — 166: G. Berthoud — 166-167: ARC — 167: G. Berthoud — 168: ARC, ARC — 169: S. Domenjoz, ARC, J. Overton — 170: ARC, G. Berthoud — 171: F. Kräling, ARC, S. Domenjoz — 172: G. Berthoud, ARC, G. Berthoud — 173: S. Domenjoz, ARC, S. Domenjoz, S. Domenjoz, S. Domenjoz — 174: Words & Pictures/B. Williams — 174-175: Photo 4 — 175: ARC, G. Berthoud — 176: P. Nygård, S. Domenjoz, S. Domenjoz — 177: G. Berthoud, ARC, S. Domenjoz, ARC — 178-179: G. Berthoud — 180: G. Berthoud — 180-181: F. Kräling — 182-183: ARC, F. Kräling — 183: ARC, A. Marzoli, ARC — 184: A. Marzoli, D. J. Cundy, Photo 4 — 185: W. H. Murenbeeld — 186: F. Kräling, Photo 4 — 186-187: Photo 4 — 187: J. Overton — 188: R. Miller, Photo 4 — 188-189: J. Potiker — 189: R. Miller, M. C. Brown — 190: G. Dawkins — 191: R. Miller, R. Miller, R. Miller — 192: ARC, J.-L. Taillade, ARC — 193: J. Overton — 194: J. Overton, J. Overton — 195: W. Eisele, Porsche AG — 196: Porsche AG — 197: Porsche AG — 198: Porsche AG, G. Berthoud, Porsche AG — 199: A. Marzoli — 200-202: A. Marzoli — 202-203: F. Kräling, D. Leroy — 204: J.-P. Decuypère — 204-205: M. Holmes — 205: A. Marzoli, A. Marzoli, A. Marzoli — 206: A. Marzoli — 206-207: A. Marzoli — 207: A. Marzoli, A. Marzoli — 208: A. Marzoli — 208-209: A. Marzoli, F. Kräling — 209: A. Marzoli — 210: A. Marzoli — 211: A. Marzoli, F. Kräling — 212: A. Marzoli — 212-213: M. Holmes, A. Marzoli — 213: A. Marzoli — 214: A. Marzoli, A. Marzoli, A. Marzoli — 214-215: P. Nygård — 215: A. Marzoli — 216: A. Marzoli — 217-219: A. Marzoli — 220-225: A. Marzoli — 226-227: Photo 4 — 227: M. C. Brown — 228-229: Photo 4 — 229: M. C. Brown, R. Miller, M. C. Brown — 230: Photo 4 — 230-231: Photo 4 — 232: Photo 4 — 233: Photo 4 — 234-235: F. Mormillo, Photo 4 — 235: R. Miller, M. C. Brown — : J. J. Jiran, R. Miller — 237: J. J. Jiran — 238: F. Mormillo — 239: F. Mormillo — 240: M. C. Brown, R. Miller — 241: ARC, D. J. Cundy — 242-243: J.-L. Taillade — 242: ARC — 243: J.-L. Taillade — 244-245: J.-L. Taillade, J.-L. Taillade — 245: Photo 4 — 246: Photo 4, ARC, Photo 4 — 247: Photo 4 — 248: Photo 4, G. Dawkins, J.-L. Taillade — 249: S. Domenjoz.

"All Clear for Light-Speed Listening."

● *BLAUPUNKT*

Bosch Telecom

It's a small point. But it makes a world of difference.

The München SCD 09 remembers what you like. It has a memory for 36 radio stations and 192 CD titles – Track-Program-Memory. It can store, for instance, the six radio stations with the most powerful transmitters in your area. Or your very personal selection of twelve different CDs.

Ready to play at the touch of a button.

The cartridge system keeps the CD well protected, even outside the player, and ensures that it's safe and easy to use. Right in the car. To give you the pure sound of digital laser technology, so you can hear its best side.

Your specialized dealer would be pleased to show you the extraordinary capabilities of the new München SCD 09. For information contact the Blaupunkt-Werke GmbH, Dept. VWB, Postfach, 3200 Hildesheim, West Germany, Btx-Leitseite ∗30396#.

Don't get any closer unless you seriously want to fall in love.

As you can see, the MX-5 is a sports car, conceived and engineered without compromise.

Touch the accelerator and you move, very, very quickly.

Flick your wrist and the gear change is positively orchestral.

In motoring's long history, very few cars have been created with such dedication to oneness between driver and machine.

The MX-5 is the breathtaking product of a philosophy referred to by the Mazda design team as Kansei, a true understanding of which can only be achieved behind the wheel.

It isn't power alone: 16 valves, double overhead camshaft, in line 1.6 litre, 4 cylinder engine.

Or ride: a rigid frame, double wishbone assembly, giving feel when you need it and comfort when you don't.

It's the spirit: in part emanating from the gleaming exterior of this beautiful two seater, but more importantly coming from somewhere deep within.

Beware.

The MX-5 is going to get you.

STYLE & QUALITÉ UN CONCEPT DE PROGRÈS

S.A. FRANCE DESIGN HENRI HEULIEZ - 79140 LE PIN FRANCE - TÉL. 49 81 33 11 - FAX 49 81 04 75

You turn the ignition key. The finely tuned Marelli-Microplex ignition starts the engine. A first strong impression arises. You can hear what distinguishes the new 16-valve engine despite its great power: its outstanding quiet running quality. You touch the gas pedal lightly and drive away. Feel the progressive power output of the 2-litre turbo engine, the rapid reaction behaviour. You push the pedal all the way to the floor, freeing the full thrust power of the turbo and the 16 valves. 177 hp. You experience the safe and comfortable feeling of power steering, single-wheel suspension, ABS, rally-proven technology and – upon request – electronically controlled suspension. After a test ride you will take a dis-believing look at the newly styled exterior and interior of the new Lancia Thema Turbo 16v. And you will wonder how it is possible to get away from it all so elegantly and so fast.

Now at your Lancia dealer's.

Detailed Thema data: 1994 ccm engine, 130 kW (177 hp), 222 kph. Electronic fuel injection Bosch LU2-Jetronic, turbo compressor, charge cooling, two-stage overboost system, opposite balancer shafts. The new 16-valve turbo technology, also to be found in the new Thema station wagon Turbo 16v.

H.S.G&L

6-year anti-corrosion guarantee.
Advantageous financing and leasing through Fiat Kredit AG.

LANCIA THEMA

THE NEW TEMPRA. WITH 83 KW/113 HP OR 57 KW/78 HP. BEST CD IN ITS CLASS (0,28). ANTI-DIVE BRAKE SYSTEM

532 KM ALREADY COVERED.

2 LITRES UNDER THE BONNET.

2 BAGS IN THE BOOT.

113 HORSES UNDER YOUR RIGHT FOOT

ONE THOUGHT IN MIND.

RUST PROTECTION FOR ALL EXPOSED BODY COMPONENTS. 500 DM³ BOOT CAPACITY. AT YOUR FIAT DEALER NOW.

ACTION
FIAT TEMPRA

Less Work, More Enjoyment.

Tension can be a good thing in moderate amounts. In fact, for safe driving, it's absolutely essential, translating as driver alertness. But just where does tension stop being alertness and become discomfort, and then fatigue?

Mitsubishi Motors, in designing the Galant, spent hours on that question, using the latest technology to measure drivers' physical reactions to various aspects of driving. One such aspect is the way driving, particularly cornering and lane-changing, requires constant steering adjustments. This results in added stress for the driver. The Galant's 4-wheel steering and Electronic Control Suspension take some of this pressure off the driver by actively controlling vehicle

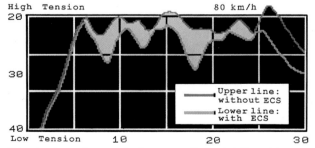

Driver tension under cornering is measured by level of skin resistance. With ECS, higher skin resistance shows lower levels of tension in the driver.

attitude. With less work, the driver can get more enjoyment from driving.

As far as Mitsubishi are concerned, human engineering is much more than a catchy phrase. It is a practical way to make cars more useful and more appealing to people.

MITSUBISHI
MOTORS

MITSUBISHI GALANT

Come to
Marlboro Country.

The number one selling cigarette in the world.

► No one has an exclusive hold on technological progress today: these days, all the serious automobile manufacturers are versed in electronics, engine construction and harmonising suspensions. This means that the way in which a manufacturer applies this technology has become all the more important.

► For instance, one approach is to equip the dashboard with flashing knobs and displays, making it resemble an aeroplane cockpit. Or you provide the driver with unlimited possibilities for tinkering with the car's suspension. A task that Formula 1 drivers frequently despair at. Others resort to the wind canal in an attempt to find what they consider to be the face and character of an automobile.

► At Mercedes-Benz, technology is never used simply for its own sake – at Mercedes-Benz, progress is associated with such terms as common sense and responsibility. And so it is that our engineers do not only have the courage and the capabilities to construct an avant-garde product such as the Mercedes World Championship sports car. They also have enough responsibility to wait before mass-producing fourvalve motors until they are

No unsigh

(Unless you

ly roll bar.

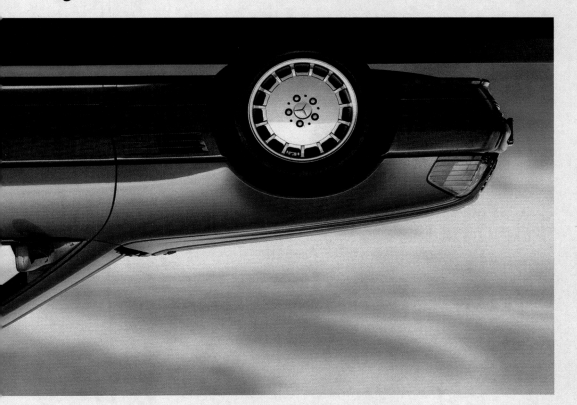

turn it over.)

convinced that these yield the desired added performance for low-rev driving in the city.

▶ Or take the SL. A car which in the public eye is frequently considered to be a "technological wonder" or a "super sports car". Yet, for all their excitement, our engineers did not permit this car to be released until it was not only the most advanced convertible in the world but also presumably the safest.

▶ To this end they invented the roll bar which is only seen when it is needed. And when it really is needed, it's there in a flash: in less than 0.3 seconds it pops up the very moment sensors and microprocessors report that the car is in a critical situation.

▶ When it comes to remaining at the technological forefront, our engineers are every bit as ingenious as any others. Yet, they are not merely concerned with being technological Number One. They are motivated equally by a sense of responsibility towards you. Have a good drive.

Mercedes-Benz
Ihr guter Stern auf allen Straßen.

F O R M A   foto G. Bellia

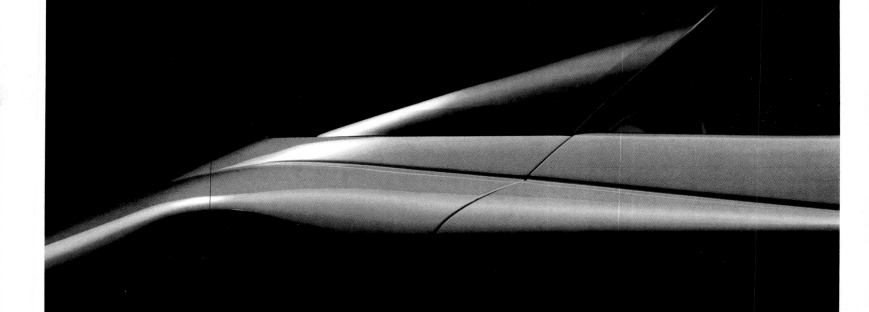

pininfarina

MERGERS AND CO-OPERATIONS

Martin Pfundner

The never-ending tale of new mergers and cooperation within the world-wide automotive industry is recorded in the economic pages of major newspapers. The reasons behind these developments range from the Japanese threat, the influence of micro-electronics, the rising research and development costs, the need for globalisation to balance political, economic and, above all, monetary risks, to the advent of 1992 and the collapse of the Soviet system of satellite states. All these factors and more have come into play to steer the industry in certain directions.

"What are the directions, and what are the changes over a longer period of time" — this is the kind of question an annual publication like *Automobile Year* should try to answer. Perhaps it serves a useful purpose to study the automotive "cosmography" of 1969, and to compare it with the 1989 situation, and take a final look at the 1990 changes before trying to assess what has happened.

In 1969, just over 20 years ago, the world automotive industry produced just over 23 million cars, and there were ten major corporations with an output exceeding half a million units. In the United States, then as now, there were the two "super powers", General Motors and Ford. The third among the "Big Three", Chrysler, had just taken over Simca and the Rootes Group in Europe. The resulting indigestion aggravated its relative weak position and led to the Chrysler crisis. In Europe, Volkswagen, Fiat, Renault, Peugeot and British Leyland were the members of the "Club of Ten", while in Japan only Toyota and Nissan/Datsun had "made it".

Apart from these, there was a multitude of small and medium-sized companies retaining complete independence, and no fewer than 15 of these reported an annual output of between 100 000 and half a million units.

Compare this with the "cosmic" map of 1989. For the record, global production had risen to 35.5 million cars, an increase of 55 per cent. The number of majors had increased from 10 to 16, more or less in line with the overall increase. The "super powers", GM and Ford, were more or less stagnant, although they had drawn quite a number of new satellites into their orbit, through take-overs or substantial acquisitions of shares. The Japanese, of course, were closing in, and Honda, Mazda as well as Mitsubishi had joined Toyota and Nissan as members of the Club. In Europe, both Mercedes and BMW entered the Big Time, together with VAZ/Lada as the first and only member from the Soviet sphere of influence. It is worth recording that Hyundai (South Korea) also exceeded the half-million mark and became eligible for membership. British Leyland had left — that was a sad story of an exploded planet.

Two members of the new "Club of 16" can hardly be termed "sovereign" corporations, in view of their strong links with other giants: Mazda is part-owned (25 per cent) by Ford, whilst Hyundai is dependent on Mitsubishi.

Leaving out the East European "nebulae" on one fringe of the cosmic map for the moment, a picture very different from 1969 begins to emerge. The universe between the big "planets" with their large number of "moons" is becoming very, very empty. There are few independent companies left. By the end of 1989, there were only four "singles" left: BMW (the smallest Club member), Subaru (mid-sized), and the two dwarfs, Porsche and Rolls-Royce. Mercedes, incidentally, cannot be rated as a "single" because of the sheer size and weight of the Daimler-Benz group of companies. Nevertheless, the agreement with Mitsubishi, a major 1990 event, signals the possible advent of a new industrial super power, albeit only partially automotive. Also, during 1990, Subaru's dependence on Nissan increased

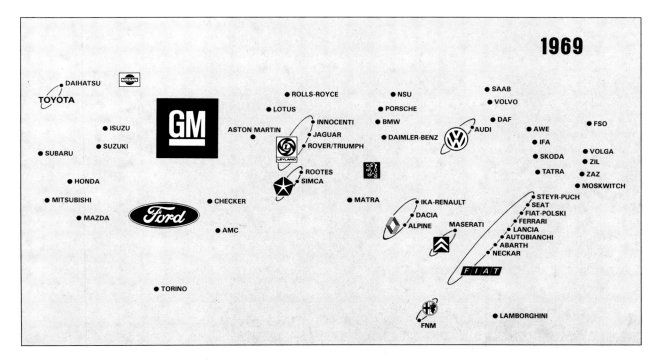

1969

The automotive cosmography of 1969 (world-wide production 23 million cars) shows the members of the "Club of Ten" with an output in excess of half a million units, plus a large number of small and medium-sized independent companies. No fewer than 15 of those "independents" had a production volume between 100 000 and half a million vehicles.

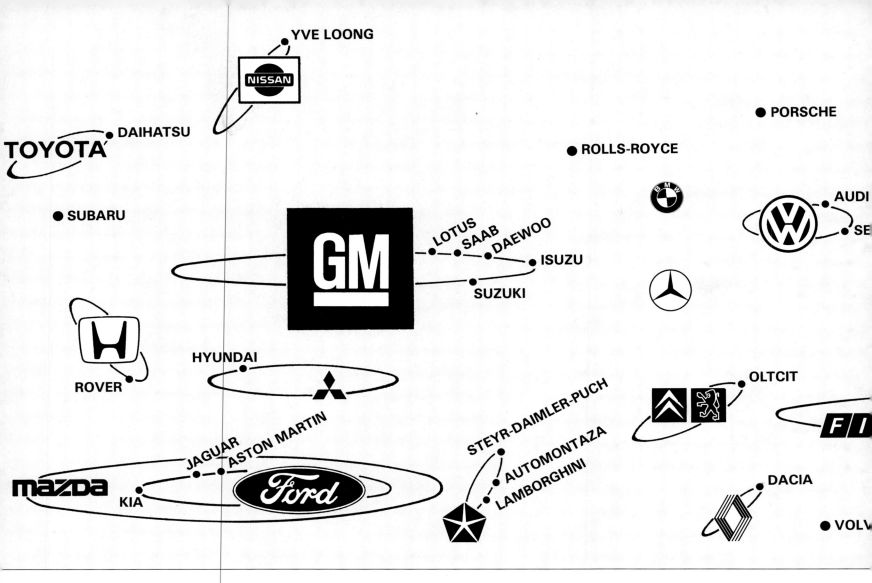

In 1989 (right and opposite, top), world production had risen to 35.5 million units, and there were 16 "Club Members" instead of only ten. The British Leyland planet was the only one to disappear. However, between the huge planets, the space is almost empty: the independents have all but disappeared. It is only on the right-hand fringe of the map that certain "nebulae" still exist. They represent the Comecon countries.

significantly, for example in the appointment of the new Subaru chief executive. Rolls-Royce is part of the Vickers group.

Thus, by the end of 1990, only three "independents" are left. Even actual or reputed mid-sized companies like Saab, Daewoo, Isuzu, and Suzuki (part-owned by GM), Jaguar and Kia (Ford), or Volvo (co-operating with Renault) are no longer "sovereign", and the famous Italian makes (Ferrari, Lancia, Alfa Romeo, and Maserati) are orbiting round Fiat.

For the enthusiast, there is some consolation in this. When famous makes lost their independence, they used to disappear. This no longer happens. The "Big Ones" gobble them up eagerly, allowing them almost autonomous status in some cases (for example, Lotus with GM, Aston Martin with Ford), or at least survival as prestigious brand names.

In East Europe, what started with a strong migration of East German refugees to the Federal Republic via Hungary in late 1989 brought down the entire political and economic system of Soviet satellite states. As one after the other East European countries swung to the system of Western democracy and more or less free-market economy, the economic system of "Real Socialism" and Comecon appeared to be heading for receivership. This was particularly manifest in the East's motor industry. Despite the fact that East European car production (including the Soviet Union) surpassed the two million mark, the Communist system somehow failed (with one exception) to master the transition to a new generation of fuel saving and environmentally compatible models and modern manufacturing methods without the aid of the West.

As the bloodless revolution gathered momentum, a new wave of migration started, this time affecting top management from the motor industry, East and West alike. Everyone talked to everybody, and a number of joint ventures between East and West reached the letter-of-intent stage surprisingly quickly. In East Germany, Volkswagen took control of the IFA works at Zwickau, a former Auto-Union plant where the Trabant symbol of East German mediocrity was built. GM/Opel countered with an agreement affecting AWE at Eisenach (BMW in pre-war days), where the Wartburg was manufactured. Vectra production has started there, and plans for an annual output of 150 000 Opel Kadetts are being studied in detail. The commercial vehicles section of IFA appears to think in terms of Mercedes...

In Hungary, where the process of liberalization had set in earlier than elsewhere, Suzuki and the Japanese trading house, C. Itoh, quickly reached the letter-of-intent stage for the assembly of the Swift, although the project seemed to become bogged down. In contrast General Motors set up a company with its Hungarian partner Raba (makers of trucks and buses) to build 20 000 engines and assemble 15 000 Opel Kadetts at Szentgotthard near the Austrian border. Ford are setting up a component plant west of Budapest.

In Czechoslovakia, things have progressed very much more slowly. Although the counry's industry is probably the most advanced of any Comecon country, legislation to permit joint ventures on a sound basis is slow in coming. The Czechs were under a stricter regime than the Hungarians, but it seems that the subsequent left-wing government still thinks in terms of a "guided market economy" as pronounced by Ota Sik and his disciples. Nevertheless, Skoda is deeply involved in negotiations with both Volkswagen and Renault/Volvo, and have even enlisted the help of Price Waterhouse to formulate possible ways of cooperation. GM, together with

1989

● AWE

● GAZ

● IFA   ● AZLK
              ● ZIL
       ● UAZ

● SKODA
     ● TATRA

              ● ZAZ

LANCIA FERRARI ALFA ROMEO MASERATI
● ─ ● ─ ● ─────── ● ─── INNOCENTI
                    ●
● ─── ● ─── ● ───
FSO/FSM ZASTAVA

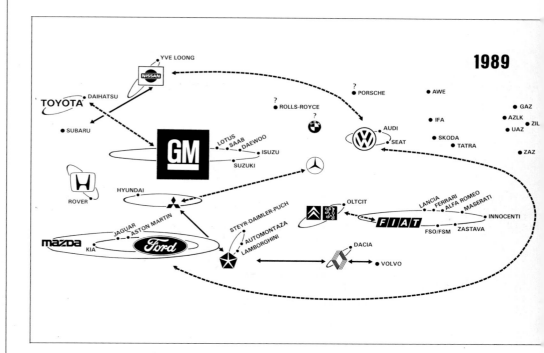

1989

the government, is studying possibilities for a gearbox plant in the country, and three minor manufacturers of commercial vehicles are hoping to survive through cooperation with the West...

In Poland, both FSO and FSM will continue their licensing arrangement with Fiat, Daihatsu having failed to establish a presence in the country. It now very much looks as if Fiat will soon have the ultimate word at Kragujevac (Yugoslavia). The Italians are no longer happy with their minority share in Yugo.

French companies, Renault (with Dacia) and Citroen (with Oltcit, at Craiova) dominate the Romanian market through their licensing agreements, yet Citroen is rumoured to be less than pleased with its 36 per cent share in the company. Balkancars in Bulgaria assembled Russian cars but feelers have been extended to Rover for a possible Maestro assembly agreement. The former satellite states, it seems, will soon be well integrated into the automotive compound of the West.

In the Soviet Union, on the other hand, the story is entirely different. Only Fiat has a firm contract, to build a new Tipo plant at Yelabuga, East of Kazan, for an initial 300 000 units, production to be doubled or tripled if and when... General Motors will supply ignition and fuel injection systems for VAZ at Togliatti, where Lada and Samara are being built, to the tune of $1 billion over a five year period. All the other Soviet manufacturers, GAZ at Gorki (where the outdated Volga is built), ZAZ at Zaporoshje (where a new Soviet-designed mini car is slow off the mark), AZLK at Moscow (Moskvich and the fwd Aleko) do not yet seem able to conclude deals with the West although these are badly needed. Virtually every Western corporation has been mentioned as a possible partner at one time or the other, but it very much looks as if the Soviet Union will remain unexplored

on the automotive map as a viable business proposition. Over the past twenty years or so, most independent manufacturers had to give up or seek refuge with one of the giants. Among the latter, there are only about a dozen huge corporations able to shoulder the cost and the risk to develop, produce and market a complete range of volume models. It is impressive to see how a number of Japanese companies made it into the exclusive Club whilst so many others fell by the wayside. Even so, the process of concentration has not yet ended, and there are still a few doubtfuls among the majors. Consequently, take-overs from now on will be fewer.

But even the "sovereign" majors are forced to cooperate with their arch-rivals, albeit for certain specific projects (engines or other components) or in a geographically limited area, like the Autolatina company, the VW/Ford joint venture to handle the tricky Brazilian market. A dense network of cooperation, joint participation and financial deals between rival corporations is so complex that it is virtually impossible to illustrate it graphically. It is in precisely this area that more and more cooperative arrangements will be concluded in the future, in order for companies to remain competitive — and to survive.

This focus on the East European "nebulae" shows the East European and Soviet motor manufacturers as they were before the Berlin Wall crumbled. The arrows indicate the rapidity of change in the former satellite countries where a number of joint ventures are being negotiated. However, in the Soviet Union no sign of definite change can be detected, although Fiat have signed a contract to build a new Tipo plant at Yelabuga, East of Kazan.

25

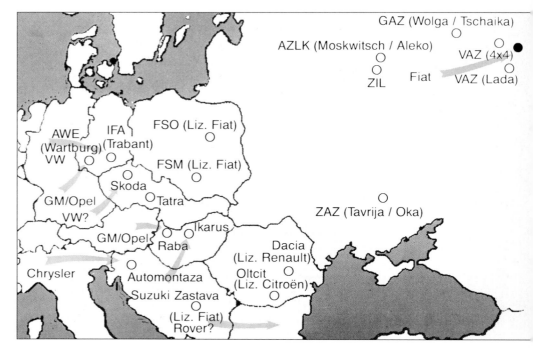

After a period of crisis due to a dramatic lack of productivity, the European automotive industry seemed to be flourishing again, as was shown by total profits for the six major manufacturers of nearly $11 billion in 1989, 7 per cent up on 1988, but then 1990 saw a sombre down turn.

In 1989, 13 325 000 cars were built in western Europe (plus 2.4 million in the Eastern bloc including the Soviet Union). Western Europe thus accounted for 37.4% of world production, or 44% including the East European manufacturers, and volume was up 6.4% on the 1988 figure. The increase worldwide was only 3.2% on production of 35.6 million vehicles.

Taking only cars into consideration, the relative production shares were 25.6% for Japan (up 8%), and 19.3% for the United States (down 4%). West Germany, with 12.9% of the total, remains the leader in Europe, followed by France (7.9%) and Italy (5.8%), while Spain (4.9%) confirmed its fourth place in the hierarchy, with its output up 12%.

The calculation will be more difficult in the future due to the Euro-Japanese vehicles such as the Nissan Bluebird/Primera/Patrol and the Santana-Suzuki (output reached 300 000 units in 1989 including the 4x4 version). Production of these vehicles is likely to approach 800 000 units in 1992/93 and to exceed a million around 1995/97. And there are more to come, with Mazda, Honda and others setting up real European-scale operations.

Based on the figures for the first half of the year, the automotive sales market in Western Europe 1990 was expected to remain stable, at around 13.5 million units, reaching nearly 15 million units if various commercial versions and light vans are included.

The Volkswagen group, with 15.2% of the market, and Fiat (14.9%) were then neck and neck for the Number One position in Europe, but the outcome depends on how the figures are interpreted. With only the Common Market nations considered, Fiat led with 15.8%, but counting the small utility vehicles and including all of Western Europe, on the face of it the two giants were almost equal with 14.5% of the market. However, by the summer Fiat had very large stocks of unsold cars as its domestic market slumped.

Despite arguments that are sometimes fierce, about tax advantages which do not conform to Common Market rules, the problem of reducing pollution from petrol-driven vehicles has been settled as far as legislation is concerned.

But the diesel question has taken its place, despite the fact that diesel is far more efficient in converting energy. Publicity over the problem caused a sharp drop in sales of diesel cars in 1989, with 1 852 000 sales representing 13.8% of European registrations. Sales were seriously depressed in two of the major markets, West Germany (down 24%) and Italy (down 30%). France, with Peugeot and Renault respectively first and second largest producers of diesel engines in the world, became the largest European (and thus world) market with 680 000 sales, 30% of all diesel registrations. There are widespread questions about the future of the diesel engine, which was not considered "clean" until very recently, but while Raymond Levy of Renault has postponed all industrial investment, PSA continued to drive forward and Jacques Calvet said he is ready to sell turbocharged and multi-valve diesel engines to anyone who wants them, even the Japanese.

The Japanese and Americans have tended to neglect the diesel in private cars, and making them illegal (in whatever manner) would statistically knock out somewhat more than 15% of the European industry's capacity. That may be a cynical view of a worldwide battle in the automobile industry, but it is an interesting thought.

USA: a confluence of conflicts

Never before have so many critical issues been threatening to turn the US new car market — and the industry — inside out.

By any account, new car sales are likely to tumble again in 1991, but as the new model-year opens, it was anyone's guess just how badly the US economy would sag. With oil prices racing heavenward, a serious recession was then seen as a distinct possibility. Combine that with tight interest rates, and the sales slide of 1990 could turn into the rout of 1991.

That, in turn, will put further pressure on the car makers to increase their already large incentives. The Ford Motor Company was spending over $1100 a car on rebates in mid-1990, twice as much as it did just a year earlier. And as a result, profit margins could collapse at a time when spending on new products and technology is running at a record high.

As if that is not trouble enough, federal lawmakers are again getting into the act, and in the months to come, the auto industry could be saddled with some of the toughest new regulations since the mid-1970s.

Just consider the homework assignments car makers, both domestic and importers, are likely to face in the very near future:

— The crisis in the Middle East is likely to lead to an increase in the federal government's automotive fuel economy standards. One proposal would boost the current standard by almost 50 per cent;

— Pressure from consumers as well as tougher govern-

SHADOWS OVER THE INDUSTRY

Paul Eisenstein, Peter Nunn, Jacques Farenc

ment regulations will call for marked improvements in vehicle safety;
— A new federal Clean Air law will force sharp reductions in exhaust emissions.

Meanwhile, California's own so-called "Super Green" proposal would go one step further, essentially mandating zero emissions by the end of the 1990s, thus effectively outlawing the gasoline engine.

It is not the first time the auto industry has faced a list of conflicting demands. In the late 1970s and early 1980s, in the wake of two oil crises, car makers had to boost fuel economy, and also meet the requirements of the original Clean Air Act.

The result was a generation of products derided by critics as "stone ponies," and auto industry leaders are quick to argue that American motorists simply will not put up with small, slow cars.

This is not the first time Detroit has sounded a note of panic. As far back as the mid-1970s, the car makers insisted they would never be able to meet the original CAFE and Clean Air standards. As recently as 1987, they were still threatening to chose big car plants if the government enforced the current 27.5 miles-per-gallon standard.

And as a result, Detroit's warnings have not been well-received on Capitol Hill during the latest round of hearings.

"When I'm testifying before Congress and telling them we don't know how to do this or that, they throw back at me the fact that we've said that before," admits Dr. Klimisch.

As a result, Detroit — and the imports — are not likely to be able to head off a round of tough new regulations.

Japan: global expansion

Now, more than ever, globalisation is the watchword for Japan Inc., with Europe, set to become the world's largest and most lucrative single market after 1992, a main contender for attention.

Toyota, Nissan and Honda, Japan's leading car makers, have already laid down their strategies for European production in the 1990s, using Britain as a base. But as these words are written, Mazda and Mitsubishi, the nation's other two major producers, have still to formalise agreements. The smaller fry — Subaru, Suzuki, Daihatsu and Isuzu — are in the same position,

although behind the scenes, the negotiations go on. The Japanese are determined not to be left behind in the fiercely competitive EC market place that will come into being at the start of 1993. However, how and to what degree they will be allowed to participate remains controversial.

It now seems likely a transitory period of continued sales restraint will follow the setting up of the post-1992 unified EC market when supposedly all limits should be lifted. And yet question marks remain as to the length of the period, whether transplant-produced cars should be included in the overall quota, the level of local content that defines "an EC-produced" car and so on.

Another sensitive issue has Honda the first of the Japanese to propose marketing US-produced cars in Europe, thus potentially swelling the influx of Japanese-badged cars in Europe to even greater volumes. The full effects of this may take some while to be felt, as all the Japanese may not be willing or able to follow Honda's bold initiative.

Nonetheless, it provides another telling demonstration of Japan's increasingly sophisticated policy of globalisation, in which definitions of a car's nationality are becoming ever more blurred. The components industry should not be overlooked, exemplified in 1990 as air-conditioning manufacturer Sanden set up its European HQ in Britain.

The liberalisation of East Germany is also providing the Japanese with food for thought. The major players have already made plans for a fresh sales assault in this large under-developed market, but so far have stopped short of local production. Nearby, however, Suzuki has signed a deal to initiate car production in Hungary, while Daihatsu continues to eye Poland.

The Japanese onslaught in North America continues unabated. Not only was 1989's best-selling car the Honda Accord, the Japanese continue to fill the top places in the much-quoted Customer Satisfaction Index reports. On the face of it, it seems they can do little wrong.

Although Japanese exports to the US continue to decline, revenues from these and other foreign car sales are rising steadily because quotas are instead being filled by sales of fully-equipped, upscale models like Lexus and Infiniti as opposed to those of less expensive cars, which are now increasingly being locally produced.

In the US, Japanese transplant production continues to accelerate, as does the Japanese penetration of the overall market, even though Japan's "Voluntary Restraint" figure of 2.3 million units remained unchanged (and also unfulfilled), just as in 1989. Analysts now feel a Japanese 30 per cent share of the US car market cannot be far off. At home, the leading producers continue to profit in a buoyant market that expanded 8 per cent to achieve sales of 7 256 704 units in 1989. A similar rise is predicted for 1990, thanks to a seemingly never-ending stream of high quality new Japanese cars appearing in the showrooms (such as the Honda NSX, Toyota Previa and Nissan Primera, to name but three), backed up by yet another record year of import sales.

With 350 cars for every 1000 inhabitants, Western Europe already has a total of 130 million vehicles, which is set to increase to 150 million in 1995. With private car sales of 15 million expected by 1995, Europe is already the world's largest market, but it is far from saturated and produces 37% of the world's cars. According to Martin Bangemann, the European Commissioner for Competition handling the automotive industry, it has never been in a healthier position in Europe: "It produced more than $10 billion profits in 1988, and some $25 billion more if the equipment and

the private hunting ground of particular or local interests." He supports the idea of free competition and flexible barriers: not cartels on the European side and transition periods for the Japanese when the Market is unified in 1993.

The committee known as the CCMC, grouping the "truly European" manufacturers, has developed into a real lobby aimed at slowing to the maximum, by all means possible, the establishment of Japanese manufacturers in Europe. It opposes "screwdriver" factories which assemble components made in Japan and seeks a com-

This photograph symbolizes the automotive gulf at the time of the greatest political event of recent years, the opening of Eastern Europe to liberal economics and freedom of thought.
Half a century separates the concepts behind these two cars — an Audi V8 and a Trabant — in front of what was Europe's Wall of Shame. In less than ten years Western manufacturers, notably the Volkswagen group, will bring East Germany's industry up to date. The potential East European market, in Western terms of 350 cars per 1 000 inhabitants, is some 12 million new vehicles.

28

accessory industries are taken into account. 1989 was better, and forecasts for 1990 are quite optimistic." (This statement was made before the Gulf crisis — ed.).

But behind this success story there is an urgent contest between manufacturers needing to establish alliances, and above all a fundamental disagreement over the presence of the Japanese constructors in Europe. The Japanese are accused of refusing to practice honest and true free trade.

Bangemann personally rejects the idea of "Fortress Europe", saying "the great European market cannot be

mitment that 80% of the sale price value of a vehicle will be represented by European-sourced parts.

The Japanese question was the major automotive battle in Brussels in 1990, with the tendency towards a liberalisation of import quotas in 1993, but under supervision for five to seven years. A major problem was, however, left unsolved: should cars of Japanese marques assembled in Europe or the United States be counted towards the quotas? It may be a long time before it is resolved, given that such a good "European" car as an Opel Kadett diesel has an Isuzu engine and a Daewoo gearbox.

WHAT OF EUROPE IN 1993?

Jacques Farenc

In April 1990, a milestone was passed, little noticed — 1000 days to the theoretical total abolition of all the barriers between the 12 nations of the European Community, an economic bloc of 320 million consumers. The New Europe presents a formidable challenge for the constructors battling in a market which is already rich but not saturated. Developments in 1990 also opened the prospect of 135 million consumers to be won over in the East European nations.

manufacturers: "They should not stay nervously locked inside their captive national markets. And they should not count on the European Commission in Brussels to support the current jigsaw market pattern."

There is cause for his concern. With the opening of the market in sight, some constructors are fighting hard to maintain the leadership of their domestic markets, and maintaining the highest possible prices in order to reap the maximum possible profits before 1993. The 1989 figures for the ratio of domestic to total EEC sales show that Fiat sales in Italy was 70% of its production despite a falling volume on its home market (Lancia's was 81.5%), Mercedes 67% in West Germany, and Rover 78% in Britain. The most "outward looking" companies among the majors were the VW-Audi group (50%), BMW (55%), Renault (40%) and PSA Peugeot-Citroën (46%). In fact, the most 'European' companies are the American-European. For example, GM makes only 35% of its sales in West Germany and Ford 41% in Britain, while Seat is obliged to rely on exports, with only 37% of its output going to its domestic market.

Leaders of the automobile industry protest loudly against the abnormal difference in automobile taxes imposed by various governments inside the EEC. But a closer look shows that the manufacturers change the pre-tax prices of their products considerably, certainly with an eye on these taxes and to keep the after-tax price moderate, but also because of technical policies or political protection. A study conducted by the BEUC (European Bureau of Consumer Unions) compares 24 widely-sold models with their average pre-tax price established in ECUs (the Community's monetary unit) and set to a base of 100 for the country where each model is the cheapest. In 1987, the spread ranged from 100 in Denmark to 143.5 in Britain. In 1989, when the price spread should have been considerably reduced by the development of the harmonisation of tax structures, it had in fact increased. Between Denmark, with its outrageous taxes on cars, and Britain, where the market is restricted by right-hand drive, it was 100 to 161.

The BEUC has also protested about manufacturers who, pleading the need to vary models for the particular wishes of customers in various countries, list very different models for different markets. The organisation claims this policy is deliberately aimed at making it increasingly difficult for clients who want to buy a car wherever it is cheapest, along with such ploys as excessive delay inproviding the necessary papers for Type Approval or refusal to honour guarantees.

Proponents of real free trade inside the Market see the whole situation as totally chaotic, for which the constructors, hiding behind a lack of harmonisation — notably of legal technical specifications — bear most of the responsibility. And Japanese manufacturers are prepared to offer buyers the choice that might be denied them by these activities.

The only conclusion which can be drawn from this situation is that the real Europe, that of a great unified market, is still far from being achieved.

Before the end of the decade, more than a million Euro-Japanese cars will be assembled in Europe by Nissan, Honda, Suzuki and later Toyota, and most probably Mitsubishi. They will add to an already spectacular over-capacity situation. According to Harold Poling, Chairman of the Ford Motor Company, there will be excess production capacity of 8 million vehicles worldwide in 1995, of which 2.2 million will be in Europe, where he believes 10% of plant is already obsolete. Bangemann is also worried by what he sees as a range of rather unorthodox procedures by the major European

Italdesign, despite a necessary diversification towards industrial products of all kinds, wishes to maintain the automobile as its flagship and increase its approaches to manufacturers not so far among its regular clients. The Kensington (opposite) is a study for a characteristic Jaguar saloon: deliberately heavy but also individual, it tries to respect the major styling criteria of the Coventry cars. "It's a very beautiful job, you immediately recognize a Jaguar, and I am very pleased with it." Jaguar's former managing director Sir John Egan said at the Geneva Show, where it was unveiled.

Bertone, in whom General Motors is always said to be "interested", devised an innovative version of the Chevrolet Corvette ZR-1 in the Nivola, using Corvette components. The name of the little mid-engined two-seater evokes that of the great Italian driver Tazio Nuvolari, whose nickname was Nivola, and its yellow colour echoes the shirt Nuvolari habitually wore when racing. It is a coupe that can be transformed into a convertible for its 'hard top' disappears into a compartment above the engine.

Overall, the Italian coachbuilders are anxious to escape from the straightjacket imposed by the term "stylist" and prove that they are real design bureaux able to contribute technological advances to giant groups.

Only specialists would recognize a Honda Concerto basis under the Rover badge on this 200. This mid-range saloon matches Japanese standards of quality, and is evidence of a real reawakening of the British automobile industry.

Volkswagen has found the right compromise between the multivalve and turbo concepts with the G supercharger fitted to the Golf G60. This powerful but flexible engine, which is also economic in these times of soaring energy prices, works wonders with the six-year-old Golf variant.

GERMANY: EXPANSION AND GROWTH, WITHOUT IMPERIALISM

West Germany is Europe's largest automotive market, with sales of some 3 million vehicles expected for 1990 but with imports taking a rising share, the Renault 19 and Mazda 626 vying for the title of leading import. The country also leads in production figures with 4 564 000 units in 1989, 13% of the world total.

Daimler-Benz has become the leading industrial group in a nation where many different constructors co-exist. Its diversification is thriving, but transport (cars, trucks and buses) still accounts for 75% of its turnover. Sales of Mercedes cars were unchanged at 3.2% of the European market in 1989 while those of its eternal rival BMW drew closer at 2.8%.

The Munich firm compensated for losses in the United States with spectacular growth in Japan looking to annual sales of 55 000 by 1995. On the eve of the launch of the new Series 3, BMW announced expansion of capacity to 600 000 units a year by simply improving productivity. Its 1989 output of 511 000 units compares to 546 000 for Mercedes.

What may be the most significant event of the European automobile year was the agreement, about which details were hazy, between Mercedes (with turnover of $48 billion) and Mitsubishi ($100 billion — 12% of Japan's GNP!). Mercedes is seeking a turnover of more than $60 billion by 1995, a 30% increase on 1989. Mercedes president Edzard Reuter said that "we are both firmly convinced that we can cooperate on a large and durable basis to the benefit of both companies." But six months after the signature, there had been little progress and the atmosphere between the partners seemed somewhat strained.

By siting its multi-valve engine plant in continental Europe rather than in Britain as first planned, Ford confirmed its European ambitions, with investments measured in billions of dollars by the end of the century (the largest commitment — some 45% — still being to Britain). The company, which produced 1 654 000 cars in Europe in 1989, linked up with VW to produce 200 000 MPVs from 1993. It does not seem over-pleased with the German investment plans of Mazda (in which it has a 25% stake) for a

200 000 unit per year plant, although the Ford-Mazda-KIA cooperation works well in North America. Mazda has already invested nearly $40 million in a research and development centre near Frankfurt. Mazda's interest comes despite the fact that labour in Germany is more expensive than in Japan, and twice as costly as in Spain, where employees work 1 776 hours a year (compared to 1 500 in West Germany, 1 626 in France, 1 643 in Britain, 1 646 in Italy, 1 847 in the United States and 2 165 in Japan).

GM-Opel's 1989 output was 1 541 000 units, but it is seeking to increase its European capacity by 25% through its agreement with Saab and developments in Eastern Europe.

Volkswagen is looking for savings, a little less than year before the launch of the Golf III and the retirement of Carl Hahn. Events in China could set back its projects there, but Japan is promising, with VW predicting 100 000 sales in 1995. It is investing in Latin America, in the Autolatina agreement with Ford and more particularly in Brazil where it has 40% of the market.

And the Beetle, born in 1936, is still very much alive, produced by the Mexican plant at Puebla which planned 1990 output up to 100 000 units, 450 per day.

Looking forward to 1993, the Wolfsburg company is considering expanding annual capacity by the order of 600 000 units, through certain projects in Eastern Europe but above all by developing its southern European strategy with Seat.

Audi is increasingly developing its exports, and acknowledged the existence of a project for an engine plant in eastern France to produce 200 000 motors a year in 1995. The failure of the V8 and quattro models to exceed 10% of production remains a problem, as do management conflicts.

As for Porsche, it changed its president, hiring Arno Bohn, 42, from Nixdorf Computers. Although 10% of non-voting shares are said to have been bought by a Swedish investor, the Stuttgart firm is still not for sale. Production was up in 1990, to an estimated 30 000 units, and profits were more comfortable.

Porsche has recovered well from a commercial disaster in the United States although it now faces a Japanese menace on the technical level in cars like the Nissan 200SX/300ZX and especially, the Honda NSX. Permanent four-wheel drive has rejuvenated the Carrera (above). The lightweight Carrera RS, introduced at the 1990 British Motor Show, is the first sports car from Porsche to officially carry an 'RS' designation since the early 1970s.

ITALY: FIAT TERRITORY

As the end of 1992 approaches, Fiat needs of break free from Italy. It has initiated negotiations with a number of companies, following the failure of talks with Ford and Saab, the latter despite the start of cooperation in a study of a common Tipo 4 platform for Fiat, Lancia and Alfa Romeo, and Saab). Fiat achieved almost total control of the Italian industry via an agreement with Alejandro de Tomaso for a 49% interest in Maserati and 51% of Innocenti. Maserati had an accumulated deficit of $130 million by the end of 1989, more than its annual turnover, and was due to be relaunched through association with Fiat's subsidiary Alfa, sub-contracting the future 164 coupe. Innocenti, producing — with difficulty — 10 000 cars a year under a technical agreement with Daihatsu, will theoretically continue this range, but has also installed a Panda line.

Fiat now controls 99.9% of Italian automobile production, and has again been restructured, under the iron control of Cesare Romiti. The automobile division has been split in two, under Paolo Cantarella and Luigi Francione. The latter is directly in charge of the car divisions, Fiat (under Alberto Fava), Alfa Romeo (Gian-Battista Razzelli) and Lancia (Ernest Ferrari).

Alfa and Lancia are concerned with battles for survival, and their images overlap too much. Playing the competition card, Alfa is back on the circuits (in the United States) while Lancia is committed to two more years in the World Rally Championship.

Lancia has been successful with the Dedra, but Delta and Thema have faltered and it urgently needs to break into other markets, predicting that its exports will rise from the current 20% of production to a still modest 33% by 1995. Alfa, after the launch of a poorly revamped 33, must rebuild its mid-range quickly and return to the sporting market which once made up 40% of its sales. Alfa production has dropped to 235 000 units in 1989, and Razzelli says an increase of 100 000 units is necessary by 1995.

Meanwhile, Fiat continues its overseas operations. In Poland, after its agreement with FSM for a 126 replacement, totally "made in Poland", Fiat is believed to have finally beaten Daihatsu to extend its cooperation with FSO in a $600 million contract for a model derived from the Tipo.

Fiat above all has scored with the impressive Oka project, a 70% joint venture with the Soviet Union. The planned Elabuga plant south-east of Moscow, calling for investment variously reported between $750 million and $1.3 billion, is to produce a small car, with three or five doors and a 1- or 1.1-litre engine, starting in 1994. Initial output is to be 300 000 a year rising to 900 000, firstly for the Soviet market where 60% of current demand is not met, and then for export.

Fiat will also start production of the Fatia, a Uno derivative, in 1993 at Tiaret in Algeria, with an investment of $260 million for output starting at 30 000 units a year and hopefully rising to 100 000. There is also a project in Iran for 150 000 Tempras per year, and considerable expansion in Turkey.

While Fiat plans to invest nearly $1 billion over the next three years in the automobile sector, its continues diversification (gas turbine generating plants, high definition television, etc.) and has registered very strong growth in other sectors such as construction, telecommunications and robotics. The car, truck and associated equipment sectors, which formerly represented 82% of the group activities fell to 77% in 1989. There has been talk of links between Fiat-Auto and other constructors: firstly with PSA, then with Ford, the old enemy in the battle to buy Alfa, fact where heavy trucks (Ford and Iveco) and tractors were concerned. The last major rumour concerned a majority stake in the capital of Chrysler Auto. There is already an agreement for Alfa 164 distribution by Chrysler's North American dealerships.

Looking at the prospects for growth outside Europe, analysts believe that apart from finally achieving a commercial presence worthy of the name in North America, the Italians would gain little from such an investment in Chrysler, unless they took a stake only in the Jeep operation. Fiat might then gain the 50 000 4x4 sales in Europe predicted for the cancelled Jeep-Renault project.

For the top model of the Fiesta range, Ford has used a turbocharged 4 cylinder 1.6-litre engine with turbo, intercooler and electronic injection-ignition power is boosted to 133bhp, giving the Fiesta Turbo (opposite) to 205kmh/127mph top speed. To handle the power, the suspension is stiffer and the 14 inch wheels take 185/55 tyres.

34

The Elan completes a strong Lotus line-up, and is a car in the traditions of Lotus founder Colin Chapman. Designed under the reign of General Motors, it has a 1.6-litre twin-cam engine from GM's Japanese subsidiary Isuzu which in normally aspirated form gives the Elan a top speed of 190kmh/120mph.

Lamborghini remains creatively free within the structure of the Chrysler group. But while the Diablo may be a technical marvel, it is not as striking as the Countach, developed from a prototype dating from 1971 which Marcello Gandini also designed at Bertone.

1990 was a strong year for new products from Renault, starting with the Clio which introduced a new era, of names not numbers. Replacing the R5, it met the new, very rounded, styling trends. With four levels of four-cylinder engine — 1.1-, 1.4- and 1.7-litre petrol and 1.9-litre Diesel versions — it is more spacious than the R5, being 3.7 metres long and approaching the general size of mid-range European cars. The Renault 19 (opposite, top) is now equipped with a four-cylinder overhead camshaft 16-valve engine, the F type, bored out from 1721cc to 1764cc and developing 140bhp. The same engine is used in the Chamade 16S version and will be available in the Clio.

THE NEW "GREATER GERMANY"

The gentle revolution of the merger of the two Germanies means the incorporation of 17 million future consumers and formidable prospects for the automobile industry — a market of 5 million cars in the 10 years to come, according to Carl Hahn of VW, while Ford's Harold Poling foresees 9 million by the year 2010.

East and West come together with quite extraordinary automotive differences: 4 564 000 million cars produced in the west, against 262 000 obsolete units in the east.

Volkswagen, in taking over Trabant at Zwickau, intends to produce 250 000 to 350 000 Polos a year by 1995 (production starting late in 1990), and to win 40% of the local market. GM-Opel acquired the AWE-Wartburg plant, making 70 000 cars a year, and plans to build Corsas, Kadetts and Vectras at a rate of 150 000 to 250 000 a year, while Mercedes sees itself as the logical partner for the IFA truck group.

The whole industry, including Continental tyres, rushed into East Germany, as did the Japanese, although they seemed more likely to aim at Hungary (where GM set up a joint venture for Opel with Raba), Poland, Czechoslovakia and Rumania, possibly taking over the Citroën-Oltoit plant at Craïova.

36

At the Paris Show, Renault displayed this striking concept car, and "out and out" roadster called Laguna, which suggest that the period of bland Renault styling maybe in the past. It is equipped with two roll-over bars which deploy automatically in the event of an accident. It is a mid-engine configuration with a 210bhp 2-litre turbo power unit (the 21 Turbo engine), giving a claimed top speed of 250kmh (155mph). The body, 4.1 metres long and only 99 cm high, is made entirely of carbon fibre Kevlar and polycarbonate panels, on a steel/aluminium honeycomb monocoque.

BRITAIN: REBIRTH, PARTLY THANKS TO THE JAPANESE?

As the 30th anniversary of the Mini was celebrated in April 1990, Honda, which since 1976 had only technical cooperation agreements with the former British Leyland, finally took a stake in the capital of Rover Group. Rover by this time was a subsidiary of British Aerospace, and BAe was under attack from the European Commission and some British parliamentarians for allegedly buying Rover at well under its value in a government-organised operation.

The Japanese company took a 20 % stake in Rover, for $930 million — nearly four times what BAe had paid for the whole group — with Rover becoming the owner of Honda UK Manufacturing. HUM plans to build another factory at Swindon with an output of 100 000 units a year.

Simultaneously, Honda's European headquarters was established in London with Osamu Iida as president, while local chief executives were installed in the subsidiaries in Europe.

Lessons have been learned from the first UK Legend programme, leading to efficient cooperation between the Japanese and the British, notably in the Honda Concerto production and in aspects of the Rover 200/400 programme. Production of the Japanese car was 30 000 units in 1990, with 40 000 planned for 1991. The Longbridge plant, where all the cars are assembled, has demonstrated efficiency and productivity by running 24 hours a day, like GM-Opel in Saragossa and Bochum.

For 1991, Rover is investing $230 million for a new "top range" production line (the AR-17 and AR-18 coupe projects) and is proving that British creativity is not dead, for example in the K-type engine. In 1100cc, 1400cc and 1400cc 16-valve versions it equips the 200/400 series, and the all-British Rover Metro. Land Rover's Discovery helped recover sales "lost" to Japanese manufacturers.

Nissan set up production in Britain independently `and is awaiting the completion of the second stage of its Sunderland plant, to produce the new Micra and double annual output to 200 000 units, while the Primera has been introduced to succeed the Bluebird (just in time, as sales of that model slipped). With a planned level of 8 500 units a month, it will be sold through Europe (there were even suggestions that it would be exported to Japan, to make up for a local short fall!).

The third Japanese constructor established in Britain is Toyota, on a green field at Burnaston. Derby, with a projected engine plant at Clwyd to produce 200 000 mid-range vehicles per year by 1994/95. This major investment of nearly $1.2 billion will increase Toyota's overseas production to 1.5 million vehicles a year.

The heads of Continental manufacturers, such as Giovanni Agnelli of Fiat, are understandably concerned about the proliferation of these "transplant" factories in Britain. But Rover has
shown how Japanese influence can be a positive spur to productivity and build quality.

Among the British companies, the major event was the sale of Jaguar to Ford for $2.7 billion, after the British Government waived its "golden share." Jaguar, revitalised by Sir John Egan, will see its production of nearly 50 000 cars a year tripled or quadrupled, according to Ford. Sir John, who would have preferred a deal with GM, resigned and was replaced by another Briton, William Hayden, vice-president of Ford Europe.

Hayden's comments on the weaknesses of the Jaguar manufacturing system were widely quoted, and improvements to working practices and productivity have high priority. Beyond that, he already seems to be 'a Jaguar man', intent on consolidating the current range, updating the XJ-S for 1991, and beyond that looking to XJ40. The association with TWR in JaguarSport continues, with the emphasis swinging back towards genuinely sporting cars rather than 'high performance' versions of standard saloons.

'High performance' tended to be played down as the summer of 1990 passed, but among the new models at the British Motor Show was the Aston Martin Volante, as if to show that during a honeymoon period Ford leaves its new subsidiaries to get on with their programmes. The Show also saw Vauxhall's astonishing Lotus Carlton make its debut — this full four-door saloon shames some so-called supercars, coupling real interior comfort with a claimed maximum speed approaching 290 kmh/180 mph from its twin-turbo 3.6-litre engine. In 'real sports car' terms there was also the sleek Griffith from TVR and the Ginetta G33.

Rolls-Royce is looking to reorganisation and the launch of a new range in 1996 with a Bentley to come earlier. With production up from 1700 cars in 1980 to 3254 in 1989 — a level forecast to be maintained in 1990, despite the slump in the American market. Rolls-Royce is also working towards a very considerable improvement in productivity. Vickers, which already owns Rolls-Royce, has bought Cosworth Engineering, which produces racing engines, including F1 units, and carries out research and development work for many manufacturers.

Peugeot-Talbot Motor Co, which has been very profitable, was to see PSA invest $180 million in the Ryton plant, to double capacity to 200 000 units a year, although this plan was 'frozen' in the Autumn of 1990. Meanwhile, almost one in every three 405s sold in France was built at Ryton, which also produces most of the 405s sold in Japan.

With GM promising Vauxhall a new plant in Liverpool to produce 85 000 engines a year from 1992 and Ford proposing that more than 45 % of its total European investment in the 1990s will be committed to Britain, it appears that the country could become one of the major European automobile producers again by the end of the century.

Two contrasts among the Italian drop-head brigade: the Ferrari 348 (opposite), very modern with its longitudinal engine — a 3.4 litre V8 with 32 valves developing 295bhp — driving a transverse gearbox; and the new Alfa Romeo spider (bottom), a new style of the Duetto spyder and still based on the 25-year-old Giulia platform, fortunately considerably improved. Two four-cylinder engines are specified, a 1.6-litre 109bhp unit or a 2-litre 126bhp unit. Still in the Fiat group, the Fiat Uno II with more fluid lines has a Turbo version (above) giving improved performance from a 118bhp, 1400cc injection engine. The Uno II has ABS as an option. The Alpa 164 Quadrifoglio Verde (centre) now has its 3-litre V6 equipped with a catalyser, boosted output from 184bhp to 200bhp, still with two-valves per cylinder. The aerodynamic extras which have been added tend to compromise the purity of its initial styling.

Aston Martin has replaced its 20-year-old V8 coupe with the Virage, a more modern two-door, four-seater coupe complemented by the Volante convertible. Both have the 5.3 litre V8, developing 335bhp. It drives through a 5-speed manual or 3-speed automatic box.

The Sapphire RS Cosworth has Ford's proven permanent four-wheel drive system, and a four-cylinder, 16-valve 2-litre turbocharged engine developing 220bhp.

Opposite: the new generation Ford Escorts introduced in the summer of 1990 are a little larger than preceding models. The four-cylinder engines are in 1300cc, 1400cc, 1600cc and 1800cc Diesel versions, with a 150bhp, 2 litre, 16 valve engine for the RS2000 to come. The convertible and three-box versions perpetuate the Orion name (opposite, top and bottom). Although the Escort RS Cosworth 4x4 will not be marketed until 1992, a rally version was driven to a debut victory in the 1990 Talavera Rally.

FRANCE: THE SQUEEZE

Despite another increase in imports, which gained two per cent to 38% of the market in mid-1990, PSA Peugeot-Citroën and Renault appeared to hold up well, at least until the Gulf crisis hit an already hesitant market. Both the groups cut production in the second half and laid off temporary staff. PSA had lost seven weeks' output from Peugeot, 60 000 cars and $530 million in turnover, in the late-1989 strike, but still produced 2 233 000 units in 1989, an increase of 6%. Renault, more broadly diversified outside Europe, built 1 966 000 units, a similar rise of 6% compared with the world average of 3% increase on 1988. Strong profits resulted, $1.65 billion for Renault (+5%) and $1.81 billion for Peugeot (+15%), which became France's largest tax-payer but more significantly cleared its debt burden entirely and built up positive reserves of $450 million.

The two French groups did, however, seem strangely isolated from the worldwide wave of alliances and agreements, until the unusual "engagement" was announced between Renault and Volvo and then in the Autumn both talked to Skoda. Following the semi-privatisation of the Regie, which became a public company after 45 years under nationalisation, the $2.7 billion acquisition of 10% of Volvo Ab involved the transfer of 45% of its truck activity and 20%-25% of the car division.

The engagement did not mean a marriage, but coordination of certain technological and industrial activities (basic research, industrial investment, purchasing, etc.) with the integrity and the personality of the two manufacturers preserved. It remains to be seen if this can lead to a group that can really become the world's leading truck manufacturer (150 000 a year) and Europe's third largest car maker.

Renault, which in mid-1992 will move out of its historic Billancourt plant, is counting heavily on the success of the new mid-range Clio, producing 2 500 a day, 16% of the European total in the sector. It had some problems with the European Commission in Brussels after the French Government wiped out $2.1 billion of debts on the 1988 accounts. After complex negotiations, Renault will only have to repay half the sum. The truck subsidiary, RVI, has been turned around and there are also fringe deals such as the agreement with Toyota in Colombia for the production of 4 000 Land Cruisers in 1991 and 3 000 Hi-Lux in 1992.

But there was a new, serious split with Chrysler, with the failure of the JJ project for a small 4x4 which was to have been produced for Europe at a rate of 50 000 a year in Renault's Valladolid plant.

Peugeot was restructured, in a manner of speaking, with Jacques Calvet as triple president: of PSA (the group), of Citroën, and now of Peugeot. Calvet talks less and less of PSA becoming the Number One in Europe, and is apparently concerned for the survival of Citroën: the two marques are parallel rather than complementary.

Peugeot sales in the United States slumped to just 6 000 in 1990 and it looked elsewhere, strengthening links with India's Mahindra (10 000 pick-ups to be assembled annually), talking of assembling 605s in the Soviet Union (possibly 160 000 a year), and projecting a Turkish plant for 100 000 cars a year. Its agreement with Iran for the assembly of 500 000 405s and 50 000 engines, although signed, had still not gone into operation.

France maintained its 3% quota on Japanese imports despite efforts to raise it to 3.5% but the importers were selling European-made cars, 30% for Nissan and by 1995, 50% for Honda, with British-made Toyotas to follow. Imports from Eastern Europe were a disaster: importers typically spent 15 to 18 hours preparing the poorly-finished vehicles for sale — longer than it takes to build a complete car in the West. François Michelin finally obtained U.S. permission to by U.S. Uniroyal and BF Goodrich for the handy sum of $1.5 billion, a significant increase in the group's debt loading as it became the world's leading tyre manufacturer, Michelin announced a revolutionary new process for tyre production, and the discreet François Michelin himself was named Man of the Year by a leading French automotive magazine for the success of his worldwide policy.

Third generation (oppo-
site) of the BMW 3
Series, which was origi-
nally launched in 1975:
this "small" BMW, with
nearly 250,000
produced each year, has
grown in size and now
has the same family
appearance as the 5
and 7 Series. From the
316 to the 325, the new
3 Series uses the four-
and six-cylinder, 100 to
192bhp, engines of the
old range and 2/4 door,
Touring 5 door and
drop-head versions will
be introduced. The 325ix
4x4 seems to have
been dropped.

The Rover Metro (oppo-
site, lower) shows that
the Rover Group has not
become entirely
"Japanesed". This little
3/5 door saloon uses the
basic structure of the
Metro, but with consider-
able styling modifications
which lengthen the body
by 11cm (4in) to 3.52
metres (138in). The new
features is the engine
range, with a four-
cylinder light alloy unit
and with one or two
overhead camshafts, the
latter on the 16 valve
1400cc sports engine
producing 95bhp. The
Rover now has a five-
speed gearbox, bought
from Peugeot, but the
suspension is by
an improved
Hydragas system.

42

In the 900 series, the
Volvo 940/960 range
(opposite) had a face-
lift: outwardly, the over-
angular lines of the rear
section were replaced
with a more classic style
with softer lines, which
also contributed to better
aerodynamics (the cd
improved from 0.41 to
0.36). At the top of the
range, Volvo no longer
uses the V6 PRV (built
jointly with Peugeot and
Renault), replacing it
with a new straight 6
"made in Sweden." This
compact and light long-
stroke 3-litre is a
24-valve unit developing
204bhp. The "multilink"
independent rear suspen-
sion is still used only on
the 760 saloon.

IBERIA: FLOURISHING SPAIN, HESITANT PORTUGAL

Spain became the fourth largest European manufacturer, and the world's sixth largest, producing 1 740 000 vehicles in 1989. The figure for the Iberian peninsula as a whole reached 1 815 000 with the inclusion of Portugal, seen by some as the "Korea of Europe" because of the low cost and high quality of its work force.

Ford saw part of its future in the peninsula, with investments of $300 million to produce electronic components at plants in Lisbon (Portugal) and Cadiz (Spain). So did GM-Delco Remy, putting $50 million into electronics components manufacture — 500 000 ignition systems annually — for European use.

Apart from Seat, the major companies involved in Spain are Renault, PSA Peugeot-Citroën, Ford, GM-Opel and the 'Spanish-Japanese' represented by Nissan-Ebro and Santana, a licensee of Suzuki (which has a 33% interest) whose production of small 4x4s will rise from 30 000 SJs in 1989 to 50 000 Vitaras in 1992. There is similar development at Ebro (Motor-Iberica) which is to receive new investment of $1.3 billion over five years from its parent Nissan, the 91% shareholder. Ebro will replace the Patrol with the ET project in association with Ford, with a target production of 50 000 per year from 1993, and increase production of utility vehicles from the current 90 000 a year to 150 000 units. When the further investment for a research and development centre is taken into account its becomes obvious why Spain worries those European manufacturers obsessed with 'Japanese bridgeheads'.

The only really Spanish constructor is Seat, although it is now 80% owned by Volkswagen, whose president Carl Hahn has given reassurances that: "The opening of Eastern Europe will change nothing in Volkswagen's southern European policy, which aims to develop Seat." The marque, born out of Fiat, produced 350 000 cars in 1989 (60% of them Ibizas), is also supported by the sales of 120 000 VW-Audis in Spain.

Seat is increasingly an exporter with particular success in Italy (more than 80 000 units) and France, where the 50 000 mark should have been reached in 1990. Seat could also subcontract production of the new Polo, but has slipped somewhat in the launch its own new Toledo, a mid-range saloon with heavy use of VW components, due out in mid-1991. Clues to the 1993 Ibiza successor appeared in Proto C concept car studies, shown at the Paris Motor Show.

There was considerable activity in the heavy truck sector in 1990: MAN, number three in European trucks, bought 60% of Enesa-Pegaso in association with Mercedes-Benz (20%) and INI, representing the Spanish government. This $440 million investment should enable Pegaso to develope a marked increase in capacity, currently static at around 13 000 trucks a year. And Scania, a member of the Saab group, is committed to a $180 million investment in northern Spain.

In Portugal, where Renault, Citroën and Opel represent the car sector, there has also been movement. Renault sold a small plant assembling Trafic vans to Reinshagen, a subsidiary of GM-Packard Electric, which started production of the Clio at a rate of 150 a day in mid-1990. Citroën, however, finally ended production of the 2CV, after 42 years, and carried out a $4 million refurbishment of the old Mangualde plant, to produce 100 AXs per day. However, there was official concern that this activity represented assembly rather than manufacture.

Uniao Metalo-Mecânica of Lisbon started modest exports of its Peugeot diesel-engined UMM 4x4 range, primarily as working vehicles for commercial or agricultural operators and taking on manufacturers of small and light 4x4 models and the mid-range Japanese models.

And the Japanese in Portugal? They are hesitant — the only company with an industrial presence is Toyota, through its 27% holding in Caetano which annually assembles 11 000 Land Cruisers with Italian VM diesel engines for near-by European countries.

UPHEAVALS IN SCANDINAVIA

In automotive terms, Scandinavia is essentially Sweden, with Volvo and Saab (of the other nations, only Denmark is remarkable, for its taxes which limit annual sales to some 80 000 cars). Sweden's position outside the EEC apparently decided the management of Volvo to transfer its legal headquarters to Brussels, because the majority of its production (400 000 cars in 1989) is already within the Market, from the Dutch plant at Born with the 300 and 400 series. One of the major events of 1990 was the "partial marriage" of Volvo with Renault after a long association, industrially through the V6 PRV engines built in France since 1971, commercially through distribution by Volvobil of the R5, R19 and Trafic in Scandinavia, and financially through Renault's 10% stake, which it sold in 1985. Details of the agreement are given in the French industry section.

The other upheaval for the Swedish industry was GM's acquisition of Saab Automobiles, after serious propositions from Ford (Trollhättan said the deal was virtually done) and then Fiat, which had long-standing links, for example in the Saab-Lancia 600, and technically in the 9000. On December 14, 1989, during the traditional meeting at Maserati, Fiat Auto head Cesare Romiti even gave some details of Fiat's strategy for Saab, which produced only 104 000 vehicles in 1989 (its capacity was 180 000) and increased its deficit by around $250 million. The lightning struck on December 15: Bob Eaton, the president of GM-Europe, had concluded the deal very quickly, the world Number One buying 50% of Saab's automobile division for $600 million. This led to a restructuring of the Swedish group with the creation of an independent subsidiary, Saab Auto Ab, of which Eaton is president but D.J. Hermann, a 44-year-old Swede, is executive managing director.

The agreement will make Saab the "top of the range" for GM-Europe, with a real image which the Senator has never achieved. It foresees output increasing to 180 000 cars a year after the replacement of the 900 — production has already ended — by a saloon derived from the Vectra (Carlton) for better penetration in Europe's upper sector. Saab will of course have access to GM equipment including at last a V6 engine — a power unit which has been desirable for the current 9000 range.

This agreement, which theoretically maintains marketing independence (always the story at the beginning), also extends to the electronic and armament sectors (Saab Missiles and Hughes Aircraft). But the Scania truck division remains Swedish and Saab has continued with investment of $150 million in an entirely automated factory at Sodertalje which can produce 150 000 engines a year with only 200 workers.

S2 will be for Audi what M (for Motorsport) is for BMW, and the coupe, aesthetically modified by using an Audi V8 type grill, inaugurates this sporting series. The Audi Coupe S2 has the 5-cylinder, 20-valve, turbocharged 2.2 litre engine from the 200. But although it retains permanent four wheel drive, it does not carry the Quattro badge.

The Seat Toledo, to be launched in spring 1991, is the first car really produced in common by Seat and VW. Designed by Giugiaro, it was previewed in a series of "styling prototypes" seen at the major European motor shows in 1989 and 1990, like this Proto TL which was shown at Geneva.

PROMETHEUS

PRESENT MYTH, FUTURE REALITY?

JEAN-PIERRE GOSSELIN

Prometheus is the most demanding joint research project on the automobile ever undertaken. European manufacturers have set aside their commercial rivalries to work together towards a major objective: to raise the level of road safety to heights never before achieved.

In 1990 only a few European drivers appreciated the significance of the Prometheus programme. Named after the Greek hero who stole fire from the Gods to give it to the human race, Prometheus stands for "Programme for European Traffic with Highest Efficiency and Unprecedented Safety" — the full title spelling out the vast range and very ambitious nature of this co-operative project.

Fourteen manufacturers from five European nations joined together in 1986 in the Prometheus project, pooling their research resources with the objective of to the organisation of road traffic on a European scale. The many systems proposed often create more new problems than they solve. It is thus clear that not all the systems will be developed to a commercial stage and that the costs of those selected will be high. But it is also already clear that Prometheus has caused a constructive revolution in thinking about road safety. Shaken by Prometheus from 1986, the manufacturers' self-centred attitude should have disappeared by 1994.

Now more than a century old, the constant development of the automobile has progressively changed society.

offering the motorist of the late-1990s safer roads and a more fluid traffic flow, which will mean more economical driving with less pollution.

They believe they will achieve those results in the first instance by modifying cars, stuffing them with powerful and "intelligent"" electronics, somewhat like the current generation of aircraft. The second stage would be to reorganize road traffic on a new basis to make it more rational and safe.

It is an enormous task, matched only by the enthusiasm of the technicians involved. It is so obviously valuable that Prometheus has been made part of the European Community's Eureka scientific project system, this bringing to the project substantial financial support and the active assistance of governments, despite the possibility that they might have felt uneasy about being stripped of certain prerogatives in the field of traffic organisation.

Conscious of the limitations of vehicles and their drivers, the manufacturers are pinning their hopes on electronics to improve both. That decision presupposes an immense and unprecedented research and development effort, its scope ranging from the design of new sensors

Mobility is now considered to be a fundamental liberty. In daily life, it seems so natural that all the benefits it brings to mankind are no longer fully appreciated. To the contrary, only the faults of the car are perceived: pollution, traffic jams, waste of energy and accidents.

An unhappy reassessment

The automobile at the end of the 20th Century is in the dock, and seems under increasing pressure because all the solutions to problems that have been put forward, principally by increasingly strict regulations, are shown to be ineffectual in stemming the hemorrhage of human lives.

Basically, the progress accomplished in development of the automobile has been incomparably superior to that seen in "driving man" and in traffic engineering. Faced with the attitude of governments which are restricted to limiting and punishing, and attempt to manage the crisis without fighting it, European manufacturers decided to react in a positive fashion.

They see safety as firstly primary and active, with the qualities of the vehicle allowing even inexperienced

This telemetry system couples laser and radar, to be as effective in curves as on a straight road. PSA even got its stylists involved to integrate the unit into the front of the Citroen XM.

drivers to avoid accidents. When an accident has become inevitable, secondary or passive safety protects the vehicle's occupants to a degree. In both these fields, Europe has reached such a level that progress will henceforth be considerably slower and of minimal effect, raising the question of what should be done next.

The fundamental idea of Prometheus is to concentrate on areas before and after secondary safety: drivers must firstly be given the means of avoiding the accident, and then, if it happens, help must reach the scene as quickly as possible.

While the logic is impeccable, achieving the objectives is considerably more difficult, because no manufacturer has ever studied safety problems which are so far "outside the bodywork".

Just a single second...

This project, ambitious but crucial if the automobile is to be saved in the long term, did not evolve by chance. It was born at Daimler-Benz, carried through by charismatic Dr. Ferdinand Panik, director of Principles and Products research, a Daimler-Benz "futurologist."

It all started from a very detailed study of accidents carried out by Daimler-Benz in 1979, and whose conclusions illuminated areas which had been ignored until then.

It showed that about 50 per cent of accidents at intersections and 30 per cent of frontal collisions could have been avoided if the driver had known of the situation he was going to encounter just a half-second earlier. With advance warning a full second sooner, the level of avoidable accidents rose to 90 per cent!

This is considered fundamental, and is a reason for optimism. It shows that the quality of cars and that of the road network is not in question. It is the driver who operates poorly, because he is poorly or tardily informed of accident situations. His reaction is limited or poor, and the accident becomes inevitable. Prometheus was created to give the driver that vital extra second.

From that basic aim, the chain of developments, while logical, starts to demonstrate the difficulties involved. Information must first be acquired and then transmitted as quickly as possible to the driver, in an easily understood fashion. That is where the questions start: what sort of information should be collected? is it all useful? should it be sifted? in what form and by what means should it be delivered to the driver? how will the information be collected — by the vehicle itself, through the road network, a satellite, other vehicles, or many sources at the same time? And how should the traffic be regulated, through individual initiative or in an authoritarian manner? If a driver panics, should the system not go beyond just giving information, and help him to control his vehicle?

Each question leads to others, in a cascade which shows the enormous complexity of the task. The challenge of Prometheus is to use the new electronic and data processing techniques to gather useful information, and

then process and transmit it. The two primary objectives of Prometheus could then be achieved.

To these ends, three major lines of research have to be pursued:
— to improve the information system on vehicle to help the driver anticipate critical situations,
— to create systems for communication between vehicles. This concept developed in the Prometheus programme is unique
— to create systems of communications between the road and the vehicles. These would have to be extremely powerful, bearing no relation to the current modest and partial attempts at distribution information by radio. These would be real traffic management.

When traffic movement is more relaxed, more fluid and safer, it is obvious that fuel consumption will be reduced. For example, it has been calculated that all standard "urban cycle" consumption figures could be improved by 15 per cent if all the acceleration and deceleration imposed by traffic lights and traffic jams were eliminated. Overall, if the objectives of improving traffic flow are achieved, a colossal annual saving estimated at 20 billion ECUs (£14 billion) would be achieved.

All the tons of fuel saved would obviously mean that much less pollution and a considerable reduction in the greenhouse effect. Given those savings for the general population, what would be benefit be for the motorist? Safety would increase and fuel consumption decrease, but the price of vehicles would increase considerably. Happily for the credibility and economic interest of Prometheus, the systems it will develop could lead to vehicles far more sophisticated and efficient than the current models and particularly well adapted to the developing needs of society.

46

A humorous explanation of a typical ISIS sequence: (1) the infra-red emitter warns the vehicle: (2) a diagram lights up in front of the driver (by classic methods or "head-up" display) with an audible signal: (3) when the driver ignores the signals, (4) the car brakes automatically.

Five steps to avoid the classic highway accident. The telemetry at the front of the car alerts the driver that a car has stopped in his lane. An audible signal supplements the visual information, but if the driver does not react, an automatic braking system (symbolised here by the robot) comes into action.

The electronic systems promised by Prometheus would offer increased comfort and better dynamic control of vehicles, meaning reduced stress while driving. They would also allow the driver to communicate more easily with the outside world. Currently, to signal his intentions, the driver has only rudimentary facilities — headlights, turn indicators and horn — which is a very limited vocabulary.

More seriously, inside the closed, moving cage which is the vehicle, very little information is received — some visual, from road signs, some audio from the radio but with only a little real traffic information. It is ridiculously limited. In terms of "communications," current vehicles are bizarrely under-developed, even taking mobile telephones into account, compared with the home or office. Prometheus will lift communication to a proper, integrated level.

Prometheus: born quickly and healthily

How was it possible to create a programme as ambitious as Prometheus and involve the majority of the European manufacturers? There was a miracle worker involved, Dr. Panik. He was the real father of the operation, which developed from his studies of the future of the automobile in Europe. In 1985, he delivered his conclusions to his company during an internal seminar, which developed them further. Given the magnitude of these studies, they were expanded to the whole group. As it was the era of the introduction of Eureka projects, Mercedes "thought European" and wished to associate Matra with the studies, Matra being a firm it was courting and with which financial links were to be formed. A good idea is rarely developed alone, and the affair became international. Internally, major groups such as VW and

PSA had similar preoccupations about the future. The telephone works well in Europe and automotive engineers, already linked through learned societies or clubs or simply by their profession, knew and respected each other.

In 1986, there was a ferment of ideas and the discussions took on a clearly European aspect, but everything was still informal, based on friendly relations between the engineers.

The senior managements of the manufacturers, far from being worried by the formation of this "international automotive engineers' club" favoured its development. To the three concerns listed above — fuel consumption, pollution and communication — which concerned governments and individuals, they added a fourth, much more self-interested but of vital importance to their strategic planning. They saw in Prometheus an opportunity to reinforce the European electronic industry through the coordination of research and development efforts, and to develop effective standardization. The European automotive industry could find new strength in this operation to increase its resistance to the Japanese onslaught.

A project which initially was almost too idealistic was thus transformed progressively into a powerful industrial weapon, on which the survival of an independent European industry may depend.

By the autumn of 1986, the informal discussions were sufficiently advanced to launch the project, and on October 1, the first Prometheus general meeting was held in France, at Nemours. All the manufacturer members of the CCMC (the committee grouping all the EEC constructors except Ford and GM companies Opel and Vauxhall, considered to be American), and their governments, were represented.

In negotiations, engineers are often more effective than politicians. Agreement was reached swiftly and the basic elements of Prometheus were laid down at a second meeting, this time at Matra, with the definitive project being agreed on August 26, 1987. At the end of 1987, the structure was in place, the only notable event intervening in that period being the withdrawal of Rover.

Eureka!

While the European manufacturers were constructing Prometheus, their governments were giving birth to Eureka. At a meeting in Paris on June 17, 1985, 19 nations and the European Commission authorities agreed to give the Eureka label, and subsidies, to worthy scientific projects.

In June 1986, one of the first projects to be so recognised was Prometheus. The programme, which could appear to be a self-defence reaction of the European automotive industry, was admitted to the Eureka system as being a major project of public interest. A long road had been travelled in a short time from the original worthy objective — saving a maximum of human lives on the road — to the mobilization of researchers on a European scale.

Automatic detection of obstacles on a road, or maintaining a set distance between vehicles in a convoy, calls for powerful electronic calculation and accurate telemetry in all circumstances, to measure distances continuously. Servo controls, the third element of the safety system, are better understood: they are close to the cruise controls already used in many cars. The major problem is in the accuracy of detection a vehicle ahead. While rain, snow or fog do not present problems, corners and echoes generating false data represent difficult technical problems. Obstacles must also be interpreted, so that emergency braking is not initiated for nothing. A variety of solutions have been tested, but none are perfect. The tendency seems to be towards the "lidar" — the word is a contraction of laser and radar — which in fact is an oscillating laser combining the advantages, rather than the faults, of the two systems.

The advance warning signal, 100 or 150 metres before a stop sign, is equipped with an emitter (infra-red in the PSA system) which warns the car. If the driver does not lift off the accelerator or start to brake, the electronics will immediately brake the car sufficiently to stop at the sign, and not carry on into a possibly dangerous accident situation.

For a car to halt at a stop sign, even if the driver does not wish to, it must be equipped with complex systems. An infra-red receiver relays the information from an intelligent road signal to the driver, and sends data to an electronic unit. This acts via a supplementary electric valve on the braking system, which must be ABS-equipped. The automatic gearbox also has a speed sensor which releases the brakes when it "sees" the car has stopped.

A second and far from negligible advantage was that a proportion of the financing would henceforth be ensured by the governments concerned, although that imposed some controls which some people would have preferred not to have.

The third advantage of the Eureka system was that Prometheus would operate in parallel with the European Community's Drive programme, which also aimed at improving the infrastructure of the road network. Drive (which stands for "Dedicated Road Safety and Intelligent Vehicle in Europe") became the indispensible complement to Prometheus, so much so that a Drive 2 programme is now being considered to continue the studies undertaken with Prometheus. A sure sign of success and good coordination is that the two programmes exchange their leading officials.

It was vital to link up also with many other programmes already in existence when Prometheus was created. Transpolis, Carminat (by Renault and Philips, which was almost a commercial proposition in 1990), Europolis, Ertis, Télé Atlas, Demeter, ERDB, Logimax and so forth often cover the subjects studied by Prometheus and are handled by the same companies. It is clear that they can only enrich the Prometheus programme.

Committed partners

When Prometheus started, it had ten firmly committed partners: four German, BMW, Mercedes-Benz, Porsche and VW; three French, Matra, PSA (Peugeot, Citroen) and Renault; two Italian, Alfa Romeo and Fiat; and a single British company, Rover, which would withdraw but be replaced by Jaguar and Rolls-Royce. The two Swedish companies, Saab-Scania and Volvo, were to join the group, which was to lose Alfa, absorbed by Fiat. Truck companies were also recruited, with MAN and Iveco, as were off-road vehicle builders with Austria's Steyr, and Opel was accepted to a limited degree. As Fiat was present under the triple designation of Fiat, Lancia and Alfa it was not clear if 14 or 16 companies were taking part, but that was not really too important. The important fact was that they were seconding personnel and paying their share.

Equipment manufacturers, the usual suppliers of the big manufacturers and much more specialised than them, were also involved — an estimated 100 companies. Further downstream were the suppliers of individual components and specialized raw materials, in all another 300 companies making a total of some 400 large and small firms.

To handle the most advanced research, Prometheus contacted 70 research centres or universities. The mobilization of brain power had spread far wider than the automotive industry and moved strongly into the electronics field.

Overall, it is estimated that 300 people are working directly on Prometheus. It is a theoretical figure and thus false: rarely does any one person work on the project 100 per cent of the time. For example, the majority of researchers and engineers merge their responsibilities in their laboratories or design centres with their Prometheus activities, so the number of people more or less involved may be multiplied by two or three.

Governments should not be overlooked as partners in the project. The Eureka label gives them the right to supervision, but their role is more importantly that involved in standardisation and the new traffic rules that may develop. The trap to avoid is a plethora of interested parties, a problem with which the French, for example, are well acquainted, for Prometheus is being observed by four of that country's ministries at the same time.

Seeking efficiency above all, the creators of Prometheus wanted the lightest possible administrative structure. Often bogged down in the heavy administration of their own companies, the engineers wanted more freedom in Prometheus, and the system seems to be operating very well. Prometheus does not even have a real headquarters. The permanent secretary-general, Dr. H.P. Glathe, and a few staff "squat" in the Mercedes-Benz offices. One can hardly imagine a lighter or less costly administrative structure.

Smooth going

The administration of Prometheus was drawn up in June 1987 at the meeting hosted by Matra, and is comprised of a Council which is in effect the Board of Directors of Prometheus, and a Steering Committee which is responsible for directing, coordinating and above all, synthesizing the results of the research. Composed of 12 members, in turn responsible for Pro Car, Pro Net and Pro Road, it meets four times a year. For the members, all senior officials from all the European constructors, there is also no set language, In practice, everyone uses English, "poor English" the non-British members would confess, but adding with a smile: "We all understand each other very well".

The majority of the work is allocated to groups working on clearly defined programmes. In the enthusiasm of its creation, no fewer than 31 groups were established. A touch of realism reduced that figure to 11 and then to seven, before another attack of realism saw the biggest programme, Pro Car, split into two, to end up with eight working groups.

For obvious reasons of practicality and cost, the temptation to create a Prometheus research centre was avoided.

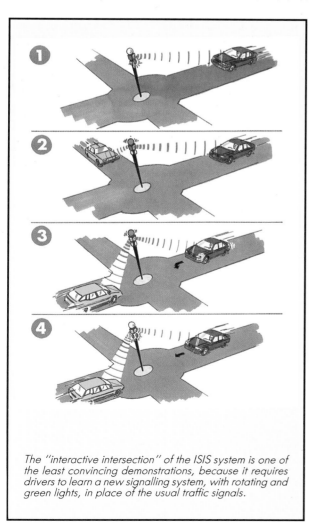

The "interactive intersection" of the ISIS system is one of the least convincing demonstrations, because it requires drivers to learn a new signalling system, with rotating and green lights, in place of the usual traffic signals.

Each partner, manufacturer, equipment supplier or research department works "at home" with its own staff and material. This makes for substantial savings in expenditure, but demands close and regular contacts between researchers over Europe's extensive telecommunications networks.

The financial structure is both simple and complicated. It is simple because the design bureaux are used to working to budgets, but complicated in regard to income. The governments subsidize the manufacturers to between 30 per cent and 50 per cent, with the constructors meeting about 35 per cent of the expenses of the equipment suppliers. The difficulty is in evaluating the expenses of the universities which are solely engaged in research projects. The system developed has been to estimate the extra expenditure due to specific work for Prometheus, and contribute 50 per cent of that cost.

Though the system of subsidies works smoothly, the manufacturers still face substantial expenses. These are calculated pro rata to their turnover, which remains the most equitable system: thus from 1989 to 1994, the French will put into the Prometheus "pot" 155 million francs (about £15 million) per year — 20 million francs (£2 million) from each manufacturer, 60 to 80 million francs (£6-8 million) from the other industrial partners, and 30 to 35 million francs (£3-3.5 million) from the universities and research institutes. It is a substantial sum, but not in comparison to the Germans, for example, who will contribute almost double that, about £28 million each year.

A new spirit

Pessimists would describe Prometheus as a wide blue-yonder programme conceived by engineers "to amuse themselves", and then if something interesting is discovered, as a "cut-throat contest" to exploit it. The creators of Prometheus, intelligent engineers, have long since thought through both cases.

The first concerns the futuristic nature of certain projects, fundamental if Prometheus is to make any sense, such as extremely complex "intelligent" cars which may worry some sections of the public. The early days of Prometheus were certainly rather hazy for the European public, even if the Eureka label was potentially reassuring. It has been better perceived since the first exhibition of demonstation vehicles early in 1989 in

The objective of the "interactive intersection" is to make traffic flow more fluid while avoiding accidents. According to whether the cars go straight ahead or turn, the lights in the middle of the intersection show green or flashing orange. Once again the connection between the lights and the vehicle is by an infra-red beam, chosen because it is very difficult to scramble, while its limited maximum range of 150 metres meets the objectives well. Existing production of millions of infra-red remote controls (for TV, video and stereo) make for low costs. But within Prometheus there is still debate over the various transmission systems. The argument that they should be unified seems logical, but is technically difficult.

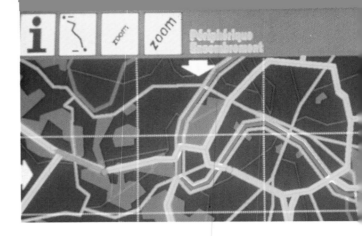

50

Munich, but all the public's fears have not yet been allayed. The rare articles that appear on the project remain prudent, their authors a little scared by the novelty and extraordinary nature of certain systems — the more so because they will call for a complete change in the behaviour of drivers, in some cases quite profoundly. Public opinion has thus not yet been won over, but a second exhibition in 1991 will have the aim of removing remaining doubts, although it could also raise further questions. To meet the commercial objection, Prometheus has developed a very strict code of ethics regarding the pooling of its research, confidentiality, the process of exploiting the results, and so forth. In fact, the pooling of research does not simply mean that a research bureau will reveal everything to a competitor. Projects which could concern the manufacturer's future products will remain secret until they have been put on the market. In the extreme case, a participant could apparently reach the end of the Prometheus project without having revealed anything to its partners.

This situation has been considered, and because the idea of the "transparency" of research cannot be absolute, all the members of the club, and the Steering Committee, have substituted the idea of balance. Each member should offer as much 'value' as he wishes to draw from the work of the others. This is also a realistic solution to the problem of the disparity of financing, and in no event will a member be permitted to deviate from this fundamental rule.

In 1994, all the participant manufacturers will be able to rummage through the stock of discoveries and among the products that have been developed, licenses being free. However, the companies will naturally remain competitors where the industrial development and sale of the products are concerned.

In the early stages, all the studies, projects and potential systems were brought together and subjected to critical appraisal. But in the end, Prometheus is basically about widespread development of electronics; that is its strength and originality, but also its difficulties.

The first organisational structure finalized, to facilitate the work, was the creation of eight "sub-programmes" and thus eight working parties.

First come three industrial sub-programmes:

— Pro Car, divided into Pro Car 1 and Pro Car 2, dealing with electronic aid to the driver;
— Pro Net, Net being an abbreviation of network, for the system of communications between vehicles dedicated to safety;
— Pro Road, a system of communications between the highway infrastructure and the vehicle.

These sub-programmes are called "industrial": they should result in concrete products, in contrast to the other four, concentrating on basic and applied research:

— Pro Art, basic research into artificial intelligence, electronic components and data processing systems;
— Pro Chip, basic research into highly integrated micro electronics;

— Pro Com, applied research into standards and protocols so that all mobile communications material will be compatible;
— Pro Gen, research into road traffic in the future and the possibility of developing mathematical models of it.

Each of the eight groups has a leader responsible for the development and coordination of the work, often carried out in scattered corners of Europe; they are called "mentors" in the industrial groups and "scientific coordinators" by the researchers. According to the wishes and strong points of each leader, the maximum number of specialists in each subject have joined the projects, but they are widely dispersed physically. The leader, supervised by the steering committee, also oversees the schedule, laid out in principle on the count-down basis familiar to engineers working on the future designs for their own companies.

The overall schedule of Prometheus has been met so far. The definition phase was completed in November, 1987, and 1988 saw the institutes and universities concerned start the research and development phase. That set in motion the exploration of a wide variety of problems and brought forward the construction of "demon-strators", still experimental systems but sufficiently advanced to allow them to be installed on vehicles. They were presented, on schedule, at Munich on January 27, 1989. The project has thus entered its third phase, that of integration, which will be completed in 1991 with the construction of CEDs, Common European Demon-strators. These will be ten vehicles with complete "func-tions" and no longer just partial systems.

For example, the research into electronic architecture carried out by Pro Car will be married to that of the same programme concerning information and control.

An operation which will be decisive for the success of Prometheus is scheduled for June 1991 — the presenta-tion of the ten CEDs. They will first be shown to the senior management of the companies involved and senior government officials, who will be able to see where their money has gone. Then it will be the turn of the media, and through it the general public who will have an opportunity to appreciate the work of Prometheus, and what it could bring them in terms of safety.

It is obvious that not all the developments will be adapt-able to mass production vehicles. Choices will be made and everything that is considered practical will be grouped in ten "synthesis vehicles" that are scheduled to be completed in 1994. The overall results will be judged then, and it may be that, as with Drive 2, a Prometheus 2 will be launched to complete those tasks that the first programme could not finish, and to undertake research in other areas.

Prometheus is rolling!

By definition Prometheus is a secret programme, and

little information has become public. It seems that secrecy may have been carried further than advisable, for fear of worrying the public. It is thus fortunate that the Munich meeting of the research departments of the major manufacturers produced some very positive reports.

The 55 "demonstrators," systems or vehicles, made it possible to further appreciate what Prometheus is about. The first lesson concerned the famous "information" which should enable the driver to avoid accidents: roads which are slippery but do not appear so, dangerous corners, obstacles on the road hidden by fog, traffic jams, unsafe distances from other vehicles, a car making a sudden overtaking manoeuvre, or the privilege of "seeing as in daylight" at night. It is evident that a great deal of electronics are indispensible to detect and quan-tify such information.

This information will be collected by "intelligent" beacons on a road network, by the vehicles themselves or by other vehicles. Some information for traffic guidance may even come from satellites, a second justifi-cation for powerful electronics, and also from radar, lasers and ultrasonic devices.

The information thus collected must then be trans-mitted. Transmission may be by a wide variety of radio wavelengths, ultra-frequencies, infra-red waves, ultra-sound or several systems combined. Drivers may receive the information by aural warning signals or through spe-cial head-up displays on a windscreen, but many systems have potential for further investigation. Developments beyond the collection and distribution of information may include helping the inexpert driver, by braking better and faster than he can, making him automatically respect a safe distance to other vehicles, or in correcting a bad line through a corner.

As ideas that had appeared to be Utopian became a reality, Prometheus began to become credible. Two general conclusions were evident:
— the creation of an electronic safety network between vehicles is possible (certain people had doubted it);
— discovering critical situations that might degenerate into accidents is also within the domain of the pos-sible: a driver could avoid an accident. That alone could make the creation of Prometheus worthwile.

The electronic highway

Some examples of the demonstration models give a good idea of the systems while at the same time highlighting their terrifying complexity. At the very least each vehicle must have sensors for position, speed, acceleration, power, and status of the vehicle in order to feed a com-puter which would manage all the communications.

Undoubtedly the most spectacular demonstration was the "highway" concept developed by Pro Net. A bus and six cars equipped with the system ran on a stretch of six-lane highway, simulating normal traffic three lanes abreast in each direction. If the gaps between the

The quality of the elec-tronic equipment and infrastructure indispens-able to meet Prometheus objectives poses the obvious problems of cost, of operation and its implementation. The electronic equipment necessary would make a small car too expensive, and would be rejected by the public, defeating the overall project. That is why some manufac-turers think that cheaper, simplified systems are necessary. This little Citroen AX (below) has a rudimentary display system for ISIS informa-tion, in black and white but sufficiently clear to be used successfully.

51

Statistically, chain collisions on roads or highways are rare. But they are spectacular and worrying, and are given priority in the programme.

One of the most spectacular experiments in the Prometheus programme was the use of video and infra-red cameras mounted on this BMW. The technique, well known to the military, brings high quality pictures on screen whatever the atmospheric conditions, even in snow or fog, as shown by these four pictures. Drivers who have tried the system have adapted very well to this view of the road on the dashboard, but the price of the cameras would be much too high for series production cars, and is not expected to drop for a long time.

The vehicle has frontal telemetry and a computer. Depending on the distance separating the two cars and the state of the road (which determines the stopping distance), the system acts on the brake or accelerator to stay within reasonable limits. Associated with automatic braking systems interconnected between vehicles in the same lane, it would enable the spacing between vehicles to be reduced without reducing safety.

vehicles were correct, nothing untoward took place. When that condition was not met, an orange light came on in front of the driver as soon as the distance was less than the calculated safety minimum — this was instantly clear to observers as lights were also installed on the roofs of all the vehicles, lighting simultaneously with those on the dashboards. If the minimum distance became very short and thus dangerous, a red lamp lit. If a driver still insisted on maintaining his behaviour at that stage, he had something of a Kamikaze mentality...

The system is sufficiently powerful and intelligent to manage a whole lane. If the first car brakes brutally, the system warns all the following vehicles at the same instant. The saving in reaction time is 0.7 second compared with the usual stop light warning. In one system, the famous one extra second's warning that would make 90 per cent of chain collisions avoidable is within reach, and that will be a really positive development.

Pro Net also manages collision risks in overtaking. If, for example, a driver wants to move out to the next lane when it is already occupied by a fast-approaching vehicle, there is a dangerous situation. A red warning light flashes in the door mirror and warns the driver in time to delay his move.

This first phase of Pro Net is the most simple, as all the vehicles are moving in the same direction. It will be extended later to the more complex case of traffic moving in both directions, and to intersections.

The manoeuvres and information involved seem elementary but conceal extremely complex situations. Firstly the distances must be measured with radar, lasers or lidars (area-sweeping lasers). Speeds and distances must then be calculated in real time and the driver warned. Several warning systems are possible — on the dashboard or the rear vision mirrors, or by a head-up display on the windscreen. Each system has its advantages but also disadvantages, and must not distract the driver from other important tasks — problems must be solved, not simply moved around.

After collection and distribution of information comes the concept of "assisted driving" with the aid of electronics. Instead of lighting up a yellow lamp, an "autopilot" would come into operation and automatically maintain the safe distance by controlling the accelerator, as in anti-skid systems. It may even be put in control of braking, a task which it can carry out much better (with mandatory ABS) and above all faster than the human driver.

In that case, the distance between vehicles in the same lane can be reduced to almost nothing, and running in sort of railway train formation could be practical. It does place a lot of responsibility with the driver at the head of the train, who might not even realize that the drivers of a whole line of vehicles behind him are relying on his abilities. However, it would multiply the capacity of a highway lane, and positive aerodynamic effects (known in racing as slipstreaming) would greatly reduce the fuel consumption of the following vehicles.

An important factor is the possibility offered to the driver of "leaving" the automatic lane control system. It is sufficient for him to activate his turn indicator to move into another lane to overtake or to leave the highway at an exit. It is a major principle of the system: the driver must always, at any moment, be able to take back control of his vehicle. It is also a lesson in humility, as the most powerful electronic system remains far less effective than the driver in conditions where its sensors cannot capture all the parameters of an exceptional situation.

Prometheus steadily becomes credible: even if it seems very complex, it is possible to see what can be developed. Car to car communication can also render important services. For example, the Handshake system allows a car travelling in the opposite direction to pass messages, "I have just passed a traffic jam (or an accident) in your lane X kilometres ahead", which gives a driver the opportunity to leave the highway and avoid the trouble spot. It is technically possible to give a similar warning of police radar checks ahead, although that may not be strictly legal! Porsche has also presented an intelligent system for an altruistic car. If it detects, through its sensors and computer, that the surface of the road is dangerous, it warns following vehicles. With a simple system, the driver is warned; with assistance, his car modifies its speed automatically at the dangerous spot.

The same information could, however, come from an "intelligent" roadside beacon. It would not simply announce "Dangerous corner", for a mini weather station would automatically inform passing cars of the adhesion coefficient of the road: drivers could then respect the speed suggested by the warning signal in their cars or, if the cars are "assisted", it would impose that speed.

The safety and fluidity of the traffic would be increased by highly developed guidance systems with extremely precise cartographic information. Very large terrestrial transmission systems are being studied, but satellite transmission is also under consideration. These networks offer a second advantage, quick detection of accidents. By a wide variety of procedures, from simple radio-telephone to Loran C navigation systems or beacons and satellites, what is already called tertiary safety can be obtained: the detection of vehicles involved in accidents, their identification and their almost instantaneous positioning would allow the rapid arrival of emergency vehicles.

Prometheus is certainly coming, at least in part. It is

The system warns the driver if he crosses the white line, or with more advanced equipment, automatically moves the vehicle back into its correct lane. It operates by the numeric treatment of images from cameras, and can be associated with an automatic braking system or a distance-maintenance function.

Drowsiness in drivers leads to serious accidents, and Prometheus foresees a system linked to the white line (diagram here) to reduce the risk of loss of attention. It could also be useful in conditions of poor visibility.

One of the best methods of warning and informing the driver is to put messages in front of him, superimposed on the outside scene, so that his eyes do not have to leave the road. This technique, used in fighter aircraft, is efficient but very expensive. It can, however, be adapted for mass-produced vehicles: using mirrors, a virtual image can be formed about 80 centimetres from the driver's eyes, behind the windscreen. This distance is sufficient for the eye to read the message without having to "accommodate", to change its focus which is already set to infinity.

Volvo is showing an ultra-violet projector (top) integrated into a classic headlight at motor shows, but Saab invited the European Press to the first demonstration. Based on classic Cibié lights (bottom), a powerful beam of harmless and absolutely invisible UV light is projected at the same time as the normal dipped beam. Where the visible light will not penetrate more than 50 metres, a pedestrian wearing a cotton garment is visible at 150 metres. The system is expensive, but much cheaper than infra-red cameras which are the ideal solution.

known that cars can communicate with each other and with the road network, and the extent to which useful information they can be collected and distributed has been determined. That a car can tell its driver, 150 metres before a blind intersection, that another vehicle is on a conflicting path is very reassuring, but the Prometheus programme still faces enormous problems. The first problems are of a technical nature. To build each of the demonstrators, the teams involved used known, efficient solutions. That is why there are a multitude of systems: one team chose ultrasonics, another opted for infra-red because it operates over short distances and thus avoids any interference. Radar works well in certain cases, lasers better in others, without considering the complexity of the electronics, sensors and the development of standards. A new phase of the rationalisation of the systems is opening, which could also benefit from the findings of the scientific programmes, Pro Chip, Pro Art, Pro Com and Pro Gen, because the electronics must be ultra-reliable and must all communicate reliably in all conditions — not an easy task.

Price is the second problem. The project must develop systems comparable with those of aircraft, but at automobile prices, that is to say, very low. Prometheus researchers do not yet know how to achieve this.

The third problem is evidently the investment that will have to be undertaken to put Prometheus into operation. To equip vehicles, roads, and centres for distribution of information and for emergency services will demand enormous sums. Where should the investment begin? By imposing these systems on all new vehicles, like catalytic converters, or by letting market forces operate, as for ABS? The second solution is obviously the more democratic because it is not mandatory, but it would mean introducing improvements little by little, reserving them for the rich and making mass production, and lower prices, impossible. The debate continues.

The fourth problem is the human being. Will being an "assisted driver" not mean completely abandoning his role and turning control blindly over to the "automatic pilot"? The experts working on Prometheus think not, but the example of ABS is there to prove the contrary. Given confidence by their anti-lock braking systems, drivers commit new faults, the more serious as they arrive on the scene faster.

How too will the owners of older vehicles live in this "new era of the automobile"? Imagine being on a highway in a car without the new systems, faced with convoys running at 70mph with gaps of just two metres between the vehicles: a driver will not react like them in a tenth of a second, but will still have to rely on human reaction time. Assisted driving also demands the use of an automatic gearbox, without which the system cannot have total control both over speed and stopping. And some drivers dislike automatic gearboxes.

All these factors are so important that market research has been and is being carried out to test how all these innovations will be received. Prometheus will have to overcome many hurdles before being accepted, but

these will just have to be overcome. Everyone now understands that there is no other solution to save the future of road communications in Europe.

The Munich meeting had a second effect, that of showing up weaknesses in the structure of Prometheus. Members of the Steering Committee felt that it is not going fast enough, and that there is a lack of coordination. Drastic steps were called for, and all 12 members met in March, 1989 with an agreement not to leave until a new organisation had been created. The result was a new structure, simpler and more efficient, based on the 10 Common European Demonstrator vehicles.

Even if Prometheus was to be halted it would already present a favourable balance sheet. It has shown the long term problems of the automobile and that manufacturers are not just salesmen but are ready to consider the problems. The programme also obliges companies to talk differently, not only about their own interests, as they do in Brussels. The Utopian dream sometimes leads to positive results, and whatever happens in the future, a new European automotive civilization could be unfolding before our eyes because of the achievements of the Prometheus programme.

SEE AND BE SEEN

A quarter of all accidents occur at night, and the fact that the traffic is only one-tenth as dense as during the day shows the seriousness of the problem. Prometheus researchers have worked extensively on the question. BMW and Peugeot have tested quite extraordinary infra-red video cameras, by which the driver can see as well at night as during the day — provided he looks at a screen. The drawback of these military cameras is the price — around £10 000 of which some £5000 is for the germanium lens alone, with mass production simply impossible. Mercedes and BMW are thinking about vision by computer, but that is well into the future.

More modest and realistic, the Swedish contribution to the problem is headlights emitting ultra-violet rays, "black light." It makes pedestrians visible with dipped headlights at 150 metres, three times the usual range of dipped lights, provided they have some reflective item on their clothing (a strip of cotton will do). Volvo has shown such a system incorporated into conventional headlights, but it was Saab that invited the European press to attend a very convincing demonstration.

Outside the framework of Prometheus, PSA, Cibie and Norma have presented new headlights with gas discharge lamps. With no filaments, the arc light starts with a 12,000 volt impulse and then functions at 80 volts, lasts 1500 hours and is incredible strong, and offers an unequalled light power. The Norma 35 watt headlight delivers twice as much light as the best 60 watt halogen light, the Norma Philips Gold, though because of the danger of dazzle it means headlights only 5 centimetres high. An advantage is that the composition of the light rays includes a certain proportion of ultraviolet, easily reflectable outside the illuminated zone. Researchers thus did not wait until the end of the Prometheus programme to produce better lighting, but the programme considerably accelerated the process.

WHAT'S IN A NAME?

RAY HUTTON

It seems a long way from multi-valve engines, exhaust emissions, and active suspension, but the badge on each new model is also the subject of intensive research. Naming cars is now a big business in its own right.

When all is said and done, the name of a car is surely not very important. After all, some don't have names at all and go into production carrying what is — or might as well be — their engineering project number. Mercedes-Benz have not used model names for 60 years. Neither have Peugeot.

But Renault, intent on improving their image in international markets, announced in April 1990 that they had decided to break with their long tradition of numbered models and give every future car a distinctive name. "Market research has shown us that the public awareness of our products and their identification would be improved by using names rather than numbers", said Philippe Gamba, Renault's director of marketing.

The first name in this new generation of personalized Renaults had been a closely-guarded secret. The new small car was known, inside and outside the company, as "X57". In the advertisements prepared in advance of the launch it was referred to as Alma. The real name was, of course, Clio.

Why Clio? According to the *Oxford English Dictionary*, the name means: "The Muse of epic poetry and history; a sea nymph; a genus of pteropod (mollusc); the 84th

asteroid". None of these have the slightest relevance to a neat little modern car. What *was* important was that it is short, catchy and internationally acceptable, presenting no problems of pronunciation in all the main languages. It remains to be seen how far Clio will improve Renault's image. But their use of a meaningless name shows how difficult it is to find a title that can be used worldwide. In recent years a whole industry has grown up around 'branding', not just for cars but for everything from chocolate bars to international corporations. Agencies specialize in suggesting names, or arranging to make them available if someone else holds the rights to them, and then protecting the chosen new brand by registration.

The commercial world has become infinitely more complex than in the earlier days of the car, when the directors of a manufacturer chose model names — and sometimes the marque name as well — on whim and personal preference.

Take the British Daimler company as an example. In 1953 they had a new 2.5 litre saloon, smaller than the Regency, Empress, and their other regally-named models of the time, but they could not decide what to call it. Finally, someone noticed the price they planned to charge — £1,066. As every English schoolboy knows, 1066 was the date of the Norman Conquest. The new car became the Daimler Conquest...

Birds and musicals

In the 1960s before the Japanese motor industry had awakened to the world-wide possibilities for its products, car names were plucked almost at random from Western culture. Nissan's president Katsuji Kawamata made a point of choosing them personally. Bluebird was a favourite from childhood fairy tales. He had been to see the musical *My Fair Lady* and enjoyed it; hence Fairlady, a title used for Nissan's sports cars in the domestic market to this day.

Henry Ford II also regarded model names as his prerogative. Edouard Seidler provides an illuminating insight into Ford's procedure in his book *Let's call it Fiesta* (Edita, 1976).

The short-list for what had been known internally as Project Bobcat was: Fiesta, Amigo, Bambi, Pony and Sierra. Ford's European management didn't like any of them much and eventually resurrected Bravo from an earlier list of suggestions. They recommended that to the Henry Ford who exclaimed that, "Bravo is no name for a car — we will call it Fiesta!"

Seidler notes that research at that time had sidelined Sierra because 10 per cent of those questioned confused it with Siesta. He also recounts an early brain-storming session when they attempted to follow a traditional Ford theme of place names — Taunus, Cortina, Granada, Capri. "What about a German name — a glamorous winter sports resort perhaps?" asked Bill Bourke, then chairman of Ford of Europe. Bob Lutz, who was to have that job five years later, playfully suggested Garmisch-

Partenkirchen, demonstrating that some place names were much more appropriate than others...

The places served Ford well in Britain, where the names had the faintly exotic flavour of holiday destinations. But Ford of Germany was not prepared to give up their Taunus line for the name of a town in the Italian Dolomites and most of their European sales organisations were happy to replace a Moorish city in Spain by the more celestial Scorpio. Evidently, when they came to research Sierra again, it did not have such sleepy connotations! In Ford's case, the names themselves were less important than the way they de-lineated the range. People talked of a Fiesta, an Escort, or a Granada, without referring to the maker's name; the model itself provided the identification and the size and type of car.

Branding specialists

British Leyland, now Rover, were envious that Ford's range had a coherence that theirs notably lacked. Sorting out their model names was the first major success for Interbrand, who can now claim to be the world's leading branding specialists. They invented Metro.

As the product of any number of mergers and rationalizations, Leyland held title to a large number of names, but all of them had associations with the past. The 1980 launch of a 'supermini' was seen as a new beginning that needed a new name. Furthermore, by linking future cars in a branding system, the company itself would seem better organized and therefore build confidence with its customers.

Interbrand had been established — originally as Novamark — in 1974 by John Murphy, who as marketing manager of Dunlop, had devised the clever name Denovo for their ultimately unsuccessful run-flat tyre. The experience taught him the difficulty of finding and establishing an internationally-acceptable brand name. Figuring that if Dunlop had struggled, other big companies must have the same problems, he decided to set up an agency to deal in names.

For British Leyland's small car they narrowed the choice down to Metro, Maestro, and Match. Since all three were thought equally suitable, it was decided that it would be a good morale-booster for the Leyland workforce to have a factory poll to christen their new baby. Metro was the winner, by a narrow margin from Maestro. Both names would be used in due course (Match later became

a special-edition Mini) and Interbrand proposed Montego as a right-sounding third member of the group. Murphy's agency has since grown to an international business with over 100 staff and an annual turnover of £10 million. They are active in every area of consumer and industrial products and sometimes even able to convince clients in different fields to use the same name. Vectra, for example, devised as a pseudo-scientific name for Opel, also finds a place in Hewlett Packard's computer range. Interbrand's automotive portfolio also includes Omega for Opel, Discovery for Land-Rover, Eclipse for Mitsubishi, Dynasty for Chrysler-Dodge, and Swift for Suzuki.

Though they have a computerized 'name bank' with some hundreds of thousands of names stored, Interbrand start every new naming project with a brainstorming session of a group drawn from a panel of some 150 creative, articulate people. This alone can generate hundreds of names, and all of them will have a relevance, however slight, to the car concerned and the manufacturer's marketing strategy for it. Artificial, computergenerated names are not usually included at this stage. "The best brands have a natural feel", says Tom Blackett, Interbrand's deputy chairman.

It is also important that a model title fits well with the manufacturer's name. "The model name must add to, not overlap with the corporate name — which will always be more potent", Blackett emphasizes.

They reckon to present between 30 and 40 possible names to the client at the first stage. These will all have been checked for linguistic appropriateness — using language specialists and their own offices around the world — and prescreened to ascertain that no identical names appear in the trade mark register for the car's domestic market.

Usually, the client then narrows 30-40 to 10-15 names and those are subjected to consumer research. Though Interbrand make recommendations based on this, the final choice is with the client company. Now that the czars of the industry have mostly gone, that responsibility usually falls to the marketing director.

Many a chosen name falls when the commercial searches begin. There was little danger of Mr Kawamata's idiosyncratic choices for Datsun being registered for use somewhere else but today most of the slicker international titles already 'belong' to someone. The trouble is, there is no international registration system. Though there are

plans for a common procedure throughout the European Economic Community, at present each country has its own trade mark laws and its own system of establishing the rights to a name. In general, common surnames cannot be registered and neither can collections of letters and numbers, nor descriptive words — mini or micro, for example. That does not prevent their use, of course. Mini is regarded as one of the best of all car names which is so closely associated with a particular product that it needs no formal protection. (It is intriguing to reflect that at the launch in 1959 Mini was only part of the name of one of the two versions — the Morris Mini-Minor — and that, trying to extend its reputation to its larger successor, the Metro was at first called the Mini-Metro.) Most manufacturers now avoid such generic terms because they do not want spend money promoting a name which could also be adopted by a competitor.

Sierra and Ciera

Quite a lot of name trading takes place between car companies. When Henry Ford selected Fiesta, the company was aware that the name had already been used by Oldsmobile in the United States. This matter was settled on a chairman-to-chairman level when Mr Ford phoned Tom Murphy, then number 1 at General Motors, who gave permission without hesitation — or payment. In other cases, there are reports of large sums of money being paid.

Sometimes the benefit to the incumbent user is more subtle. When Ford eventually decided to use the name Sierra the company knew that there was another clash with Oldsmobile, who had a car with a badge spelt differently but pronounced the same: Ciera. But Ford had not reckoned on a challenge from Dutton, a British specialist car manufacturer, already using the name Sierra for a glass-fibre kit to rejuvenate tatty Ford Escorts. Dutton was unlikely to be able to resist Ford's lawyers but took the matter to court and in the process gained a lot of valuable publicity — and it was to become Britain's best-selling kit car manufacturer.

Name clashes are not just a problem with other cars. In the early 1970s, Lord Bernstein, chairman of Britain's Granada Television, took exception to Ford's use of his company's title, though the council of the Spanish city that gave its name to both was so delighted that it sent a gift to Henry Ford.

Even synthesized names can present difficulties. In 1988 Nissan and Toyota both signalled their intention to enter the luxury car sector in the United States. Both commissioned the Lippincott & Margulies agency in New York to find suitable names and create identities for completely new marques, to be sold separately from their mainstream products. They settled for Infiniti and Lexus respectively. But at the time of their launch in January 1989, Toyota found themselves in the US courts fighting an objection from a computer data service called Lexis. After a few anxious weeks, the case was thrown out.

Lexus and Infiniti are strictly nonsensical (though Nissan are happy with the 'limitless' connotation of their name spelt with a 'y'). But they sound right; high class and technological. "A little bit of meaning, just something in there, is better than none at all", says Interbrand's Tom Blackett, who dismisses a lot of other Japanese car names as "simply daft".

Many Europeans, puzzled by the mis-application of familiar words on some Japanese products, would agree. But it as well to remember that in most cases the same names are used in the Japanese domestic market, where customers can hardly be expected to understand the nuances of Western languages. Sunny and March, long used by Nissan for popular small cars, were both selected by a public ballot. Nissan's Langley, which not only seems odd to us but is particularly difficult for most Japanese to pronounce, seeks to indicate European sophistication.

So, one suspects, does the Mitsubishi Starion. Officially, the name has its roots in astronomy but the real story is thought to revolve around a mis-spelling and the Japanese inability to pronounce the letter 'l'. Ferrari's prancing horse would have suggested Stallion as a potent, macho name for a sports car...

Presumably pronunciation problems also brought us the Subaru Loyale, while it is said that Honda wanted to call their biggest car the Regent but the Japanese found that too difficult to cope with, so it became the Legend (try saying it the Japanese way to see how one could have led to the other).

Toyota have, helpfully, issued an explanation of some of their model names. From it we learn that: Camry is "the English phonetic spelling that sounds most like the Japanese word for a small crown"; Celica is the Spanish word for 'heavenly' (though the symbol used on the badge is a swan); Corolla is the outer envelope or

crowning portion of a flower; Cressida is the female Trojan character from *Troilus and Cressida*; Tercel is a male hawk used in falconry, known for its compact size; Supra means 'to surpass or go beyond' and Previa, their innovative new 'people carrier' is from the Italian for 'preview' or 'looking ahead'.

Other Japanese names defy logic. The latest Isuzu sports truck is known as the MU; the full name is 'Mysterious Utility'. Daihatsu have a 4x4 called the Rugger Sports Afield and one domestic-market version of the Mitsubishi Minica is called the Lettuce.

Nationale preferences

Interbrand's research indicates that there are national preferences in car naming. Germany and Holland prefer the more rational approach with names that mean something; France and Italy are happy with something more abstract. What is clear though, is that if a name has a meaning, the interpretation should be clear. Names are tested by asking the public what kind of images they conjure up. It is not much good labelling a new sports car with a word that brings to mind hearts and flowers.

Cuddly ones like Panda (even if applied to an inappropriately boxy Fiat) crop up less frequently than the powerful big cats (Jaguar, Cougar, Tiger), birds of prey (Eagle, Skyhawk), snakes (Cobra, Viper), and wild horses (Mustang).

Aggressive names have become rather unfashionable of late. Sometimes they have been applied to surprisingly mild cars. Remember the Avenger? Diablo is a supremely appropriate name for Lamborghini's latest supercar but, surprisingly, was held by Rover, with whom Chrysler had to negotiate for its use.

It is all-too-easy to get caught in the language trap. Rolls-Royce have an enthusiasm for etheral names linked to 'Silver': Silver Ghost, Silver Wraith, Silver Shadow, Silver Spirit. They came close to settling on Silver Mist for a new model until someone pointed out that 'mist' in German means manure. Vauxhall thought Nova a better name for Britain than Corsa used by Opel. But they could hardly use Nova where it is built, in Spain; *no va* translates as "doesn't go"!

Sometimes names take on a different meaning from that originally intended. The most celebrated case is that of Volkswagen, who as part of the 'new deal' in the mid-1970s when they finally produced a generation of cars to succeed the Beetle, decided to name them after some famous winds. The trouble was that they are not quite famous enough in countries where they don't occur and the spellings vary in different languages: Scirocco, Passat, Golf. More people understood the latter as a game played over 18 holes, so Volkswagen quickly adopted the golf ball as a motif for the model and started thinking in more sporting directions — hence the introduction of Polo.

Animals have always had a place in car nomenclature.

Those organisations that complain about the promotion of speed and power in car advertisements, claiming that they increase driver aggression, cannot be pleased with the American industry's fixation with deadly weapons. General Motors offer Le Sabre (Buick), Cutlass (Oldsmobile) and Beretta (Chevrolet). Reportedly, the gun-maker was not too pleased about the latter either.

Places were a safe bet when car makers were more insular. American manufacturers must have used every up-market resort in the United States for a model name but — like most of the cars — they did not travel well overseas. They also adopted exotic sounding place names from Europe, sometimes seeking associations to which they were really not entitled. Pontiac has never played any part in the *Vingt-Quatre Heures du Mans* but shamelessly use the name Le Mans, first for big, powerful but unruly saloon and now, even less appropriately, for a version of the mild Opel Kadett made by Daewoo in South Korea.

In Britain, Austin and Morris monopolized the names of the more prestigious English cities — Cambridge, Oxford, Westminster — and counties — Devon, Hampshire, Hereford, Somerset, carrying on a tradition from

HOUSEHOLD NAMES

Strictly speaking, corporate identity has nothing to do with names but signs, symbols and a consistent presentation of a company name are also important factors in product recognition and image.

Henrion, Ludlow & Schmidt, a London consultancy that specializes in corporate identity, commissioned a study by MORI, the British market research firm, to learn the attitudes of industrialists to their business. 243 senior executives of Europe's largest companies were asked which company's corporate identity they most admired. The winner was Mercedes-Benz.

The three-pointed star was regarded as the best symbol of a European business by respondents in Austria, Germany and Spain and featured in the top ten in the United Kingdom and Scandinavia; it had a low rating only among French businessmen.

Mercedes was the only motor manufacturer to feature in this poll of corporate identity. The other companies quoted most frequently by respondents were IBM, Nestlé, Philips and Shell.

speak Italian and evidently also works well in Italy where it was voted 'top brand name of the year'. That is surprising; in English, a car named 'type' would not have the same appeal...

Fiat's Lancia division have not found it as easy with their Greek roots. They go back to the origins of the company — there were Betas, Gammas and Deltas in 1911 — but they present some problems today. For obvious reasons, it is not now appropriate to use Alpha (Alfa). Spelt out, some of the other letters of the Greek alphabet neither look nor sound good, so Thema was devised as a complementary artifical name.

And then came Dedra, which Lancia say "reflects the strong and elegant geometry of the car's form". Spoken in Italian, the name has a certain ring to it, but in English it evokes images of mortality rather than morphology. Fiat Auto UK considered changing it — as they had Ritmo to Strada some years before — but eventually decided not to.

Does it really matter? Tom Blackett of Interbrand admits that a name in itself will not sell an indifferent model but he thinks that the opposite may be true: "A bad name can damage the potential of a good car".

the 1930s. These were comforting for buyers at home in the British Commonwealth, which were their main markets in the immediate post-war years, but confusing for everyone else.

Oxford was at least Morris' home town. Fiat tried linking factory and its product with the Mirafiori, the meaning of which was lost on most of their customers. Their subsequent use of Uno — understandable universally as 'number one' — was brilliant but *due* and *tre* did not have the same ring to them and Quattro was already spoken for at Audi. Tipo sounds good to those who don't

FASCINATION WITH Z

Why are so many car makers attracted to Z? Somehow, it has a technical cachet. When BMW Technik built a sports car using advanced materials, the company had no doubts that it should be called Z1.

Similarly Alfa Romeo's extraordinary 'limited edition' became SZ (though since Alfa has used it before, it could also be claimed that the Z stood for Zagato, who make the bodies).

In America, there is the Camaro Z28, Cavalier Z24, Corvette ZR1, Beretta GTZ, Daytona Z.

Nissan is generally credited with introducing this nomenclature with the 240Z in 1969. Today it is explained that this is a potent symbol in Japan, the last letter of the alphabet representing 'the ultimate'.

The original reason for the name was rather more expedient. President Kawamata had decreed that the sports coupe should be called Fairlady. Yutaka Katayama, the chief of Nissan's US subsidiary, thought that Americans would regard the name as a joke but he could not reject the president's choice. It was a tricky problem of protocol, eventually solved by using the car's project number — 240Z. Since this was an official internal designation, Katayama felt able to adopt it — and remain confident of keeping his job!

It is hard to imagine this car standing still. The Bolero is the latest show car from GM's Buick Division, and if the past is any indication, the design could give a hint of what Buick is planning for the mid-1990s. There may not be much chrome, but the Buick signature is still there, in the vertical bar grille, and the wrap-around rear lights. To keep the lighting surfaces small, the Bolero uses fibre optics for everything from those tail lamps to the instrument panel display.

Only a decade ago, virtually everyone was predicting the death of the muscle car. The V8 was as dead as a dinosaur, the pundits prognosticated. Well, a quick look at the spec sheets will prove that performance is actually alive and well. American drivers can choose from more new V8s than at any time since the early 1970s. In fact, 1991 models like the Corvette ZR-1, the Acura NSX and the Dodge Stealth may be the hottest machines ever to race down great American road. They will keep pace with most of the fashionable European imports, perhaps more convincingly than their fore-runners in 1970. But they are hardly "all-American" — Chrysler may announce its design and engineering input in the Stealth, but under the skin most of it is Mitsubishi 3000GT (Starion GT in some markets), for example, while there is Lotus input in the ZR-1.

But there is a big difference between the early 1970s and now. Today's performance cars are built to a different standard from the straight-line sleds of the past. Technology now plays a bigger role than brute displacement, with a growing emphasis on twin overhead cams, port fuel injection and multi-valved engines. The NSX, for example, punches a blistering 270 horsepower out of a

seemingly modest 3.0-litre V6, while the top Stealth has 300bhp from a twin-turbo 3-litre V6. And with rack-and-pinion steering, tuned suspensions, traction control and anti-skid brakes, today's muscle cars can brake fast and corner like slot cars.

Ironically, as performance reaches a new zenith, a possible death knell is beginning to sound again and the blame once again belongs on the Middle East. As oil prices rose, there came a growing interest in raising the nation's fuel economy standards. And even a peaceful resolution of the Iraqi crisis is not likely to soften the mood in Congress. A 40 mile-per-gallon standard (it is currently 27.5mpg) would likely force the typical American driver into a car no bigger than the Ford Escort or Toyota Tercel.

On an individual basis any one of the new regulations for fuel economy, improved safety and reductions in exhaust emissions poses a very tough technological challenge. But industry officials fret that trying to meet them all at the very same time may create a technological nightmare.

Take the effort to reduce tailpipe emissions. The technology used to clean up exhaust usually results in a

HOW WRONG WERE THE CRYSTAL BALLS

PAUL EISENSTEIN

Like the little Dutch Boy trying to plug up a leaky dike, the US automakers hardly know which hole to patch first. Not since the early 1970s have they faced the threat of so many new and often conflicting Federal regulations: a tough new Clean Air bill, the threat of a big increase in fuel economy standards and the call for improved vehicle safety. But when they try to solve one problem, they just make another one worse. Add in an uncertain US economy, and the new decade already looks tough.

reduction in fuel economy. So as a counter balance, and to meet any government-mandated increase in the Corporate Average Fuel Economy standard, "We would take out all the (vehicle) weight we can," says Dr. Richard L. Klimisch, Executive Director of General Motors' Environmental Activities Staff.

But that creates yet another conflict, according to Dr. Klimisch, since "There's no question if you are in an accident you'd rather be in a heavier car." And some of the safety regulations now under study will almost certainly add to vehicle complexity — and weight —, which will not help reducing fuel consumption.

Fighting back

Conveniently, a wave of new subcompacts make their bows in 1991, including all-new updates of the Escort and Tercel, the Nissan Sentra and General Motors' long-awaited Saturn. So the battle for market share will be fierce — as it will in virtually every segment of the American new car market, from minicars to sport-utility vehicles.

With cars like the Saturn and Escort, Detroit hopes to

finally reverse its decade-long slide in market share. But that is going to be a difficult task. The Japanese have invested billions in "transplant" assembly lines which, by the mid-1990s, will be capable of producing 2.5 million cars and light trucks a year on American soil. Combined with imports, the Japanese could regularly take a 30 per cent share of the American new car market — on a one-month basis, the Japanese took a 34 per cent share in August 1990.

While Japan keeps gaining ground in the car market, the Big Three have regained some in the booming "cross-over" light truck market, thanks to some exciting new minivans and sport-utility vehicles. But the Japanese are not going to give up and have got their own new models on the drawing boards. By the mid-90s, they could even tackle one of Detroit's most hallowed and protected markets, for full-sized pick ups.

The Big Three will not be the only losers as the Japanese continue their march. With luxury cars like the $60 000 NSX and the $40 000 Lexus LS400, Japan has successfully invaded the highest reaches of the market, stealing away share from the lines of Mercedes-Benz, Porsche and BMW.

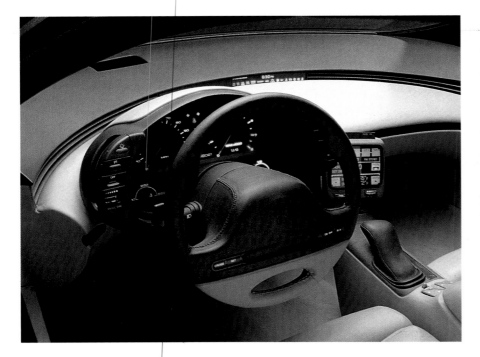

Fibre optic lighting illuminates the Buick Bolero's easy-to-read instrument panel (above). This is a show car built with the family in mind, so it includes a rear-seat cooler for soft drinks and sandwiches, and even a separate radio for the kids.

This the ultimate Expression of Oldsmobile (top, centre), a show car that blends the sleek styling of a futuristic sports sedan and the convenient roominess of a more conservative station wagon. The Expression boasts a bevy of electronic gadgets, including CD player, cellular phone and a Navicar navigation system.

There is more to Cadillac's Aurora show car (opposite, top) than just its svelte silver shape. The advanced prototype features all-wheel-drive and Traction Control, both designed to improve its road handling, an electronic navigation system and other techno-goodies designed to appeal to the urban road warrior.

This is the Pontiac Sunfire (right), a radical 2+2 prototype with a body built of advanced carbon fibre composites. The forward portion of the Sunfire's unique, two-part doors open conventionally, but the smaller half-doors open rearward for easy entry.

GENERAL MOTORS FIGHTS BACK

How far is down? For nearly a decade, General Motors seemed determined to find out. Despite spending upwards of $77 billion on new plants, products and technology, the giant car maker's US market share was steadily slipping away — it lost nearly a dozen points during the 1980s. In turn, a dozen body and assembly plants have been closed, and GM has had to cut its workforce by tens of thousands.

"Just wait," company officials have kept insisting, "the investments will eventually pay off." If GM's big break is ever going to come, 1991 may be the year.

It has already begun showing at least some encouraging signs of recovery. It has scored well with the Geo "division-within-a-division," a line of small, stylish cars and trucks sold through Chevrolet dealers, but aimed at young import-oriented buyers. The Geo Storm is one of the hottest cars in the tough but fickle Southern California market.

Geo shows GM is ready and willing to fight fire with fire. Its products are almost all produced by General Motors' Japanese allies, including Suzuki and Isuzu, then given Geo badging. The Pontiac Le Mans turns out to be an Opel Kadett/Vauxhall Astra built in South Korea by Daewoo Motor! GM is also scoring with some of the cars coming out of its own design studios. Its restyled 'full-sized' Caprice has buyers rushing into the showrooms.

Meanwhile, the Cadillac Division has begun to reverse a nearly decade-long sales downturn by emphasizing traditional styling and lots of muscle.

The world's largest automaker still has some serious problems to resolve. Its Oldsmobile Division is, to put it kindly, a basket case. Sales have plunged from more than a million units in 1986 to barely 500 000 in 1990. In a desperate bid to pump Olds up, the division got into the booming light truck market in 1990 with its first minivan, and for 1991, there is the Bravada sport-utility vehicle.

But the biggest challenge — and potentially the biggest opportunity — for GM comes with the introduction of its long-awaited Saturn subsidiary. Like Geo, Saturn is aimed at the young, entry-level buyers who all but ignore American automobiles. But unlike Geo, Saturn is designed to win them over with a domestically-built product. If Saturn succeeds, it could add another point or two to GM market share in 1991. More significantly, it would prove that the giant company's massive investments of the 1980s may ultimately pay off. This division is taking on manufacturers with a sure grasp on the US small-car market, and in the background there are unhappy memories of past attempts that persuaded the Big Three to surrender it to the Far East. The mixed reception for Saturn could mean GM faces even more of an uphill task.

What is 50 years old and brand new? The Oldsmobile 98. The classic Olds luxury sedan takes on a completely new look for 1991. The windswept exterior is only one of the many changes, for under the hood there is a 170bph V6 mated to an electronically-controlled four-speed automatic. The Regency Elite also gets ABS brakes and Olds' new Computer-Command ride, which automatically adjusts to the roughness of the road.

It is big, bold and completely reskinned for 1991. And who says traditional American big car buyers are not looking for a little sizzle in their style? The aerodynamic update of Chevrolet's full-sized Caprice and Caprice Classic got an early jump on the 1991 model-year, and were soon ringing up big sales.

The return of the Roadmaster. After a 30-year retirement, Buick brings its classic name plate back in the form of the 1991 Roadmaster Estate Wagon. In early 1991, Buick adds two more models to the line-up, the Roadmaster and Roadmaster Limited sedans (right).

Sleek and silver, the Cadillac Aurora could be the shape of things to come from Cadillac. This concept car breaks the stodgy Cadillac mould with its windswept shape. It also features a number of technological breakthroughs, such as all-wheel-drive and Traction Control, features designed to improve its handling, and an electronic navigation system. Cadillac officials say the Aurora will not make it into production "in its present form," but reaction has been so positive, they hope to use the basic design to influence a car for the mid- to late-90s.

Buick is GM's "traditional American" division, but that does not have to mean square, stodgy styling. Witness the Park Avenue. Completely redesigned for 1991, this sedan is sleek yet roomy, with a just a dash of the chrome that many Buick buyers still expect. Both the Park Avenue (left) and the upscale Park Avenue Ultra feature an electronically-controlled four-speed automatic and the new 3800 V6 engine with tuned port-injection pumping out 170bhp.

Buick's Regal line is now available in both two- and four-door models, including the Regal Limited Sedan. This is one of GM's most aerodynamic models, with flush glass, a swept-back grille and inset door handles. The optional 3800 V6 is the production version of the successful Buick racing engine that won eight national championships in 1989.

Who says American luxury cars have to be stodgy? The Lincoln Town Car is one of the most popular products in its class, but for 1990, it took on an entirely new feel with the aerodynamic Ford aero-look. Critics no longer call these "jelly bean cars." It's hard for Ford to keep up with the demand. For 1991, the big change in the Town Car is under the hood, where there is a more powerful 4.6-litre V8. This is the first in a new line of "modular" engines, a basic design that can be easily modified to meet the needs of future car lines. Alongside the Town Car's 2-litre iron block four-cylinder powerplant, there will eventually be a performance version, with the SOHC and DOHC models available in both aluminium and iron.

Hello from Down Under. The first of the Australian cars arrives in America. The long-awaited, oft-delayed Capri is being built on Ford's Australian assembly lines, but it is a product of global cooperation, styled at Ford headquarters in Dearborn and engineered by Ford's Japanese ally, Mazda. The Capri's manual convertible top makes it easy to go topless, and there is also an optional hardtop. The XR2 provides some real kick, thanks to its intercooled, turbocharged 1.6-litre engine.

Ford shook up the automotive design world with the swept-back look of the Ford Taurus and the Mercury Sable (shown here). The cars continue to define the shape for the 1990s. Ford is using the aero-look throughout its model line-up, from the new Escort to the re-skinned Lincoln Town Car. This is also a shape that other carmakers continue trying to copy.

The Mustang GT convertible combines the best of both worlds: Ford's popular Mustang convertible, and the awesome 5.0-litre engine. Together they can put a lot of wind in the hair...

FORD – LOSE SOME, WIN SOME

The opening years of the decade could be critical for Ford. After steady gains, in the 1980s, the company is suddenly starting to lose some ground.

Several things went wrong for Ford in 1990, but by far its biggest problem was with the update of the subcompact Escort, based on Mazda's new 323/Protege. Long the best-selling car in the United States, the old Escort slipped into the number two spot in 1990, behind the Honda Accord. The all-new Escort was exptected to again leap to the lead in the sales chart. Instead, volume has lagged far below expectations. Ford blames unexpected production delays at assembly lines in Wayne, Michigan, and Hermosillo, Mexico. But the new Escort is simply going up against a lot more competition, such as Mazda's own 323. And Honda will weigh in with a new version of the Civic, while General Motors will introduce its long-awaited Saturn.

The Escort has not been Ford's only problem. Declining sales of Ford's long-popular Mustang have cost in market share terms. And after four wildly popular years, Taurus and Sable sales have also begun to soften. Just when those models are to be updated is a matter of question — and concern. Re-skinned versions are likely to show up sometime in 1992, but Ford may not introduce complete redesigns until the second half of the 1990s.

To boost interest in its passenger car lines, Ford is putting a lot of attention into what goes under the hood. The Lincoln Town Car gets a brand-new "modular" V8 for 1991. The term modular refers to the flexible design, which can be quickly and easily adapted to the size, shape, and marketing needs of individual Ford product lines. There will eventually be at least four different aluminium and iron, two-valve and four-valve versions of the Town Car's 4.6-litre engine. A V6 is another member of this family of engines. In its 4.6-litre sohc form, the V8 is more powerful than the pushrod 5-litre engine it replaces — power in this case means only some 200 bhp — quieter and more economical. The Town Car which it propels is large by any standards, but at least revenue from its high price helps offset engine development costs.

While Ford may fret over its recent passenger car problems, executives can remain smug about the truck side of the business. The company is scoring with its newest sport-utility vehicle, the all-new Explorer, which is eating into the market share of rivals.

The Explorer, incidentally, breaks ground by becoming the first "captive export." It is common for US manufacturers to market products built for them by a Japanese ally. But a two door version of the Explorer will be sold by Mazda's American dealers under the Navajo nameplate.

MANAGEMENT CHANGES

This has been a big year for shaking up the old management order at the Big Three.

At Ford, many view the early retirement of Donald Petersen as a major loss. In the early 1980s, with Ford on a desperate, downward spiral, Petersen championed of quality and policies that led to successful products like the Taurus.

Petersen's replacement is anything but unknown, Harold "Red" Poling, previously Ford's president. Tight with the budget, Poling is likely to follow Petersen's basic game plan. But at General Motors, it clearly won't be "business as usual" for new Chairman Bob Stempel, who in August, succeeded Roger Smith, GM's controversial chief executive. Smith was an autocrat with a firm belief in technology, but despite more than $70-billion invested in new plants and products, and the purchase of two huge high-tech subsidiaries, Smith presided over the biggest loss of market share in GM history. He admits his inability to motivate people. In contrast, Stempel is spending a lot of time convincing people to join his GM "team".

Chrysler still has Lee Iacocca at the helm, but in recent months, a growing number of underlings have abandoned ship, including heir-apparent, Gerry Greenwald.

The Jeep Wrangler Renegade (above) is for those who seek their adventure in the great outdoors. The appeal is in an affordable, no compromise sport-utility vehicle designed for serious off-road fun. The Renegade has a new 4.0-litre in line six for 1991.

Bravo Bravada. The new entry is the first sport-utility from General Motors' Oldsmobile Division, and sound marketing strategy as several million Americans have traded in their sedans and station wagons for light trucks like this. With its four-wheel-drive, anti-lock brakes and upscale options such as leather seats, the Bravada shows that sport-utility vehicles can be more than just utilitarian.

When it comes to sport-utility vehicles with the family in mind, Ford has scored the big hit of the year with its all-new four-door Explorer. Quick and tough, yet stylish enough to take to the theatre, the Explorer features plenty of leg room and cargo space, and a 155bhp, 4.0-litre V6. There is also a smaller two-door. And, in an unusual move, the Explorer becomes the first "captive export," with Ford's Japanese ally Mazda marketing its own version under the Navajo nameplate.

LEXUS/INFINITI UPDATE

Rocks and trees apparently don't sell many cars, but good customer service does.

After their first year, Toyota's new Lexus luxury division and Nissan's upscale marque, Infiniti, have had distinctly different experiences.

First to reach the market, in September 1989, Lexus quickly achieved big sales. But three months later, potential disaster struck in the form of a recall. Rather than run and hide, Lexus took the lead, even sending mechanics to pick up recalled LS400s late at night. They were back in the driveway the following morning — with a little gift for the owner.

The nightmare turned into a coup, helping send first year sales soaring to the 60 000 mark.

Infiniti, on the other hand, just has not got into gear.

Part of the blame goes to a zen-like ad campaign that conveyed images of pastoral nature scenes — rocks and trees, but no cars. "We stayed with (that) campaign longer than we should have," concedes Infiniti's general manager, Bill Bruce, and as a result, first year sales were pathetic 17 000 units.

Bruce is hoping to more than double that number in 1991, thanks to several new models.

Millions of American drivers are turning to sport-utility vehicles, minivans and pickups. The Oldsmobile Expression (opposite, centre) is designed to offer them an alternative, a halfway point between a conventional passenger car and a light truck.

69

The American Baby Boom generation has fallen in love with the minivan. But Chrysler, which created the minivan concept, still owns the market with products like the 1991 Dodge Caravan (opposite, top). Beyond the streamlined grille, it might be hard to tell from the outside that Chrysler invested more than $700-million updating its minivan line. But inside and the new interior is not only functional but surprisingly attractive, with the type of layout and materials that have won converts in the past for the Japanese.

The Ford Aerostar (left) is one of those tough competitors, with a new 'Sport Appearance' package for 1991. With the optional four-wheel-drive, and anti-lock brakes, the Aerostar is a go-anywhere, do-anything vehicle.

The Dodge Spirit R/T (right) is a wolf in sheep's clothing. To outward appearances, it is a conservative four-door, front-wheel-drive sedan. But its turbocharged, 16-valve, DOHC 2.2-litre engine makes it one of world's fastest production sedans, and the fastest built in North America. The Spirit R/T, incidentally, features Chrysler's first domestic multi-valve engine.

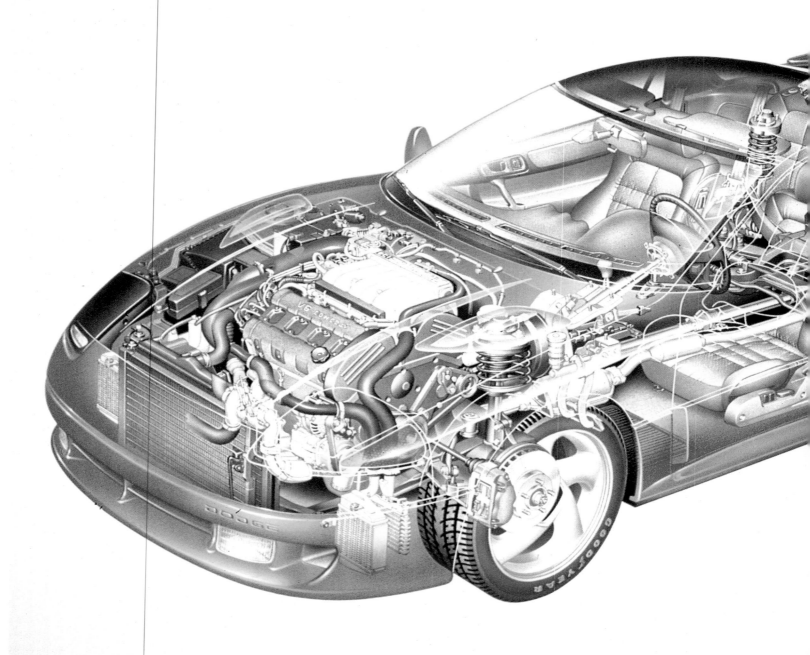

A convertible does not have to be expensive. With a price tag of around $13000, the Dodge Shadow Convertible (left) is aimed at young buyers who are bored with boxy hardtops. It also boasts a driver's side airbag, an appealing feature for the safety-minded.

Named the Stealth (opposite), this new entry from Chrysler may easily take you by surprise. That sports car skin doesn't lie. This is a fast car that can hold its own on most winding roads. This limited edition sports car is being offered in four different versions and two distinctly different body styles. The ultimate configuration is the R/T Turbo. It has a 3.0-litre, 24-valve V6, with twin intercooled turbochargers that produces 300 horsepower and 307 pound feet of torque. Four-wheel-drive keeps those ponies under control. It also has anti-lock brakes and four-wheel-steering tuned for high-speed handling. The Stealth is a joint venture between Chrysler and Mitsubishi, which is marketing its own version, dubbed the 3000GT.

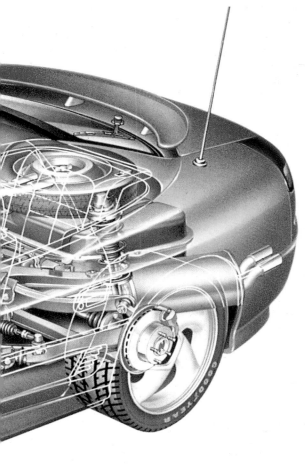

CHRYSLER – FUTURE UNCERTAIN

If nothing else, Chrysler Chairman Lee Iacocca is the consummate salesman. To demonstrate the effectiveness of his company's airbags, Iacocca offered to be filmed driving into a brick wall. Ultimately, he was replaced in the commercial by a trained stuntman, but it illustrates just what lengths the Chrysler Chairman is ready to go to in order to turn around a worsening slump in sales.

Iacocca has remained the central star in Chrysler's increasingly aggressive TV and media sales campaign. Much of the blitz has been aimed at the Japanese, quoting company-sponsored surveys that found a select group of motorists preferred Chrysler products to those of Honda and Toyota. But despite the costly campaign, and billions of dollars in incentives, Chrysler's sales and market share has been on a steady, downward spiral.

Why have things been going so badly?

Some point to the absence of the Omni and Horizon subcompacts. Sales have also been weak for other entry-level offerings built by Chysler's Japanese partner, Mitsubishi, and badged as Dodge or Plymouth models.

And then there is the fact that depends more than its Big Three and import rivals on low-income and blue-collar workers, the type of buyers who are particularly vulnerable when the US economy goes sour.

However, Chrysler continues to dominate the Jeep and minivan market, despite the best attempts of its many competitors. The best-selling Chrysler minivans get a facelift for 1991. There is little outward difference, other than a smaller more aerodynamic grille, for most of the changes can be found on the inside. Gone, for example, is the clumsy, truck-like dashboard with flimsy buttons and knobs hidden beneath the steering wheel.

"We started from the inside because we think our customer is more interested in functionality than in breaking new grounds in styling," says designer Trevor Creed.

Chrysler is not ready to write off the passenger car market, and is taking steps to overcome its stodgy, ho-hum image with cars like the new Dodge Stealth. The high-tech, high-performance sports car is part of a joint development program with Japanese ally Mitsubishi.

But perhaps the biggest news is that the Viper has been given the go-ahead. Unveiled as a prototype at the 1989 Detroit Auto Show, the Viper is a paean to the great sports cars of the past. And with its brutish V10, it could give modern muscle machines like the Corvette ZR-1 a real run for the money. Vipers will not be built in large numbers, but the real value of the project is to provide a halo for Chrysler that could translate into a sales rebound.

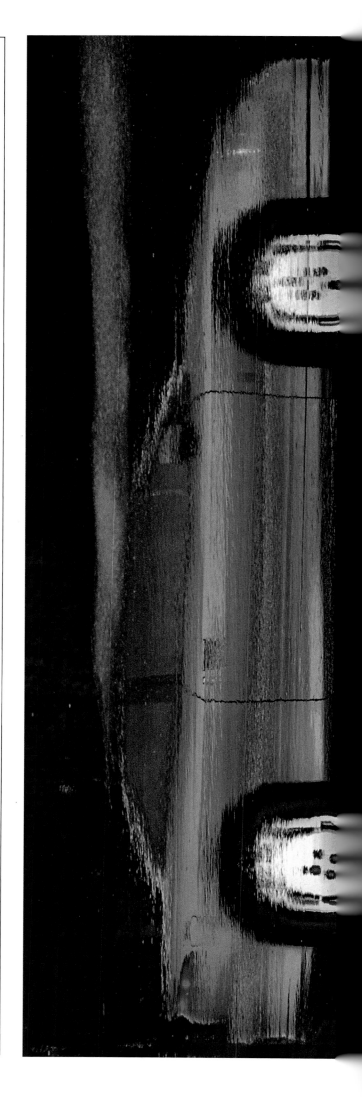

There is a lot riding on GM's new Saturn division. This $2.5 billion project was given the lofty goal of creating a new generation of products that would win over the younger, import-oriented buyers who never set foot inside an American new car showroom. Saturn makes its auspicious debut with two models. The coupe is the more radical of the pair, with a sharp, tapered nose that sweeps back over a surprisingly roomy passenger cabin. Critics lament that the design does not really break new ground, bearing a noticeable resemblance to the Geo Storm. A little more conservative is the Saturn sedan, with a look that may recall the Oldsmobile Cutlass Supreme. The body panels on both models are thermoset plastic, which resists corrosion, and which Saturn people claim can withstand the types of parking lot bumps that would put a dent in a conventional metal body panel. Styling is secondary for Saturn. The emphasis has been on designing vehicles that could match the best of the Japanese in terms of quality, reliability, features and performance. Buyers have a choice of single- or twin-overhead-cam 1.9-litre aluminium block engines which can be mated to either manual or automatic transmissions. There is an extensive list of standard features, and options such as anti-skid brakes.

SATURN:
TWO... ONE... ZERO... IGNITION!

When Roger Smith drove a Saturn subcompact off the assembly line in Spring Hill, Tennessee, late last July, it marked both the beginning and the end of an era for General Motors.

It was the last act for the controversial Smith, now retired at age 65. During his decade-long tenure, GM's market share plunged roughly a dozen points, and in the process, a dozen assembly plants were closed, with tens of thousands of jobs lost. But it might also mark the beginning of GM's long-sought turnaround.

Perhaps no automotive project in history has attracted as much attention. In January 1985 General Motors announced plans to create an entirely new subsidiary intended to produce the type of small car that would drive the Japanese back into the sea. In the following months, a stream of politicians, like Greeks bearing gifts, rolled up to GM headquarters offering millions of dollars in subsidies if the automaker were only to build the Saturn plant in their state.

After an initial flurry of attention, Saturn was wrapped in a shroud, to reappear five-and-a-half years and $2.5-billion later.

Saturn is finally in production. But is it up to the standards of a Honda Civic? Initial reviews are mixed. Clearly, it is the best small car GM has ever built. The general consensus is that the look and feel of the interior is highly refined, with a careful attention to detail, to touch, to fit and finish. The engine, however, is not nearly as smooth and quiet as the best of the Japanese competition.

Saturn was introduced with just two models, with looks which broke no new ground: a sporty coupe with styling reminiscent of the hot-selling Geo Storm, and a more conservative sedan, with a design that puts it in the same family as the Oldsmobile Cutlass Supreme.

Buyers have a choice of single or twin overhead-cam 1.9-litre aluminium block engines which can be mated to either manual or automatic transmissions.

The power train design illustrates some of the ways in which Saturn differentiates itself from the more conventional General Motors passenger car.

To start with, Saturn is the first high-volume manufacturer to use lost foam casting, a technique in which a short of hot metal is poured into sand wrapped around a styrofoam mould. The styrofoam bubbles off, leaving a perfect aluminium block.

In a unique move, Saturn engineers designed both the manual and automatic transmissions so they could be rolled down the same assembly line, making it easy to change the mix in response to market demand.

Big differences can be seen almost everywhere in the Spring Hill plant. Surprisingly, it is not as highly automated as many other new assembly lines. The emphasis is on automating jobs that are boring, dangerous or difficult to do right.

Among the 2500 or so workers, it is almost impossible to tell who is a union and who is management, for hourly workers have played an active role in almost every stage of the Saturn project. They even helped picked Saturn's advertising agency, and had the chance to veto potential dealers.

The distribution system is in itself unique. Dealers are being granted a wide geographic franchise in which they are expected to open several different stores. Some will handle everything from sales to service, but others may only serve as new car showrooms or as repair centres.

Fittingly, Saturn mechanics will rely on an advanced computer diagnostic system designed to leave little to chance — or guesswork.

When the Saturn project was initially unveiled, GM planned a $5-billion investment capable of producing 500 000 cars a year. Cautiously, those numbers were cut in half. Saturn will be going up against some of the toughest competition in the auto industry. But if it lives up to expectations, GM plans to double capacity — to the original target — by adding a second line in the next few years.

Perhaps the station wagon is not dead? With many buyers switching to minivans, Buick is betting that some buyers may just want something a little bit more all-American. This full-sized battle wagon has a lot of kids and cargo capacity, and the muscle to haul it around, thanks to a 5-litre V8. It revives the classic Road-master name, and also marks the first major redesign of the Buick Estate Wagon since 1978.

JAPANESE INVASION

Japanese auto imports have long been a mainstay in the California market, but now they are also beginning to play significant roles in Peoria, St. Louis, and even Detroit for that matter.

A decade ago, the Big Three vowed to push their Japanese competitors "back into the sea," but as the 1990s opened, the import beachhead extends deep into the American heartland, month after month, translating into new records in market share.

In the coming year, Honda may push past Chrysler as the number three passenger car company. Toyota intends to capture 10 per cent of the American new car market by mid-decade.

The Japanese are very different companies compared to 1980. In the wake of an energy crisis, they then made their mark selling small, reliable, fuel-efficient and inexpensive cars.

Their products still have a reputation for reliability, but today they cover a much broader range, from minicars to sport cars, midsized sedans to minivans. With its new NSX, Honda's upscale Acura division is challenging the world's best sports cars. The Lexus LS400 is stealing sales from Cadillac and Lincoln, as well as BMW, Mercedes-Benz and Jaguar.

As for price, as a result of the steadily appreciating yen, their vehicles are anything but cheap. But no matter. Especially as when buyers under the age of 45 are concerned, Japanese products have become as American as apple pie.

That is not such an absurd statement as it might seem, for virtually every Japanese car manufacturer now operates at least one "transplant" assembly line in the USA and Canada. Toyota took its first tenuous step into North American production through a joint venture with General Motors. It has since added two of its own assembly plants and recently announced it will build a third. By the mid-1990s, the Japanese will have capacity to build 2.5-million vehicles a year in North America.

But Detroit is fighting back. General Motors has had some success this year with its trendy new Geo line. But, ironically, all but one of the Geo products are really "captive imports," produced by GM's Japanese allies, Isuzu and Suzuki. The other vehicle, the compact Prizm, comes from the GM-Toyota joint venture.

The ultimate test for Detroit may be another General Motors bid for the small car market, Saturn. GM is counting on this domestic subcompact to convince young buyers there really is a reason to buy an all-American car.

The Caprice Wagon (right) is another option for family buyers looking for a minivan alternative. Like the Caprice sedan, it has an all-new aerodynamic look for 1991. It also boasts a choice of a 5.0-litre or 5.7-litre V8, a stiffened suspension package and anti-lock brakes. For the kids, there is even a special interior fabric that resists stains.

The classic American muscle car, the Pontiac Firebird gets a facelift for 1991 with a new front fascia, redesigned rear deck spoilers and an aggressive Sport Appearance Package. The SLP Firebird shows its talons with a "Street Legal Performance" package that stops just short of the race track. For the timid, the base Firebird model comes with a more modest 3.1-litre V6.

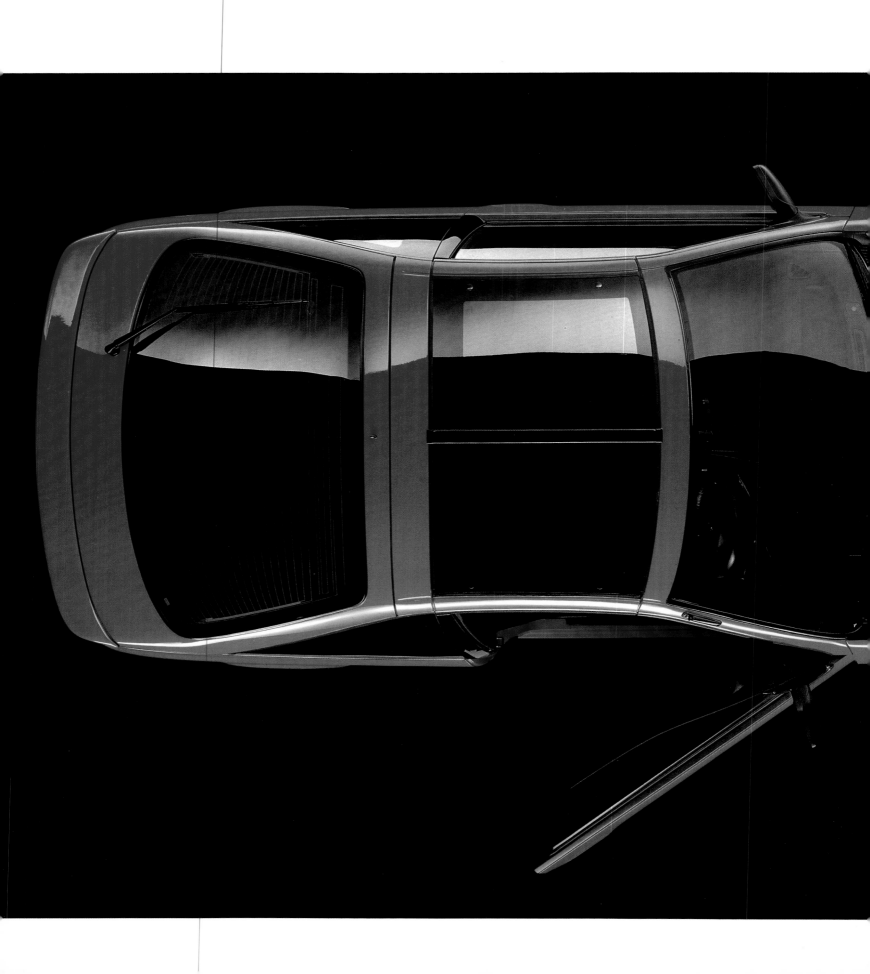

JAPAN'S INDUSTRY

BUILDING ON STRENGTH

<u>Peter Nunn</u>

Japan's mighty auto industry moved several gears higher during 1990, consolidating its home base while at the same time laying down expansion plans for wider world production in the decade to come.

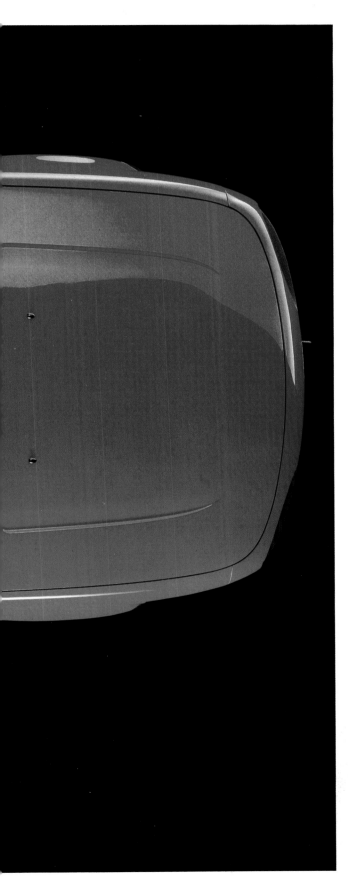

At the start of the 1990s, the old maximum about the strong getting stronger and weak becoming weaker seemed especially true of Japan's domestic car producers.

At the top of the tree, Toyota, not only Japan's largest company but also the most profitable of all (for the third year in a row), once again turned in record sales and set of awesome financial results.

In stark contrast, for Fuji Heavy Industries, makers of Subaru cars, 1989-1990 resulted in a damaging Y29.6 billion loss in operating income and the likely prospect that 1990-1991 will not be much better.

Nissan in number two spot was another company to blossom, with an increased market share plus a healthy balance sheet. Isuzu, meanwhile, stands as the only Japanese car maker whose sales continue to go down instead of up, and this despite the launch of the brand new and important Gemini mid-range series.

The introduction of the new 3-6 per cent VAT rate, in April 1989, continues to have a marked effect on Japan's domestic registrations, with those relating to cars in the over 2.0-litre sector showing the sharpest growth. There, the best sellers continue to be Toyota's Mark II (Cressida) series and Crown, the Nissan Laurel and Mitsubishi's newer and well-received Diamante/Sigma series.

In the top sector, Toyota's Lexus LS 400 (sold as the Celsior in Japan) has been a spectacular success. So much so, that a number of wealthy Japanese businessmen have been prepared to pay a premium to have LS 400s *reverse-exported* from the US to Japan, to short-cut the year-long Japanese waiting list. Toyota, it is said, is not amused.

Importers, once again, are benefitting from this continued and lucrative Japanese demand for upscale cars. BMW, Mercedes and VW seem to take it in turn to be market leader from month to month, while renewed efforts by US manufacturers (including Honda USA and Mitsubishi/Chrysler's DSM) are starting to pay off, putting them in second place in the burgeoning import league table. Japanese importers finished 1989 with a record 180,424 registrations and it will be a surprise if there is not a jump to well over 200,000 units for 1990. In the midst of these glowing sales figures and record domestic production of 12 953 790 vehicles during fiscal 1989, one sector, that of Japan's unique mini-vehicle category fell away, then regained strength. The introduction of the allowance for enlarged (660 cc) engines plus another 100 mm in body length breathed new life into the car side of the business. However, the mini truck and van market has been severely hit by tax law changes.

Although 1990 does not compare to the incredible output of top quality Japanese cars in 1989 — the year the Toyota Lexus, Mazda MX-5 Miata, Nissan Infiniti, Skyline GT-R and 300ZX all appeared — the growing Japanese ability to produce spin-off variations of different cars, and in quick succession, too, was once again an eye-opener.

The Toyota Sera, Mazda Revue, Nissan Presea and new President were all examples of this 1990s genre. Rest assured, they certainly will not be the last.

Left: 1990 was Nissan's family car year. As well as this Californian-designed NX coupe, launched in Japan in January, the year also saw the arrival of the Primera and Pulsar, Nissan's replacements for the European Bluebird and Sunny. The NX, Nissan's answer to the Honda CR-X, highlights the new Sunny range.

NISSAN: CONSOLIDATION

After the hectic rebuilding years of the late 1980s, Nissan had a relatively quiet time during 1990. Even so, the company still managed to chalk up significant increases in sales and profits to stay healthy and to consolidate its strong number two position in Japan.

In comparative terms, the pace at which new Nissan models appeared slackened noticeably. But then it would be difficult, even for Nissan, to top the achievements of 1989 — the year of the Infiniti Q45, 300ZX and Skyline GT-R all.

In 1990, Nissan concentrated on remodelling its family car line, the 'bread and butter' Sunny and its close cousin, the Pulsar. Nissan also introduced the Primera and its estate cousin, badged Avenir in Japan. Another model — the Presea — arrived in mid-year as a small speciality saloon.

For Japan, Nissan launched a conservative new Sunny saloon and US-designed NX coupe in January, both receiving new generation twin cam engines, drivetrains and suspensions, quite apart from new shells and interiors. This Sunny saloon later went into production in the US as the 1991 Sentra.

In August, Nissan launched the mechanically similar (but sportier) new Pulsar and this will double as the next generation European Sunnys in early 1991, when they challenge the Escort-Tipo-Golf set.

The flagship of the new Pulsar range, the be-spoilered 2.0-litre turbo 4WD GTi-R, forms the basis of a renewed Nissan WRC attack starting in mid-1991. With 230 PS, it is also quite some road car...

The Primera also went on sale in the US as the G20, the third model in Nissan's Infiniti luxury division. Infiniti has been conspicuously slower off the mark in the US than Toyota's Lexus, having been dogged by controversial TV ads and weak production recognition, among other things. Whether the Peugeot-lookalike G20 will provide more action remains to be seen. But mid-year rumours of a 1992 mid-engined Infiniti supercar, derived from the stillborn Mid-4, sounded very exciting.

Two other events put Nissan in the news in 1990: an unprecedented, full-scale attempt to be the first Japanese to win Le Mans (Nissan finished fifth, the highest ever by a Japanese team), plus the acquisition, in all but name, of troubled Subaru. Isamu Kawai, former head of Nissan Diesel, is the new Subaru president.

On the technology front, Nissan unveiled a sophisticated new manufacturing system in Japan called IBAS, which primarily allows for much speedier and accurate body assembly. Latterly, the company also began marketing VW's new Passat under licence, prior to initiating local production in 1992.

Right: Toyota's gullwing Sera caused a stir when it appeared, instantly becoming one of Japan's hottest cult cars. Based on the new Starlet, the 1.55-litre Sera's ingenious doors open out and up. Below: New 2.0-litre, second generation MR2 received mixed reviews in Japan. Though fast and comfortable, its handling needs care — especially in the turbo version.

Above: Powered by the 4E-FTE 1.3-litre dohc 16-valve turbo engine, the new 135 PS Starlet Turbo does not lack for performance. An aggressive body kit adds to the sporting image.

TOYOTA: CHALLENGING FOR TOP SPOT

For Toyota, the challenge to be the world's number one manufacturer is definitely on: Japan's most affluent company is gunning for an annual six million unit target by the late 1990s.

In 1989, Toyota produced 4.32 million cars and commercials and through new plants in Japan and overseas plans a dramatic rise in production to challenge Ford and GM.

Toyota's new plant in Fukuoka, western Japan, is set to be the world's most advanced assembly facility and will be one of a new group situated outside the company's traditional central Japan base.

Toyota certainly has the finance to fund this towering expansion programme. With record profits for fiscal 1989, it became the first Japanese company to announce a pre-tax income of over Y700 billion.

Toyota continues to dominate its home market with a market share of around 42 per cent and giant model line-up. In 1989, Toyota sold 2.3 million cars, trucks and buses in Japan, yet has reportedly earmarked a sales drive to hike that to 3.0 million by the mid 1990s.

Lexus, Toyota's new luxury division, has proved an outstanding success. The exceptionally refined V8-engined LS400 won the 1989-90 Japanese Car of the Year title at a canter and, right from the start, demand has remained strong both in North America (its main market) and Japan, although critical acclaim when it was introduced into Europe in 1990 was less than ecstatic.

Marketed in Japan as the Toyota Celsior, the LS400 will spawn a wider range of profitable Lexus products, including a luxury coupe to rival the Mercedes SEC and possibly a long-wheelbase V12 saloon. While the smaller, Camry-based ES 250, its sister car, has been much slower in the showroom, there is no doubt Lexus has shaken the establishment.

Toyota was kept very busy with new product during 1990. The new twin cam Starlet came on stream early in the year, then the gullwing Sera speciality coupe which, beneath the skin, is Starlet-derived. Overnight, the tiny Sera became one of Japan's hottest cult cars.

In company with new versions of the Land Cruiser — dubbed the 80 Series and 70-Series Prado — Toyota also launched a new Camry for the domestic market, the acclaimed Estima (Previa) minivan plus a rebodied Tercel/Corolla II/Corsa series. In 1991, Toyota is expected to produce a separate run of wide-bodied Camrys at its US Kentucky plant.

Also significant was the Autumn introduction of a new 1JZ-GTE 2.5-litre twin turbo, straight-six engine. First seen in facelifted versions of the Supra and Mark II in Japan, this high power 2.5 is destined for Lexus and other top Toyotas.

Left: Specialised interior of the gullwing Sera features unique dashboard and fittings. Car is basically a slim 2+2, its low roof being made largely of glass.

MAZDA: AMBITIOUS PLANS

The momentum Mazda built up during 1989, establishing not only two new sales channels in Japan, but also a policy of launching new and varied niche products (such as the MX-5 and MPV minivan) continued to gather pace during 1990.

In the home market especially, Mazda is very much the profitable company on the rise. The new Honda is how some have described it. And yet 1991 will see Mazda even more preoccupied, with no fewer than three major new model introductions.

In the coming year, Japanese buyers can expect a new 929/Luce and 626/Capella, as well as new, third generation RX-7 in the autumn. In the case of products such as the 626, Mazda is likely to 'add' cosmetically-related variations to the line-up, to be offered through separate sales channels in Japan.

It is with developments such as this that Mazda is said to be developing rivals for BMW's 3.5 and 7-Series during the early 1990s.

Mazda's plans for the Japanese market are ambitious. In 1989, the company sold 490 000 units and the forecast for 1990 is 560 000 units. By 1992, Mazda hopes to be up to 800 000 units and a 10 per cent share in the car sector — ahead of Honda.

Mazda intends to get there with a continual stream of fresh and interesting new models, by extending the breadth of its five

domestic sales channels and by dramatically hiking production. An extension of its Hofu plant is being readied specifically for that purpose and will be responsible, in part, for the production of one or more of the new luxury models under wraps.

Mazda is widely believed to have an upscale Lexus-class saloon under development, which in the US will be marketed through a separate luxury division, possibly to be called Pegasus, in 1992. Mazda's flagship triple-rotor Cosmo coupe went on sale in the spring, backed up by a cheaper two-rotor version. With 280 PS on tap, the top, twin turbo three-rotor Cosmo ranks as an fast, luxurious 2 + 2 coupe. In due course, Mazda may offer the Cosmo for export, perhaps through its new luxury channel.

In 1990, Mazda upgraded its new 550cc Carol minicar to 660cc in line with new Japanese K-car regulations and introduced the Revue, a small 1.3-1.5-litre speciality saloon.

In Europe, Mazda's intention to initiate production with Ford in West Germany has been agreed in principle but, as these words are written, yet to be formalised.

In the US, a second production plant to add to that in Flat Rock, Michigan is under review. Ford and Mazda now collaborate more closely in product development: witness the co-designed US Escort and increased plans for engine sharing.

Right: Mazda's Cosmo coupe, the first production car with a triple rotor Wankel engine, is marketed through Mazda's sporting Eunos channel in Japan. Exotic, 280 PS twin turbo Cosmo might be described as a 'Japanese XJ-S'. Below: The Toyota Previa, rebadged as the Estima in the home market, is Japan's critically-acclaimed new mid-engined MPV. The rounded styling came from North America.

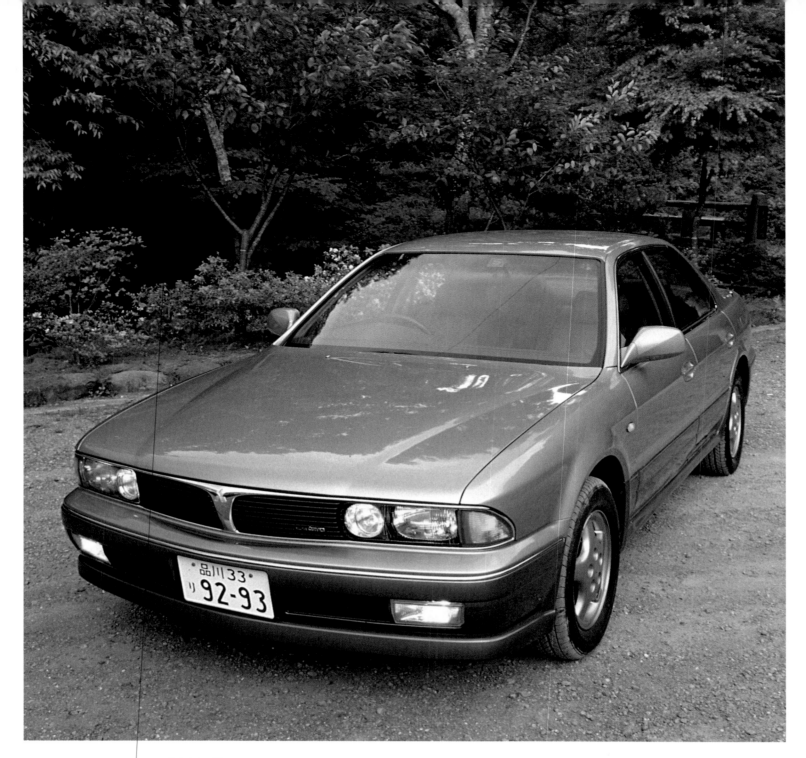

Diamante is Mitsubishi's brand-new 1990 saloon. Offered in a wide variety of forms, with engines from 2.0-litre four cylinder to 3.0-litre V6, the Diamante is likely to be renamed for its European launch in 1991. Styling unashamedly apes former BMW 7 Series. Interior is spacious and comfortable and in top specification it is exceptionally well-equipped.

MITSUBISHI: MOVING UP

Mitsubishi, a long time prominent player in Japan's bustling truck and commercial vehicle sector, gave its car division a major boost in 1990 with the mid-year launch of the Diamante, a compact luxury saloon. In some ways, a cleverly enlarged, pillarless version of the Galant, the V6-engined Diamante provides Mitsubishi with its first real ammunition in that upper market sector. In Japan, it targets the strong-selling Toyota Mark II-Nissan Laurel set, while at the same time opening up a whole new market for Mitsubishi in Europe: that of the prestige Rover-Alfa-BMW-Saab group. On the strength of looks, packaging, performance and equipment, the Mitsubishi is likely to make waves in North America, against the Legend and Camry in particular.

For export, Mitsubishi plans to change the name to Sigma and to modify the body with increased rear headroom and conventional framed doors. Both two and four-wheel-drive systems are available, the latter having the benefit of Mitsubishi's TCL Traction Control system, which curbs understeer and wheelspin.

The arrival of the Diamante has had a very positive effect on Mitsubishi sales and profits in Japan. Another new model — the 3000 GT VR-4 — Mitsubishi's high image replacement for the ancient Starion — looks all set to build on this new-found im-

provement. This powerful 3.0-litre twin turbo V6 two-seater, renamed Mitsubishi GTO for the home market is aimed primarily at the North American market and has Chrysler's charismatic Dodge Stealth as its close cousin — the two cars build side-by-side by Mitsubishi in Japan.

Adding impetus to Mitsubishi's upmarket aspirations is the behind-the-scenes completion of a prototype V8 to power a possible Mitsubishi Lexus rival in the near future. Not that Mitsubishi is likely to rush into such an operation.

Throughout 1990, the industry watched and waited as Mitsubishi apparently came closer to Chrysler, thus fuelling speculation of a partial or complete take-over. Mitsubishi, however, deny it, along with rumours that it intends to take a controlling interest in the joint-owned Diamond Star Motors plant.

By the beginning of October, Mitsubishi's straight-talking president, Hirokazu Nakamura had still to name a site for local EC production. However, now the Mitsubishi group is renewing links with Daimler-Benz on a variety of issues, a joint-production plan could be realised. Mitsubishi also announced plans for a new group of factories in Japan, to lift sales of cars, trucks and buses well above that of the 1 268 million of fiscal 1989.

In Japan, Toyota's third generation Camry is sold alongside badge-engineered Vista cousins and with either pillarless or conventional framed doors. Pillarless (Hard Top) Camry, left, with 2.0-litre V6 power is flagship of the entire range while the Vista Hard Top, below, is an alternative to new Camry saloon for the domestic market.

Top: One of the many faces of the new Toyota Camry. This saloon, with framed doors, will probably be the version exported, to markets including Europe. A separate run of wide-bodied Camrys will be produced in the USA from 1991. Below: one of the 1989 Tokyo Show stars, Suzuki's Cappucino sports car is still only at the "maybe" stage. Prototypes have been built, but production still seems a long way off.

SUBARU, SUZUKI: PROBLEMS AND PROGRESS

In time, Subaru insiders and stockholders could look back on 1990 as their darkest hour. In the financial year to March 1990 Subaru posted an operating loss of Y30 billion.

As a result, Subaru chief Toshihiro Tajima vacated his presidency in favour of Isamu Kawai, president of Nissan Diesel. The tough, well-respected Kawai faces a difficult restructuring job, particularly in North America. He has already said the company will post another operating loss for 1990-91. He has also sensibly axed Subaru's shambolic F1 participation with Coloni. On the product front, the Legacy is going well for Subaru, both in the showroom and in rallies. But until the next Leone/L-Series appears, Subaru will remain exposed in the vital, middle market sector. A new Alcyone, based on the exotic SV-X coupe shown at the 1989 Tokyo Show, will debut early in 1991.

By way of support strategy, Nissan could well re-commission Subaru to undertake local production on its behalf, starting with Japanese production of the next generation March/Micra in 1992.

With Japan's K-car class moving up to 660cc, Subaru duly introduced a new, upgraded version of the Rex in 1990. However, the class leader continues to be Suzuki and following the dismal K-car results of 1989, Suzuki regained lost ground with new versions of the Alto, a completely restyled Cervo Mode in late summer and continued supplies of K-car engines and technology to Mazda (for its Autozam minivehicle channel).

The Cervo Mode, in top SR-Four guise, is the most developed of Japan's new generation K-cars, boasting a four cylinder dohc 16 valve intercooled turbo engine — of all off 658cc — plus four wheel drive.

While there is still no news of the little Cappucino sports car, displayed at the 1989 Tokyo Show, Suzuki released a stretched five-door version of the Escudo 4WD/utility vehicle in Japan in September. Called the Nomade, it allows Suzuki to side-step the stiff US import tariffs imposed on two-door utilities. The 1.6-litre sohc 16 valve engine is the same as that of the Escudo (alternatively called the Vitara, Sidekick or Geo Tracker in export markets).

Although best known for its minicars, Suzuki is steadily expanding its model mix and production capability. In January, Suzuki entered a joint-venture agreement to build 1.0-1.3-litre Swifts in Hungary, the project set to start in 1992 at the initial rate of 15 000 cars per year. Although the cars will be mainly for local distribution, company president Osamu Suzuki has not ruled out the possibility of exports to neighbouring EC markets at some point in the future.

Left: New bodies and interiors characterise Isuzu's reborn Gemini saloon, shown here in Handling by Lotus trim and BRG paint finish. The 1.6-litre dohc 16-valve engine is shared with the new Elan and America's Geo Storm.

Above: The Presea is Nissan's answer to the perennially successful Toyota Carina ED speciality saloon. But with that styling, perhaps it should also be an Infiniti for North America.
Left: The Primera is the new Nissan Bluebird for Europe and will be built in England as well as Japan. In America, it doubles as the entry-level Infiniti G20.

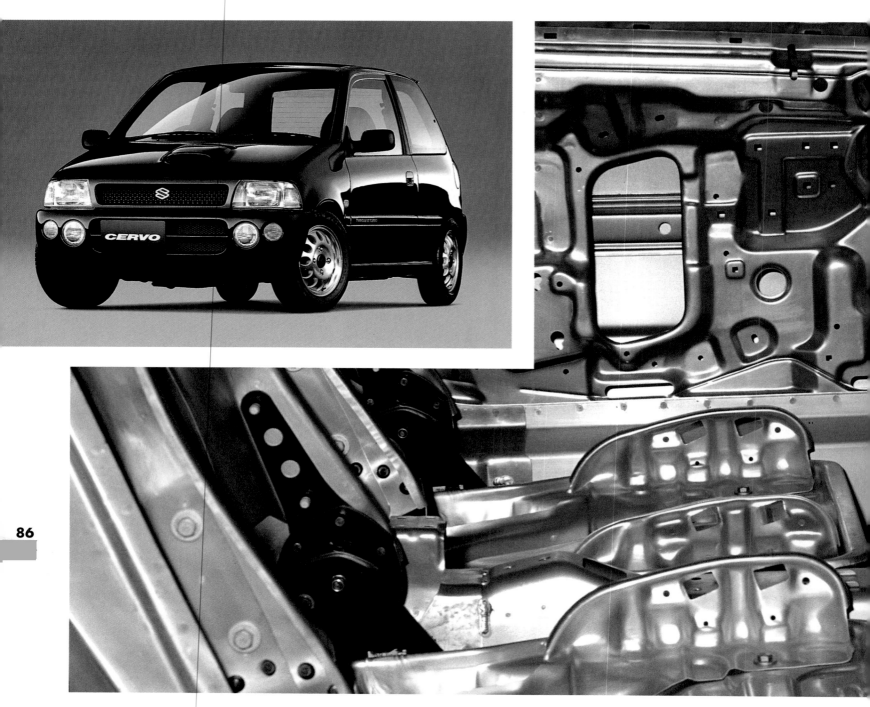

New for 1990, Suzuki's Cervo Mode SR-Four ranks as the most developed of Japan's new generation microcars. With four cylinders, a twin cam 16 valve head, turbo + intercooler plus the availability of full-time 4WD, the tiny 658cc Suzuki is a riot.

Nissan's new Pulsar will double as the next EC Sunny early in 1991. Three and four-door versions are available alongside this X1R five-door, all powered by brand new 1.3-2.0-litre twin cam engines. Aimed squarely at VW's Golf, the new Pulsar will be built in Japan and also Australia, while the top 2.0-litre turbo 4WD GTiR stands as Nissan's new WRC contender.

HONDA: STAYING AHEAD

After a year on the international show circuit, Honda finally put the NSX sports car on sale during the summer of 1990 and set new parameters for top flight exotica. The NSX, new from the ground up, came without the compromises normally expected of cars in its class. Superbly designed and crafted as well as enthralling to drive, the mid-engined, aluminium-bodied NSX was hailed as the user-friendly supercar and Japan's first fully-fledged rival to Europe's sports car greats.

Launched first in North America in late summer, then in Japan in September (at Y8 million, making it Japan's most expensive domestically-produced car), the NSX provided a perfect launch platform for Nobuhiko Kawamoto, Honda's technical chief who moved up to become company president at the end of June, succeeding Tadashi Kume.

Time will tell what changes, if any, Kawamoto proposes to make to Honda. The company remains Japan's best-loved car maker in the US — the Accord was actually 1989's best-selling car — and Acura, Honda's US pioneering luxury division, continues to figure strongly in the prestigious J.D. Power Customer Satisfaction surveys.

For the next generation Civic, expected in 1991, Honda is moving to have US suppliers extensively involved in parts sourcing, thus raising the local content and allowing the cars to qualify as "US-made." In that instance, the Civic should theoretically be allowed free access to the otherwise restricted EC market. Honda's US-built Accord Wagon is believed to be another such candidate for the EC.

Here, once again, Honda is ahead of the other Japanese in trying something new. However, with its main rivals now moving increasingly faster, Honda is having to be that more agile to stay ahead.

Honda's considerable expenditure on new plants in the US and Japan, coupled with sluggish motorcycle sales, foreign exchange losses and increased selling costs all contributed to a generally 'flat' set of financial results for 1989-90. Consolidated net income actually decreased 16 per cent.

With the NSX filling the headlines in 1990, the new Legend saloon and facelifted 660cc Today tended to be overlooked. Meanwhile, the second generation US-built Accord Coupe (that is reverse-exported to Japan) continued quietly on the successful path of its predecessor. It is, however, another conservative Honda.

On the new technology front, an ingenious passenger-side airbag and seat belt pretensioner were both unveiled by Honda in Japan during the summer, debuting on the new Legend, while a new deal to sell Chrysler Jeeps through its domestic Primo dealer chain was formalised.

Honda spent a fortune developing not only the all-aluminium body for the mid-engined NSX sports car, left, but also the brand new factory in Tochigi to build it. The two-seater NSX body, designed from scratch, has a light but rigid structure. Even main suspension parts are fashioned out of aluminium to reduce vehicle and unsprung weight. Expressly designed with clear all-round visibility and sound ergonomics in mind, the NSX interior is also beautifully crafted. A long 2530mm wheelbase allows for generous cabin space and excellent high speed stability, while comfort and equipment are both top class.

The aggressive Mitsubishi 3000 GT VR-4, left, is the replacement for the long-running four cylinder Starion and in the US, it has Chrysler's Dodge Stealth as its close cousin. For Europe, the 3000 GT name changes to Starion GTO and in Japan, it's just GTO. In top guise, the Mitsubishi's specification is awesome: a twin turbo 3.0-litre V6 providing 300 PS is matched to a full-time 4WD, 4WS chassis that also boasts electronic suspension. 240kmh/150mph top speed sees Mitsubishi competing head-on with other new wave Japanese exotics such as Nissan's 300 ZX, the Mazda Cosmo, Honda NSX and Toyota Supra 2.5.

DAIHATSU, ISUZU: SMALLER SUCCESS STORIES

Daihatsu was one of those affected by the fluctuating fortunes of Japan's K-car sector during the latter half of 1989 and early part of 1990. Although upgraded 660cc versions of the Mira and cheeky Leeza helped stem the tide, keeping Daihatsu close behind first-placed Suzuki in terms of overall sales, the slumping K-truck and van sector depressed Daihatsu's performance.

In Japan, Daihatsu is now very much back on course. But the Applause, Daihatsu's new 1.6-litre saloon, was the subject of a number of embarassing recalls soon after launch which did little for the car's reputation or that of Daihatsu's top management. Daihatsu continues to have strong links with Toyota. Japan's number one company holds a 14.3 per cent stake in Daihatsu which could quickly grow to a more supportive 20 per cent should the smaller company face more difficulties.

Looking to expand into North America and also Europe, Daihatsu is said to be considering a plan to initiate local production of the Feroza-Rocky off-roader in the US, possibly in co-operation with Toyota, while in Italy, a preliminary deal has been struck with Piaggio for the joint-production of small Hijet trucks. Starting in 1992, the latter could be expanded to include car production in the future.

At Isuzu, a new and complex range of mid-range Geminis bowed in during 1990, to brighten up the company's old, tired model line. The surprise is that even with these in the showrooms, Isuzu's home car sales continue to decline. Substantial commercial vehicle sales make a major contribution to Isuzu's balance sheet, as do those of the company's popular sports/utilities.

Though a curvaceous new four-door saloon is the main seller of the new Gemini group, the range also encompasses a pair of swoopy 2 + 2 sports coupes, the PA-Nero and the Gemini Coupe. In top form, these are powered (as is the 4dr) by the same 1.6-litre twin cam engine featuring in Lotus' celebrated new Elan.

In the US, the PA-Nero becomes GM's Geo Storm (or, with heavier nose treatment, the Impulse XS), while the four-door Gemini changes its name to Stylus.

Isuzu is still said to be nuturing plans to put its stunning 4200R Tokyo Show supercar into production, although replacements for the aged Piazza and Ascona-based Aska would seem to be of more immediate importance.

Isuzu is the smallest of Japan's nine car makers, but security comes through ever closer links with the giant GM.

A new type of rechargable battery was unveiled by Isuzu during 1990, with an output density 20 times greater than that of a conventional lead-acid battery. Sales are set to start in 1992.

88

Toyota's third generation Tercel family arrived in Japan in the latter half of 1990, slotting in between the Starlet and Corolla on the prodigious Toyota family tree. Created with younger buyers (and particularly Japanese girls) very much in mind, this curvaceous and significantly enlarged 1.3-1.5-litre Tercel comes in three-door hatchback and four-door saloon forms and also as the badge-engineered Corolla II and Corsa. Interiors, suspension and equipment are all new, making the Tercel unusually refined and luxurious for its class. A Stand-By 4WD version adds to the Tercel's versatility.

Conservative looks for Honda's new generation Legend saloon, which debuted in Japan in October. Powered by an all-new 3.2-litre, all-alloy V6, the Legend makes use of the 'front-midship' configuration first seen on the domestic five cylinder Accords (this places the engine's centre of gravity behind the front wheel centre line for optimum weight distribution and handling). The new sohc 32 valve V6 produces 215 PS and 30.5kg/m of torque but does not get Honda's latest VTEC technology. Launched in Europe in spring 1991, Honda's flagship saloon is expected to appear alongside the next Legend coupe.

ONE EUROPEAN APPROACH

Erhard Spranger

In 1985 a prediction that sales of cars imported into Japan could reach 500 000 units by 1995 would probably have been considered bizarre, could even have become a joke in the industry. And that would have been understandable, for in 1985, imports into Japan only just exceeded 50 000 cars, and these were driven by eccentrics, or maybe members of the Japanese underworld. Five years later, anybody not predicting that sales of imported cars will reach 500 000 units by 1995 is considered a pessimist, out of touch with the realities of market development as the 1990s opened. Today, however, ownership of a foreign car is no longer evidence of eccentricity, or an activity the law might frown on. It is en vogue, like wearing an Armani suit or carrying a Louis Vuitton bag — it has become an expression of a life style Japanese aspire to, and indeed can afford in a country where consumption tends to be conspicuous. Underlying this spectacular development, quite obviously, is the nation's increasing economic prosperity. A strong Yen, a stock market that save for very occasional fluctuations caused by outside factors such as oil crises has been steadily booming, high savings and ready access to money at low interest rates all fuelled the appetite for foreign goods in Japan. In addition, the Japanese government has responded to the pressure of criticism because of the aggressive export tactics of Japanese companies and its protectionist strategy and has begun to encourage imports in order to pacify overseas trade partners. Red tape has at least been reduced and regulations modified, to make it easier for a foreign manufacturer or importer to gain a foothold in the market.

This new enlightenment does not yet apply to all sectors of the economy, as negotiations between the United States and Japan have shown. But it has certainly been to the benefit of automobile importers, and many have taken aggressive advantage of the changed situation. Furthermore, in May of 1989 the taxation system was completely revamped. A commodity tax on cars which, depending on engine capacity, had amounted to 18.5-23 per cent of the landed cost, was replaced by a consumption tax and surcharge totalling 6 per cent on the retail price. One effect was that the prices of imported cars fell. Taking advantage of this, most importers re-appraised their pricing policy and some made further price cuts in the hope of achieving higher volume sales. More importers offering cheaper models appeared in the market, too — previously, the tendency had been to offer top-of-the-range versions, or cater for the niche areas where the small specialist British manufacturers have been so successful.

Jiro Yanase had been among the first to foresee eventual success for car imports — he started importing Mercedes-Benz in 1952, Volkswagen in 1954 and General Motors products in 1962. Of the 50 000 cars imported into Japan in 1985, 40 000 came out of German factories and 27 000 of these were handled by the Yanase Group. Volkswagen/Audi, Mercedes-Benz and BMW were the leaders at that time. In 1989, imports reached approximately 195 000, and two thirds of these cars originated in Germany. The same manufacturers still topped the list, and more than 80 000 units were handled by Yanase.

Until quite recently, Mercedes-Benz and VAG still relied on an importer to represent their interests, but BMW decided in the early 1980s that a wholly-owned subsidiary should manage BMW business in Japan. The fact that BMW sold more than 33 000 units in 1989 more than justified the decision, and BMW's current massive operation in Japan.

The German share of imports peaked at more than 75 per cent, but as a percentage of the market German-sourced imports have recently shown a decline, as other manufacturers have entered the market. However, there are no indications that the very strong position of German manufacturers will be seriously eroded in the near future.

History suggests that over many decades Japanese and Germans have developed 'haragei', a tacit understanding of each other and respect for institutions and methods. In Japan there is a deep-rooted appreciation of most things German, and 'Made in Germany' is synonymous with quality, with high standards of engineering,

A German success story, as its major manufacturers take the lion's share of import sales in 'the most difficult market in the world'. Growth potential in the 1990s encourages Opel to enter market, where it becomes well established in less than two years, and looks toward expansion. Coming to terms with local conditions is a real challenge for European manufacturers.

workmanship and durability. All are to be found in cars. The many Japanese motoring magazines spread the message of the innovative engineering in Europe, and of course sound engineering in Germany. Through their education, from secondary school to university, Japanese learn to methodically assemble facts and absorb information down to the smallest detail, appreciate that European cars are built to criteria different to those applied by their own industry. Functional design, high speed and excellent handling and ride characteristics are attributes of European cars. As far as the Japanese market is concerned they are also 'different', and they set a driver apart from most of his fellow road users. German cars offered just the right combination of engineering quality, performance and image, so the road to success was open.

The customers

In a society that could hardly be termed individualistic in the past, economic prosperity has shaped a new type of consumer, rich with cash and ready to spend it, one looking to break out of the traditional mould, wanting to

be different and prepared to be ostentatious with it, the 'shinjinrui', or new rich. As these people regard themselves as trailblazers for a new life style they obviously show a keen interest in new products.

Most 'DINKS' (double income, no kids), have no obligation to save for their own house — which is probably out of reach even for them — have money to spend and do spend it in their search for new life styles and self realization. They are the people who most readily buy foreign cars, and they are most important to the success or failure of a new product.

One of the most recent automotive newcomers to Japan is Opel, at least in its own right. The company was represented in Japan as far back as 1936, and again after the Second World War by Toho Motors Corporation, which in the Japanese fashion stood loyally by Opel even when the German company could not supply vehicles suitable for the market. In 1988 Opel felt ready to enter the Japanese market on its own account, with cars that were selling well in Europe and new products in the pipe line. These had the virtues of functional yet appealing lines and were sound in aspects such as aerodynamics, while the engines were suited to Japanese requirements

The Senator CD is Opel's flagship in Japan. It is marketed as a "new representative of German automotive engineering".

To immediately identify Opel as a German manufacturer, Opel vehicles are shown in a German environment, signalling to the audience the class, heritage and history of the make.

and Opels enjoyed a reputation for quality and reliability. Thus they met the physical requirements for success in perhaps the most demanding market in the world. In Europe or the USA car dealers are usually businessmen or investors who in choosing a manufacturer or importer to do business with are concerned with the availability of a franchise in a selected location, almost to the exclusion of anything else. In Japan, however, retail outlets are in many cases either directly owned by the manufacturer or importer, or are financially dependent on the franchiser. So it would be almost unthinkable for — say — a Toyota dealer to take on another marque as an additional franchise. With many alternatives available for investors to make money, the automobile business is not the most attractive, and this is why some importers needing a distribution channel have turned to department stores or supermarket chains. Thus Saab is associated with the SEIBU chain of department stores, for example, or Ford with the JUSCO supermarket group.

For Opel the establishment of a distribution organisation did not pose major problems. In Isuzu Motors, to a degree like Opel part of General Motors (GM actually

SUCCESSFUL SPECIALISTS

In overall terms, Britain has been running a distant third to Germany and the USA in exports to Japan, but apart from the not insubstantial sales of the Mini as a cult car most have been in market sectors least likely to be affected by a down-turn in trade — top-end luxury cars or specialised sports cars.

Among the specialist constructors, archetypical traditionalist Morgan does not sell many cars — averaging around two a month — and as in other markets expects its customers to wait for two years between order and delivery, a situation the loyal importer (Takano) seemingly accepts.

Caterham Cars' Graham Nearn has followed a one-model policy with the one-time Lotus Seven, slow evolution leading to the Super 7 HPC with a 175bhp 2-litre Vauxhall engine in 1990. The annual production rate falls just short of four figures, and looking to 1991 Nearn anticipates that a fifth of production will go to Japan. Modern Lotus sales may not seem impressive in total, but the real returns reflect the high value of each unit, for example in the 32 Turbo Esprits sold in 1989. The value of tradition? When finance from the Wary House Company of Minato-Ku under-pinned Ginetta in 1990 the contract initially meant that cars from around a quarter of a century ago were to be put back into production.

In its visual approach, Opel maintains as much uniformity as possible between the various merchandising activities. Also, the identity of the car line finds its visual interpretation in both a brochure (above) and a poster (left).

ACCESSORIES

AUTOMOTIVE DISTRIBUTION IN JAPAN

The automotive distribution system of Japan is basically structured on the same lines as the U.S. or European systems. Manufacturers supply cars to dealers who in turn sell them to the end user. The franchise agreements normally include reference to the product lines, the area of primary sales responsibility and the annual sales objective.

Seven of the eleven passenger car and truck manufacturers in Japan divide their product lines into two or more "sales channels", comparable to the "Divisions" of a U.S. automotive manufacturer. The number of sales channels differs from manufacturer to manufacturer as a result of product variety and sales volume. While manufacturers generally try to avoid product overlaps between sales channels, low volume models might be sold by more than one channel.

For optimum geographic coverage, domestic manufacturers strive to contract at least one dealership for each one of the 47 "prefectures" (administrative districts) in Japan. Large metropolitan areas like Tokyo, Osaka or Nagoya will, obviously, be serviced by several dealers for a given sales channel. Dealers, in turn, will operate a number of "sales outlets", which usually comprise a showroom and a service area. In many cases, the dealer's network is supported by a number of "independent outlets", which might be workshops, used-car dealers, and other small businesses acting as "bird dogs" for the dealership.

Imported vehicles, on the other hand, are distributed and sold somewhat differently from domestic cars. Imports find their way into Japan through one of two channels.

One is 'the official channel', constituted by wholly owned Japanese subsidiaries of foreign manufacturers, importers franchised by a foreign manufacturer, or importing companies, some of which are joint ventures between Japanese firms and a foreign carmaker. More recently, Japanese automobile manufacturers themselves have become active in importing foreign cars, either of their own production overseas (Honda, Mitsubish, Nissan, Mazda) or from other manufacturers (Isuzu/Opel).

The second channel is through independent importers who purchase from overseas dealers for resale in Japan. While these parallel imports initially flourished due to the growing popularity of imported cars, the volume is declining as a consequence of the strengthening of the 'official' import sales channels.

While many Japanese industries are characterized by a multi-tiered distribution system with retail sales generated mainly by a multitude of small "mom and pop" shops, the distribution of cars is rather simple and straightforward, on lines familiar elsewhere.

VECTRA QUALITY

パワー、走り、居住性。どれも高性能セダンに欠かせない要素。オペルはこの三要素をみごとにブレンドして、極めつきのドライブをお約束します。

Power, handling and comfort – the three elements of quality demanded of a high-performance sedan. Opel perfectly blended these three traits for your total driving pleasure.

owns some 40 per cent of Isuzu, in contrast with its complete control of Opel or Vauxhall) a potential partner was already waiting. A distribution network was almost immediately accessible, while some other GM facilities could be shared. By the middle of 1989 just over 100 Isuzu dealers were handling Opels, and the 1990 target was 200.

Meanwhile, Opel also showed that it had learned lessons about doing business the Japanese way — rather than cancelling the distribution agreement with its long-term partner Toho Motors Corporation as it teamed up with Isuzu, Opel maintained the bonds with the loyal partner. In any case, Toho has some 80 outlets, and was to take some models from the Opel line which otherwise would not be marketed in Japan.

Outlets and models

Since relationships once formed are not easily terminated, Opel was careful to select from the Isuzu dealer network only those outlets which from their location, appearance and facilities, attitudes and abilities of their personnel, matched the expectations of potential cus-

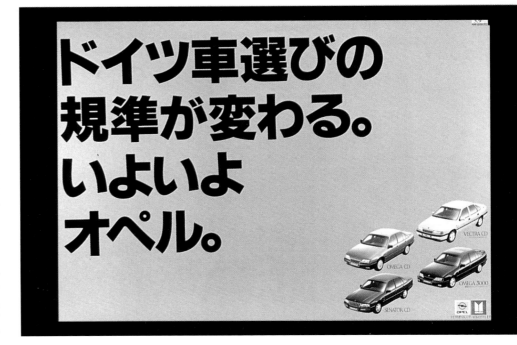

ドイツ車選びの規準が変わる。いよいよオペル。

Direct Mail is an important merchandising tool for both the importer and the dealer. It is heavily used throughout the year. As well as addressing prospective clients already known to them, dealers also target specific groups.

Magazines play an important part in the media mix, since they are widely read and usually provide very good and topical information on the developments in the automotive world. Opel has used magazines extensively to create awareness for the Omega 3000.

94

Millions of people pass through Tokyo subway stations every day, and these are ideal poster sites for creating awareness for a new product. Posters like this are usually displayed for a week at a time.

OPEL発見

The most important medium for any advertiser in Japan is certainly television. With eight stations broadcasting nationwide and regional stations to supplement coverage, television has become the favourite medium of the automotive industry, and an area of original creative competition between manufacturers or importers. Opel's launch spot for the Vectra CD (opposite) presented the car in its German environment, yet with an eye to a favourite Japanese pastime activity — fishing. Narrative was kept to a minimum, leaving the pictures to arouse a response in the audience.

ALLEGRO MA NON TROPPO...

To the clear soprano of an opera star a car soars majestically through the clouds, past Neuschwanstein and into the rising sun. The incantation reminds a viewer of a "Deutsches Lied". The text is German, the car is German, the commercial is for a German automobile manufacturer — in Japan.

In rhythm with the typically Parisian sounds of an accordion, two little cars jump like grasshoppers across a Seine bridge. The cars are Japanese, the location is Paris, the advertising is for a Japanese automobile manufacturer — in Japan.

To the Western viewer who lacks the cultural background to properly interpret them, Japanese commercials and advertisements can be seen as surreal collages, pseudo-intellectual phantasies, or nonsensical puzzles. Sometimes, they seem just childish. But advertising carries encoded messages. The viewer, as a result of his or her cultural heritage is in a position to decipher the code and to ultimately get to the intended message. The Japanese code is just different from the Western code language. But, nevertheless, many foreign elements have found places in Japanese advertising. Coke started it with "I Feel Coke", only to be topped by "Speak Lark". Both slogans have caught on in Japan, making Coke and Lark — each one in its field — the two best-selling international brands.

In Japan, a "stopper", an eye catching visual is extremely important, but so are music, "catch phrases" and actors. Many film and TV stars are striking it rich in Japan by advertising for cigarettes (Roger Moore), cars (Eddy Murphy), whisky (Mickey Rourke); the list is very long.

Advertising in Japan and Dentsu go hand in hand. Dentsu, "the number one advertising agency in the world" as the appendage always reads, presently employs more than 5800 people and handles approximately 3300 corporate clients, including such heavyweights as Toyota, Nissan, Honda, Matsushita (Nations/Panasonic), Toshiba, Sony and JVC — all at the same time, which does not seem to bother these clients. Dentsu's largest account bills more than 20 billion yen per year, whereas the smallest spends only 50 000 yen each year for the design of a leaflet for local distribution. Dentsu, the humble giant.

While Western advertising is direct and favours the hard sell approach, subtle "soft-sell" is preferred by the Japanese audience. Forget the notion that products can be sold in Japan on the basis of facts alone. Image and imagery are more important. The beauty of the visual, the lull of the music, a copy that is suggestive rather than direct, the product an afterthought rather than the centrepiece... Advertising in Japan is different. But it works!

Top: To capture the attention of an audience which is inundated with advertising, "dramatic" photography is often used in attempts to distinguish a product. "Opel hakken" — discover Opel — was the message used in the Omega 3000 launch campaign.

tomers. In appointing the first agents, emphasis was naturally on the urban centres of Tokyo, Osaka and Nagoya, where most imported cars are sold.

The same care was taken in selecting models for Japan. While the Opel range could offer an opportunity to cover much of the market, research suggested that the Senator and Omega 3000 would be acceptable in the 'High Car Group', while the Vectra would ideally fit into the 'Small Car Segment'. In terms of price, these cars could be positioned to compete with other models just as they would in European markets. Opel also decided to offer only the top-of-the-range versions, a strategy that was realistic in supporting the objective of becoming a volume seller in the market.

The Japanese are careful customers. They expect the degree of quality in a product that their American and even European counterparts might only hope for. And they want to know about the product they are thinking of buying — awareness is important. When Opel moved into the Japanese market, the awareness level was very low; Opel was just not known to potential customers, whereas marques like Mercedes-Benz and BMW featured in the 90 per cent range in every market survey.

This called for a brand awareness programme, to be implemented quickly. Dentsu, the largest advertising agency in the world, was commissioned to put Opel on the map in Japan. The briefing was to firmly establish Opel as a German manufacturer, and Opel cars as high-performance automobiles that would reflect the modern life style of their owners.

'Opel Hakken' was the theme adopted by Dentsu and the client, suggesting 'Discover Opel', the new representative of German automotive engineering. Several thousand customers got the message, visited dealers, and discovered the car they wanted in the Opel range. In 1989 Opel was the fastest-growing import, and so built a base for its Japanese expansion programme in the 1990s.

Doing business in Japan

The perception of 'Fortress Japan', a closed market for many years, has receded. It was never accepted by some European car companies, and more seem to have found the key to the market. As remarked, given normal trading conditions, recent trends suggest that the market could absorb half a million cars annually by 1995. That is roughly equivalent to the total Dutch car market in 1990. A number of foreign companies have tried to impose their Western business practices onto Japanese partners and customers in the past. Many of those companies are no longer in the Japanese telephone directories. Japanese business practices are different, primarily in longer-term thinking — an impressive bottom line is not necessarily the prime objective for Japanese management.

Business is a quiet affair in Japan. One prefers to be inconspicuous. Relationships, human bonds, are more important than written documents.

This is particularly true in selling automobiles, when customer and salesman form a bond that in many cases lasts an entire lifetime. A customer buys on the recommendation of a salesman and the salesman would rather forsake the chance of a quick sale than risk upsetting the relationship with his long time customer. There is no "fast buck" in selling automobiles in Japan, but customer satisfaction does count.

At the root of everything, however, is a high-quality product, that boosts the (self) image of its owner, is marketed in the subtle, non-direct, subliminal "Japanese" way and is taken good care of after the sale... until the next sale. Automobiles can be the perfect example.

IMPORTED CAR SALES

	1983	1984	1985	1986	1987	1988	1989*
Total	35,286	41,982	50,172	68,357	97,750	133,583	129,906
Growth rate (per cent)	−0.6	+19.0	+19.5	+36.2	+43.0	+36.7	+36.9
From Europe	31,396	38,016	46,171	62,724	88,025	111,806	106,608
Growth rate (per cent)	+1.6	+21.1	+21.5	+35.9	+40.3	+27.0	+32.0
From USA	2,646	2,382	1,816	2,345	4,006	14,511	15,194
Growth rate (per cent)	−25.7	−10.0	−23.8	+29.1	+70.8	+262.2	+66.3
Japanese car market ('000s)	2,937	2,902	2,943	3,007	3,147	3,563	2,992
Import share (per cent)	1.2	1.4	1.7	2.3	3.1	3.7	4.4

* First nine months.

Source: Japan Automobile Importers Ass., Japan Automobile Dealers Ass.

PROBLEMS OF SIZE

PEDR DAVIS

Australia is a vast country, thinly populated away from the main centres. In global terms, it is a small market for the motor industry, and a difficult one for manufacturers, for geographic, economic and bureaucratic reasons. It has been a harsh market for some companies, rewarding for others. Now there are just five Aussie manufacturers, controlled by US or Japanese majors. They account for 75 per cent of sales, and some ranges include fascinating 'model-sharing'. Pedr Davis reviews the market, and looks at the long historical background to the Australian motor industry.

Australia's vibrant motor industry is a case study of how a dedicated and enterprising group of companies can survive in the high-tech era despite geographic, demographic and bureaucratic difficulties.

Although the country's motor market is small by world standards, over 16 million Australians own nine million road-registered motor vehicles, not including motorcycles. Vehicle ownership has increased sharply since the Second World War and continues to accelerate. The figure jumped from one million vehicles in 1948 to two million in 1956, from four million in 1967 to seven million in 1979. About 600,000 new vehicles are registered each year, some 75 per cent being passenger cars, the rest commercials.

Australia has very long distances between major centres, with the bulk of the population living in coastal towns and cities, but inland areas play a major role in development because the country depands heavily on rural and mining industries for its economic well-being.

The average vehicle probably travels further in a year in Australia than in most countries and, in the main, has to handle worse road conditions and greater extremes of climate. The harsh environment has led to the development of cars and trucks which are tougher than their overseas counterparts, and last longer.

The unusual local conditions and relatively high level of demand means that Australia needs its own manufacturing industry. If it depended purely on imports, the pressure on the trade balance would be prohibitive, with the annual drain on foreign currency being at least $5 billion, a figure the country cannot afford.

To encourage local manufacturing, the federal government has operated a series of industry plans since the Second World War, using high import tariffs to persuade major car companies to invest in local facilities. Whilst the intention has been laudable, the plan — and hence the ground rules — has been frequently changed and car makers complain they cannot instigate long-term planning.

The best sales year ever was 1985 when 695,000 new cars, light commercials and trucks were sold. Sales dipped sharply in 1986, following high interest rates, a battered Aussie dollar and the introduction of a tax on business cars. By 1987, sales were down to 450,000 units — the lowest in 20 years. The market has since partly recovered and industry analysts expected the 1990 demand to be 600,000 new vehicles. Of these, about 160,000 would be light commercials, trucks or buses.

Five companies manufacture cars — Ford, Toyota, General Motors-Holden, Mitsubishi and Nissan. Together, they account for about 75 per cent of all passenger vehicle sales. Surprisingly, virtually all commercials are fully imported, the vast majority from Japan. The exception has been the Aussie-made Ford Falcon van and utility which was joined in 1990 by Holden's Commodore ute.

The competition to gain a bigger share of the car and commercial market is intense. Some European and Japanese companies are prepared to subsidise their Aus-

tralian operations because they see Australia as a potential growth area. In all, 27 firms import cars from Japan, Europe and Korea. Including the local output, 280 different passenger models are listed.

Despite the choice, eight firms share the bulk of the market, leaving the others to scramble for the crumbs. Major companies such as Citroën, Renault and Audi sell only a handful of cars annually but are in Australia for the long haul (Fiat has withdrawn from the market).

Australian retail prices are high. Imported cars are subject to a stiff import tariff and both local and imported cars are charged a minimum of 20 per cent sales tax (assessed on the wholesale price). The tax on luxury cars (priced over $43,000) is an astonishing 50 per cent.

Local manufacturing costs are high compared with Japan and Europe because of the relatively small output. The import duty was originally imposed to help the local firms remain competitive but now applies not just to cars but to truck-type utilities and four-wheel drive vehicles which are not made locally. Import quotas have been removed.

Currently, the duty on passenger cars is 42.5 per cent, based on landed cost; Australian cars with a minimum of

The Ohlmeyer 'Jigger' was built in South Australia in 1904 using a British-built single-cylinder Automotor engine. It had a combination of belt and chain drive, a system which powered one wheel at a time. The 'Jigger' was one of many home-made cars produced in Australia in the early 1900s.

Another example of the low-volume cars which proliferated in Australia in the early 1900s, made by engineering and cycle factories, was the two-cylinder Australis. It was produced in Leichhardt (New South Wales) in 1906. Volume production was planned but only a few were built.

Previous page: The FE series Holden, launched in 1956, was the first Holden model wholly developed in Australia. It retained most of the mechanical components of its predecessors (the 48-215 and FJ models) but introduced a lower and longer body plus a 12-volt electrical system.

IF YOU CAN'T BUY IT, BUILD IT —
AUSTRALIA'S EARLY DAYS

No one can be absolutely certain who produced Australia's first horseless carriage. One known fact is that a local petrol-driven tricycle was publicly demonstrated in 1893, just seven years after the original Benz three-wheeler made its debut in Germany. H. Knight-Eaton, manager of Brisbane's Austral Cycle Agency, built a small petrol engine and mounted it at the rear of a pedal tricycle, which he rode uncertainly along side streets.

As early as 1885, David Shearer of Mannum, South Australia, had started work on a steamer but this was not road tested until 1899. The 20 HP Shearer had seating for eight and was more a carriage than a car. On its maiden voyage it travelled 160km (100 miles) without mishap, cruising at 24kmh/15mph, and was used by the Shearer family for many years. This vehicle survives.

Few people recorded motoring events at the time but numerous claims later surfaced relating to early Australian cars including an interesting tale of an 1880 steamer. The story, published in a cycle magazine in 1904, recalled that during a royal tour in 1881, Prince Alfred and Prince Edward visited a residence near Adelaïde where they met Frederich Gilden, who was driving a large steam-driven three-wheeler of his own make. He proudly puffed ahead of the royal procession at eight miles per hour.

Herbert Thomson of Melbourne, Victoria, planned to put a lightweight steam car into production and talked about having several factories to keep up with the demand — a far-sighted view at the time! He started work on a relatively small 5 HP car of his own design and had it running in 1896. Thomson and a friend, Edward Holmes, undertook the country's first interstate motoring trip. They shipped the four-seat car to Sydney, drove inland to Bathurst then set out on the long drive back to Melbourne, taking ten days for the 790km/490 mile journey. Thomson formed a company to make his steam cars and took 150 orders. Only 12 were delivered and one survives.

During the late 1890s, Harley Tarrant of Melbourne built a Benz-powered four-wheeler with a view to producing it in volume. He sold only 12, and again one survives.

The most ingenious early designer was Melbourne's Henry Sutton who built a three-wheeler in the late 1890s. His next car, a four-wheeler, was powered by a single-cylinder engine and was probably the world's first front-wheel drive car. It also had four wheel steering, an ignition advance-and-retard mechanism, a recoil-type hand starter for the engine and a full differential. Unfortunately this highly original car was scrapped many years ago.

An ambitious attempt to create a motor industry was made when twelve Melbourne businessmen formed the Australian Horseless Carriage Company in 1896. They engaged a local firm to install a stationary engine in what was otherwise a horse-drawn carriage. The result, the Pioneer, was a magnificently decorated vehicle with a kerosene-burning engine. It was widely publicised with photographs appearing around the world. But only one Pioneer car was completed.

Several Australians built cars from scratch, using local foundry and machine shop facilities to make components. For example, Bruno Hammer of Mount Torrens, South Australia, had never seen a car but he managed to build one using drawings from overseas magazines. He made the chassis, wheels, engine and carburettor himself, completing the job about 1900.

Alfred John Swinnerton was 26 years old in 1906 when, he built a car in Sydney, NSW. It took him a year to complete it and he made everything himself, including the engine. The most unusual feature was that the body and chassis were integrated into one unit — a original idea that was later widely adopted.

These were just some of the pioneers who built their own cars and bravely tried to start production in a country remote from the European "home" of the automobile.

From top to bottom: The oldest surviving Australian 'car' is the massive Shearer steam carriage. The Shearer brothers of South Australia started work in the 1880s but the vehicle was not completed until the late 1890s. The top speed was 24kmh/15mph, restricted more by the primitive roads than power.

The kerosene-fuelled Pioneer of 1897 resulted from an ambitious manufacturing plan launched by a syndicate of 20 Victorian businessmen. It failed. Adelaide cycle manufacturer, John Bullock, produced a few motorcycles before building this one-off car in 1902. It was powered by a De Dion-Bouton engine.

Of the many early Australian cars, those built by Harley Tarrant (Victoria) most deserved success. Only 16 Tarrants were built but they won races and rallies and were acknowledged as being the most attractive local designs of the day. This 1905 example is the only Tarrant known to survive.

Far right: Taken at Railway Square, Sydney, in 1920, this photograph shows that traffic and pedestrian discipline had yet to be established. At the time there was an estimated 15,000 motor vehicles in the city. Notice the driver-less car parked in the middle of the street and the indiscriminate jaywalking. The 1920s was a hectic decade for motoring in Australia, with the launches of around 15 home-grown marques and the production of hundreds of thousands of motor bodies for imported chassis. The motor market peaked in 1927 with a total of 103,637 new vehicles, which brought the number of vehicles on the road to just over 480,000, or one for every 15 persons. From then on sales declined, slumping to just 13,921 new vehicles for the year 1932, the height of the Depression. They climbed steadily thereafter.

This shot of a car driving through water in the 1920s shows conditions that were not untypical of country motoring in Australia at the time. Few roads were paved and many country and city thoroughfares became virtually impassable in bad weather. Not surprisingly, it was not until the mid-1920s that a car — a baby Citroën — successfully circumnavigated the continent. As a result of the harsh conditions, ordinary touring cars were expected to handle mud, open country and broken surfaces, often in extreme temperatures. Many imported cars had modified cooling systems and strengthened suspension systems. Although local attempts to build cars specially for Australian conditions were not financially successful, local designers produced such innovations as four-wheel drive (1913), an engine-driven winch (1908) and an extraordinary number of unusual suspension systems.

THEY TRIED TO START AN AUSSIE INDUSTRY

There were 75628 motor vehicles on Australian roads by 1920, equivalent to one for every 71 persons. By the end of the decade, the vehicle population had jumped to 571417, one for every 11.3 people. The vast majority were imported, the Model T Ford being by far the most popular. From 1919, Model Ts were assembled in Geelong, Victoria, and fitted with Australian bodies. Eventually there were no fewer than 250000 Model Ts in Australia and as in other countries the car transformed many facets of business and social life.

The 1920s boom encouraged several ambitious attempts to launch local designs. All were financial disasters. It was not that the locals lacked skill but they could not compete with the low-cost imports — notably Fords and Chevrolets — which became cheaper with each passing year.

The failures included Frederick Gordon, who designed the Australian Six, and Charles Innes, who built the six-cylinder Lincoln. About 900 Australian Sixes were sold before the firm dissolved in bankruptcy. Lincoln's output was smaller, probably around 200 units. Both enterprises, however, represented serious attempts to produce the type of vehicle that most Australians were buying — fairly large, six-cylinder, conventional tourers with a strong top-gear performance. The Australian Six for example had a 3.8-litre Rutenber engine developing 45bhp, giving a top speed of 80kmh/50mph.

Charles Innes assembled his first chassis in the USA, using a Continental engine, Zenith carburettor, Borg and Beck clutch and a gearbox made in Detroit. He drove the chassis from Detroit to San Francisco then shipped it to Sydney where the body was fitted.

The seven-seater tourer was ambitiously trimmed in hand-enamelled buffalo hide and went on sale at $1050. At the time, the Australian Six sold for $990 and a Model T for half as much. The Lincoln could not compete.

Another 'high volume' car was the Sydney-made Summit. Powered by a four-cylinder Lycoming engine, it had an unusual suspension comprising a series of leaf springs running down each side of the chassis. The Summit was extremely well equipped for its day, having electric stop lights and a cigar lighter. The makers offered a full 12-month warranty. It was in production for three years and over 200 were made.

Although it was evident that Australia needed its own motor industry, the government did nothing to assist by way of import tariffs. The local industry did not really get under way until 1948 when General Motors-Holden launched the first successful all-Australian car, the Holden.

The Australian Six was an ambitious attempt to mass-produce an Australian car. It richly deserved to succeed but failed largely because it could not be produced in sufficient numbers to compete against American cars of comparable size and power. Based on an American design, the Australian Six was a mixture of imported components and local parts, with 60 per cent Australian content. Frederic Hugh Gordon, the man who established the factory in Ashfield, New South Wales, had planned to progressively manufacture all parts himself. After around 900 cars had been built, he sustained such large losses that he was forced to close down the project. The Australian Six was launched in 1919 in the expectation that the Federal Government would subsidise the project or at least help by imposing an import duty on overseas cars. It declined. And so, like the Lincoln Six — another local car sold in the 1920s — the Australian Six carried a retail price twice as high as a Model T Ford. Had tariff protection been available, it is probably that the Australian Six would have prospered.

As a car, it was a good but orthodox design and many examples operated successfully with hire car companies and as company vehicles. The engine was an imported 3.8-litre Rutenber unit which developed 45bhp and gave the car a top speed of 80kmh/50mph. In a pioneering export programme, at least one batch went to New Zealand.

In a final burst before the factory closed in the mid-1920s, the company entered motor sport and one car was timed at 112kmh/70mph when being raced at Victoria Park, Sydney.

Six complete Australian Sixes survive in working condition.

THE GREAT DEPRESSION

By the mid-1920s, new vehicle sales had reached the magic figure of 100,000 per year and Ford and General Motors had local assembly operations. They were going well until 1930 when the world depression hit Australia and new vehicle sales plummeted to 40,000 units for the year. Not until 1949 did the annual demand again exceeded the 1927 level. Most firms recorded huge losses during the 1930s, but stability was eventually restored and sales slowly improved, from 20,654 in 1933 to peak 79,218 in 1938. Ford's domination slipped progressively during the 1920s because the Model T was outdated. At the height of the 1927 boom, Ford held only 13 per cent of the market, compared with 26 per cent for General Motors Australia (later GM-Holden) which sold Chevrolet, Vauxhall and Bedford vehicles. Chrysler (Plymouth and Dodge) had 9 per cent, Hudson Terraplane 8 per cent and British-made cars (other than Vauxhall) 7 per cent. Despite the failure of several more new Australian cars, the Federal Government took steps to establish a motor industry. Of the companies which had survived the 1930s depression, GM-H was in the best position to pursue the concept of a truly Australian car. In all probability, the Holden — or something like it — would have been launched in 1940.

Australia's Own Car...
HOLDEN

Patriotism has long been a good selling point in Australia. No-one has exploited it more than Holden, which became known as 'Australia's Own Car'.

The first Holden, officially called the 48-215 but later known as the 'FX', quickly attracted a long waiting list when launched in 1948. The combination of comfort, power, room and rough road durability was unbeatable at the price.

102

The 1960 FB Holden introduced an American appearance that was not as acceptable as previous designs. Sales remained strong, however, due to the car's good performance. In 1961 the FB evolved into the EK which introduced Holden's first automatic transmission. Before the FB was phased out, major competitors had arrived in the form of Ford's Falcon (introduced in 1961) and Chrysler's Valiant early in 1962.

Although the styling of Holden's 1956 FE model was Australian, it was heavily influenced by the Chevrolet and Opel models of the day.

Below: During the early to mid-1950s, Holden was the only local car to be volume produced but numerous other makes and models were locally assembled.

Bottom: The 1957 Lloyd-Hartnett was a local version of Germany's front-wheel drive Lloyd 600. The project was launched by Laurence Hartnett who had conceived the Holden project and subsequently left GM-H. Around 3000 Lloyd-Hartnetts were built before the German company closed and the supply of components dried up.

THE BOOM YEARS AFTER WWII

The insatiable demand for cars after the Second World War took the Australian government, the industry and the public by surprise. Cars were shipped in as rapidly as the boats could be loaded and the shrewder companies brought in parts to assemble cars locally. GM-H started building Vauxhalls in 1945 and, in the same year, Morris announced an assembly operation. Sales of all types were so brisk and the vehicle population reached the million mark in 1948.

That year, Austin acquired a factory in Melbourne and announced a major expansion plan. Although rivals at the time, Austin and Morris jointly dominated the market for several years, partly because GM-H could not produce enough of the all-Australian Holden launched in 1948.

In 1951, Austin and Morris accounted for over 30 per cent of new car sales, compared with 23 per cent for GM-H and 15 per cent for Ford. Soon the public displayed a growing preference for the larger six-cylinder Holden.

Based on a Chevrolet design which never went into production, the Holden was developed and manufactured locally. Sensationally successful, it enabled GM-H to expand production to 100 cars a day and, later, to over 100,000 a year GM-H expanded as rapidly as it could and Ford introduced plans which led to the local Falcon. This was based on a none-too-robust US model but later became (and still is) uniquely Australian.

During the 1950s the government announced a long-term plan to force more local production. This led to more schemes to manufacture or assemble cars, mainly from British firms. GM-H replied by announcing plans to boost output to 400 Holdens a day by 1958. BMC — the next largest producer — increased the Australian content of Austin and Morris vehicles. Ford and Chrysler did the same and the marketplace became a battleground. The main losers were the UK manufacturers.

Volkswagen commenced local assembly in Melbourne in 1954 and 'Beetlemania' swept the country. Chrysler also did well with a range of locally-assembled large US cars. During the 1960s, the industry became larger, more diverse and more sophisticated. A lively export industry developed and, at one time, Holden shipped 25 per cent of its output abroad. Ford's locally-built version of the US Falcon came on stream in 1960s and Chrysler introduced the Valiant sedan in 1962. The early Valiants were locally-assembled US models with some minor modifications for Australia. Sales went so well that Chrysler decided to lift production to 50,000 units a year, with a progressive increase in local manufacture.

Of the marques which thrived in the 1950s and 1960s, only Holden and Ford were still in business in the 1980s.

Despite enormous sur-
taxes on imports (50 per
cent Value Added Tax
for a car worth more
than $43,000 and 42.5
per cent Customs duty),
Australians are still very
much attracted to presti-
gious European cars,
even if the prices of
Mercedes, Porsches and
Ferraris are almost
doubled.

104

THE JAPANESE INFLUENCE

*The 1960s proved a watershed for the local industry.
Meticulously made, inexpensive, fully-equipped cars started
to trickle and then flood into Australia from Japan. They
proved more robust and better value for money than anyone
had expected. The Government was forced to hoist defence
barriers. In 1964, it limited duty concessions to those firms
selling over 7500 cars a year only if they undertook to raise
the local content to 95 per cent within five years.*

*This meant the Japanese companies had to establish local
production facilities if they wanted a larger market share.
Three firms took up the challenge — Toyota, Nissan and Mitsubishi. Mazda and Honda decided to continue importation
and pay the duty involved. As a further measure, the Government moved in 1966 to raise the rate of import duty from 35
to 45 per cent.*

*Meanwhile, the market continued to boom. GM-H remained
the best seller but fresh competition arrived in the shape of a
much improved version of the Falcon. Due to early mechanical problems, the Falcon venture had proved incredibly
expensive for Ford but its long-term success gave the company market leadership by 1982.*

*Toyota was the first Japanese marque with an Aussie accent.
Tiara sedans were assembled in 1963 by a Melbourne company, Australian Motor Industries (later acquired by Toyota
Motor Corporation). The Corona followed and proved very
popular. By 1969, Toyota was selling 50 000 vehicles a year.
In 1972, Toyota decided to install manufacturing facilities
and, six years later, the first Australian-made Toyota engine
was fitted to a car.*

*Nissan had been the pioneer Japanese car company in Aus-
tralia, with a pilot shipment arriving in 1934. Its postwar
products came on the market in 1961. Nissan established its
own local subsidiary in 1966 and had some cars assembled in
Sydney by contract. Two years later, Volkswagen Australia
— which was making cars in Melbourne but not running at a
profit — agreed to assemble Datsun/Nissan products. While
Nissan went from strength to strength, Volkswagen did not
and Nissan acquired its Melbourne plant in 1976.*

*Mitsubishi came to the market in a similar way. Chrysler Aus-
tralia had started to assemble and market Mitsubishi Galants
in 1971 as an adjunct to the succesful Valiant operation. The
Galant sold well and, when Chrysler ran into financial
problems in the late 1970s, Mitsubishi bought the company
lock, stock and barrel. Production of Valiants continued for
a while but they were phased out in favour of a succession of
Mitsubishi designs and the Chrysler presence vanished from
the Australian market.*

85 per cent local content are not subject to import duty
on the remaining 15 per cent.

As a result of the car plan announced in May 1988, import
duties are progressively coming down. The Federal
Government hopes that the threat of more overseas
competition will force the locals to become more efficient. Only time will tell if the theory is correct. Unhappily, the rules keep changing, as in the May 1990 imposi-
tion of a 50 per cent sales tax on luxury cars.

The latest plan also provides for import duty to fall
progessively to 35 per cent for cars and 15 per cent for
light commercials and 4WDs by 1992. This will undoubtedly make life harder for the local companies and possibly force them to import more cars and make fewer
locally.

An objective of the plan is to reduce the proliferation of
locally-made models and so improve the economies of
scale. The government says that no firm should produce
a model range unless they can sell at least 40 000 units per
year. This will reduce the models made locally to one or
two per company, compared with the two, three or four
which had been the case.

By imposing a minimum production run, the govern-

ment expects manufacturers to share components and complete cars and become further involved in export sales. Several firms successfully sell components overseas but, so far, only Ford and GM-H export cars in reasonable numbers. Ford's Capri convertible is shipped to North America, Holden's Commodore to New Zealand.

Although cars as diverse as the small Capri and the big Holden V8 Caprice are manufactured locally, the effective choice is falling as model-sharing becomes a fact of life.

In 1989, Toyota introduced a rebadged clone of the Holden Commodore V6 sedan and Holden reciprocated by rebadging Toyota Corolla and Camry cars, calling them Apollo and Nova. Ford launched the Corsair — which is identical to the Nissan Pintara — and Nissan put its badge on the Falcon utility. In addition, Ford sells a rebadged Nissan Patrol 4WD and builds modified Mazda 323s which are sold as Lasers. Mitsubishi is the only local car maker not sharing a model with a competitor.

Interchange of components between the local firms is widespread. The Nissan Pulsar, for example, uses a Holden-made engine and both Holden and Ford make mechanical parts and body panels for their competitors. A lesson learned from the model-sharing programmes is that customers have a distinct preference for the original brand over the rebadged model, even though both are identical apart from some equipment.

In the main, the locals combine Australian and overseas engineering. Until the late 1970s, US-based designs dominated the market but the Japanese influence took over. Currently, 56 per cent of cars and wagons are imported from Japan or made locally using modified Japanese designs. However, top-selling Holden Commodore and Ford Falcon have very high local design contents and are more European than Japanese in concept. Currently, Holden is the only firm manufacturing a V8 engine; Ford and Holden make 'sixes'; Holden, Nissan and Mitsubishi make four-cylinder units.

A significant factor in passenger sales is the popularity of four-wheel drive vehicles. Australia is said to be the world's second largest market for off-road vehicles with a record 68,000 4WDs imported in 1989 alone.

In terms of vehicles sold, Mazda and Honda are the biggest importers. BMW leads the luxury car segment and Hyundai imports the most small cars.

Some 80 per cent of the population of Australia live in four major cities and with a car ownership rate of 1.7 vehicles per inhabitant, traffic jams — here in Sydney — are not rare, nor are they about to disappear.

Jac Nasser is the director general of the Ford Motor Company of Australia, which holds second place in the Australian market with 1,680,212 cars, 235,023 utilities and 4x4 vehicles registered (in 1988).

American Bill Hamel (above) was called in to head General Motors Holden Automotive Ltd in 1990 as chairman and managing director, replacing an Australian, John Bagshaw.
Left: derived from the Commodore, the long-wheelbase Holden Statesman is equipped with a fuel-injected 5 litre V-8, built in Australia.

The major Ford factory at Broadmeadows, north of Melbourne, received considerable investment at the end of the 1980s to robotise its lines (above). It produces the Ford Falcon EA, of which the Series II (opposite, bottom right) is the best seller in its category, and the Capri (opposite, bottom left), which has been exported to the United States since June 1990.

The Ford Fairlane (opposite, top) is the top of the range version of the Falcon. The Ford Corsair (opposite, centre left) is produced for Ford by Nissan Australia while the Ford KF Laser Ghia (opposite, centre right) is derived from a Mazda but assembled by Ford.

The Holden Apollo (left) is actually a locally produced Toyota Camry. It is sometimes difficult to distinguish the 'Australian' products of GM-Holden and Toyota...

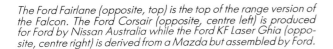

GM-Holden was restructured in 1986 into two companies (Holden Motor for cars and Holden Engine for motors), both subsidiaries of GM Overseas Corporation. Since May, 1988, it has established a joint venture with Toyota called United Australian Automotive Industries. Holden Motor production is split among the group's five factories, but the sales networks remain independent. This does not prevent the factories exchanging models, and thus the Toyota Lexcen is a badged version of the Holden Commodore V6, while the Holden Nova (left) is built by Toyota and is almost identical to a Corolla.

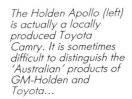

HOLDEN

Bob Johnson, President of Toyota Motor Corporation Australia Ltd.

More than 20 variants of the Corolla are sold in Australia by Toyota, including this high-performance SX version with a 134bhp normally-aspirated engine. Three body styles (hatch, lift-back and sedan) and a variety of twin cam engines are built locally, with a 4WD wagon variant being imported.

INTO THE MODERN ERA

At the beginning of the 1970s, Australia enjoyed one of the world's highest living standards. There was an average of more than one car for every family and buyers could choose from 292 basically different models representing 58 marques.

The proliferation of new models continued, with Sweden joining the American, British, Japanese, German, Italian, French and Czech firms.

In 1973, British Leyland took the step which brought about its demise: it launched the P76, a completely new locally-designed sedan sold with six-cylinder and eight-cylinder engines. The P76 won the Wheels magazine 'Car of the Year' award but, unfortunately, the Leyland structure tumbled due to poor quality control and circumstances outside its control.

Meanwhile the new vehicle market was running at about 572,000 units annually. In July 1976, a new Australian Design Rule significantly affected the engine design and the price of cars. It required an exhaust emission level which was similar — but not identical — to the US 1973 emission standards.

A momentous year for the motor industry followed. Ford launched the XD Falcon, the design which soon made it the unchallenged market leader. GM-H persuaded the Federal Government to agree to a radical Export Complementation Scheme which meant that any firm exporting whole cars or components could import an agreed amount of cars or components without paying duty on them.

Ford concluded a deal which led to fully-imported Mazda light commercials being sold with Ford badges. The agreement also meant that variants of the Mazda 323 and 626 were assembled as Ford Lasers, Meteors and Telstars.

The 1980s started with massive price hikes, due not just to changing economic circumstances but to the increasing sophistication of family cars. Alternative vehicles — such as four-wheel drive types and minibuses — became popular.

New rules effective from 1984 allowed manufacturers to import up to 30 per cent of their components free of duty provided they exported cars or components to an equivalent value. Import quotas were increased to 105,000 in 1985, with the possibility of unlimited quotas by 1992.

The most obvious result of these changes was that the local manufacturers tried to get export projects under way. As the 1980s drew to a close, Ford Australia announced it would send Capri convertibles to the US and Holden continued to sell four-cylinder engines around the world. Mitsubishi sold a few Magna wagons in Japan and Nissan planned to export its Pintara.

Although it bears a visual similarity to the Japanese Sigma Galant, the Mitsubishi Magna was developed in Australia with a widened body and a transversely mounted 2.6-litre four-cylinder engine. It has received many awards since its debut in 1985 and is destined to be replaced in 1991. In 1989, the front-wheel drive Magna was the biggest and best-selling four-cylinder model on the market. It competes against the mid-sized fours and several locally-made 'sixes'. A sedan and an Australian-developed wagon are produced, the latter being exported to Japan in small numbers.

SALES OF IMPORTS – 1988

Category	Type	Number
Small	Mazda 323	2 482
	Daihatsu Charade	2 906
	Holden Barina	4 481
	Honda Civic	4 491
	Hyundai Excel	5 327
	Others	8 607
Medium	Subaru	3 090
	Mazda 626	3 941
	Others	9 600
Medium/Large	Others	8
	Toyota Camry	830
Luxury	Jaguar	1 055
	Saab 900/9000	1 964
	Toyota Cressida	2 176
	Mazda 929	2 256
	BMW (all types)	2 757
	Mercedes-Benz (all types)	3 307
	Toyota Celica, Supra	3 346
	Volvo (all types)	3 853
	Others	5 333
	Honda (Prelude, Accord Integra, CRX, Legend)	9 122
Imports, total		80 932
Total sales		403 723

yacht which won the America's Cup). Toyotas range from the MR2 to the Lexus, plus the best-selling 4WD (LandCruiser) and light commercial ranges.

Holden's Commodore (available with six- or eight-cylinder engines) is currently Australia's favourite sedan. Two extended wheelbase models — Statesman and Caprice — were launched in April 1990 and should be strong competition for the long wheelbase Fords. Other Holden models are the rebadged Toyotas and the imported Suzuki-built Barina.

Recently, Holden's light commercial models have been imported from Isuzu, but a locally-made Commodore utility comes in late 1990.

Mitsubishi has ceased making the small Colt and concentrates on the wide-bodied Magna (a very successful four-cylinder car) and a range of Lancer and Galant imports. It does well with the imported Pajero 4WD, with some models having Aussie-built engines.

Nissan claims most improvement in recent years and manufacturers the four-cylinder Pulsar, four-cylinder Pintara and six-cylinder Skyline locally (the latter using an imported engine). It also imports the 300ZX sports car and the highly successful Patrol 4WD.

All local firms are wholly owned (in the case of Toyota, almost wholly-owned) subsidiaries of overseas companies. Holden and Toyota are in the process of merging their operations into a new firm, United Australian Automotive Industries, to be jointly owned by General Motors Corporation and Toyota Motor Corporation. Holden and Toyota will maintain their identities through separate dealer networks and brand names.

Ford is the largest local manufacturer and in 1989 achieved 24.2 per cent of the new vehicle market. Next came Toyota (19.7 per cent), GM-Holden (17.5), Mitsubishi (11.9) and Nissan with 11.1 per cent.

Ford's most popular model is the six-cylinder Falcon but the company does well with the Mazda-based four-cylinder Laser and Nissan-made Corsair. An extended wheelbase version of the Falcon, the Fairlane, is the best-selling big car. Ford also imports the Mazda-built Telstar TX and light commercials, Nissan's 4WD and the US-made F1500 truck.

Toyota's most popular model is the Corolla, followed by the larger Camry. The company has been disappointed by the sales of the six-cylinder, Holden-made Lexcen (named after the late Ben Lexcen, designer of the Aussie

NOW FOR THE FUTURE

Australian firms are likely to continue to buy rebadged cars from their competitors as part of 'shared model' programmes but the experience so far indicates they will need to change some of the sheet metal to provide a more distinct identity. Ford is going this way with the 1990 Laser (based on the Mazda 323 and US Escort) and the trend will continue.

Australian firms will also turn increasingly to their overseas parent companies for new technology and updated designs. Because of increased complexity and sophistication, the cost of developing uniquely Australian cars has become prohibitive for the volumes involved: Australian firms can expect to sell only 40,000 to 80,000 of any one series annually.

The concept of a new kind of world car, in which variations of the basic design are produced at a number of countries, is inevitable and Australia stands to gain more than it will lose from such practice. However, as in the past, many models need to be modified to suit the Australian road and weather conditions as well as personal preferences.

There seems no alternative but to import much of the design technology. Unhappily, this means the end of the era in which cars have been wholly conceived and designed in Australia.

Top: The Australian Nissan Pulsar is unique, being powered by 1.6 and 1.8-litre versions of Holden's Family fuel-injected, four-cylinder engine. More expensive models incorporate viscous coupling differentials. Their spritely performance and handling qualities have been highly praised. A Holden version called 'Astra' has been discontinued.

Above: The managing director and chief executive of Nissan Australia, Ivan Deveson. Under his leadership, the company has invested heavily in new plant and equipment, has sold complete cars to Ford Australia and announced ambitious export plans centred around the four-cylinder Pintara model. The Nissan Pintara is a locally-produced variation of the Japanese Bluebird, available with 2-litre and 2.4-litre four-cylinder engines. It is also sold in Australia as the Ford Corsair with slightly different bodywork. An estate version of the Pintara is slated for export to Japan.

onscious that he was responsible for the continuation and development of his father's creation, Sergio has never missed an opportunity to evoke his father's memory, when many other people would have publicized their own accomplishments.

He has now turned over responsibility for the management of important sectors of the group to his sons Andrea and Paolo, and the time to discuss his own *œuvre* with him seemed opportune. This conversation was held at the Paris Show, which Pininfarina has often honoured with prestigious creations.

I had the good fortune to meet Sergio first in the early 1960s, so I was interested first in knowing more about his early days in the company as a young engineer in the 1950s, newly graduated from the Politecnico of Turin, and in understanding the nature of his professional relations with his father.

Were they relations of father to son, or of boss to employee?

Our relations were exactly the same of those I have today with my sons. Which means that beyond the normal relations which unite a father and son, they were, in the company, exclusively the relations between a chairman and his directors.

There was no weakness. Any other way would not have been constructive. I even think that ideally, if you have the strength, you should be even tougher. I find that one's love of one's children is directly proportional to the hoped-for results, and that is why mistakes are less well tolerated.

I remember that my father had a very strict attitude towards me, but there were moments, which to tell the truth were rare, when he opened up to me. He would say: "But you don't understand why I am so tough with you, it's because I love you." In saying that he said everything: when you love someone, you are the more demanding because you seek perfection. A memory: I was working at the Esperienza, the design bureau at that time, an annex of the factory. That day my father was very critical of everything that I had done, that I was doing, and that I said, and he wouldn't stop criticizing me. At one moment, one of the heads of the bureau addressed him familiarly in Piedmontese, the local dialect: "Don't say that, your son knows his job very well!"

I believe now that my father wanted my qualities to be recongnized by the people who were working for him. He was right. The situation of a son protected by his father naturally creates animosity because the workers understand very quickly that this boy is unjustly privileged in comparison to them. On the contrary, if they can see clearly that there is absolutely no favoritism for the boss' son, they will judge him on his own merits. It can't have been easy for my father to be so tough, so distant, but in treating me in that fashion, he did me a service. I won't say that at the time I appreciated his methods very much.

In a way, he sent you into battle without protecting your flanks.

On the face of it, yes. But if there was really a need to protect my flanks, I could count on his support. As that didn't happen very often, people really thought that I operated without his protection. Which was exactly the result he sought.

When your father handed over the responsibility for the company to you, he had established the conditions for its development and provided the means, but the development still had to be achieved.

I will divide the history of Pininfarina in the 1960s into four parts. The first period was that of my father, a period during which he was immensely self-confident in his talent. My father did not look closely at anything, he was not preoccupied with the financial state of the company, or the resources and assets available to him. He simply had an unshakeable confidence in the success of his venture. There is a major compliment behind those words: he believed in his success. He always behaved in that way with me, with the staff, with the clients, with his social contacts. My father was recognised as one of the greatest coachbuilders in the world, but this international recognition was nothing compared to his human qualities. He was worth a lot more as a individual. When you fight for the World Championship in Formula One, you have at most three rivals at your level. When you are in the race of life, you have to beat thousands of people My father did not envy anyone, did not criticise anyone, he was tough with himself and understanding with others, he liked youth, he had an instinctive sense of progress and of technology. In this first period in the history of Pininfarina, my father created everything and took responsibility for everything. It was like a liquid which covered us all. There was no way to break surface alongside him.

I consider his severity as the essential factor. From the age of three or four already... People talk of tough educations, I received one!

The second period starts at the moment that my father handed over the day to day running of the company to my brother-in-law, Renzo Carli, and myself. From that moment, you have to speak of the two of us. We are two very different personalities. That is undoubtedly the reason that we have got on so well together. He has qualities that I lack, and I have a few qualities too. We are really very well matched. After having worked together for dozens of years, our relationship is still as good as it was then. I think that is pretty rare.

THE SERGIO YEARS

PHILIPPE DE BARSY

Together, we lived through this second and relatively brief period from 1955 until the death of my father on April 3, 1966. From that moment, one of us had to take the lead. It was impossible to have two chairmen, two managing-directors. My brother-in-law said, by nature and by temperament: "You carry the name, it's yours, go!"

He then retired considerably into the background as far as the outside world was concerned, the clients and the press too. But not in relation to the real world of the company. He seemed to amuse himself by working, inventing, criticising, by driving us mad...

He played the dilettante, in a way.

Yes, a little like the English play sport! Somewhat detached... He worked like an Englishman. I am the opposite to an Englishman — I take work seriously, even too seriously.

This period, the third, is that of the Sergio years. In the eyes of the world I did personify Pininfarina. This position of Number One was reinforced over the years, undoubtedly because I also had activities outside the company.

I had the courage and the merit to test myself in environments which were not those of the factory: in politics, or the Cofindustria (the Industrial Association, the CBI or NAM of Italy — Ed.). It was a question of courage because at the factory, whether it was in relation to the suppliers or the personnel, I always had an advantage. That was not so in the economic or political world. There I could count only on my own faculties of thought, of reasoning, of consistency, of behaviour. I was able to earn the esteem of others through my own merits. This experience strengthened me enormously, and it also made me more of a celebrity. My position as Sergio, as a man, and not as an industrialist or in terms of the production of automobiles, grew steadily to a peak which was reached two years ago with my nomination to the presidency of the Industrial Association.

It is a difficult presidency with the task of bringing together the interest of all those industrialists who are so much individualists. There are small, medium and large companies. They don't have the same ideas or the same interests.

So you consider that experience enriched your personality, your capabilities and your knowledge.

Absolutely. It was extremely stimulating and positive. I fully recommend it. It enriched me for my personal work. It was in no way negative for my work in the context of Pininfarina. It was an opening to culture, to new arguments, to new environments...

With that presidency, I also entered the fourth phase of the company.

When I accepted that task, I stepped aside from the programme that I had laid down. I am a person who tries to follow a programme once I have established it. I had planned to hand over the responsibilities to my sons and to my directors.

Pininfarina is not a small company in which the father hands over the reins to his son. From father to son, yes, but only if it is sensible. If these sons are worthy of it. The bigger the company, the more difficult the hand over. I had foreseen giving up the responsibility of day to day management towards 1992/93 — not the leadership, but the operational responsibility. I would have been 65, my father's age when he handed over the same responsibilities to us. I wanted in the meantime to put a "Prova" plate on the backs of my sons. If everything went well, they would have had increased responsibilities. If not, I could change my plans and look for alternatives. My presidency of Cofindustria meant that it was no longer possible to carry out this experiment.

So you took the risk of speeding up the process.

Exactly. It was less dramatic than it seems, because I was sure of my sons. It was an impression, a favourable feeling, but not a mathematical certainty. Now, two years later, I am much more relaxed because I have been able to verify that the combination of son and director has became a reality, that the tangible results are there, that the company has been strengthened and not weakened, and I can thus see the internal life of the company in a rosier light. I stress internal, because the external environment of our company is quite another matter. There are certainly problems. Italy's problems are big enough to give you sleepless nights but that's another subject.

So, I have lived through three of the four periods in the life of Pininfarina: one with my father, another with my brother-in-law including a part in which I had to act rather more alone, and finally the last period, where I progressively concerned myself only with the major strategic decisions and no longer undertake the operational management.

During the second and third periods you really were very close to the automobile.

It's true that over the past two years I have lost contact a little, but not in the field of design. If I am still involved to a degree in an area, it is certainly in design. But I am there as a wise man, a counsellor, a critic, not as the person who leads the project.

Of all those creative years, which were your best moments?

The years spent alongside my father gave me enormous satisfaction. I introduced into the company the weight and experience of the technical studies I had undertaken. My father worked instinctively, I had technical training. I introduced some rationality into the company. If you examine photos of cars created in the early 1950s, when I was still a kid, you will notice that they were often eccentric, novel and sometimes open to criticism for bowing to fashion. When my influence was expressed, they became more rational, less bizarre and more related to technical themes.

I carried through this process under the direction of my father, and I am immensely proud of having influenced him. I didn't copy him, I really influenced him. It is a period which I consider as very personal.

My brother-in-law and I worked together. One designed, the other criticised, and the final decision was always

111

gerous", he said. But I had lived through the period during which Bertone had the mid-engined Lamborghini Miura with which to express himself, and I was still building cars 15 centimetres higher. I've got nothing against Bertone, on the contrary I admire him, but we were competitors and I had the impression of fighting a war without an air force. And then that Dino came along to make a dream into a reality. It introduced concepts that no one had presented previously: the form of the rear window which solved the problems of getting rid of the engine heat, of visibility and of noise. I was the last to arrive in that mid-engined car category, but at least I had some new developments to offer. That's why I attach special importance to that car. But there were all the rest, too, because at Pininfarina there is never one person's car. It's the work of a school. I started as a student, I finish as chairman. Men change, one retires, another dies, some come and some go...

If there really is a characteristic of Pininfarina design, it is that continuity, with perhaps a few exceptions, for example that strange NSU R080...

I claim to be the father of that continuity to a certain degree, because of my consistency, my rationality, and my attention to and love of the product. It's true that that R080 is a contrast to the rest, but it has its own internal history.

That continuity is really an extraordinary success when you consider the number of people who have worked with you.

It will continue. Yes, it will continue. It really is the result of a school of thought. It will continue for many years, and then a moment will come when I won't be able to do anything more...

You will have put the Pininfarina rocket into orbit, and others will control the trajectory... But to get back to the product, I believe that if there are so few cars that you consider out of the ordinary for one reason or another, it means that all the others have given you equal satisfaction.

Absolutely.

However, there are one or two more to pick out. For example, there was that remarkable Lancia Beta Montecarlo which should have been the Fiat X1/20. It had superb proportions, a bodywork structure of sculptural beauty.

The Montecarlo was Pininfarina's greatest lost opportunity. From a technical point of view, Pininfarina gave

The Ferrari 275/GTB was a star of the 1964 Paris Salon. Its strong lines were to stand the test of time, although in the mid-1960s they seemed exaggerated with the long bonnet pushing the cabin back towards the rear wheel line. The 275/GTB precisely matched Ferrari's idea of a Grand Touring vehicle.

taken jointly. We marked those years by the real expression of a style. Pininfarina expressed its beliefs, developed themes. Not all had the development or the success that they merited, but they all had the merit of existing, and of inspiring later ideas or creations.

It's true that many themes were adopted.

But of course. For example, our safety car, the Sigma, expressed a belief. The same for the Sigma Grand Prix concept and many others. The day I retire, I will be able to leaf through the books devoted to Pininfarina and say to myself that I have achieved something. If I have to express particular memories, I would cite the Lancia B24. She was something of a daughter of the Giulietta, but personnaly I didn't do much work on the Giulietta. Then there was the Fiat spyder, then the Fiat 124 spyder and then all the Ferraris...

Of all the Ferraris, the one closest to my heart is the Berlinetta Speciale Dino, presented at the Paris Show of 1965. It wasn't just a simple design, it was the precursor of a new generation of Ferraris. Commendatore Ferrari — I don't say Engineer Ferrari but specifically Commendatore — did not want a mid-engine layout. He accepted it for competition cars but not for his clients: "Too dan-

The Ferrari 365 California drop-head dating from 1966-1967 brings together various themes, including that of the Superamerica.

everything it had. The credit goes largely to my brother-in-law, Renzo Carli. It was the first car for which we had created all the body. It was entirely created by us. It had innovative elements like the integrated bumpers, the type of hood in the convertible version. It also had rational dimensions: neither large nor small... But it was born at a bad moment!

We coachbuilders often have the chance to produce cars which, for example, have excellent mechanical elements, where the sales network is dynamic and the marketing astute, where everything combines to create an enormous success even if the design of the bodywork is not exceptional. It's rare, but it happens. But on the contrary, it happens that one creates a thoroughbred — I could cite two or three, but you know them as well as I do — and then it happens that the mechanical elements are at the end of their life, or the model from which they are taken is dropped, or the margin on the model is too small, or it is only sold in certain markets and not others — in short, this rare flower does not bloom as it should! The Montecarlo is a perfect example of a marvellous object with an unhappy destiny. It was born without being a Lancia, or a Fiat. I remember that when it was

transferred to Lancia, it seemed to be an excellent idea. The Fiat executives welcomed it going to Lancia. After a year, total fiasco, and Fiat executives asked: "What idiot gave that car to Lancia?" — and quite often they were the same people. Those are human stories. Only the bitterness remains, and a certainty: a car like that, produced at the right moment, backed by a courageous development policy, would have become the great car that it was, but also a great commercial success. I accept the reality sportingly...

Isn't the Cadillac Allanté another example of a beautiful car born at a bad moment in the life of a marque?
The Montecarlo is finished, but the Cadillac isn't. Cadillac and Pininfarina have a product improvement programme. It's true that there is room for improvements and obvious progress has been achieved already. The Allanté has a future. It also symbolises a unique international cooperation and has supported an image remarkably well. It's an experience of which I could say a thousand good things.

Wouldn't it be an opportune moment for Cadillac to promote its sale in Europe?
When you have an excellent product, one should say

The Jaguar XJ displayed at Birmingham in 1978 never went into production with the British company, to the regret of many. It was built up on XJ-S components and restated Jaguar's sporting image after the E-type years.

The Ferrari 365P with a central driving position and three front seats was a concept car built to a special order from Giovanni Agnelli in an effort to provide an elegant solution to the problems posed by the mid-engined configuration.

The PF Modula on the basis of a Ferrari 512S was one of the more extreme styling exercises in Pininfarina's history. Shown in the Italian pavilion at the International Exposition at Osaka in 1970, the prototype played a similar role to that of an haute couture creation: pure aesthetic provocation!

114

that its success would be a boost for the whole range, and thus one should choose to push that product.

Another approach is to calculate that that product costs so much, add a margin of so much, and sell it. But that's not always the ideal way.

What personal influence have you had on Pininfarina's engineering?

For a small organisation, Pininfarina has shown signs of great vitality in two fields. The first is in the field of numerically controlled machine tools. We were the first to use a numeric machine capable of picking up the data from the shape of models, of optimising them and of controlling other numeric machines. If it had been Ford or Fiat, it would have been normal. But coming from a small company like Pininfarina, it was amazing. I remember that one day Henry Ford was in Turin to visit Fiat and meet Gianni Agnelli, who was his host. He asked Gianni Agnelli if he could visit our plant to see this machine he had heard about. One Sunday morning, these two legendary characters arrived together. Renzo and I led them to the famous machine. It was an extraordinary scene, almostsurrealistic. We were there, explaining to them how the machine worked, until Henry Ford said: "Listen, I understand the interest of the system, but I'm not a specialist. I'd really like my guys to see it. Is that possible?" Two months later, a whole team of Ford technicians arrived at our factory. They weren't the only ones. It's much less well known than our wind tunnel.

Aerodynamic research is something I rather had in my blood. In 1935, my father had already created a Lancia Aprilia with a stretched wheelbase, which with the production engine was capable of exceeding 160 kmh/100 mph on the Rome-Ostia *autostrada*. It was a good 30 kilometres faster than the production car. My father had understood the importance of aerodynamics, which was a field that had been very little explored until then. He had also understood that it was a field in which the coachbuilder could play his role freely. The engine was not our domain, nor the tyres, nor the suspension, and the driver even less! Aerodynamics was our private hunting ground. My father had understood that in 1935. He was 42 and had not had a classical technical training. He simply had intuition.

I was a kid at the time. But at the Politecnico, I was involved in aerodynamics, and as I said, I also had it in my blood. To that I was to add my experience with Ferraris. I followed the development of each one of them closely, and I tested them all on the Turin-Ivrea road. It was desperately dangerous. To test, for example, the behaviour of the windscreen wipers at hight speed in the rain and traffic was insane. Maximum risk and minimum result. As another example, to define the position of a upright which divided two glazed surfaces required an enormous amount of work. To compare two solutions in the same conditions required a lot of time, too much time, and often intuition replaced scientific testing.

The idea of building a wind tunnel just came naturally. It was a major project. We started to study it the year my father died, in 1966. Three years of studies were followed by three more years for the construction. Then there was a year of fine tuning it to standardize it in relation to the others. Then we really started to work for third parties.

The wind tunnel was my project in many respects. I believed in it, I pushed for the project to be carried through, and in the end, it didn't cost us anything. Moreover, building it brought us enormous prestige. It enabled us to develop relations at a much higher level. It allowed us also to train specialists. A short time ago, one

And there was a friendly atmosphere at Pininfarina. Our Alumni Association is fantastic. I am the Honourary President of the Alumni since the death of my father. We have been through all the tough times together for the last 24 years. We had everything: in the 1970s, terrorism; in the 1980s, the Fiat strike when I was President of the Industrial Union of Turin. It couldn't have been worse. Through all those difficult moments, I always got a wonderful welcome from them. Those people have always understood that managerial decisions were taken to protect the whole enterprise. That is a great personal success, because the group is open to everyone, without distinction. For me, every one of our meetings is like passing the final examinations at University.

Those difficult years were also marked by the brutal change of policy by Fiat towards coachbuilders.

You're talking about the Ghidella period. He was convinced that everything at Fiat was worthless. That wasn't completely wrong. He thought everything had to be completely overhauled, completely changed, including the personnel, the suppliers, the products. Everything there, absolutely everything, had to disappear.

The result was that Fiat lost all the market niches where it had a prime position, and also its most prestigious products. And it decided it could afford to do whithout any expansion into the off-road market.

Yes, but now that position has been reviewed and there is again open and constructive dialogue. All the constructors have understood the importance of niche markets.

So the future of coachbuilders in general and of Pininfarina in particular is safe?

Without a doubt, but there are so many external factors which mould the future of the sector that very great vigilance, active vigilance, is essential.

The Peugeot 605 represents a particular aspect of the creative activity of Pininfarina as a coachbuilder. The role here has been to progressively create a line that the French manufacturer has taken over, to the extent of labelling its own projects as "in the style of" and "in association with" Pininfarina, which carried out the interior design.

of our young technicians won an international prize for the best technical paper written by a technician aged under 40. I wrote him a letter of congratulations. Isn't it wonderful that one of our youngsters wins at an international congress? It means that the company is young, not me or our specialist, Cogotti.

We're not stopping there. We are progressing in aerodynamic modelling. That brings us prestige in our relations with General Motors and our clients in general. Here's another memory: Fiat decided to build a wind tunnel when the press wrote about the inauguration of ours. Engineer Montabone seized the opportunity to obtain finance and break down internal resistance. Isn't that marvellous!

Listening to you telling all that, it's clear that you have had a magnificent life and that you are still passionately involved with the automobile.

Yes, even if it's no longer on a minute to minute basis. Now I am involved with the automobile and design through my sons. The strategy of the company remains my domain. It hasn't fired me yet. But I'm afraid that one day I'll find a sign on the door of my office: "Closed because of unjustified, repeated absence". The truth is that today, my value is seen through my sons. It should no longer be measured against me. There is a period of life in which to learn, another to create and struggle. I struggled a lot. Then, a period in which to teach. Not to teach as I did at the Politecnico in a lecture hall, but teaching by example. People watch you, observe you, judge you and come to conclusions. Essentially the value of the master is judged by the quality of his students...

Like the great painters whose students formed a school. In the end it is hard to distinguish between the work of the master and that of his students. You really did achieve that.

THE REALITIES OF ALTERNATE ENERGY

Jean-Pierre Gosselin

The Gulf Crisis has revived a question first addressed during the oil crises of the 1970s: the eventual replacement of petrol by other sources of energy. Scientists are still far from solving all the problems involved. Petroleum remains indispensable and there is no indication when it might be replaced. In the meantime, the solution is surely to develop new engines to use it more efficiently.

Replacing the used hydrides in a hydrogen-powered vehicle is theoretically not dangerous, but it is a complex operation. The exhausted hydrides must be removed and replaced in the tank with fresh material. Service station equipment would be complicated, as each refuelling operation would involve handling hundreds of kilos of hydrides in liquid solution.

Alcohol produced from sugar cane is the "national" fuel in Brazil. The hot climate make this ethanol fuel possible, but it is expensive and corrosive in engines. To force its use, the government went to the lengths of ordering traditional petrol pumps to be shut at weekends.

A t a series of motor shows, BMW and Japanese hydrogen engines continue to stimulate a public interest which is no longer impressed by internal combustion engines using methanol, alcohol or vegetable-based oils: the expectations raised about these fuels after the 1973 and 1979 oil crises were very far from being realised. However, there is heightened interest in electric and hybrid cars and for the first time, a European manufacturer, Peugeot, has taken the plunge and has started series production of electrically-driven utilities.

The contrasting positions are easily explained. Projects developed on the basis of petroleum being very expensive were rapidly abandoned or slowed down when the oil price dropped quickly and substantially. The anti-pollution campaign then took over to such a degree that an anormalous situation developed: engines equipped with catalytic converters consume more fuel that their predecessors. In the name of pure air and the survival of the planet, its fossil energy resources are being wasted — a nice paradox of modern society.

The past decade has seen research into substitute energy sources become more complex, with the quality of emissions and their low levels becoming as least as important as availability or cost. But the results have been very modest and there has been little real impression of progress, the automotive industry marking time whenever the question of freeing itself from petrol arises. Without examining every area in detail, it is safe to comment that this situation will continue for some time, even if massive investment follows the Gulf Crisis.

Historically, electricity was a tough rival for petroleum early this century, but the lead-acid battery unfortunately lost out, and even now insufficient progress has been made with it for it to drive vehicles adequately. In contrast, however, electric motors and their electronic

management systems have been developed to give very high levels of performance, and production of urban vehicles with lightened classic batteries can be considered. These are relatively slow, with a top speed of barely 100kmh (62mph), and a maximum realistic range of around 100 kilometres (62 miles). But this limited range is sufficient for town use by fleet vehicles housed in garages equipped for re-charging, which could last almost all night (as indeed it does with urban delivery vehicles).

Though the modest performance has changed little for many years, there has been a real revolution. The price of these vehicles, and that fact that their batteries can now accept 2000 charge-discharge cycles, makes their urban performance now financially acceptable. Peugeot actually reduced the technology level of its J5 and 205 utilities from their prototype designs to make series production possible. The high performance nickel-cadmium batteries in the prototypes were replaced with standard lead-acid batteries to enable them to be sold at a reasonable price. The electronics were simplified because a conventional gearbox was introduced, and the high priced prototypes became economically viable vehicles, even if they still cost more to operate than a petrol-driven equivalent.

Fiat has followed the lead with a project for an electric Panda, and the Italian company Volta is selling electric Seat Marbellas. This market, held up to now by specialised firms, seems to be taking off in Europe, as it is in Japan where the use of electric vehicles is increasing.

But the problem for all alternative fuels remains that of storage. For example, the little Marbella carries 360kg/792lb of batteries, rechargeable over eight hours, giving it a top speed of 80kmp/50mph and a range of 100 kilometres/60 miles at 50kmh/30mph. It is frankly

This Peugeot 205 electric prototype has an integrated battery charger. It can be plugged in at night and recharges over six to eight hours. This is a reasonable method for fleet vehicles, operating over fixed routes which are known in advance (like urban delivery vehicles need for most of the 20th century). The problem is more complex for a private car user who must calculate a route carefully, including his return trip to the charging point, or risk being stranded. The joke is that these 205s still have a petrol tank — for the heating system. It quickly became apparent that running the heating system in winter of electricity was impractical, as it used almost as much power as the drive mechanism and thus dramatically reduced the range. Peugeot turned to blown air truck heating systems running on petrol or diesel.

ridiculous, because the same performance can be obtained with a conventional engine using just four litres (less than a gallon) of petrol weighing about 3kg/6.6lb. Engineers and scientists are well aware of the problem, and are seeking to improve the power to weight ratio of batteries, and particularly their energy to weight ratio, by reducing their internal resistance at a steady current output. They are also seeking the least possible battery maintenance and the maximum life. Batteries demonstrating these improvements exist already, built of nickel-cadmium or nickel-iron combinations, and all the manufacturers have used them in their prototypes as they have twice the energy to mass ratio of lead batteries. But they are, alas, seven times more expensive than conventional batteries and their price will only drop if they are produced in large quantities — which is not possible as they will be too expensive for the consumers for some time. It is a classic vicious circle and may finally only be solved by outside intervention in the form of sodium-sulphur batteries, with twice the energy capacity of cadmium-nickel. The drawback here, however, is that they operate at high temperatures (300 to 400°C), which poses further problems. The next step may be polymer batteries without solid metals, much lighter and more powerful than any current units.

All forecasts concerning the future of electric vehicles must still be hedged with caution, and announcements of spectacular results treated with reserve. An example is the publicity concerning the famous GM Impact. It is claimed that the Impact can reach 160kmh/100mph and accelerate from 0 to 100kmh/60mph in 8 seconds, with a range of 190 kilometres/120 miles at 90kmh/56mph — all with cheap lead batteries that can be recharged in just two hours. It is apparently the perfect electric vehicle. While it is true that it has a Cd of only 0.19 and runs on Goodyear low rolling resistance tyres, engineers around the world remain sceptical about the reality of its claimed performance, unless three different cars were built, one for each achievement! For example, calculation shows that once it had accelerated to 100kmh/60mph its batteries would be flat. In fact, GM seems to have used batteries with ultra-thin plates, a system which is as old as the automobile itself. The Belgian Jenatzy used such batteries in 1899 to break the 100kmh/60mph "barrier" in his car *Jamais Contente*. The problem is that such batteries have a life of only a few weeks!

BMW's liquid hydrogen option is explained by the desire to maintain similar engine power to that of a vehicle equipped with a petrol engine. General layout remains the same, and research has shown how such engines could be produced economically. The injection of liquid hydrogen is through injectors operated by oil pressure: changes in the pressure are created by a simple in-line diesel injection pump. With the reheated oil and this indirect system to open the valves, freezing of the controls is avoided despite the fuel being stored at a temperature near absolute zero. The engine in this BMW 745i develops 200bhp (against 252bhp in the petrol version) and the 45 litre tank gives a range of about 400km/250 miles).

With its ultra-low Cd, very light weight and low rolling resistance tyres, the Impact should theoretically not use more than 3 litres of fuel per 100km/94mpg with a thermal engine. Its performance with batteries and electric motors should thus be evaluated on that basis, which makes them somewhat less spectacular, and little more credible.

Some manufacturers are developing turbine engines to produce around 100 Kw or 136bhp (here, Toyota's), which would be adequate to drive a car in the 2-litre class. They are also faced with problem of efficiency, which is a function of the internal temperature and will only be solved by using ceramics.

In short, pure electric vehicles will be restricted to urban use for some considerable time to come. The next step has been to consider producing the electricity aboard the vehicles in two different ways. The first has been advocated recently by VW and Audi with hybrid cars. Out of town, a diesel engine drives the vehicle to a maximum of 150kmh/93mph while also recharging the batteries, which are fewer but adequate for pollution-free driving in town at a top speed of 60kmh/36mph. This is a short-term solution, that for the longer term being the replacement of the diesel engine with a turbine which can burn all types of fuel, coupled with increasingly efficient alternators and electric propulsion motors.

It is hoped that as the turbine will run at a constant speed, it can be tuned to operate extremely economically with low pollution on any variety of carburant. The first European prototype (VERT) is due to run in the mid-1990s with an existing micro turbine, an aircraft starter motor, until the Agata turbine, being developed as an EEC Eureka project, is ready.

Solar power appears to be the most direct and the cleanest way to produce electricity, with renewable, limitless energy sources in place of fossil fuels. It would be perfect if the 1000 watts per square metre offered by the sun could be collected with 100 per cent efficiency, but that is far from the case. One square metre of mass-production solar cells, which should be enough to run an household iron, produces just about 100 watts, only enough for a light bulb!

Certainly gallium arsenide photocells improve the efficiency to above 20 per cent, and Boeing has recently achieved a record 37 per cent, but at a price only just affordable by the space industry and impossible for the automobile industry or car owner. The only efficient sun-powered vehicle, GM's Sunraycer, did cross Australia at an average of more than 110kmh/68mph but carries only one person, uncomfortably, stretched out on webbing and in torrid heat. It is 6 metres (nearly 20 feet) long and cost $3 million... Unless, like batteries, there is a spectacular breakthrough, solar energy will remain a supplementary power source for automobiles, for example to run air conditioning when the car is at a halt. Thinking otherwise is utopian.

There remain the "traditional" alternative fuels, the eternal outsiders such as methanol, vegetable alcohols, vegetable oils, gas of all types, wood, coal and so forth. It must be said that since the oil crises of the 1970s there

has been absolutely no progress in the automotive application of these, even for those said to be low pollutants. Some people have attributed the stagnation to lobbying by the major oil companies, but nothing could be more wrong. All the lobby does is recall the well-known and major technical problems of availability, price and distribution which consistently hold back these substitute fuels.

The most significant example is the clear failure of the Brazilian alcohol system, produced from thousands of acres of sugar cane and managed by the national petroleum company Petrobras. Every possible effort was made to encourage manufacturers and consumers, sometimes verging on duress, but nothing availed and the operation was a failure. Furthermore, because of its social and economic implications, the plan was irreversible and in the end, inefficient. If oil prices rise substantially over a long period, the alcohol system may yet give Brazil some relief, but so far it has only proved that even on a large scale, experiments of this type are risky. That is why in Europe and the United States, ethanols of agricultural origin, mainly from beetroot or corn (the latter making American "gasohol" to use up surplus grain stocks) are considered no more than complementary to hydrocarbons. As they remain two or three times more expensive to produce than petrol, their distribution remains limited and "political" in the sense that they can be used to absorb farm surpluses.

In the temperate, but sometimes cold and humid climates of Europe and northern America, they also have a tendency to absorb water and separate out from the carburants which they are supposed to improve, notably where pollution is concerned. With these disadvantages, it is certain that promotion of ethanol will make little progress and that unless there is a particularly serious oil crisis, these fuels will never take off.

These difficulties do have one advantage, in that they tend to silence the unrealistic. The supporters of biomass, for example, discovered that the energy recovered from wood chips and other forestry debris was just sufficient to run the collection vehicles! Realism is in vogue and sets the limits for the future of ethanol, which cannot be regarded as brilliant. It is the same story for those who foresee operating diesel engines with vegetable fuels. Surpluses have disappeared, particularly in Africa, and the engines do not use the fuel well. It is clear to anyone who has seen the excellent Elko diesels

running on colza oil: the thick exhaust smoke and nauseous odour are forms of pollution which produce stronger reactions because they are more easily perceived.

Fuels of vegetable origin, including those derived from wood through gasproducers, could not save Europe from shortages during the Second World War. They are still discounted today, even if in exceptional circumstances they could provide some complementary energy, useful if of low quality. Our civilization does, however, produce an increasing amount of waste of which it is increasingly difficult to dispose. It is estimated that a town of 100,000 people produces about 15,000 cubic metres of sewage a day. Properly treated, it can be turned into 200 cubic metres of mud and 2500 cubic metres of gas of good quality, because it contains 72 per cent of hydrocarbons. Here at last is a tangible reality, quantifiable and realistic, even if it only applies to developed economies.

Bio gas, or manure gas, has been an operational reality on an industrial scale for 20 years, notably with Fiat's Totem system. The figures show that 30 cows produce two tons of shredded waste, which after fermentation and purification create bio gas containing 70 per cent methane and equivalent to 15 tons per year of domestic fuel oil. Once again it is an additional energy source, but though available in considerable quantity and at reasonable cost it can never become a major energy source for cars.

Technically, current cars could run on bio gas, because some already run on natural gas. Apart from some particular periods when coking gas or low-quality charcoal gas was used, natural gas always dominated this small market. In Italy and France in particular, natural gas was compressed and liquified to save space and give vehicles a range identical to that offered by their petrol tanks. It has now been replaced, however, by LPG, a mixture of butane and propane produced in large quantities during the refining of crude oil. These gases, an automatic product of the distillation process, are popular with drivers as their cars do not lose power compared with the petrol version. LPG has never needed added lead to have a high octane rating, and indeed these gases are used to increase the rating of liquid fuels. The low resultant pollution has made LPG popular for taxi fleet use, notably in the Netherlands and Japan.

Thouth they are already in use, these gases, easily liquified under pressures of only 3 to 5 bars, can be also be considered a fuel of the future, as proven gas reserves far exceed those of crude oil and will still be producing when crude oil has been exhausted. But there is an argument that says they are not a fuel of the future because they are part of the classic energy system based on hydrocarbons.

Another advantage of gas, and particularly natural methane, is that it can be converted into excellent liquid fuels. New Zealand covers a third of its fuel requirements with a synthetic petrol of excellent quality produced by the Mobil MTG (methanol to gasoline) process. Methanol, another carburant which is very popular in Europe, can also be produced from gas or from coal, of which the Earth has reserves estimated to be sufficient for some 500 years.

A number of projects have been based on methanol since the first oil shocks, and some carburants already contain up to 15 per cent. But to use it, internal combustion engines must be modified as methanol attacks some metals violently, and also quickly degrades some rubbers and plastics. It is much more difficult to run on pure methanol, but Volvo recently resumed its initial M85 programme (an 85 per cent methanol fuel) with its B230F FFV engine which was optimised to burn fuels with a variable percentage of methanol. Given the necessary changes to the storage and distribution equipment, methanol thus could be a fuel of the future independent of petrol. Although it has a lower specific energy and is more expensive than hydrocarbons, its use appears viable in both the short and long term, and is even probable. The pollution caused by certain industries such as cement production in exhausting CO_2 into the atmosphere, engendering the greenhouse effect, can be reduced by requiring them to produce methanol from the waste gases.

It remains true that in all the alternatives considered, including the most exotic solutions of making synthetic petrol from sunflowers, cacti or water haycinths, produce fuels containing carbon. That molecule remains the best "trap" for hydrogen, which is the real fuel. Their combustion necessarily produces CO and CO_2 which are not welcome as they contribute to the greenhouse effect and planetary warming.

The ideal fuel from the point of view of avoiding pollution is certainly hydrogen: its combustion with oxygen from the air produces a lot of energy and only water vapour — lots of water vapour — as a by-product.

It may look like an UFO, but it is actually the very real GM Sunraycer, currently the most advanced ground vehicle in the field of solar powered electric propulsion. Every division of the huge GM empire contributed considerable know-how to the Sunraycer, and exotic materials and advanced aerodynamics are employed to exploit the gallium arsenide photocells. The photocells had previously been used only in high performance cameras. Limited by the competition regulations to a maximum length of 6 metres, the Sunraycer crossed Australia from north to south at an average speed of more than 60kmh/ 38mph. It was a remarkable performance, but the vehicle ran only by day, and in a country with abundant sunshine — and it cost $3 million, factors which show the true nature of the sun solar power problem.

The Sunráycer driver's cockpit is even less comfortable than an F1 car's. Savage weight-paring means that he is half reclining on simple webbing, and sees the road going past under his seat, for the vehicle has no floor at that point. The peculiar position makes driving difficult, but the major problem is the heat in the cabin. Solar heat, plus that generated by the engine and electronics, make the cabin temperature almost insupportable. Drivers in the Le Mans 24-hour race have had similar problems, solved as in Sunraycer by bringing fresh air in through tubes aimed at the face. The fact that the energy source for this "automobile" is free does little to make it viable. The Sunraycer covers the same surface area as an old Cadillac while carrying only one person, and with safety almost non-existent.

The calorific value of hydrogen is 30,000 kg-calories per kilo, compared to 11,000 for petrol and only 5400 for methanol. On another scale, hydrogen produces 3100kg-calories per cubic metre with completely clean combustion involving no lead or sulphur and 40 times less nitrogen products, the famous NO_x range. If the 0.2 litres of water produced per 100 kilometres (one drop every metre) is not considered as pollution, it would appear to be the ideal fuel for the future.

Hydrogen is virtually inexhaustible as it can be extracted from the oceans which cover two-thirds of the world's surface, and the water produced by its combustion returns to the ocean. But the hydrogen solution is still extremely far distant for the automobile, although it is used successfully as a carburant in all the major rockets and missiles.

This gas poses a number of very difficult problems for everyday use, because the qualities of hydrogen are at the same time its faults — this highly energetic gas is dangerous. Mixed with about 4 per cent of air, it explodes violently. One cubic metre of hydrogen produces an explosion comparable to two kilos of TNT. Its very low density (it is 14 times lighter than air) is also a handicap, because an equal volume in the engine delivers much less power than conventional fuel. This characteristic also poses enormous problems of storage on board vehicles, because it must be compressed or liquified to provide sufficient energy for a decent range. That in turn leads to a series of problems of feeding the engine and above all of security — the car becomes a rolling bomb.

BMW has faced up to the problems of liquified hydrogen. The fuel tanks in which it is stored at − 253° C, not far from absolute zero, are robust and heavily lagged. Injection in the liquid phase had been mastered, because it is the only known way of achieving a power loss limited to 10 per cent, without increasing the engine size. The remaining problems are outside the vehicle: they concern the problem of liquefaction which demands very high energy input, of distribution and of storage. Service stations for hydrogen would have unusual installations, and handling would be difficult and risky.

Storage in bottles with the gas compressed to 200 bars (1 litre of petrol equalling 1.5 cubic metres of hydrogen) is marginal for automobiles although standard procedure in industry, and also poses distribution problems.

The range of problems is so great that some companies, like Mercedes and Peugeot, have explored the possibility of producing hydrogen on board the vehicle. The gas is held in the form of salts hydrides, in a sort of metallic sponge. Problems of storage and transport are eliminated as are those of safety. The problems come in using the gas efficiently. The hydrides are heavy, supply little hydrogen and must be heated. That can be carried out with the engine cooling water, but it is a slow process. Engine power is cut by half and not all the hydrogen can be extracted from the metallic sponges.

The problems of distribution, of the increased weight of vehicles and the modifications necessary to utilise hydrogen in that form have so disheartened the researchers that they have shelved the projects, awaiting new "hydrogen sponges" which may be made from titanium hydride. Each litre of such a material can contain 1700 litres of hydrogen, six times more than in the current iron-lithium or magnesium-nickel compounds.

Paradoxically, hydrogen could help revive the Wankel engine. Its major fault, the voluminous combustion chamber which slows the combustion of hydrocarbons, becomes an advantage with hydrogen which has a tendency to burn too fast and poses a problem in conventional engine design.

There is a better way of using hydrogen, however. The fuel cell which produces electricity and water directly by "slow combustion" has been vital to the exploration of space. It would be perfect combined with electric drive mechanisms, save that hydrogen fuel cells are very expensive, as are those operating on methanol or petrol. There are also turbines which can run on almost anything, including powdered coal, but they are well out of reach. Hydrogen is expensive to produce and difficult to distribute and store, particularly in the compressed and liquified forms which are suitable for vehicle engines. These are weighty handicaps — without adding that of nuclear power. Production of large quantities of hydrogen at low cost would have to be done by electrolysis of sea water using cheap electricity, most probably low tariff power produced at night by nuclear power stations. This scenario immediately brings protests from those who affirm that actual pollution should not be removed only to be replaced by potential pollution from nuclear sources. It is hardly realistic to suggest covering vast expanses of the country with solar mirrors to produce the power for the hydrogen process.

Given all the problems, the future of hydrogen as a fuel for the automobile is extremely uncertain, and it will certainly need a very grave shortage of other fuels to bring it in to use. But its qualities as a fuel are obvious, which is why VW continues its research into on-board production of hydrogen, not with hydrides but from methanol. The one problem that VW will have to overcome is that the exhaust gas is the disagreeable ammonia, more aggressive than the usual pollutants! The future may simply be a choice between many forms of pollution.

There is no miracle solution in sight to free us from the need for petroleum and its derivatives, at least in the short term. But fossil energy resources will not run out tomorrow. Increased energy prices will make other sources of crude oil viable, from oil shales and tar sands, deep off-shore wells and gas, with coal as a final fall-back position. There are still hundreds of years of supply ahead of us — which is why the research is unhurried. Only a serious increase in pollution could bring the problem into critical focus, but the reduction of pollution by the automobile is now receiving considerable attention throughout the world. For moral, social or financial reasons, the number of vehicles powered by alternative fuels may increase in the coming years, but the vast majority of motorists will still be absorbed by headlines reporting changes in petrol and diesel prices.

THE INSTITUTE OF DEVELOPMENT IN AUTOMOTIVE ENGINEERING

CREATING IDEAS

JACQUES FARENC

.DE.A. is one of those "mini" design bureaux, covering the gamut from styling to production methods, which thrive in an automobile world where mergers and rationalization rule the day. Franco Mantegazza, the owner and driving spirit of I.DE.A., regards it as a "commando of engineers" who maintain a sharp creative and analytical drive, forming the sort of group which he emphasizes can perform a useful advisory role for the big battalions, for these can become bogged down by their sheer size.

Turin is the Detroit of Italy, and everyone lives for and by the automobile. But there is a major difference. One group reigns supreme in Turin: Fiat, with its army of suppliers.

However, the magnificent 18th Century chateau on the hills on the other side of the River Po, the Villa Cantamerla, is not just one more Agnelli family mansion. It is the heart of I.DE.A. (The Institute of Development in Automotive Engineering) which despite its origins in Turin maintains its independence from its giant neighbour.

That is the position Dr-Ing Franco Mantegazza, its lively, multilingual, ever-smiling founder, wishes to preserve

industrial concept. The idea was a basic structure on which mechanical systems could be assembled more quickly, easily and economically than on conventional assembly lines.

It was thus the forerunner of the "off line" assembly of complete sub-systems (engines, transmission systems, suspension steering systems, dashboards, rear axle units, etc) and it also favoured the flexibility of decentralizing production. The concept was built around the idea of separating two major elements, the structure and mechanical units on one side, and the bodywork and styling elements on the other. The structural cage, which was from the first designed to be very rigid, was created to receive a "skin" of advanced plastic. The vehicle could then be produced in two- or three-box forms, or with an estate body, and the concept allowed re-styling at relatively low cost.

Mantegazza outlines why his Institute is able to exist independently. It reflects his own position as an outside observer of the industry, an engineer who also understands industrial realities, who can analyse automotive problems objectively and clearly. "In the big automotive groups, destabilized by an excess of vertical integration",

121

A Ferrari Testarossa was remodelled by I.DE.A. for the PPG paint com-pany, which sponsors the CART series in the United States and introduces a number of distinctive pace cars each season.

for his company, which was founded "quietly in 1978", and whose first major commission was for the VSS project, for Fiat.

Mantegazza describes I.DE.A. as "an organisation creating and selling ideas, at the service of all manufacturers, having the advantage of a different vision of the future of the automobile, making these new ideas practical, and creating these improved products which will make the difference for the manufacturer."

I.DE.A. was born with the VSS project, the Vehicle with Sub-Systems, which was the ancestor of the modular

he says, "there may be 5000 engineers in the technical services of one major marque. It is understandable that these specialists have neither the time, nor sometimes the ability, to stand back from a situation and speak out."

"To make an automobile, you must be both very sensitive and a great engineer, we need to recreate small groups, with people capable of reasoning like Leonardo da Vinci, while communicating better among themselves to achieve the benefits of improved analysis and creativity."

From his tiny base, Mantegazza applies his objective

FRANCO MANTEGAZZA

Franco Mantegazza impresses everyone who meets him with his strong and remarkably dynamic personality. A mechanical engineer with diplomas from the universities of Zurich and Aachen, he started his career at Bofors as a production engineer before moving on to bodywork projects at Volkswagen, during the reign of the celebrated Prof. Nordhof. After a period with VW of America, Mantegazza returned to Italy with Magneti Marelli. Working with advanced technology and the newly emerging plastics materials gave him the idea of developing new products in a realistic industrial situation. He then moved to Fiat France SA, before working with Unic-Fiat trucks and Somaca public works vehicles. Returning again to Italy, he established a factory specialising in sub-contracting production of plastic materials and light alloys, before the concept of I.DE.A. finally emerged, as a mini-industrial company rather than just a design bureau, which would take concepts from the original idea to its industrial-scale production. Since it was set up a dozen years ago, it has never lost a minute through the strikes that often seem endemic in dynamic but troubled Italy.

Dr. Ing. Franco Mantegazza, the founder, leader and motivator of the Institute of Development in Automotive Engineering, in his office at the Villa Cantamerla.

The Villa Cantamerla, the home of I.DE.A., is a magnificent 18th Century chateau in the hills south-east of Turin.

I.DE.A. has 320 employees, the majority being engineers and technicians. The 24 drawing office staff, of widely varied origins and nationalities, are more nearly "designers", aware of the industrial realities of the automobile.

122

I.DE.A., as an independent design bureau, works for many constructors from around the world. Research is carried out in a number of different locations, for obvious reasons of confidentiality, and the few visitors admitted to the workshops see only carefully covered cars.

Despite the formidable processing power of computer aided design, Italian artistry can still find expression through wooden models on which real craftsmen shape metal panels by hand to produce the bodywork of the first rolling prototypes.

In the future I.DE.A. intends to reduce its dependence on the automobile by developing in other industrial design directions, shown in this study for a television set ordered by Toshiba.

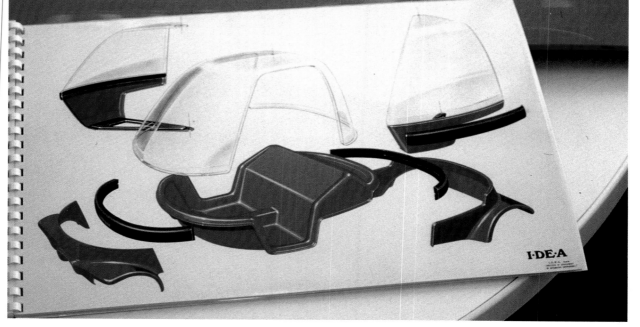

An organization like I.DE.A. normally has to be at the leading edge of advanced technology and engine design, although in its broad principles this study for a two-seater mini-vehicle (2.3 to 2.5 metres long), with electric power and plastic bodywork, conceived for the "red zones" of major cities, was not new. The idea is that the vehicle, rented on presentation of a credit card, would be picked up and dropped at rental stations spread throughout an urban area.

I.DE.A. can proceed to the creation of "white cars" and rolling prototypes. All the components, such as the rear lights here, can be built in its own workshops.

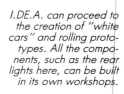

This project for a coupe, which I.DE.A. designed for Alfa Romeo (below and top centre) was not followed up. It was known by the name of the manufacturer's first factory, Portello, which was in the centre of Milan.

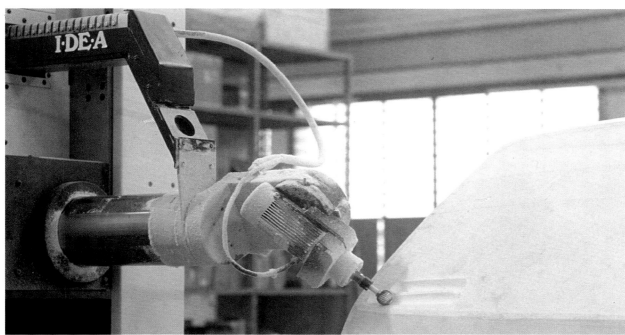

A modern design bureau is obliged to have the latest computer-controlled machine tools, like this numerically controlled milling machine. But the craft of the panel beater, in the highest sense of the term, that of the sculptor who works in wood and metal, helps to maintain the standing of European stylists.

Until the Fiat Tipo launch in early 1988, I.DE.A. was virtually unknown in the world of automobile design. The Tipo design caused some surprise, but it was an outstanding compromise of internal space and external size. Using the same mechanical elements, the Tempra is in contrast a conventional saloon. Three-quarter front sketches at two stages of the design are shown here. The Dedra (top sketch) marks a return to original thinking, with a nod towards the styling of the Mercedes 190 as a reminder that in the Fiat range, Lancia is an elite marque.

126

views to the major constructors. Like Raymond Levy of Renault, who has described the huge complexes as "unsteerable ocean liners", Mantegazza sees the mega-constructors "gamble vast capital on the launch of a new model. Just imagine that simply for the bodyshell of the Tipo, Fiat invested nearly $1.8 billion: there is no room for a mistake in these huge enterprises." And executives in these organisations can suffer from "a tragic illness," says Mantegazza — they can be so specialized that no one can see errors in another specialist's area.

A convinced European before it was fashionable, Mantegazza can also view Italy, that dynamic if often illogical country, with an objective eye. He feels that it is rare for a large organization to operate as well as Fiat, "a company created by Piedmontese, the Prussians of Italy." This just reinforces his belief in the necessity of an organisation like I.DE.A. "When I launched the idea of I.DE.A., the general trend was to make the big grow bigger. I had the feeling, however, that great talents were refusing to be locked into these mega-organisations and their sometimes radical management of human resources."

Very much influenced by German culture, Mantegazza recognised the need to understand how to unite talents in a "Bauhaus" comparable to a guild of masons, with the spirit of a Masonic lodge. "In an environment in which the big companies can work to self-paralysis, a group of enthusiasts can develop perfect osmosis. My institute is a challenge to develop a new approach to engineering for the automobile, truly capable of synthesizing multiple techniques in the spirit of an enterprise culture."

Looking at a most basic aspect, Mantegazza reflects, "a person buys a car perhaps 20 times in his life: we must give him functionality, rationality, style and pleasure in his driving, without ever falling into the temptation of attempting to achieve the 'perfect car'. We must also respect the manufacturer's policy and image."

Mantegazza believes that the notion of a "perfect car," developed from the concept of the "world car" which evolved a dozen years ago for obvious economic reasons, could dramatically mislead constructors. It gives him another justification for the existence of I.DE.A., as a truly independent design bureau: "The big groups may find here the breath of fresh air which they perhaps no longer have in their own organisations."

I.DE.A is thus a design bureau with several facets, employing only 320 people in its own buildings "spread around the suburbs of Turin, for obvious reasons of confidentiality." The company philosophy is to build on a spirit of synthesis, directed by people "with good brains rather than well-stuffed brains."

An example is Mantegazza's leading advisor, Ing. Rudolf Hruska, one of the leading conceptual automobile engineers of the last 30 years. He may well be seen to have been one of the last engineers capable of pulling all his ideas together in his head and not in his computer.

I.DE.A is not just a styling bureau "where all the designers are truly engineers" (a favourite idea of Renault's Patrick Le Quément), but is seen as a complete organisation with a sales division (prospecting for clients, with two new offices opening in Detroit and Tokyo); a technical division to establish the detailed requirements of a constructor-client which can undertake structural calculations and full engineering activities; and a division described as 'production' which is responsible, before the final cost estimate is made, for the production of models and rolling prototypes built on a mini assembly line in conditions as close as possible to industrial reality.

In its compact structure, I.DE.A. thus offers a complete service, ranging from styling, the major activity with its

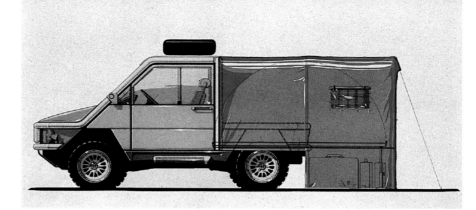

Conceived as a joint study of a mini 4X4 with Nissan, the Alfa 148 project — developed before the liaison between the Japanese manufacturer and Fiat was broken off — was a highly flexible vehicle, the chassis, cabin and platform being covered in canvas or sheet metal and useable for professional or leisure purposes of all kinds, for example as an extendable camping car for long distance "raids", a beach buggy, or a carrier for trials 'bikes.

128

24 designers of all origins and nationalities, to concepts of industrial production methods, and cost estimation.
As an Italian organisation, the shadow of Fiat undoubtedly looms over it. I.DE.A.'s reputation has been spread mainly by its work on the Fiat Tipo series, the second generation Fiat Uno (the first having been the work of Giugiaro), the Fiat Tempra and the Lancia Thema II and Dedra.

But Franco Mantegazza has other faithful clients, including BMW and Nissan, and inside the Villa Cantamerla are displayed the logos of other disparate constructors which have commissioned work from the institute: Karmann, Toyota, Subaru, Volvo, General Motors, Chrysler, Kia of South Korea and Bajaj of India.

It is obviously important that Mantegazza becomes more independent of Fiat. "Previously, Fiat accounted for 70 per cent of our turnover; today it is 40 per cent and I want to adjust the balance of my automobile activities even more, to work with other constructors, especially French companies. There is also industrial design in the broader sense, which currently represents only 10 per cent of turnover but which offers enormous potential," he says.

In 1985, 12 years after its foundation, I.DE.A. has a turnover, thanks to Fiat and Alfa Romeo, of $20.5 million. "In 1990, if all the prospective programmes come through, we will finish up around $55 million," says Mantegazza, revealing that his turnover has almost tripled in five years, and increased on average by 50 per cent per year.

Mantegazza defines the role of I.DE.A. in relation to each marque as that of respecting its image while developing its character. "Above all," he insists, "there must not be cars without character. The only advantage of such a vehicle, if one can call it such, is that it would not displease."

I.DE.A., whose direct competitors are styling bureaux such as IAD, Porsche Weissach, Lotus Engineering, Matra Automobile and Ital Design, "does not wish to impose its image, but to blend into the mould of its client."

Franco Mantegazza concludes: "You must not be superclever among the clever; institutes of research and development like mine will play an increasingly important role in defining the automobile, where they can bring in really new ideas. I do not want to sell by image simply for money, nor to lower myself to design macaroni; I want to remain a real creator of really new concepts."

GROWTH THROUGH DIVERSIFICATION

Creative people in all sectors of industry are increasingly influential, and most of them have come out of the specialized world of the automobile.

Design, as conceived by specialists such as Pininfarina, IAD, Bertone, Giugiaro or I.DE.A. is international and multidisciplinary. It is not confined to the automobile; for example Mantegazza's team also works in areas such as clothing, housing and so forth. I.DE.A. has thought through this diversification and created an "industrial design" department. Its work outside the automobile field has included a Toshiba television set, Komatsu civil engineering vehicles, the Phenix sportswear range, and Citizen watches and glasses (all made in Japan). It has also designed boats for Balietto, furniture, aircraft interiors and seating, Recaro automobile seats and Wesumat car wash bays. Franco Mantegazza and his engineers have a multitude of projects in hand, ranging from crash helmets to kitchens and suitcases.

It is interested in everything that moves: new requirements for engine power sources and advanced technology of all kinds, throughout the world. "You don't have to be the CIA, which collects information on a world scale but does not always pull it together systematically and thus does not fully understand it," says Mantegazza.

Among the Institute's novel projects are "a new layout for a moped, which is characterised by a more logical ergonomic position that that of a 'traditional' bicycle, and has a removable motor." This is a 1 horsepower two-stroke engine, weighing a maximum of 3 kilos, with chain drive and very low fuel consumption. Discussions about this project are in progress with the Indians and the Chinese, who have major potential markets for such a simple vehicle.

At the other extreme, the major projects currently under development are said to include a sub-contracted study for a super sports car, a coupe with a central engine, for a well-known European constructor.

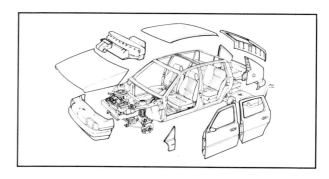

ULTIMATE CARS OR ULTIMATE FOLLIES?

PHILIPPE DE BARSY

In the best of all possible worlds, what would you choose — a Ferrari F40 which is a handful in traffic, a Lamborghini Diablo, unusable in town or up a mountain pass, or the reincarnation of a real pre-war Grand Tourer or of a light *barchetta* of the Mille Miglia era? Today's real supercars are not quite what people believe.

During the 1980s, the generation of men and women born 40 years ago reached professional maturity and financial ease. It is a generation whose childhood lullabies were the songs of the V12 Ferrari, the 6 cylinder Maserati, the MG TC and TD, Jaguar XKs and C Type, Porsche 356 and 550, Aston Martins, Mercedes 300SL, Triumphs and many other fascinating automobiles. It was a magic period in the renaissance of the car from the ashes of pre-war promise epitomised by the Alfa Romeos, Bugattis, BMWs, and in Grand Prix racing, the fabulous Mercedes and Auto Unions with their magnificent engines.

The Second World War put an end to some projects for early supercars such as an Auto Union coupé with a mid-mounted V16 engine, and on a smaller scale, the VW Type 60 Berlin-Rome coupés laid out on the same lines by Porsche. With the rebirth of the sporting automobile in the last years of the 1940s and the start of the 1950s, the classic design for a sports car with a front engine and rear driven wheels was dominant. This was simply because it was easier to locate existing mechanical units in elementary chassis under a lightweight bodywork than to launch into the production of innovative designs

which had not yet been perfected. The market was too small and finances limited.

Racing sports cars of that era lived up to their name. After a major race it was not uncommon to see a Ferrari 166MM *barchetta*, a Jaguar XK120C or an aluminium-bodied Porsche coupé of the "Gmünd" series being driven home on the public roads. It was also an era when closed public roads were more frequently used for racing.

An important factor, often overlooked nowadays, is that the roads of that time were far from crowded, and sports cars could and were really used to the maximum for long distances on open roads, an unimaginable situation today except perhaps in certain exceptional and completely illegal circumstances in the small hours! Possible exceptions are the German "autobahns", but by definition "autobahns" only offer the sports car driver very limited pleasure. The sports car was born before the First World War, in cars such as the Audi Alpensieger, Vauxhall Prince Henry and the American runabouts and really came into its own in the 1920s, despite the fact that events like the Le Mans 24-hour Race were initially run for four-seater touring cars.

The six-cylinder Alfa Romeo 1750 Sport Zagato was a great commercial success in the early 1930s, in sales and sporting terms. Its supercharged engine was the basis, with two extra cylinders, of the famous 8C Alfas.

129

UW 3761

The racing climax for these true sports cars came in the 1950s, in events such as the Mille Miglia. For example, the 1955 Mille Miglia had 533 starters, cars large and small that were sent off over a period of 20 hours on a course that covered half of Italy. That year, Stirling Moss, driving a 3-litre 300bhp Mercedes 300SLR and accompanied by journalist Denis Jenkinson, covered the 159km/992 mile course in 10 hours 07 minutes and 48 seconds, at an average speed of 157.650kmh/97.96mph.

Cult objects

There was an extraordinary diversity of cars in the Mille Miglia during the 1950s, from the smallest sub-750cc Osca, DB, Stanguellini, Giannini or Moretti to Ferraris with 4.9, 4.1 or 3.5 litre V12s or the 4.5 litre Maserati V8. Major manufacturers competed with small specialist builders, and touring cars, modified or not, raced in the same event with the most prestigious GTs of the day, the Ferrari 250GT or Mercedes 300SL.

The characteristics of all these vehicles were such that they could still be handled by a competent amateur driver, even if in the rain (and it rained often in the Mille

Miglia), they demanded considerable skill to keep them on the road at a competitive speed. The braking distances and the G-forces in corners bore no comparison to those involved in modern rally cars, let alone a sports-racing car.

It is not surprising that these cars, restored so meticulously that they are often more beautiful and much better finished than they were originally, have become such cult objects and that the Mille Miglia Storica has become a modern classic for many lovers of nostalgia, invariably wealthy. They have to be...

These cars can give great pleasure to a driver of normal ability who appreciates things mechanical. The engines are lively, noisy and sometimes brutal, the gearboxes call for precision, and the brakes need to be treated with care. These cars demand to be driven, and in return provide immense pleasure just from simple acceleration and gear changing.

In their day, with the tyres available then and with their rudimentary chassis, the most powerful cars like the mid-1950s 4.9 litre Ferrari, had some 340/350bhp under the driver's foot and were already completely unsuitable for the Mille Miglia course. But the engines were com-

From 1924 to 1931, Mercedes developed a range of big six-cylinder sports cars. The 38/250 SS seen here (the bodywork is not original) was very similar to the SSK which finished second in the 1931 Le Mans 24 Hours. The legendary SSKL represented the most extreme development of the series. Its supercharged 7-litre engine produced 265bhp.

W.O. Bentley built an extraordinary reputation with his fabulous straight four and straight six engines, the former of 3 and 4.5 litres (opposite), the six being best known as the 6.5 litre unit used in the Speed Six.

Bugatti pushed the Mercedes SS and SSK theme that big is beautiful into the realm of the absurd with the 12.76 litre Royale, but created a more reasonable car in the Type 57 — this is a 1937 Atalante coupé. It was, however, just an elegant expression of a concept that was already outdated.

parable in power terms to modern touring cars such as the Mercedes 500E with 326bhp, and not far short of supercars like the new 5.7 litre Lamborghini Diablo with its 492bhp.

The heroic days of the great racing sports cars are long over, but they created deep and lasting impressions in their young contemporaries, which grew stronger through the following years. The development of the series production automobile progressed steadily during those years, with increasing performance being matched with greater comfort. The progress of the so-called family car was such that the manufacturers of GT and sports cars were forced into a steadily narrowing niche. In a 'traditional' vein, companies such as MG and Triumph continued to build sports cars well into the 1970s (and in a carefully limited way others such as Morgan still do), but the adequate market that once existed dwindled...

As sports cars evolved towards competition vehicles, not suitable to be driven on public roads or even on the "real" Nürburgring, for example, the image of the sporting automobile changed profoundly. Sport-prototypes have for many years been coupés with closed bodywork, bulky and broad, and for that reason alone they could hardly be used on the road circuits of the past. The mid-engined layout became the norm, and that have inevitably influenced the thinking of potential buyers, hence the approaches chosen by the designers of current supercars.

No realistic use

The increase in performance of average saloons, and derivatives produced by specialist tuning firms, had in the meantime given these cars potential performance levels bordering on the absurd. It was absurd because human beings had not changed — the average driving skill of buyers had not increased perceptibly — and the priority in most countries had been on repressive measures against the motorist rather than the active and large scale training of highly competent drivers.

The development of the touring car has caused supercar designers to go to extraordinary lengths in their creations, which nowadays are far removed from true Grand Touring cars that are their forerunners and sometimes verge on the ridiculous.

Examined cooly and rationally, a machine such as the

The Porsche 356 Speed-
ster (above, a 1955
model) drew perplexed
comments at its launch,
but enthusiasts quickly
revealed its full potential.

After the Second World
War, Jaguar was the
first manufacturer to
introduce a series-
production twin-cam. It
was the 3.5 litre straight
six-cylinder unit, installed
in the elegant XK120
roadster of the same
name (left) as the saloon
for which it was intended
was still in the
design stage.

A 2 litre V12 engine, a
few large tubes for a
chassis, large diameter
drum brakes and above
all, superb bodywork by
Touring was sufficient to
create the Ferrari myth
in 1949 with the 166MM
(bottom).

Opposite, top: the Mer-
cedes 300SL was the
result of a new approach
to the sports car. The
classic chassis was
replaced by a multitube
frame, and as many
components as possible
were taken from the
series 300. The project
was developed in only a
few months, for competi-
tion, with small-series
production following,
1400 being built
between 1954 and
1956.

Opposite, centre: the
Aston Martin DB2 is
representative of classic
GT car of the 1950s,
very straightforward in its
engineering and very
English in its character.
Opposite, bottom: the C
Type Jaguar was the
competition version of
the XK120 — a superb
body on simple and
robust mechanicals, and
carefully controlled
weight.

Opposite, top: the Jaguar XK SS was a spin off from the famous D Type, but only 16 of these road-equipped two-seaters had been completed before a factory fire in February 1957 spelled the end of the programme.
The AC Ace had the elegant lines of the Touring "barchettas" for early Ferraris, and together with the chassis was used for the Cobra (opposite, bottom), a simple idea which added the power of a US Ford 4.7 litre V8.

Left: the Ferrari 250 GT in its SWB (short wheel base) form was one of the most famous 3 litre V12s, with a classic layout under the superb bodywork, designed by Pininfarina but built by Scaglietti.

The Ferrari F40 (below) owes much of its fame to Pininfarina, and to the death of Enzo Ferrari. It belongs to a generation of Ferraris with no sporting achievements outside the Grand Prix arena, a car designed to be gazed at, a sort of sculpture in homage to the concept of the mid-engined sports car.

final version of the Lamborghini Countach was quite simply totally inefficient in going from A to B without an escort to clear the road ahead. A Diablo, 2.40 metres (almost 8 feet) wide, is not particularly suited to charging over an Alpine pass or weaving through city streets! Even a more sporting car such as a Ferrari F40 is grotesque in many situations. In its standard form, little realistic use can be made of such a supercar — its owner probably cannot race it or tour comfortably in it, can perhaps tour 'sportingly' with difficulty, maybe get some sheer out pleasure of driving it. These are vehicles which their owners use to assert a social position at gatherings of like-minded, or at stylish events. In the second half of the 1980s some were acquired just as investments, and it seems probable that by the end of this decade it will no longer be possible to drive them on the public highways of many countries. But meanwhile development of the breed continues, and some supercars do blend the best in design, technology, construction and performance.

The frenzied development of supercars with progressively greater brute potential could attain its apogee in the project for the new Bugatti 110. Technical Director Paolo Stanzani carried the project forward for three years

few years it will be advisable to take the car to the circuit in a transporter. There will be no call to find the best compromise between the competition car and the Grand Touring car, and as now there will be every incentive to use a true racing car for racing. No other car of this type has been intended to be so close to the performances of current competition vehicles. Between this Bugatti and a turbocharged sports-prototype of the very recent past the only difference would be the active safety promoted by the four wheel drive of the Bugatti and the fabulous power curve of its four-turbo engine.

Other current supercars projects, for example from Jaguar and McLaren, may well reach the market too late; others such as the March have been abandoned. The magic moment of madness in the generation aspiring to this kind of these rich mens' toys will pass, and the next generation of enthusiasts will want manufacturers to go back to first principles as far as sporting cars are concerned.

This view is supported by reactions to the current sporting car that most nearly reflects the image of the sports-prototype — the Honda NSX. Honda's engineers have opted for a marvellously efficient 3 litre 273bhp

Jaguar perhaps made a mistake in not giving the XJ220 concept car (above and opposite) a body closer in style to that of the real racing XJR, which has an impressive record. The initial project was perhaps only a styling exercise, but this rather large car generated enormous interest.

until it reached the testing stage in the summer of 1990. Stanzani, who by his contract had the right to buy a considerable interest in the company, quit as he seemingly failed in that, and before the Bugatti Automobili SpA factory at Campogalliano was formally opened, with a 'teaser' announcement of the 110 as tests continued at Michelin's Clermont Ferrand test track.

This Bugatti 110 gives a indication of just how far the supercar concept is being pushed today. The project is for a hi-tech two-seater coupé, a four-wheel-drive car powered by a reasonably sized 3.5 litre V12 engine, boosted by four turbochargers to give 550bhp at 9500rpm, with a carbon-fibre/Kevlar chassis.

The car is small and low by recent supercar standards, 4 metres (157in) long and 1.10 metres (43in) high, and the body design is by Marcello Gandini, of Lamborghini Countach fame.

Back to basics

Stanzani's dream was to create a supercar which could be driven to a circuit and then raced. The motoring environment is changing so quickly and so negatively that in a

atmospheric engine, mounting it in an aluminium chassis weighing only 210kg, and with reasonable overall dimensions: 4.40 metres/173in long, 1.81 metres/71in wide and only 1.17 metres/46in high. The car has been so well designed that even an inexperienced driver feels perfectly at home driving it, in any circumstances, including city traffic. For an experienced driver, there is nothing more efficient on the market.

The Honda NSX could sweep the market in the very narrow and very exclusive sector of supercars which can be used every day, if realism on the part of buyers is the only criterion. Only Porsche with the Carrera and Turbo, based on a design concept from another era, have occupied this niche so far. Some commentators have expressed regret that the Honda is not as imperfect as a Ferrari, does not have some supercar traits — it does not require the driver to constantly fight against it breaking away when driving fast, that it does not demand brute strenght to change gear, and so on.

Such reactions actually display a lack of ability to handle the machine in some cases. It would be better if manufacturers accepted quickly that the prestige of a supercar in their ranges is not an ultimate goal. Honda has realised

this in the 3 litre NSX, which is a remarkable synthesis of all the best features of high-performance cars, without the extravagences of a supercar. Furthermore, no manufacturer in this sector has ever before offered a two-year, unlimited mileage, parts and labour guarantee!

There is no longer a 2-litre Ferrari, or even a 3-litre Ferrari. The Alfa SZ is a 3 litre with the power of a good 2 litre, there is now no Jaguar comparable to an E Type (but new E Types are being built by a specialist constructor, to individual requirements and at enormous prices), the Lamborghini Diablo has a 5.7 litre engine, Mercedes is preparing a 6-litre V12 SL to reply to the 5-litre BMW, Porsche Carreras' engine capacities are now up to 3.6 litres — this can be seen as an automobile world gone mad. Manufacturers appear to think that a sports car must be faster in absolute terms than the fastest saloon cars, but a large touring car such as a BMW 750, Bentley Turbo R or Vauxhall Lotus Carlton, however fast it may be, will never provide the same pleasure on a country road or a mountain pass, as a light little spyder or coupé with a turbocharged 2 litre engine delivering, say 185-220bhp.

Top speed will not be the ultimate selling point for the

sports car in the future — it is a statistic that is rapidly becoming outmoded. The German manufacturers already have a voluntary limit of 250kmh/155mph, which in any event is far too high for the vast majority of drivers who have never had any real high speed training.

A speculative market

In the completely unrealistic period of the past few years, manufacturers have listed vehicles which may fall outside a real market demand, basing projects on the needs of a speculative market. In many countries there have been three-year waiting lists for a Ferrari 348, but even before the Gulf crisis broke these were evaporating, just as the astronomic auction 'values' for older cars were falling. What will happen to all these cars which were ordered to be re-sold or stored, and all the new cars which already are rarely seen except in museums or private collections?

It needed Mazda to launch the little Miata MX-5 for manufacturers throughout the world to realise that there was an enormous gap in the market for a very simple little sports car. The Mazda was selling at a considerable

premium in the United States at a time when Porsche had difficulty meeting its sales targets!

Chrysler, under the impetus of Bob Lutz, went for nostalgia with the Dodge Viper project, over the top but nonetheless attractive. This car takes us back to square one (which the Corvette had never left!), with a front engine, and an almost exaggeratedly retro body over a classic drive train — a car which looked quick even when it was parked. The 8-litre V10 makes little sense in this day and age, but it fits well into the American nature of the project, and with the objective of being the last folly of the famous Cobra generation. If it really does go into production, the Viper will be the 1990s reincarnation of the Mercedes SSKL.

There is really no longer any reason to build all sports cars along the classic theme of competition, and the motor industry might look to the example of the motorcycle world. In recent years, major manufacturers built hyper-sport machines, each one more gorgeous than the last and increasingly close to endurance or superbike racing models. This was fine, for the tiny minority capable of exploiting them to the maximum, but the motorcycle market has now rediscovered with delight

Giugiaro designed a model on the basis of the Bugatti chassis demensions laid down by Stanzani for his personal pleasure.

Opposite: in the Mythos, Pininfarina recreated the "barchetta" concept of the 1950s. Based on a Testarossa chassis, he designed a bodywork with exceptionally clean lines. It was an elegant expression of the idea that because such a car is created for pleasure and not for pure performance, the stylist is free to experiment in areas such as aerodynamics.

The Ford GT40 was a landmark, certainly one of the most beautiful street-legal closed sports cars. A quarter of a century before the F40, it was the real sports car of the mid-1960s, laid down as a circuit car — a field where it was very successful — which could be used as a road car, albeit with severe limitations in aspects such as luggage accommodation.

The Subaru Caspita concept car was shown at the 1989 Tokyo Show, with the Subaru Motori Moderni engine — which hardly shone in F1. This may be another of the "supercar" projects destined for the museum before even being put into production.

the pleasure of simpler 'bikes. They are lighter and not streamlined, with the mechanicals clearly visible, there is a well defined seat for a pillion rider, and the rider has a much less of a "racing" position. The marketing effort is concentrated on the choice available, and maintaining a certain realistic level of practicality.

Current sports cars have the level of comfort and equipment of the best touring cars, and not the least paradox in the whole affair is to see their owners dream of the seductive simplicity of a MGT or a Ferrari 166MM "barchetta".

They forget that those cars were absolutely spartan, with no accessories whatsoever and were, in a sense, like four-wheel motorcycles. My best memories of the era are of the marvellous Porsche 550: its engine developed only 110bhp but it only weighed 600 kilos. Will we ever see mini supercars created, and above all put into production, with engines up to 2 litres and all the marvels of modern technology, fully equipped but with weight pared as far as possible? The 16-valve VTEC-engined Honda CRX 1.6i VT already suggests the potential of a car on these lines, which would bring back the pleasure of escaping from the motorways and of really driving.

THE AGE OF THE STRATEGIST

EDOUARD SEIDLER

Calvet

Men like Louis Renault, Henry Ford I, Carl Benz and even Enzo Ferrari must be spinning in their graves. Express astonishment today to a managing director in the automobile industry that he could have risen to the highest position without any technical training, and the reply will invariably be: 'I am a manager, an umpire, a strategist.'

Cesare Romiti, the strong man of Fiat, puts it in particularly vivid terms: "My role is that of the conductor of an orchestra. I have with me musicians of quality. I have only to motivate them, to guide them, to harmonise their playing."

It is a statement that brings to mind another one, already a quarter of a century old, made by Giovanni Agnelli, the head of Fiat, at our first meeting: "If you have come to talk to me about technical questions and cars, I'm not the right person to talk to." And pretending to open the door of his vast office again, he added: "Behind this door I have a thousand engineers whom I pay to concert themselves with that kind of problem. They will answer you more intelligently than I..."

In fact, the automobile industry is turning more and more to the strategists. The car of today, while still conceived in the design studios, is above all a matter of accountants' figures — viability, productivity, investment, market fluctuations, profit margins, forecasts — and even of politics, although some of the more overtly nationalistic aspects have faded.

Decision makers

It is the managing directors in the industry who have taken, and are still taking, the responsibility for swingeing cuts in their work forces. They have to make the decisions on investments, be it the amounts, the method of financing them, or their geographical location. Taking up a political role, it is up to them to negotiate their decisions with government and the unions. And they also have to act as spokesmen for their companies, which turns most of them into media stars, under the spotlight on television or on the glossy covers of news magazines. They are in frequent contact with their engineers, but it is now rare for engineers to rise to the managing director rank. "War," it was once said, "is too serious to leave to the generals." Similarly the automobile industry has become too political at its highest level to be a business left any longer to the engineers.

Engineers thus have become much rarer in the most senior posts in the industry. There is only one in Europe, since Fiat let go its 'ingeniere', Vittorio Ghidella, and he is Ferdinand Piech, the nephew of Professor Porsche, at Audi. While technically competent, he may suffer by being less astute as a financier, as the leader of a company, a motivator and a strategist, when the time comes to replace Carl Hahn at the head of his group. And while Raymond Levy, the president and managing director of Renault, had the training of a Polytechnicien and at the prestigious Ecole des Mines engineering school, his

professional career in the oil industry and in steel makes him far from a 'car man'.

When the French Government had to find a replacement for the assassinated Renault head Georges Besse — it is responsible for the choice and appointment of the managing director of the state company — it very naturally looked for a 'manager', even from outside the company, rather than seeking to promote someone who had made his career in the Regie, and thus in the industry. The Government's choice, Raymond Levy, had the same background as his predecessor and friend, Georges Besse.

Against the swing

Two recent appointments outside Europe have somewhat reversed the trend. The first was the most astonishing: in promoting Bob Stempel to be its president, General Motors broke what had been its rule of always giving the presidency to a financial man and the managing directorship to a technician. In the event, Stempel, who formerly ran Opel in Germany, is undoubtedly 'the right man in the right place' at a time when GM must face up to ever-increasing Japanese competition and regain positions which an obsolete product line and outdated production techniques have deeply eroded.

The other notable exception to the domination of the money men over the automobile industry comes from Japan. Nobuhiko Kawamoto, formerly in charge of research and development at Honda, succeeded another brilliant technician, Tadashi Kume, as the head of the company. Honda, indeed, is the only one of the Japanese constructors to have complete confidence in its engineers. Toyo Kogyo (Mazda), which had chosen a specialist in the Wankel engine, Mr. Yamamoto, as its head, went to the length of replacing him with a former diplomat aged over 65.

Approaching retirement

In Europe, where strategists dominate, most of the leaders of the automotive industry will give up their posts over the next five years. Some indeed have already passed the normal age of retirement, for example the two leaders of Fiat, Giovanni Agnelli and his right hand man, Cesare Romiti, whome many fear may not be able to infuse the group again with the innovative technical vigour that was provided by Ghidella. The men that Romiti has put at the head of the group's *marques* — Lancia, Alfa Romeo and Ferrar — are also more managers than technicians. And the silver-haired financier de Tomaso still calls the thune (which more often than not is flat) at Maserati and Innocenti.

With the exception of Fiat, the leaders in their 60s are preparing to turn over responsibility to younger men. It is true for all the great captains of the German industry, Hahn at VW, Reuter and Niefer at Daimler-Benz and Mercedes, von Kuenheim at BMW and, in France, Levy at

Saint-Geours

Barbé

141

Day

Kawamoto

Possible successors to Jacques Calvet as the head of Peugeot SA include the young financier Frédéric Saint-Geours, and Yves Barbé. Graham Day remains in charge of the Rover Group. Kawamoto, recently named to head Honda in Japan, is one of the rare engineers to preside over a major constructor.

Bohn

Ulsberger

Goeudevert

Hahn

Piëch

Stempel

Eaton

Reuter

Werner

Renault. In Germany, the shareholders and the supervisory boards will chose the successors, on the suggestion of the outgoing managing directors. (Hahn, for example, has promised to express his preference for his eventual successor in the spring of 1991.)

German situations vacant

The race for the leadership is thus under way in all these groups. Goeudevert, the former head of Ford Germany now in charge of purchasing at Wolfsburg, the head of Audi, Piech, and their younger colleague Ulsberger, the financial director who also came from Ford, are eyeing Hahn's position. Only one of them, Ferdinand Piech, is a technician — which may limit his chances.

Carl Hahn himself, after studying Political Science, was an official of OECD and then a 'merchant' at VW. He only returned to Wolfsburg after a period as president of Continental tyres.

It was not until Edzard Reuter, originally a journalist, became the chairman and head of Mercedes-Benz in succession to the engineer Werner Breitschwerdt that the process of diversification of the German group started and its expansion was accelerated. Helmut Werner, who was trained as a 'salesman' and like Carl Hahn presided over Continental, was expected to succeed Reuter: the assassination of his mentor Herrhausen, the head of Deutsche Bank who selected him, may reduce his chances.

Wolfgang Ritzle, the young and brilliant head of the design bureau, has ambitions to succeed Eberhard von Kuenheim at BMW, but with no certainty of achieving his aim. Indeed it appears that the Quandt family, major shareholders in BMW, may prefer a financier, if, of course, the right person can be found. If not, Ritzle may be one of the exceptions who like Bob Stempel prove the 'rule'.

Porsche, known above all for its technology, decided to give its top job to Arno Bohn (after the financier Branitski). At 42, Bohn is the youngest president of all and appears above all to have concentrated on the commercial side, given his educational background and the functions he occupied previously at the Nixdorf computer company (he conforms closely to the profile of a modern motor industry boss).

In France, Raymond Levy's post is coveted by a top civil servant, Louis Schweitzer (who was chief of staff for

Carl Hahn will soon choose who will replace him as president of Volkswagen. Goeudevert, Ulsberger and Piëch top the list, but could be upstaged by Werner, who was tipped as the probable successor to Reuter at Daimler-Benz before the assassination of his "mentor", Herrhausen, the head of Deutsche Bank. He may now move to VW.

In a rare situation, two engineers now lead General Motors, Bob Stempel presiding over the whole Corporation, and Bob Eaton over GM-Europe.

Laurent Fabius when the latter was Prime Minister), and by Philippe Gras, a graduate of the prestigious School of Higher Commercial Studies who has been at Renault for 27 years. The former is more particularly expert in planning and in financial and strategic aspects. Gras, who owes his rise in Renault to his talent at turning round loss-making operations, as he demonstrated at the head of Renault Vehicles Industriels, oversees all technical functions (design, research and development, methods and production.)

The French approach

It was generally expected that Jacques Calvet, 59, would stay in office at PSA for six more years. To general surprise, he announced that he would give up the presidencies of PSA, Peugeot and Citroen in 1994 and that, by that time, he would establish the necessary structure for his succession. The question is who can succeed Calvet, a top civil servant and banker who was chief of staff for Valery Giscard d'Estaing, when he was Finance Minister, and the president of France's leading bank, the B.N.P. The two current favourites were both senior civil servants before moving into industry: the young (40) financial director of PSA, Frederic Saint-Geours, and the former number two of Aerospatiale, Yves Barbe. They are both newcomers to the automobile industry, Saint-Geours joining in 1986 and Barbe in 1987. A third candidate is still an outsider — Yves Helmer, another young and brilliant manager who is currently responsible for the technical development of PSA after having worked in international trade. It is likely, however, that he will first succeed Xavier Karcher as head of Automobiles Citroen, having already taken one job over from Karcher.

Varied backgrounds

Other industry leaders had only remote connections with the car business earlier in their careers.

Canada's Graham Day was a specialist in shipbuilding before, at the request of Mrs. Margaret Thatcher, he took the reins of the Rover Group in Britain. Spain's Juan-Antonio Diaz Alvarez was trained as a chemist and worked on the commercial side of the chemical industry. In the United States, financial and sales experience is also preferred to a technical background, although most of the senior executives have trained in both the commercial and technical fields. Apart from Bob Stempel, however, the major figures in Detroit — Harold Poling at Ford, Lee Iacocca at Chrysler — developed their careers in finance and sales before reaching the top posts. Iacocca, whose role in developing the Ford Mustang was probably less decisive than he has claimed, had the virtue of knowing how to sell. A matchless communicator, he still has the reputation as the best 'salesman' at Chrysler. He is the star of his company's television advertisements and the author of two best-sellers devoted to his personal achievements.

Iacocca was due to retire in 1991, but made known in

von Kuenheim

Ritzle

Karcher

Gras

Lévy

Schweitzer

Romiti

mid-1990 that he might extend his career past that date, staying in office well past his 65th birthday. There are two considerations that may induce Chrysler's board to accede to his wish. The first is the precedent created at Ford by Poling, who will still be heading the company at the age of 67. The second is the unexpected resignation at the end of May, 1990, of Iacocca's designated successor, Gerry Greenwald, another graduate from Ford, who left Chrysler to become president of United Airlines. Was he tired of waiting for Iacocca to be kind enough to give up his post?

Or did he wish, like many senior officials of Chrysler, to leave the sinking ship before it disappeared under the waves? Chrysler is undoubtedly in trouble as the 1990s open, whith Honda apparently on the way to dethroning it as the third largest constructor in the American automotive industry.

While Chrysler allowed its shareholders — and Iacocca personally — to regain what they had los (and more) during the company's first crisis, it has invested too little in its product line. It announced a return to substantial profits, but in so doing, neglected to carry out sufficient renewal of its range. The group only survived thanks to one brilliant commercial idea, that of the 'van', to the continued success of the Jeep, bought back from Renault in the framework of taking over AMC, and through technological assistance from Mitsubishi in providing a V6 engine which Chrysler did not develop itself — a far cry from the company's past!

Bob Lutz and Frenchman François Castaing — a refugee from AMC — were put in charge of an emergency programme to revive Chrysler at the technical level (the attention-grabbing but low-cost and proposed low-volume Viper project is theirs). But it seems clear that Lee Iacocca will be more likely designate Robert S. Miller, from the financial side, as his successor, rather than Lutz, the brilliant 'car man'. If Lutz is to preside over anything at Chrysler in the future, it would only be the Chrysler Motors automobile subsidiary. The destinies of the whole Corporation would more likely be put in the hands of a 'bean counter', as the Americans say, like Miller.

Paths to the top

The royal road to the top in the early days of the industry was engineering. Today, it is more likely to be via the arcane world of finance. The money men now have the last word in all aspects of the automobile business, including the choice of future models. A specialist in production problems, Englishman Bill Hayden, replaced Sir John Egan at the head of Jaguar when the British *marque* was taken over by Ford. But it was the president and managing director of Ford Europe, Lindsey Halstead, more a strategist than a technician, who negotiated the deal in conjunction with his bosses in Detroit. And it was another strategist, Bob Eaton, the head of GM Europe, who with his predecessor Jack Smith negotiated General Motors entry into Saab.

One of this group of managers with primarily financial backgrounds, who now dominate the automobile industry, has confessed: "I am surrounded by competent people, by engineers who know how to build cars, by marketing men who know how to define them, by salesmen who know how to sell them. I don't know much about what they do. But I know how to count, I know how to umpire, I know how to speak in public and how to negotiate with the authorities, national and international — and I know how to face up to my responsibilities."

These are the men who are chosen in preference by the coards, representing the shareholders, when it comes to designating those who will top the pyramid, who will sit in the presidential office. They are all-powerful, received by the great and powerful of the world with whom they generally speak as equal to equal, earning fortunes and hardly finding the time to spend them: such men work 12 to 14 hours a day and reign over empires. The most recently promoted among them, Bob Stempel, has 750 000 men and women under his command — the equivalent of the whole population of the Netherlands' capital, Amsterdam.

Agnelli

Like the other leaders of the German automobile industry, Eberhard von Kuenheim must soon step down at BMW, and may be succeeded by Ritzle, an engineer.

At Citroen, another engineer, Karcher, is Calvet's number two.

There are two rivals to succeed Lévy at Renault, Louis Schweitzer, a senior civil servant, and Philippe Gras, a marketing man.

After the departure of Ghidella, Fiat's affairs are in the hands of two men aged over 65, Giovanni Agnelli, the majority shareholder, and his right hand man, Cesare Romiti.

Ghidella

FORMULA ONE

SENNA GETS HIS OWN

John Blunsden

Formula 1 racing had seemed to be entering the 1990s in less than the best of health. The 1989 season had ended in acrimony, the World Championship had been settled in dubious circumstances, relationships between some of the star performers had deteriorated seemingly beyond repair, and yet despite all this more money was being poured into the sport than ever before. Why was this so? Because despite — or perhaps because of — the disputes, Formula 1 had never enjoyed such a high profile, and consequently, for the sponsors who continued to provide its life blood it had become an even more effective marketing tool than ever before.

Nevertheless, its image had been tarnished during the winter months and there was a widespread eagerness among those most closely involved for the new season to begin — in Phoenix, Arizona — if only so that the talk and the written words could finally be diverted from the politics and the wrangling and back to the activities on the race track.

Not all of the expectations for 1990 were destined to be fulfilled — for example, the McLaren-Hondas and Ferraris were rarely to be matched in race pace by the Williams-Renaults and Benetton-Fords, which usually chased them from a respectful distance, and although there was some closing-up of performance among the teams towards the front of the grid, the disparity between one end of the grid and the other was, if anything, wider than ever.

The latest in high technology continued to reap a rich harvest for those who were able to pay for it, and although teams remained as reluctant as ever to disclose the true cost of running their operations, it is likely that 1990 marked the beginning of the era of the $100 million per season Formula 1 budget.

Further advances in aerodynamics also ensured that it

As if to put the quarrels with FISA that had brought him to the brink of retirement firmly behind him, Ayrton Senna opened the 1990 season with a flourish, adding the Phoenix and Monaco (above) races to his laurels. But there were low points, too. A collision when trying to lap Satoru Nakajima cost him a dearly-sought victory at his home race at Interlagos, and a fractured wheel rim forced him out at Imola. But the Senna-McLaren-Honda combination was still the one to beat.

marked a potentially dangerous escalation in cornering speeds and consequent G-loadings on drivers, and before the season was over FISA had put forward a list of proposed radical changes in car regulations aimed at addressing the problem. President Jean-Marie Balestre probably had his tongue in his cheek in September when he inferred that such fundamental changes as extended flat bottoms to chassis would be introduced for the 1991 season (by then, most 1991 designs had been finalised) but the scene had been set for at least some modification of regulations in the short term, while a more serious attempt to curb speeds was sought for 1992 and beyond. Of equal importance, in the view of many people, was the seemingly genuine effort to address the environmental implications of Formula 1 in a public relations context, one line of approach being a proposed modification of the fuel regulations with the aim of removing some of the more exotic performance-enhancing brews used by certain supplier and their customer teams, the unpleasant fumes from which had been pervading the pits and paddock area's in increasing quantities. The 1990 season, therefore, might not go into the record book as one of great change, but it was one during which

a significant amount of groundwork was done for some necessary remodelling of Formula 1 in the years ahead. It was an altogether more constructive season than the embittered one which had preceded it.

Senna versus Prost

Although he was still not clear in his mind that he wanted to remain in Formula 1, and had only backed off reluctantly, in the interests of the 150 or more people at Honda Marlboro McLaren who had been supporting his racing, in his dispute with the sport's government over what he saw as unfair victimisation which had robbed him of the 1989 World Championship, Ayrton Senna gained a certain amount of grim satisfaction from being first across the finishing line at the United States Grand Prix in March. However, not until he returned to his home town of Sao Paulo, Brazil, two weeks later, for the second of the season's 16 Grands Prix, and he heard the noisily enthusiastic welcome from the crowd at the remodelled Interlagos circuit, was his motivation to continue his racing career properly restored.

Ironically, it was his former team partner and arch rival

Senna's motivation had been affected by a long-drawn-out conflict since the 1989 Japanese GP, but his duel with the surprising Jean Alesi in the streets of Phoenix restored his spirits. In the course of a few very intense minutes, it once again became a pleasure to race.

Second at Phoenix and Monaco, Jean Alesi was an instant revelation early in the 1990 season, then his fortunes slipped. His talents had been already noted in 1989, and in the opening event of 1990, around in the streets of Phoenix, he confidently held first place, through half the US Grand Prix.

Alain Prost, now with Ferrari, who was victorious on that occasion, after Senna had tangled with a backmarker when in the lead, and it was to come as no great surprise that once again the battle for the Drivers' World Championship would be contested primarily between these two old sparring partners. Nor was it unexpected that the honeymoon period between Prost and Nigel Mansell, who had sacrificed his number-one status at Ferrari to enable the Frenchman to join the team, would be short-lived. Prost's ability to manipulate people into his own way of thinking is unsurpassed, and it was not long before he had gathered around him a coterie of supporters at Maranello, all dedicated to his cause. Mansell, meanwhile, thwarted by mechanical unreliability at a time when Prost was finishing race after race, three of them in succession in first place, was beginning to think that he was being regarded as something of a second-class citizen.

By the halfway stage of the season, at Silverstone, Prost had taken a narrow points lead over Senna in the World Championship whereas Mansell had so far scored in only three races. It was at this point, having just retired from the lead of the British Grand Prix, that he decided that

Seen as the "third force" of the 1990 World Championship, the William team started the season well, often splitting the McLarens and the Ferraris. The FW013 chassis had appeared at the end of 1989, and was developed through the winter, not altogether successfully, while the new version of the Renault V10, the smaller, lighter and more powerful RS02, was virtually competitive from the outset.

Derek Warwick achieved a long-held dream when he was signed by Lotus, but it was a big gamble. The team, totally reorganised since 1989, was in desperate need of good results. The association with Lamborghini and its V12 engine was still developing, and Warwick and his fast young team mate Martin Donnelly, a graduate from F3000, could realistically only hope to lead the bunch behind McLaren, Ferrari, Williams, Benetton and Alesi's Tyrrell. For most of the world's television viewers, Warwick's 1990 season will be remembered above all for his spectacular accident on the first lap at Monza, from which he stepped unharmed. Once again the remarkable strength of modern composite fibre monocoques had been demonstrated.

PATRESE PUTS THE RECORD STRAIGHT

Riccardo Patrese drove the short distance from his home in Padua to the Imola circuit with the same thoughts which had haunted him for seven years. This was where, in 1983, he had come so close to fulfilling one of his greatest ambitions — to win the San Marino Grand Prix on his 'home' circuit — only to throw it all away.

He had led for much of the race in his Brabham, then been delayed by a long pit stop, and had fought his way back into the lead again with six laps remaining, only to momentarily lose concentration two corners later and understeer off into a barrier. What made it all so hard to bear was that his retirement brought a huge cheer from the Italian crowd because it had handed victory to a Ferrari — Patrick Tambay's car. Ever since, Patrese had wanted to win that race like no other, but had never seemed likely to do so until this year. Driving better than ever before and with his Williams-Renault in excellent form, he challenged hard all the way, taking the lead just over 10 laps from the end. The rest of the race was mental torture for Formula One's most experienced competitor and on the final lap he could scarcely see because his eyes were overflowing with tears... and this time the cheers were all for him.

A promising start to the Williams-Renault season culminated at Imola where Riccardo Patrese won a victory he dearly wanted. The success of the Italian driver was helped by the problems which hit McLaren: Senna was eliminated early on by a fractured wheel rim and Berger inherited the lead, but a fall-off in the power of his engine, a problem for Honda since Phoenix, meant he could not hold back Patrese.

The revolutionary aerodynamics of the new Tyrrell 019, with its reverse dihedral front wing almost doubling the ground effect, was a sensational innovation in a field where change is rarely radical or even visible. Its characteristics allowed the car to use the Pirelli tyres to best advantage, the combination giving Jean Alesi many opportunities to star, although he did throw chances away. The most favourable circuits even saw the innovative Tyrrell, which had to rely on the modest Ford Cosworth V8 prepared by Brian Hart, battle on equal terms with the V10 and V12 engined cars.

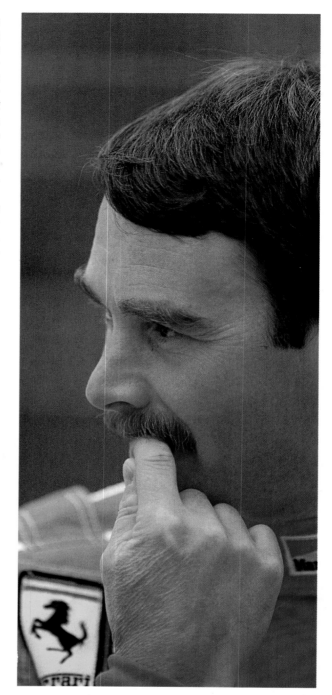

Nigel Mansell was biting his fingernails with impatience, expecting great developments with the arrival of Alain Prost at Ferrari, but he was soon disillusioned. Ferrari's efforts were quickly concentrated on the triple World Champion, and the dogged Mansell discovered that his total commitment on the track was perhaps less important than team mate's political flair. Mansell had seen 1990 as his year to star, but while the Ferraris improved steadily following major engine development, Prost was the main beneficiary.

enough was enough, and while Prost was still enjoying the cheers of the crowd, and without any prior warning of his intention, he announced to a stunned audience his decision to retire at the end of the season. He said afterwards that he felt as though a great load had been removed from his shoulders, but he was to find it very difficult to make the decision stick, and after weeks of conjecture, punctuated by regular assurances from him that nothing had changed, he finally succumbed to one of those offers which racing drivers find so difficult to refuse, and in early October he revealed that he would be returning to his old team Williams, with whom he had scored the majority of his previous victories.

Meanwhile, Prost had also found the going getting tougher. Senna's fourth victory of the season, in Germany, where Prost could only finish fourth, had taken him back to the top of the points table, and after a second place in Hungary, followed by two more wins in Belgium and Italy, where Prost was runner-up on both occasions, Senna was seemingly poised to regain the title he had lost to Prost in 1989.

Ferrari, however, were back on top form in Portugal, but it was Mansell, scoring his first win of the season, not Prost, whose progress away from the grid had been blocked by his team partner's lurid start, who beat Senna across the line. Prost was furious, not only with Mansell for ruining his chances of a victory which he had been confident would be coming his way, but also with the Ferrari team for failing to agree before the race on a strategy which would have best assisted him in his by now desperate efforts to retain the championship.

Over the next few days, the tension between Prost and Cesare Fiorio, Ferrari's team manager, remained high until top-level intervention from Fiat helped to diffuse the situation. Prost simply had to win in Spain if Senna's championship charge was to be blocked, and win there he did, overwhelmingly, with Mansell's unequivocal on-track support in second place on a day when Senna's luck ran out. The previous day the Brazilian had been full of emotion at having achieved his 50th pole position in Formula 1. He then made good use of it to lead the race until the first tyre-change pit stop, but then he picked up a piece of debris from a crashed AGS, which punctured a water radiator, and when the water had drained away his race was over.

So Senna had failed to secure the title before leaving Europe after all. Honda, however, were doubtless

Andrea de Cesaris' Brazilian GP ended in the sand trap on the first corner at the magnificently re-vamped Interlagos track. Starting from a good grid position, de Cesaris had tangled with Jean Alesi. Yet again he was to be criticised for his track behaviour on and off through the year. Dallara in any event had a difficult season, like most second-level using "customer" Judd or Ford-Cosworth V8s.

Alain Prost was the major architect of the Ferrari revival, playing the leading role in development and regularly producing the team's best results. Sticking to his usual tactics of sitting back and awaiting developments, he profited from Senna's and Boutsen's problems to win in Brazil, taking his record of victories to 40. At Monaco (above), a brilliant qualifying lap put him on the front row, although he could not match Senna in the race.

delighted that for the second year in succession the battle could now be resolved in Japan, only this time preferably in their favour.

Although the racing during 1990 had in general been closer than in the previous year, the pre-season expectation that at least four teams might be in contention for victory at every race, and therefore for the Constructors' World Championship, was destined not to be fulfilled. While McLaren-Honda and Ferrari continued their title fight as a largely private affair, Williams-Renault and Benetton-Ford became engaged in an equally lonely battle for third place.

It was an interesting contest, the slight power advantage seemingly enjoyed on most occasions by Williams more often than not being offset by the chassis superiority of the Benetton. Riccardo Patrese's emotional victory for Williams in the San Marino Grand Prix finally wiped out his memory of the race he had thrown away through loss of concentration after taking the lead in 1983, while his team partner Thierry Boutsen's leadership of every lap in Hungary was convincing proof that he could win in the dry as effectively as he had managed on two occasions in 1989 in the wet.

However, Alessandro Nannini might well have been first across the finishing line in Hungary had his Benetton not been punted out of the race a few laps from the end by Senna's McLaren. This collision, which was followed minutes later by a carbon-copy incident in which Gerhard Berger's McLaren performed a similar disservice on Mansell and his Ferrari, was indicative of a growing aggression on the part of Formula 1 drivers which had been evident for some time. It was to lead soon afterwards to a formal warning by the governing body that driving standards would in future be watched more vigilantly and that transgressions would be dealt with severely.

Other contenders

Berger's move from Ferrari to McLaren at the end of 1989 had been expected to reward him with a higher win-rate than he had managed to achieve with the Italian team, but it was not to be, although his finishing rate was little short of that of Senna. Conversely, Nelson Piquet surprised many people with the major role he played in Benetton's fortunes after his lacklustre period with

The Canadian GP was run in particularly difficult conditions. Ayrton Senna's brilliance as a "rain-master" was equalled only by his team mate, Gerhard Berger, who crossed the line first but had a one-minute penalty for a jumped start. Overall it was a good day for McLaren; the mysterious power loss problem which had made the later stages of races difficult since the start of the season had apparently been solved by the Japanese engineers.

Lotus. Although Nannini was usually a little quicker, Piquet had by far the better finishing record and he also made a considerable contribution to the team's chassis development during the season.

Jean Alesi, whose spectacular arrival on the Formula 1 scene had been a feature of the 1989 season, continued to amaze by taking his Tyrrell-Ford into the lead of the opening 1990 race, and even regaining first place momentarily after he had been overtaken by Senna, the eventual race winner. Certainly Alesi was no respecter of reputations, but during the year he also did his own no favours when it was revealed that his Tyrrell contract, which extended into 1991, had not deterred him from signing another (conditional) one with Williams prior to the start of the 1990 season, which in turn he would subsequently reject in favour of a third offer on Ferrari notepaper.

Alesi and his Tyrrell, the performance of which was enhanced by probably the best aerodynamic package in Formula 1, as well as some outstanding Ford DFR engine preparation by Brian Hart on what was basically a 23-year-old design, was invariably an exciting combination to observe, but all too often fast laps led to grief

Senna's luck deserted him in Mexico, where a slow puncture — and his failure to judge it correctly — forced him to retire, while Alain Prost drove a superb race through the field from 13th on the grid to victory, Mansell making it a surprise one-two for Ferrari. Prost had taken a chance in setting up his car with minimum downforce to get maximum speed for overtaking. His tactics paid off beyond expectations.

Playing at most only supporting roles with the V8 Cosworths, the Arrows of Alex Caffi and Michele Alboreto (below) were basically working for the future, for Porsche returns to F1 in 1991, under an exclusive agreement with the Japanese-owned team.

The early summer was a particularly successful period for Alain Prost, who repeated his Mexican success in his home race, the French GP, run for the last time on the Paul Ricard circuit. It was also a special day for Ferrari, with Prost scoring the Scuderia's 100th Grand Prix victory. The race was won and lost in the pits, both Senna and Berger suffering from what were, in current terms, dramatically long pit stops for fresh tyres.

The European season saw surprises from the outsiders. Ford introduced its second generation V8 at Paul Ricard, and the Benettons of Alessandro Nannini and (above) Nelson Piquet were up with the leaders. But the sensation in France was produced by Ivan Capelli (opposite). His Leyton House Judd V8 was outstanding on the billiard-table Ricard track, and he was able to go the distance without a tyre stop. Only a ruptured fuel line three laps from the finish deprived him of a sensational result.

LEYTON HOUSE MARCHES BACK

In Mexico the Leyton House team had been in despair. For the second time in the season neither car had qualified, the team's managing director Ian Phillips had long been absent, seriously ill with meningitis, there had been some disruptive changes of management and now their chief designer Adrian Newey was about announce his resignation.

Two weeks later the picture was rather different. Not only did Ivan Capelli and Mauricio Gugelmin qualify for the French Grand Prix, for 20 laps of it they ran first and second. Then Gugelmin's engine expired, but Capelli's held together and he finished second to Alain Prost's Ferrari in the most dramatic team comeback in recent Grand Prix history.

By that time Newey was on his way to Williams, but before he left his former team he had been the architect of its sudden and remarkable return to competitiveness. It was all to do with a stiffer monocoque and a revised underside to the floor section, with a different formation of air-extraction tunnels, which had transformed the cars' aerodynamics. Subtle changes in the direction and intensity of airflow, it seemed, could transform a car from a no-hoper into a potential winner. For Leyton House this knowledge had been the light at the end of the tunnel.

155

Silverstone, July 15, 1990, 3.15 p.m.: Nigel Mansell's steady decline throughout the year reached its nadir before "his" fans. He had produced one of those exceptional Mansell/Silverstone laps to take his second successive pole through sheer courage on the daunting circuit that was being used for a GP for the last time in its old form. But he was forced to retire for the fifth time in eight races while his team mate Alain Prost headed for his 43rd victory. Demoralised, Mansell took everyone by surprise by announcing he would retire from Formula 1 at the end of the season, although that decision turned out to be less than final...

The McLarens have never been really comfortable at Silverstone and the British GP 1990 saw their worst defeat in the first half of the season. The MP4/5 chassis, particularly sensitive to set-up changes, reached its limits in the very fast corners of the British track. Senna even spun after having to let Mansell through into the lead, and for the first time the Ferraris were clearly superior. Gerhard Berger (opposite) retired, for only the second time since Phoenix, when an accelerator slide broke three laps from the finish.

rather than points, of which there were to be none for 10 races after Alesi's second place between Senna and Berger at Monaco. In mid-season he admitted that the pressures of early stardom had become difficult to handle; driving for Ferrari as Prost's No 2 is bound to give him a lot of practice in doing so in 1991.

For every other team, 1990 proved to be an uphill struggle with major rewards difficult to come by. Gerard Larrousse started the season justifiably optimistic of his team's chances. The Lola-Lamborghini had been developed into quite a competitive package, the team had the financial strength from his new association with a Japanese partner, in Eric Bernard and Aguri Suzuki he had two of the better drivers around, and a lavish new facility close to the Paul Ricard circuit in France was in course of construction. But fourth and sixth places in the British Gand Prix were to be the high point of a difficult European season, prior to the end of which came the disturbing news that in 1991 the Lamborghini V12 engines would be going elsewhere.

A similar message was received by Lotus, soon after it became clear that its Camel sponsorship would also not be renewed. The team had had a dreadful run of misfortune, and there was worse to come. Derek Warwick and Formula 1 newcomer Martin Donnelly had offered a potentially exciting combination of experience and 100 per cent dedication on the one hand and thrusting exuberance on the other. Interestingly, time after time their lap times would be almost identical as they explored the limits of their cars, but all too often their efforts went unrewarded.

Warwick had scored just three points from 11 races when he crashed at 150mph on the opening lap of the Italian Grand Prix at Monza and he had a miraculous escape from injury as his car slid to a standstill, inverted, in the middle of the track. Three weeks later, in Spain, Donnelly was a lot less fortunate, other than the fact that he escaped with his life from an accident at a similar speed, which utterly destroyed his car, projected him from it back on to the track and left him lying there, unconscious, attached only to his seat. It was considered a miracle that anyone could have survived such an explosive impact, which was so reminiscent of the tragedy which had taken the life of Gilles Villeneuve in Belgium in 1982.

Anyone with a sense of motor racing history will wish for a change of fortune for Lotus, whose personnel should at least be able to draw some encouragement from the sudden mid-season return to form demonstrated in 1990 by the Leyton House team. They had failed to score a point in the season's first five races, then had failed to even qualify for the Mexican Grand Prix, yet two weeks later Ivan Capelli was to lead the French Grand Prix before ultimately finishing second to Prost after a storming drive. Unfortunately for Capelli and for his driving partner Mauricio Gugelmin, this level of performance was not sustainable, but at least the team's second half of the season was a great deal less depressing than the first, and both drivers were prevailed upon to sign new contracts for 1991 after Capelli had been shortlisted for a move to Ferrari prior to first Nannini and then Alesi being offered the drive.

The first season for the Arrows team under their Footwork ownership was singularly lacking in success, Michele Alboreto and Alex Caffi, the latter twice having to stand down because of injury, often finding it difficult to qualify their cars and Caffi's fifth place in Monaco providing a modest high point of a European season in which Alboreto failed to score. However, the prospect of a 12-cylinder Porsche engine in 1991 and a new chassis to carry it was sufficient encouragement for the team and

McLaren reacted quickly to its defeat at Silverstone. By the next race, the German GP at Hockenheim, the red and white cars had various aerodynamic changes and new front suspension. Honda's contribution was a new "version 5" of its extraordinary V10, running at higher revs and giving more power. Ayrton Senna (opposite) resumed his customary pole position on the grid and won the race, to take the lead in the championship again.

Gerhard Berger was often seen deep in thought in 1990 — while he greatly admired the performances of his team mate Ayrton Senna, these also posed serious questions for him. Driving alongside Senna, he realised he still had a lot more to learn than he had believed when he left Ferrari to join McLaren. But there was a good relationship between the two drivers, who worked together effectively in a healthy atmosphere of sporting rivalry.

At Hockenheim the Benetton-Fords, rather than the Ferraris, posed the greatest threat to the McLaren-Hondas. Although Nelson Piquet had the better early season, Alessandro Nannini progressively gained confidence. Starting on hard compound tyres at Hockenheim, he built up sufficient pace to take the lead after the leaders' pit stops. He held off everyone but Senna, who had a tough job passing him towards the end of the race.

Thierry Boutsen won a superb and unexpected victory in the Hungarian Grand Prix, the second of the season for Williams-Renault, leading from the start and holding the lead doggedly. Boutsen was not the fastest driver on the track that day, but he exploited the advantage of his pole position fully on the sinuous circuit to take a narrow victory (left) from Ayrton Senna. The Brazilian had come back splendidly from a puncture in the opening laps, but the problems of overtaking meant the race was unusually rough with the McLarens involved in two controversial incidents.

Ferrari Team Manager Cesare Fiorio and President Fusaro had Fiat chief Giovanni Agnelli as a surprise visitor during qualifying at the Hungaroring. Outwardly calm, the Scuderia was busily preparing for the future. Alesi, Senna, Capelli? The choice depended on Prost's decision on renewing his contract and eventually Alesi was signed.

159

MANSELL PUTS HIS FAMILY FIRST

Nigel Mansell needed to win the British Grand Prix with his three main rivals failing to score if he was to retain any realistic hope of winning the 1990 World Championship. It was an unlikely scenario, and thoughts of retirement had been with him long before he announced his intention at Silverstone, within minutes of his Ferrari team partner Alain Prost scoring his third consecutive Grand Prix victory to go to the top of the points table.

Those who thought it was a snap decision provoked by the latest in a series of disappointments on the track — in this case a failure of his transmission's control system — were wide of the mark. Mansell had achieved all his racing objectives other than winning the championship, he had wide business interests in the UK and on the continent of Europe, and his passion for golf was undiminished and needed to be fed. But most of all, Mansell, a devoted family man, wanted to spend more time with Rosanne, his wife, and their three children. She had been his most loyal supporter throughout his career and had shared uncomplainingly in the acute financial hardship of his early racing days. Despite his many injuries she never asked him to give up. Now, he decided, it was time.

its two drivers to remain together for another season. Despite troubles concerning its ownership, which had been the subject of prolonged court hearings, the 1990 season began well for the Brabham team when Stefano Modena brought his Judd-powered car home in fifth place in Phoenix. But there was little else to smile about during a year when mechanical problems and handling difficulties time after time stranded the cars at the trackside, David Brabham's Formula 1 debut season being so fraught that merely qualifying for a race came to be regarded as something of an achievement.

But Brabham were not the only team to leave 1990 almost empty-handed. Minardi, for whom Pier-Luigi Martini had ended 1989 on a high note by qualifying third fastest and finishing sixth in Australia, were ill-rewarded for their efforts during the following season, as were Scuderia Italia, whose BMS Dallara cars proved reasonably competitive on some occasions but on others were the first to retire from a race through driver error. Ligier, too, had another miserable season, but its patron's good connections have again come to his aid, and in 1991 Guy Ligier's cars will be Lamborghini-powered and for three years from 1992 the engine power is to be

"Order and Progress". The motto on the Brazilian flag could well be Ayrton Senna's. For Thierry Boutsen and Alain Prost, the Brazilian's McLaren was more often than not just a little red and white speck on the horizon (opposite). In the majestic setting of the Ardennes, Senna confirmed McLaren had solved its problems, winning for the third successive time at Spa-Francorchamps, still one of the most demanding circuits for a Grand Prix driver.

After a sensational debut, Jean Alesi (left) went through a very troubled period: major negotiations about his future were under way and he was unsettled. Often brilliant in qualifying, he threw away opportunities to score precious points in races.

The crucial moment of the Belgian GP: separated by a little less than four seconds at the start of the 23rd of 44 laps, Ayrton Senna and Alain Prost stopped simultaneously to change tyres. And as the McLaren mechanics were as fast as those of Ferrari this time, Senna and Prost left the pits in the same order, and with the same gap.

Minardi expected great things this season after promising performances in 1989 (opposite: Pier-luigi Martini duelling with Nannini in a Benetton). The small Italian team suffered, however, like other teams equipped by Pirelli, from direct comparison with the Tyrrell 019, which used its tyres most effectively. But there was a major consolation as Minardi was chosen to receive the Ferrari V12 in 1991, the first time in Maranello's history it has supplied engines to another team.

By announcing at the British GP that he would be retiring, Nigel Mansell (left) committed a tactical error. His position with Ferrari declined further in Belgium, where his decision to abandon the race might have cost him his seat immediately. As his race car was damaged during the first of the three starts, Mansell had to race in the spare car, which was set up for Prost and had a different engine. He retired after 19 laps, saying it was "undriveable."

provided by Renault, to the dismay of Gerard Larrousse, who thought his team had done sufficient to deserve similar support.

Hard living

For AGS, Osella, EuroBrun and Coloni, the hurdle of pre-qualifying always proved difficult and sometimes impossible to clear, but they persevered gallantly, then when they did make the grade they had their work cut out restoring their cars from qualifying to normal practice/race trim in the short time available in order to carry out their necessary chassis-tuning and other pre-race preparations. It was no surprise that very few pre-qualifiers actually got through into the race itself.

Prior to 1990 the Onyx team had changed ownership and become Monteverdi, but not for long because the team, or what was left of it after numerous defections, had taken its leave of Formula 1 prior to the Belgian Grand Prix after an almost farcical series of performances during mid-season. However, these were as nothing compared with the pathetic efforts to pre-qualify the so-called Life, with which the seasoned Bruno Giacomelli

was entrusted for a few minutes on Friday mornings before the car expired having lapped at about the speed of a good Tijuana taxi.

An expensive feature of the 1990 season was the growing intensity of the tyre battle between Goodyear and Pirelli and the expanded test activity which this generated on both sides. There was little doubt that Pirelli's best qualifying tyres had set the standard at the start of the season, but Goodyear fought back and by the end of the year the performance of their own qualifying tyres had been raised significantly.

The picture as regards race rubber was very different, with Goodyear consistently setting the pace even though one or two avenues of development which had been encouraged by certain of their contracted customers proved to be less successful than anticipated. As in 1989, the race performances of Pirelli's customers varied considerably, and the general impression given was that whilst their best tyres were very good, there were still insufficient for all who might have benefited from them. The tyre battle, however, is unlikely to go away, and it may well prove to be one of the most crucial elements influencing race victories in 1991.

Japan's Aguri Suzuki (above) created a strong impression in his first full F1 season. Very fast on a flying lap, Suzuki sometimes paid for his natural vigour with off-track excursions. But in the Larrousse-Lamborghini team he matched Eric Bernard, Gerard Larrousse's other young recruit, very well. His lively personality also meant that Suzuki was quickly accepted in the Grand Prix paddocks.

The first start of the Italian GP, and Ayrton Senna already leading the race. This was a characteristic of the season: faster off the mark than any of his rivals, Senna often opened up a noticeable lead in the first seconds of the race. Monza confirmed his superiority: with pole position, fastest lap and victory, the Brazilian ended his run of bad luck at the Italian circuit, where he had never won previously.

Another will be the relative performance of the many new engines which will be added to the technical fascination of Formula 1. McLaren will be switching over from a V10 to a V12 Honda engine and the V10 will be re-routed to the Tyrrell team, with which McLaren has established commercial ties through its marketing division, which is now responsible for Tyrrell's sponsorship negotiations.

Two more 12-cylinder engines will also be making their Formula 1 debut, Porsche's with the Arrows team and Yamaha's, incorporating their five-valves-per-cylinder technology, going to Brabham, while a further developed version of the Lamborghini V12 will be supplied to both Ligier and the new Modena Lambo team.

Ferrari have also become Formula 1 engine suppliers for the first time and will be powering the new Minardi as well as retaining yet another development of their V12 engine for their own cars. Through Cosworth Engineering, the Ford V8 engine will be appearing in new Phase 5 form in the compact new Benetton chassis, while the Phase 4 version which the team raced during the second half of 1990 has been earmarked for Eddie Jordan's first venture into Formula 1.

At the Italian GP meeting and in the days that followed, Alessandro Nannini (left) found himself a centre of speculation. Ferrari led him to believe he could join the team in 1991, and with that in view, the amiable Sandro endured the Monza weekend, denying everything while the rumours abounded. He finally stupefied Italy by turning down Ferrari and remaining with Benetton. Within weeks, terrible injuries in a helicopter accident put his racing career very much in doubt.

Development of its new transverse gearbox cost Brabham dearly in 1990 in the performance and reliability of its cars. David Brabham (below), called in to replace Gregor Foitek, found F1

BRUNDLE REJOINS BRABHAM

It was with very mixed feelings that Martin Brundle turned his back on Formula 1 for the second time in just over two years when he parted company with the Brabham team early in 1990. He had left Zakspeed at the end of 1987 for the lack of a competitive drive, and as in 1988, when he was to turn to Group C and win the World Sports Car Championship, he took his talents to Tom Walkinshaw's Silk Cut Jaguar team. Brundle had been happy at Brabham, but the team was in turmoil, its ownership was still in dispute, and he was owed a lot of money (which was subsequently paid). Once again he did a fine job for Jaguar, but the cars met tougher opposition from Mercedes-Benz and at season's end there was little to show for his efforts apart from a share in the winning car at Le Mans. Brabham, meanwhile, were also having a tough time, and they never really recovered from their early-season disruptions. They also missed Brundle's input, but at least they had the promise of the new Yamaha V12 engine for 1991. It was an attractive proposition on paper, attractive enough to entice Brundle back to the fold as team leader. "I'm delighted," said team director Herbie Blash. "With Martin's and Yamaha's help and a lot of hard work I'm sure we can get Brabham back to where it belongs."

life particularly hard. But again the team's thoughts increasingly turned to 1991 and the prospect of having the new Yamaha V12. When he started in F1 in 1989, driving in two Grands Prix as a stand-in, Eric Bernard showed real potential, and Gerard Larrousse had no cause to regret signing him up for the 1990 season. Efficient, discreet and very professional, Bernard got the maximum out of its Lola-Lamborghini, scoring his first World Championship points after having helped the team escape the pre-qualification trap into which it had fallen in mid-1989. The team made steady progress to join the leaders of the "Third Division", Suzuki scoring a third place at Suzuka.

162

Well, look who's back! Nigel Mansell was centre stage again at Estoril, winning the Portuguese GP in a tremendous battle. Though he stopped Senna, second, from scoring three further points, Mansell did hinder his team mate Prost with a start that was enthusiastic, to say the least. In a bitter dispute Prost then attacked Mansell and Ferrari.

After Monza, the performance of the Italian cars seemed to improve dramatically. A new qualifying engine enabled Ferrari to monopolize the front row at Estoril, Mansell scoring his third pole of the season. The Ferraris were in command of both Iberian races, Mansell (opposite) at Estoril and Prost at Jerez a week later. The Championship was wide open again!

The Ligier team struggled yet again in 1990, giving its drivers little chance to display their talents. But the consistent Italian Nicola Larini regularly finished races, and his seventh place at Jerez was the best finish for a Ligier this season! It was not enough, however, for him to be asked to stay with the team in 1991.

MANSELL HAS SECOND THOUGHTS

It is not unusual for a Formula 1 driver to make a racing comeback. Even World Champions like Niki Lauda and Keke Rosberg have done it. But Nigel Mansell scored a 'first' in October 1990 when he announced his comeback a month before he had been due to leave.

From the moment he had sprung his retirement decision on an unsuspecting world three months earlier he became the recipient of a barrage of offers inviting him to change his mind. At one stage he counted 15 of them, some from Formula 1 teams, and others from sports car entrants and Indycar racing.

For a while he looked to be resisting them. Then came the 'definitely no more Formula 1' phase, which suggested 'maybe something else'. But as late as race morning in Spain he insisted that nothing had changed since Silverstone. It was not quite a lie, but it was not the whole truth. He had not signed the contract to rejoin Canon Williams, but it was awaiting him, and he would put pen to paper hours later.

It could well have been a difficult decision for him. It was certainly not easy for Rosanna, his wife, who was at the circuit when Martin Donnelly suffered his terrible accident. No wonder she found it difficult to smile that weekend.

The Williams team had moments of glory at Imola and Budapest, but the rest of the season was disappointing for Thierry Boutsen and Riccardo Patrese. The handling of the Williams chassis meant that it was extremely hard on tyres, and this dictated their race strategies. Boutsen (opposite) finished fourth in Spain.

Estoril, April 1985: a promising young Brazilian, newly recruited by Lotus, scored the first pole position of his career. Estoril, September 1990: Ayrton Senna speeds towards what could have been the 50th pole of his remarkable career. A tenth of a second — and Ferrari's qualifying engine — ruled otherwise. But he did not have long to wait, achieving an emotional 50th pole position a week later in Jerez with a stunningly courageous lap after Martin Donnelly's horrific accident. It was another story for the championship. Senna was beaten at Estoril and forced to retire at Jerez when his radiator was holed by an undertray support lost from Dalmas' AGS. In a week, his lead over Alain Prost had melted from 18 to nine, with only two races to go.

A newcomer to Formula 1, but widely known and respected in Indycar circles through its connection with Chevrolet, Ilmor Engineering will be supplying a new V10 engine to the Leyton House team, while John Judd's new V10 has found a home in the BMS Dallaras of Scuderia Italia. Meanwhile, the venerable Ford DFR and the younger Judd V8 will continue to play a valuable role amongst the teams helping to fill the remainder of the starting grids.

Of all the driver changes, the most significant and potentially exciting is Nigel Mansell's return to Williams, while Jean Alesi's life with Ferrari will also be watched with particular interest. His successor at Tyrrell, Stefano Modena, should have ample opportunity to reveal his full potential in what should be a highly competitive car, while it is to be hoped that Thierry Boutsen's leadership of Ligier will help to restore some of that team's former competitiveness, although 1991 will inevitably be something of a transitional year for Ligier prior to its three-year link with Renault from 1992.

Both McLaren and Ferrari set a remarkably high standard of performance during 1990 and it will take a team of exceptional merit to break the mould of their dominance. It is not entirely down to finance, although that is a crucial factor in their success. Motivation, dedication and tireless industry on the part of a highly skilled staff and workforce are equally vital ingredients, and during 1990 both these teams were given the opportunity to demonstrate these qualities in full measure when they went through something of a trough — McLaren during mid-season, Ferrari a few weeks later — and proved their ability to react swiftly and come out of it stronger than ever.

Championship challengers

Williams and Benetton remain the two teams most looked upon to match the overall performance of the current pacemakers, perhaps with Tyrrell joining them from time to time. The remainder probably have too much leeway to make up to be able to achieve a major breakthrough in 1991, although 12 months from now there could well be a few surprises in the order of seeding further down the grid. Red and white, therefore, are likely to remain the dominant colours at the front of the field, but now that Camel sponsorship has moved

Red light for Alain Prost, a symbolic image of the end of the triple world champion's season, which was punctuated by start incidents. He was almost pushed into the pit wall by Mansell in Estoril, then his 1990 World Championship hopes were snuffed out in Japan — just as a year earlier on the same Suzuka circuit, in a collision with Ayrton Senna.

Collisions were not uncommon in 1990. The return of atmospheric engines levelled out performance and chassis design improvements forced drivers to take more risks in overtaking. Road holding was dramatically better through ever more efficient use of ground effects (leading to more spectacular displays of sparks from rubbing strips), braking distances were reduced by carbon brake disks (above, centre, Emanuele Pirro in a Dallara), and the rivalry between Goodyear and Pirelli accelerated tyre development.

Another round in the stormy relationship of Nigel Mansell and Ferrari: the determined Englishman led the Japanese GP from the Benetton-Fords of Piquet and Moreno (the latter replacing Alessandro Nannini after his terrible helicopter accident) and seemed set to win a crucial victory for Ferrari. His transmission failed as he left the pits after a tyre change, depriving the last GP, at Adelaide, of any championship interest: it meant McLaren-Honda had also won the Constructors' title at Suzuka.

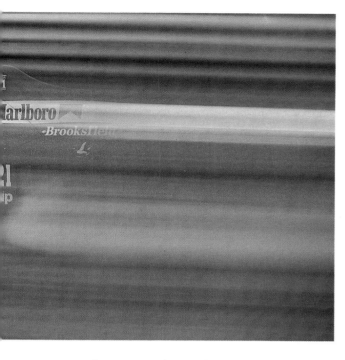

across to Benetton and, to a lesser extent, Williams, yellow should become a rather more visible element in the kaleidoscope of F1 during the season ahead.

Motor racing at this level continues to be the highest-profile activity in the world which can be put under the heading of sport, even surpassing the Olympic Games and the football World Cup because of its constancy as distinct from being a once-every-four-years occasion. Its business administrators will work to ensure this continues.

Its massive worldwide support by television has assured it of an audience of immeasurable size, which in turn has attracted the inflow of sponsorship money on the colossal scale which is essential for its survival in the form into which it has been allowed to grow. Without this annual injection of cash its foundations would crumble, but there seems little fear of this happening. As the 1990 season drew to a close and 1991 contracts were being negotiated it was evident that the financial tap was still flowing freely and that the rewards for success at the highest level had reached the barely credible. For all its imperfections, Formula 1 was still cash-rich, and likely to remain so.

FISA CLIPS FORMULA 1'S WINGS

Long before Martin Donnelly's horrific accident during qualifying for the Spanish Grand Prix, which involved him in an impact from which it seemed impossible that anyone could have survived, the sport's government had been seeking ways of reducing Formula 1 cars' cornering speeds. Even before the season began, Nigel Mansell and others had been predicting the need for G-suits within a year if nothing was done to slow things down.

Proposals for several radical regulation changes for the 1991 season were announced in September in Italy, but this was too late to gain the support of teams whose next-season cars were already well advanced. Instead, agreement was quickly reached for a set of interim measures, including a reduction in the size and a change in the positioning of wings.

But car speeds were not the only concern highlighted by Donnelly's accident. The closeness of the barrier on the outside of a 150mph curve contributed to the speed and violence of the accident; this would henceforth be given special attention during circuit inspections, as would the quality of the impact-absorption protection on the track side of barriers, of which there had been none at that spot prior to the accident.

"No failure": the sign on the digital readout which constantly indicates key parameters on the World Champion McLaren-Honda was another symbol of the season. The MP4/5B had reached the limits of its development, and was not the best car of the 1990 season, but its reliability was rarely in question. The talents of its drivers, particularly Ayrton Senna, did the rest. Although he won his second world championship in controversial circumstances in Japan, this was nonetheless a logical outcome for a wide-open, hotly contested and... sparkling season.

165

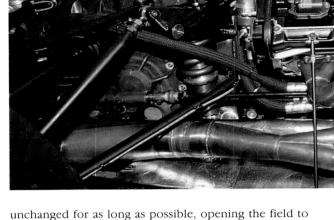

POWER BATTLES

Patrick Camus

The expected horsepower battles took place during the 1990 season, when there was an equally important contest in progress, that of configuration. The season was the setting for a contest between the V10 and V12 concepts, in which the Japanese held the V12 at bay with their V10. But paradoxically, Honda switches to a V12 in 1991.

The Honda V10 was not the most powerful engine of the year, but it was the most flexible and the most reliable, and it was also the engine which received the most development attention, with no less than five different versions appearing. The Japanese proved the viability of the V10 concept with the RA100E.

In banning turbocharging at the end of 1988, FISA sought to put an end to the extravagant horsepower race it encouraged. Starting as quite simple technology, it had become increasingly sophisticated and complex as engine designers explored it more deeply, and it followed that only the richest constructors could fully exploit its potential. After a transition season in 1989, a new era was born but despite FISA's good intentions, the new generation of atmospheric engines does not seem to have met the objective of broadening the competition and reducing budgets.

It is no surprise that Honda and Ferrari have maintained the dominant positions in the new era and maybe Renault and Porsche will return to that level, or others attain it. Whatever level of technology is involved, the design and computer facilites available, the analytical laboratories and the production capacity of the major manufacturers will normally exceed the facilities available to independant companies. The same reasoning applies to the budgets put into the engine projects, over which there can be no control. There is still room for specialists — witness the Indycar success of Ilmor — but a main hope must be that the current regulations remain unchanged for as long as possible, opening the field to other engine manufacturers and broadening the customer base, which too often is served under exclusive deals. Such developments could lead to a cost stability that has not applied in Formula 1 since the omnipotent days of the Cosworth DFV in the late 1960s and early 1970s. Technically, the 1990 season was marked by the confrontation of V8, V10 and V12 designs, with the future of Formula 1 at stake.

The Ferrari V12 lived up to its thoroughbred background, at least in terms of simple power. Appearing first in 1989 as the 036, it was credited with 600bhp at 12,500rpm, which was increased to 645bhp by the end of the season. Further major development over the winter wrung out 665bhp at 13,200rpm by the end of its life. The 037 V12 followed, still with five valves per cylinder but with a modified bore to stroke ratio which immediately raised the revs limit to 13,800rpm, while the weight dropped from 141kg to 125kg. The new engine was first used only for qualifying, when it was rated at 682bhp and later 703bhp, with the output reduced to 674bhp in race trim. Constant improvements brought the power to surprising levels for an atmospheric engine:

712bhp for qualifying and 684bhp for the race version. The 'barrier' of 200bhp per litre had been broken.

Honda adopted a different approach, and never produced an engine specifically designed for qualifying. Japanese company preferred a very sophisticated race engine which they modified with special electronic programmes and some low-level external changes, such as different intake and exhaust pipes. But it was far from a timid approach. Their RA100E engine which appeared in the 1989-90 off-season spawned a host of evolutions. The Version 2 engine appeared at Phoenix, Version 4 at the French GP, Version 5 at Hockenheim, and the final Version 6 at Suzuka. From an initial 694bhp, McLaren reputedly had 718bhp on tap for the German race, this was, however, said to be a theoretical figure derived from testing and the maximum effective power of the Honda was said never to have exceeded 700bhp.

Honda thus put itself in position to win another World Championship against V12 technology by using a V10, which will be passed on to Tyrrell for 1991. Like Ferrari, Lamborghini and Yamaha, and Ford in the longer term, Honda has now opted for the 12 cylinder format. It seems a curious decision, implying that Honda, Renault,

Judd and Ilmor were wrong to choose the V10 configuration in the first place. But the engineers had been unable to make a positive decision for two years. The question was more why Honda should abandon the V10, seemingly still in full development with strong potential ahead. The answer from Honda F1 Project Leader Osamu Goto was clear and candid: "Because we believed that the V12 was a better solution for the future. Because a V12 can produce more power."

So is brute horsepower the game, and has Goto succumbed to the Ferrari complex? The principle of the atmospheric engine is simple enough: the more the capacity is split into smaller cylinders, the higher the permissible revs limit and the more horsepower produced. But the disadvantage is in fuel consumption. For every 200 extra rpm, in identical engines, consumption increases by 3 per cent, and extra fuel means extra weight. In the near future, the graphs of power on the bench and chassis performance will cross, and because of the weight of fuel it is obliged to carry, a F1 car will not be able to use the engine power to the maximum.

The lesson was clear this season, with the more powerful Ferrari V12 not able to pull clear of the V10 Honda and its combination of power, reliability, good consumption and excellent flexibility. Goto kept his enthusiasm for the latest technology under firm control. From the introduction of the Version 5 engine at the German GP onwards, he offered the team the use of the Version 4 engine at every circuit. It gave a little less power but considerably more torque. Ferraris were in trouble on circuits where their brilliant chassis should have given clear superiority, and McLarens starred where no one expected them to be competitive.

Rarely has an engine helped a chassis as much as the Honda V10 has helped the MP4/5B. In contrast, Prost

The challenge taken up by Lamborghini (opposite, the V12 in a Lotus 102) was not easy. Mauro Forghieri preferred to go for reliability rather than outright performance, and this was a handicap for the Larrousse and Lotus teams, which also suffered from the problems in the associated equipment, the electronics, gearbox and clutch in particular.

The development of the Renault RS2 was similar to that of the RS1 in 1989 — steady and effective. Overall, the French engine gave little away to the Honda, and despite problems with the Williams FW013 chassis the combination was "best of the rest" behind the two dominant teams of 1990.

and Mansell were often penalised by the excessively narrow power band of the exquisite Ferrari engine. This was particularly true in starting from the grid, despite the theoretical advantage of faster gear changes by the semi-automatic electronic-mechanical gearbox.

Honda will thus abandon the V10, which some observers see as being almost over the hill — or at height of its glory — while others believe it still has development potential and overall potential superior to a V12.

Theories exist to explain the decision. Honda is known to want to make a new impact on the world market, and to do it by moving its range of road vehicles up-market, topped with a prestigious V12. Solid technical confidence is undoubtedly behind this commercial thinking — and a desire to match the European 'nobility' such as Ferrari and Lamborghini, representatives of the last market sector remaining for Japan to conquer. FISA's proposal to increase the minimum weight of F1 cars to 540kg will considerably modify the overall F1 design philosophy because it will give a major advantage to the 'big' engines, which are powerful, but long and fuel-hungry. If the project goes through, Renault, Judd and Ilmor may have some re-thinking to do...

A young Honda technician checking the cylinders on an RA100E. Apart from the purely sporting challenge, Honda went into F1 to demonstrate its technology and instill into its young engineers the need to constantly be alert, and flexible, and question assumptions. It achieved its objectives, and a steady rotation of staff meant the ideas spread through the company.

MIXED FEELINGS

The Honda and Ferrari engineers dominated the 1990 season strongly — the opposition was simply unable to match their equipment. The logic seems impeccable, but do their rivals really deserve such a harsh judgment? Take the case of Renault. Behind the overall disappointment of the season's results is the reality that the Williams FW013 chassis was not competitive. Second place in the 1989 World Championship inspired Bernard Dudot's engine team and the opening stages of the 1990 season appeared promising. The engine showed good reliability from the outset, performance increased progressively, and Riccardo Patrese won the San Marino GP. But the situation then deteriorated, raising questions about the engine. Of all the parties involved, only the drivers can truly judge the whole package, and their opinion absolved Renault: the Renault V10 was often the equal of the Honda V10 in respect of reliability and acceleration, while ceding perhaps 10bhp to the Japanese engine in overall terms. Their real complaint was against the Williams chassis, although this was poor only by the standards of the two dominant teams and Benetton and Tyrrell, and certainly not by those of the secondary French and Italian outfits. The fault lay, they tended to suggest, with Patrick Head, describing some sort of barrier between drivers and engineers. Head preferred to blame overwork due to Frank Williams' accident (in 1986) and the departure of many of Williams' technical staff to other teams. Head eventually conceded — at the Spanish GP — that the FW013 suffered from imbalance between the closely-linked areas of aerodynamics and suspension.

In such a situation it is difficult for engine men to compensate for the weakness of a chassis simply by the quality of their power unit, as Dudot would recall from the last seasons of the Renault GP team. A good chassis can be worth lap time advantages against a poor one of the order no engine can overcome. Honda has frequently shown that a top engine can help a chassis to overcome some minor, passing difficulties, but never major shortcomings.

Renault's frustration serves to underline the fact that the atmospheric engine does not play the all-important role that the turbocharged units held in overall performance. Chassis designers again play the most important role in F1, as teams other than Williams have demonstrated. Leyton House is an example, in its failure to find the answer to controlling the relationship of the car to the track surface at all times, the vital element in the notoriously tricky field of racing car aerodynamics. Those who have found the answer have proved that with only 700bhp and the correct aerodynamics, the records set with 1200bhp engines can be shattered.

168

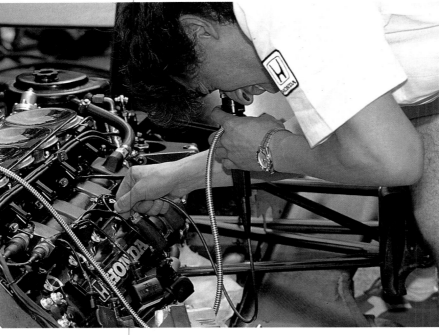

The astonishing Rocchi W12 was the flop of the season, despite the theoretical advantages inherent in such a design. It could hardly have been otherwise, given the lack of financial, technical and human resources involved. Its replacement by a Judd V8 did not help Life's pathetic situation.

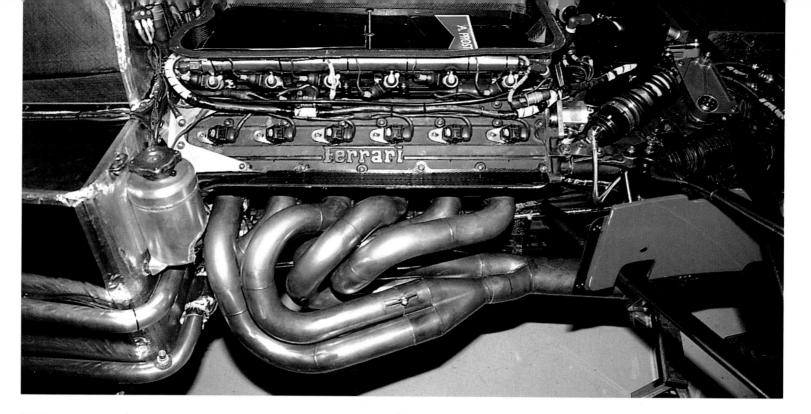

NEW GENERATION

When FISA signed the death warrant of turbocharged Formula 1 engines, it certainly did not expect the "straightforward" atmospheric engines would so soon develop 200bhp per litre — though it should have had the foresight to realize this.

The 1990 season showed clearly that the engine designers have developed a completely new generation of engines.

It was not that any made miraculous breakthroughs. They simply based their research on the information produced by the turbo generation on new alloys, better understanding of thermodynamic phenomena such as combustion chamber processes, and engine management systems. Only three or four years ago a 3.5 litre V12 would not have developed 700bhp. Now average engine speeds have increased, 13,000rpm being the usual figure for the best current engines in race conditions, friction losses have decreased and cooling has improved. Engine dimensions have been reduced (the Porsche V12 is little longer than an old generation V8), as has weight (125kg for the Ferrari V12), and fuel consumption.

The best illustration of the progress achieved was offered this year by the astonishing Ford V8/HB, run exclusively by the Benetton team. Only slightly longer, but lower and narrower than the classic V8 Cosworth DFV/DFR, it caused no little surprise with its power. It was so successful that Ford, after having initiated a V12 programme, began to wonder if it was really worth it! The weight, dimensions, fuel consumption and low-speed torque made the V8 engine an attractive package, even if its power output (of the order of 650bhp) was not that of the Ferrari, Honda or Renault. It remained a considerable gamble, given the friction and inertia imposed by this layout, which leads to big bore dimensions, but the designers again were able to draw on their turbo experience in finding solutions.

The Ford V8 apparently has a long future — provided the stability of the technical regulations is maintained, but not if there are changes, particularly to the minimum weight of F1 cars. Increasing the lower limit to 540kg as proposed would penalise the Ford V8, as the opposition equipped with V10 and V12 engines would be able to design a chassis with a larger fuel tank. The main advantage of the V8 would thus be reduced. That may explain the fuel consumption proposal put forward by Mike Kranefuss and John Barnard, purportedly on ecological grounds, and rejected by everyone else.

On the engine front, constructors will shortly have to face a further evolutionary development, which engineers have already dubbed "Generation 2". This will introduce new carbon and ceramic composite components into engines, where such materials are now used only sparingly.

The wail of the Ferrari V12 is a siren song for the true lover of the Maranello marque technology. The power output was around 700bhp, but the power band was very narrow and fuel consumption high. The engine was the Scuderia's main problem — and was kept a well-guarded secret (left).

The dominant Honda V10, seen here in the version which appeared at Silverstone, has a second lease of life at Tyrrell in 1991. At McLaren it is replaced by a V12 which ran track tests in the Autumn of 1990. This will give gains in power at some cost in flexibility — a change which may owe more to prestige than technology.

A MIGHTY PRESENCE

HELMUT ZWICKL

Each time Alan Woollard, Bernie Ecclestone's sergeant-major in the Formula 1 army, opens his leather briefcase packed with passes reserved for VIPs, dozens of Japanese faces smile at him from the plastic cards. It is a measure of their country's growing involvement in Grand Prix racing, but the Japanese desire to invest in the sport/business is far from being satisfied.

As well as the McLaren-Honda team, in which the Japanese manufacturer reputedly invests 120 million dollars annually, there is a substantial investment in the Leyton House, Footwork-Arrows and Espo-Larrousse team, with a strong resence in others such as Brabham and now even Tyrrell. At Coloni, the Rising Sun flag dropped to half-mast in mid-1990: the Fuji Heavy Industries group and its Subaru division ended their association with Enzo Coloni's Italian team.

Subaru had wanted to participate in the prestigious world of Formula 1, but on the cheap, paying for its entry ticket with an outdated 12-cylinder boxer engine designed by Carlo Chiti. The undertaking looked ludicrous alongside the total commitment of Honda, or the entry of Akria Akagi and his Leyton House Group when it took over the March F1 operation.

Akagi, whose interest in Formula One had been awakened by Ivan Capelli, has major financial investment in property (Marusha Kosan), menswear (Boss), restaurants, hotels, theme parks, travel agencies and golf clubs through his group. For a little more than $13 million, Akagi acquired the March F1 and F3000 interests, and through 1989-1990 the teams took on their own identities as the March origins receded — this allowed him to add some single-seaters in his own colours to his collection, which includes a Ferrari F40, Porsche 959, Lamborghini Countach and top line Mercedes (Leyton

House colours are also carried on Formula 3 Ralts raced by Japanese drivers).

Akagi would also have become involved with Porsche in the development of its new F1 engine if one of his fellow countrymen had not snatched the prize from under his nose.

The man responsible was Waturo Ohashi, whose Footwork group of 42 companies with 11 000 employees has an annual turnover of $1 280 billion. It includes transport operations, fast food chains, civil engineering and building companies, and metallurgy and chemical firms. Footwork Formula Limited had been set up in 1988, when it own F3000 cars appeared, with little success.

"At the beginning of October, 1989", recalls Jackie Oliver, the co-owner of Arrows, "I was contacted by John Wickham, who was taking care of Formula 3000 for Footwork in Japan. He had been mandated by Mr. Ohashi to buy a Formula 1 team. I wasn't really interested, but I have a few ideas about how to put together a good package in Formula 1 these days."

At the end of October, 1989, at the Japanese Grand Prix, the marriage between Footwork and Arrows was announced, and in December when it was completed, it was clear that Jackie Oliver and his associate Alan Rees had done the deal of their lives: for nearly $12 million, they had sold their Arrows team, which could certainly not be described as being amoug the best in Formula 1, to the Japanese. Ohashi became chairman, Wickham became a director while Oliver remained as managing director and Rees continued as team manager.

Was it a defeat for them, or the only possible way to survive? Jackie Oliver's view is clear: "For the past 11 years, we have been trained in survival techniques and we could have continued like that until the end of time! But we could never have hoped for real success. Alan Rees and I were always hungry for victories and we did not want to abandon our dream of one day seeing the team become World Champion."

When the Belgian Jean-Pierre van Rossem was unable to honour his first payment to Porsche on January 1, 1990 (out of a total of $6.4 million due to the German company in 1990), Porsche reached an agreement with the Footwork-Arrows team. In 1991, this has the use of the Porsche V12, and in Stuttgart, the word is that "we are associates, and not simply engine suppliers."

The connection between the Larrousse team and the Japanese group Espo goes back to the autumn of 1989.

Tetsua Tsugawa, born in 1949, is the veteran Japanese mechanic in Formula 1. He worked for Surtees, Ensign and Theodore before joining Toleman, now Benetton. His expertise is such that he has published three technical books on F1 in Japan.

The Footwork group has taken over the English Arrows team (right, Alex Caffi) which used Cosworth engines in 1990 and as so often in its history played a supporting role. But Japanese finance has ensured that it has the exclusive use of a new Porsche engine in 1991.

Akira Akagi's team has only performed strongly on rare occasions in its first season fully under the Leyton House banner: Mauricio Gugelmin (left) was unlucky at Imola, the Brazilian retiring when his fire extinguisher went off and his Leyton House team mate Ivan Capelli was the victim of a first lap accident.

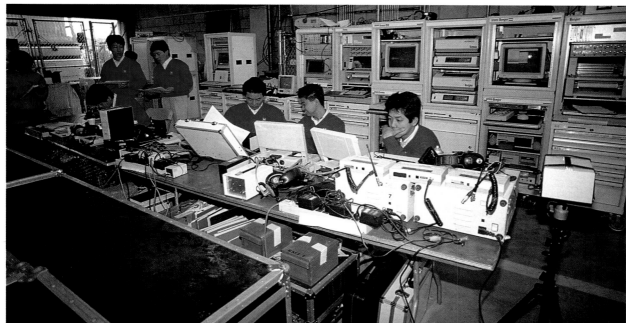

For Honda, a Formula 1 team is above all a training ground for its young engineers and technicians, as well as a technical showcase. Involvement in this most demanding of all automobile disciplines demands accuracy, flexibility and a sense of teamwork and obliges them to listen as much to the drivers as to the orders of their chief engineers.

The Japanese ESPO Corporation linked up with Gerard Larrousse on condition that he gave one seat, and a solid contract, to a Japanese driver. Aguri Suzuki (below) filled that seat competently in 1990.

Aguri Suzuki, the most Parisian of Japanese even if he does not speak the language fluently, impressed observers with his speed, although his excellent times were often marred by incidents.

Osamu Goto is in charge of the Honda F1 operation "in the field", although he was not involved with racing engines until 1984 (his previous experience was of research into exhaust gases). He now has a staff of 15 to 20 engineers at each race, a Honda enclave in McLaren territory.

Aged 37, Satoru Nakajima is the best known Japanese driver and the object of a cult of personality in his own country. On the track he has often been a victim of his own stubbornness.

Espo, a large group presided over by Kazuo Ito, produces such profits from its shareholdings in property, video, hi-fi and compact disc operations that the $15 million invested in Formula 1 hardly strained its budget. But Ito imposed on Larrousse a condition Honda had once demanded of Williams — the requirement to sign a Japanese driver. Gerard Larrousse agreed, the more promptly as, like everyone else in the business, he knew that Frank Williams had lost Honda's support because he would not agreed to have Satoru Nakajima in his team. More diplomatically, Larrousse took Aguri Suzuki on, and the driver gave a good account of himself in 1990, when he scored his first World Championship point. Even Ken Tyrrell has fallen into the 'Japanese sphere of influence', his 1991 020s being powered by the Honda V10 which was previously used exclusively by McLaren. Through the TAG-McLaren Marketing Services company, Ron Dennis arranged for Tyrrell, then sadly in need of sponsorship, to receive support from Japanese sponsors — Nippon Shinpan (a bank which controls 20 million credit cards), Angle Group (a clothing company), and PIAA (automobile equipment). And Saturo Nakajima brought in $7 million from the electronics giant Epson. In one of the minor deals, the Minardi team is to have access to Keiki high technology group know-how in data processing and composite materials in a mere $700 000 deal, covering two years. The Italian team will in particular have the use of a ultrasonic device with which any faults in any kind of material can be detected instantly. The once celebrated Brabham team has also fallen into the hands of the Japanese. After a long legel imbroglio between its owners, the British team was taken over by the Middlebridge Scimitar, fortunately retaining independence within the group as the Scimitar element has since gone into receivership. The new owners of

HONDA'S MAGIC FORMULA

Honda got involved in Formula 1 not only to add lustre to its image as a manufacturer but also to train its young engineers — Formula 1 is the best training ground imaginable: in no other sphere is the pressure so intense or the competition so tough. Formula 1 improves the reaction time of technicians, sharpens their judgment and improves their teamwork. It is an accelerated apprenticeship.

Every morning of a race meeting, 15 to 20 technicians go into the McLaren-Honda pits and power up batteries of computers and plug into their databanks.

Throughout the day, Senna and Berger receive the comparative graphs which the Honda printers spit out and which cover every deal of every lap: each driver can see at what part of the circuit he was faster or slower than his teammate. Not even at Ferrari is the quantity of data received by telemetry or from on-board memory cards so voluminous.

The head of Honda's F1 operations is Osamu Goto, aged 41. Before 1984, he had never been involved in racing engines, being a specialist in exhaust gas problems. Now Engineer Goto commands respect, and his colleagues politely stub out their cigarettes when he talks to them.

After each race, the Honda engineers take part in a debriefing, with each participant giving a report on his activities. The smallest problem is studied in detail to determine how it may be resolved before the next race. The construction of the engine, the electrics and electronics, engine management and data processing are all reviewed by the team. Attention to detail, discipline, precision and experience are the factors to which the Honda engineers owe their success in Formula 1.

Despite the extensive computer information, the McLaren drivers work very closely with the Japanese engineers and take a active role in their work. "No one at Ferrari would ever have asked me what the Honda people ask me about my engines", says Berger with astonishment.

Brabham soon had to face reality: sponsors were not providing sufficient support and each month of operation was costing about $1.9 million. "We underestimated the effort that was needed to find new sponsors", admitted Dennis Nursey, the British associate of Nakauchi. The team, however, continued its association with Yamaha to supply engines in 1991: the Japanese company's first experience of Formula 1, in 1989 with the German Zakspeed team, was less than fruitful, but for reasons that should not apply with Brabham.

Japanese companies will undoubtedly look for more slices from the Formula 1 cake, but Jackie Oliver, for one, sees no danger in this: "If the Japanese invest correctly, if they parcel out the responsibilities carefully and their investments prudently, it can only be good for everyone." Ford's competition chief, Mike Kranefuss, believes that "if the Japanese learn to exploit the Formula 1 medium better than everyone else, they will once again have shown us what we could have done ourselves...".

"The Japanese really have no idea what Formula 1 is all about," was the line that was heard around Williams when the team still had its Honda engines, and the idea can still be heard today from those who are not receiving yen in their bank accounts. FISA executives seem concerned by the extent of the Japanese penetration, and hence their influence, and seem to feel that major European manufacturers should redress the balance. Those Europeans know the value of Formula 1, and in the 1990s few will contemplate spending astronomic sums for unquantified returns. Similarly, the Japanese majors will stay in Formula 1 only so long as it suits their purpose, and not a moment longer...

"European interests, and contracts between English-speaking people are still more numerous in Formula 1", says Jackie Oliver. Undoubtedly — but for how long?

The increasingly visible Japanese presence in Formula 1 has led to constantly growing Grands Prix coverage by the Japanese media. Television crews, journalists (often accompanied by interpreters) and photographers have swelled the ranks of the European and American press corps, to serve dozens of specialized magazines, eight television networks and numerous sponsor publications. More Japanese VIPs are also to be seen in F1 paddocks.

The Japanese Rheos company, originally a producer of motorcycle crash helmets, has put two specialists at the disposal of the McLaren-Honda drivers at every race (centre, left). They take care not only of Senna's and Berger's ultra-light helmets (1.4kg) but of all their personal racing equipment including overalls, seats and dorsal and lateral protection in the cockpit.

Racing's heroes in the four decades of Grand Prix racing straddling the Second World War, from Nuvolari, Rosemeyer and Caracciola, von Brauchitsch and Lang to Farina, Ascari, Fangio and Moss, were household names in some countries but they were hardly household faces. They were perhaps glimpsed at a track, in the pages of magazines, or a week or two after a race in cinema newsreels.

For tens of thousands of dedicated fans, there is nothing like being at a Grand Prix (right, the tifosi at Imola). The rest must make do with television, hopefully live, at home.

FOCA-TV crews at each race shoot extensive footage from which TV networks can select material, at a price.

TELEVISION AND F1

AT ALL COSTS

HELMUT ZWICKL

Today, television shows all 16 Grands Prix, live or delayed, in the most obscure corners of the world. Via geostationary television satellites, rotating at 36,000 kilometres per hour above the same point on the earth, every instant of a race — be it at Interlagos or Budapest, on the streets of Monaco, in the Belgian Ardennes forests around Spa or the smog of Mexico City — is transmitted at the speed of light to television sets across the globe.

Satellites are the bridges between continents. Ayrton Senna drives at the same time on the screen in a Swiss farmer's mountain hut as in the *favelas* of Rio de Janeiro. Formula 1, live, is available to the privileged few in Mozambique or the masses in Asia, to Russians, Japanese, Germans or Americans.

The man who recognized the power of television for motor racing, early in the 1970s, was Bernie Ecclestone, the one-time motorcycle dealer who eventually took effective control of Formula 1. Within a year of that, he had stitched together a joint FOCA-FISA operation which drew its strength from television.

Bernie Ecclestone reigns almost unchallenged over Formula 1 as FIA vice-president and commercial director. He promotes many of the races and influences on the calendar, sets the prize money and negotiates the television rights.

Through FOCA-TV and FOCA-Communications, and the Geneva-based AllSport Management company which handles advertising, the whole of Formula 1 is now virtually under contract.

It is no longer possible, at least in theory, for anyone with a Super-8 or video camera and the right passes to shoot footage in the pits for his personal use. Only professionals are admitted, from TV stations which have signed long-term agreements with Ecclestone to transmit World Championship Grands Prix.

Not the least paradoxical element of the situation is that Bernie Ecclestone, who seems to have a strong aversion for any form of personal publicity, should have created a worldwide television show which is half way between sport and light entertainment.

"An exciting new decade…"

Largely thanks to television, Formula 1 has become rich, because television attracts sponsors and manufacturers. And as Ecclestone, after fierce battles in the heart of Formula 1, failed to overthrow his great rival Jean-Marie Balestre, they joined forces. Now FISA is a 30 per cent partner in the TV rights.

"There is no doubt that an exciting new decade lies ahead. I hope you will help us to make it even more successful than the last," says Ecclestone in concluding his preface to a booklet given to potential clients of Formula 1 — manufacturing or sales compagnies, which may be sponsors. The leaflet is packed with figures demonstrating the worldwide impact of televised Grand Prix. The figures, from the broadcasting organisations themselves, claim to give the totals of actual viewers of all the

Grands Prix and their associated news and feature items. Other sports make similar viewer claims, but the figures are so enormous that they give rise to some scepticism. In 1980, 37 countries took Formula 1 television transmissions, for a total potential audience of 907 million. By 1989, according to the latest FOCA-TV booklet, the figures had increased spectacularly. No fewer than 102 countries were taking Grand Prix transmissions, 76 of them being exclusive network contracts. On average, says FOCA-TV, 250 million people watch each Grand Prix, and the potential worldwide audience over a year is a staggering 17.4 billion people.

Question marks

Even a country like the Ivory Coast shows 25 minutes from most Grands Prix, though not live. In Brazil, the audience for each race varies from 4 to 16 million viewers, and in Mexico the figure reaches 19.5 million. If an average of only 55,000 viewers watch each of the 15 Grands Prix shown in the Ivory Coast, that is still a total of 825,000 each year. For Germany, the total is 168.6 million, according to FOCA.

Television is the financial heart of modern Formula 1, a fact Bernie Ecclestone (above) well understood in the 1970s. Today, all the TV and advertising contracts go through companies established for that purpose.

Access to Formula 1 is granted only to accredited crews from networks which have long-term contracts to transmit Grands Prix, negotiated with Ecclestone's companies.

THE SHOW MUST GO ON

In Dallas in 1984 and in Adelaide in 1989 there were threats of strikes by drivers, because of the state of the track in Dallas or the torrential rain in Adelaide. In the long run these could be seen as just revolts by a troupe of actors who for too long had been considered simply puppets. Television was mainly responsible for this attitude: the sponsors pay because television shows the races. Ecclestone has his contracts with the stations, in 47 nations at the time of Dallas, and more than 80 nations now. There is so much money at stake that nobody, least of all Bernie Ecclestone, wants to break the contracts. So the show must go on, come rain or snow.

It is not surprising that the number of viewers plays a primary role in determining the price many sponsors must pay to climb on board the F1 train, particularly when their products are for mass consumption. When the onboard camera shows a sponsor logo, and it is transmitted, it can cost the sponsor more than $50,000. Cigarette companies are in Formula 1 primarily to by-pass restrictions on conventional TV advertising for their products. But in Europe, forthcoming legislation will eventually ban all sports-related cigarette sponsorship, and F1 teams will have to play the television card even harder to replace it.

The eye of the television camera is everywhere: atop giant cranes located at key points of the circuits, above the pits (here, at Silverstone) with remote-controlled cameras, and on the shoulders of cameramen among the pitlane crowd. One aim is to give maximum coverage for the sponsors who invest millions of dollars in the sport.

The most popular of all the races is usually the Monaco event, taken by 73 nations and watched by an estimated 260 million viewers. But the Japanese Grand Prix of 1989 is said to have set the record, the booklet claiming that 267,712,000 viewers watched that event on "Ecclestone-TV".

Only the 1990 soccer World Cup drew more viewers, being shown in 118 nations. The potential viewing figure, given the number of matches involved, was some 26 billion, more than five times the population of the planet...

TV rights for almost all first-class motor sports are now in the hands of FOCA-Communications, a London company reached through the same telephone number as FOCA. Anyone wishing to transmit Formula 1, F3000, World Sports Car races, World Rally Championship events or 500cc motor cycle races must deal with FOCA-Communications.

Price increases

The F1 television rights were ceded by FOCA to the UER, the European Broadcasting Union, for a six year period from 1985. Under the agreement, the UER paid FOCA 1,221,000 Swiss francs at the end of the first year for the rights for European events, and 429,000 Swiss francs for the races outside. For 1990, the figures increased to 1,517,000 Swiss francs and 533,000 Swiss francs respectively.

Inside the UER, the rights were sold to each nation wishing to take the transmission, with the figure being renegotiated each year. A small nation like Austria, for example, which showed all the 1990 Grands Prix, had to post a guarantee of 154,163 Swiss francs at the start of the season.

In the future, FOCA wants to deal directly with each of the state television networks, rather than through the UER, and with the increasingly numerous commercial stations which are not members of the UER. Some agreements have already been reached, with the races being "shared" in Italy, for example, between state-run RAI and private Canale 5.

Until 1990, the spectacle of Formula One could be bought at a relatively low price by the networks. From 1991, things will change and FOCA has warned there will be serious price increases.

THE THIRD EYE

Since the mid-1970s Bernie Ecclestone had dreamed of equipping every F1 car with an on-board television camera to enliven telecasts with the driver's eye view of the race, but there were no cameras then capable of doing the job.

Major electronic companies were approached, but for years they could only offer cameras that were too heavy, too bulky and too sensitive to vibration and interference from the car's ignition.

FOCA eventually decided to go on alone, and through an Australian named David Thomas, succeeded where the industrial giants had failed. He integrated a miniature camera, with a lens hardly bigger than a thumbnail, into a small wing fixed on the body to the right of the roll-over hoop. Since then, producers have had at their disposal the sometimes spectacular scenes as the driver sees them. They included the collision between Prost and Senna in Japan in 1989, and from a backward-facing camera, Senna emerging from the spray to crash into the back of Martin Brundle's Brabham in the rain-soaked Adelaide race. Having invested heavily in the system, FOCA keeps the technical details of the camera, and its cost, very secret.

The eye of the television camera is now on board cars, through research financed by FOCA to develop miniaturised cameras. One is mounted on a mini-wing (top, left) and protected by a transparent film which slides across the camera lens, another can be in the cockpit (above, left). Their images are relayed by a helicopter hovering over the circuit at 4500 feet and are bounced back to a control room, where the director can choose to cut them into the transmission. The same picture is seen by all the commentators, working in cramped commentary boxes (left).

Repeat performances. The Sauber-Mercedes team's cars were as competitive as the C9s, a perfect synthesis of equipment "Made in Switzerland" and a car which officially carried the name of the great Stuttgart company, at last. There was more success for the drivers, too, even if in 1990, Jean-Louis Schlesser had to share the laurels with his 1989 rival, Italian Mauro Baldi.

A CHAMPIONSHIP NEVER IN DOUBT

MICHAEL COTTON

A watershed year for sports-prototype racing sees Mercedes dominate the championship, Jaguar well beaten into second place, Porsche just fades away, Spice gathers strength and Peugeot shows its hand.

Mercedes won the World Sports-Prototype Championship in 1990 for the second year in succession, but it was a more satisfactory season for the Swiss-German Sauber team because the opposition was of higher quality. In 1989 the Jaguar team was badly divided between the ageing V12 and the troublesome new V6 twin-turbo, and Nissan was too young to hope to topple any mature teams.

Both Jaguar, which won at Silverstone and at Le Mans, and Nissan, which led in Mexico and finished there in second place, could draw a good deal of satisfaction from the 1990 season, although of course Tom Walkinshaw's Silk Cut Jaguar team had its sights set on further victories, and another championship.

Toyota struggled with fuel consumption throughout the year and failed to capitalise on the fourth place earned at Suzuka back in April, while Mazda withdrew to concentrate on the All-Japan Sports-Prototype Championship, appearing only at Le Mans.

Porsche was clearly finished as a major force in sports car racing, but Reinhold Joest's factory assisted team made the old 962C go faster than ever, and achieved some minor results. Rather, it was the young team of Spice Engineering that finished fourth in the Teams Championship, behind Mercedes, Jaguar and Nissan, having finished third overall in the two British rounds at Silverstone and Donington.

The 'fuel consumption formula' was effectively ended in Mexico City in October on a bizarre note, as the winning Mercedes C11 driven by World Champion drivers Jean-Louis Schlesser and Mauro Baldi was disqualified for being overfuelled, team director Peter Sauber himself allowing one-tenth of a litre too much petrol to flow into the tank! The fact that 25 litres were drained from the C11's tank afterwards made no impression on the stewards, and their unpopular decision was declared to be "unnecessary and unsporting" by Mercedes' Jochen Neerpasch.

Earlier in the season, at Donington, both Silk Cut Jaguars were disqualified for being marginally over-fuelled, and there was a distinct feeling that the decision in Mexico was made to 'even the score'. It was a very sad way to end a formula that had merit, as originally devised, but had long since failed to impress the public as an environmentally satisfactory medium of entertainment.

As the formula drew to a close, there was more talk of the need for 'green' racing, with low emissions and perhaps with catalytic converters. All the major manufacturers involved in the sport believe that while Formula 1 is to do with absolute performance, and personalities, sports car events should be more concerned with the environment, and should set realistic development goals for the participants.

Mercedes won eight of the nine World Championship races, failing only at Silverstone in May when one car was disqualified on technical grounds (outside assistance, on the track) during free practice, and the other broke its camshaft timing chain tensioner in the race, with serious consequences to the V8 engine.

Controversially though, Mercedes did not send a team to the 24-Hours of Le Mans, since the Automobile Club de l'Ouest had failed to reach any agreement with the FISA and the prestigious event was, therefore, run outside the World Championship. A welcome accord was established in September.

The FISA declared that it would press on with the introduction of the 3.5 litre sports car formula in 1991, with naturally aspirated engines not controlled by fuel consumption, in cars weighing 750kg. Mercedes, Jaguar, Peugeot and Spice declared that they would be ready for the first events — Peugeot, in fact, raced the new V10 powered 905 in the last two races of the 1990 season — but Porsche had not even begun the development of a new sports car, while Nissan, Toyota and Mazda lagged behind in their design departments.

Simply, the Japanese manufacturers had believed, or persuaded themselves, that the FISA would postpone the introduction of the 3.5 litre formula until 1992 or 1993 and planned accordingly. Early in 1990 the controlling body conceded that the existing turbocharged cars would be allowed a year of grace but with an additional penalty established at 100kg, meaning that the Porsche 962C, Nissan R90C and Toyota 90C-V would have to weigh 1000kg at scrutineering, instead of 900kg; furthermore the cars would still be subject to strict control on fuel consumption.

Immediately, Porsche recommended their customers to keep away from the new World Sportscar Championship (thereby robbing it potentially of half a grid!), and Nissan and Toyota decided to engage in low-key programmes while preparing their new 3.5 litre cars.

It appears therefore that the FISA might be struggling to find two dozen registered entries for the 1991 World Sports-car Championship, although ten of them — two-car teams from Mercedes (C291 flat-12), Jaguar (XJR-14 V8), Peugeot (905 V10), Spice (SE91 Lamborghini V12) and Brun (Judd V8) — have the potential to provide better and more varied racing than the WS-PC series ever offered.

Necessarily, the late-season *rapprochement* between the FISA and the ACO, returning the 24-Hours of Le Mans to the World Championship for the next five years, involved some heavy compromising. The ACO has conceded all television rights, and the privilege of controlling pit and paddock passes, while the FISA has to relax its tight rules about eligibility, to allow registered teams to bring as many Group C cars as they wish, including for example the 1990 model Mercedes 011, and the twice successful V12 powered, 7-litre Jaguar XJR. In the end common sense had to prevail, as was always apparent to the participants.

The season of 1990 was inevitably a watershed, comparable with 1967 when the big Ford, Ferrari and Chaparral models ended their careers, and 1971 when the Porsche 917s and Ferrari 512s were phased out.

We will, of course, mourn the passing of the magnificent 5-litre, twin-turbo Mercedes C9 and C11 models, the V12 powered Jaguars, and particularly the Porsche 956/962C models which were so dominant in the early years of the formula, but all good things must come to an end eventually. Some will say, for reasons explained in another article in this edition of *Automobile Year*, that the FISA missed a golden opportunity to restrict the volume of *air* going into the engine, rather than the volume of *fuel*, on the grounds that air is never exhausted so the spectators are rarely disappointed.

That, though, is now history, although it was pertinent to review the political features of 1990 as a background to the explanation of what happened on the circuits. Even though it was the last year of the current Group C for-

Peter Sauber without his beret is a rare sight. The independent constructor from Hinwill, near Zurich, is normally seen with his head carefully protected, and more in the French than the Swiss-German style. It is questionable whether Mercedes would have returned to top-line competition without Sauber's ground work.

Jan Lammers and Andy Wallace (even with the help of Franz Konrad) were not able to repeat their 1988 success at Le Mans. But second place in the 24-hour race was the best result of the season for this TWR pair, behind their team mates in a Jaguar 1-2.

By taking the lead at around two-thirds distance, Geoff Brabham, Chip Robinson and Derek Daly gave Nissan some hope of victory at Le Mans in its first really serious attempt on the race. But, as at Daytona, the NPTI team, the North American branch of the Japanese manufacturer, could not quite bring it off. However, with pole position, the lap record and worthy fifth place, Nissan left Le Mans with honour.

In a strong position from the start of the 24-hour race, Price Cobb and John Nielsen (right) took over the lead in the middle of the night. It was not until dawn that they were reinforced by Martin Brundle.

In 1952, Louis Rosier retired from race when he was leading with just an hour to go. In 1990 Jesus Pareja (below) retired when his Porsche was on the same lap as the leading Jaguar only ten minutes before the finish.

Mazda expected great things from this 24-hour event, its only international race of the season, but the two new 787s retired in the 12th and 15th hours. Before the start, the team had brought a touch of charm and tradition to the grid (opposite, centre).

Nearly 50 000 British spectators came to support Jaguar, and during the final hour (opposite, bottom) they provided a fascinating show for the Continental fans, with songs swelling out over the roar of engines.

The 1990 Le Mans 24 Hours is one race Reinhold Joest, the official Porsche representative in the prestigious event, would prefer to forget. The team lost one car during practice and chose to run long-tail bodies, though they were less efficient on the modified circuit. It also had problems in balancing aerodynamics and tyres. Stuck, Jelinski and Bell just failed to make the top three finishers.

Jacques Laffite's return to Le Mans was a welcome move by the popular driver. His successful early morning stint as a mechanic was an example of what a driver can achieve in the special circumstances of the 24 Hours. But it was not enough for Laffite and his friends Jean-Louis Ricci and Henri Pescarolo who finished in an obscure 14th place, hardly fulfilling expectations of the Joest team for which they drove.

After a good debut at Suzuka (where Lees and Ogawa placed fourth), the early part of the season was so catastrophic for Toyota that Dumfries and Ogawa even had to revert to an 89C for Silverstone.

WHAT POLITICS?

The turmoil of the previous winter seemed far away when the Group C teams went to Le Mans in June. Despite the absence of Mercedes, making an empty political gesture, there was a full entry with works or works-assisted teams from Jaguar, Porsche, Nissan, Toyota and Mazda. The contest was the best for some years.

Jean-Marie Balestre had, it seemed, done the Automobile Club de l'Ouest a great favour in promoting the 58th edition of the 24 hour races. Even those who felt that the ACO had been tardy in completing safety work, officious with competitors in years gone by and parsimonious with prize funds, rallied to support the event.

There were more people at the Sarthe than in any year since the 1950s, a quarter of a million over five days. The competitors seemed to care little that the race — or is it now an institution? — counted not for the World Sports-Prototype Championship. It was there, like Everest, so it had to be attempted once again.

Ironically, the two chicanes which M. Balestre insisted had to be built, in the interests of safety, actually increased the risk of accidents and put far more strain on cars and drivers, in braking three times from top speed instead of once.

The leading cars were nearly as fast as before on the Mulsanne Straight. The magic '400' kmh was always a fluke but 380kmh was once a good speed for a car in qualifying trim, and now the quickest were peaking at 350kmh not once, but three times per lap. In 24 hours the leading cars braked heavily from maximum speed more than 1000 times, and it was estimated that there were 4300 more gearchanges on account of the chicanes.

On the positive side, Jonathan Palmer had a very lucky escape when his Joest Porsche crashed heavily from 320kmh due, it was believed, to a failure of the rear suspension. During qualifying on Wednesday the 962C veered suddenly to the left midway between the two chicanes, and would have been travelling much faster had the first one not been installed.

As usual the antiquated pits were a nightmare for everyone. The acceleration lane was narrow, the working areas woefully cramped, and there were far too many hangers-on around the fashionable pits. Within weeks those old pits had been razed to the ground, and in future teams will benefit from spacious, modern working areas, improved safety and palatial hospitality areas. FISA may have the last word about the overcrowding...

Beaten in advance on fuel consumption, the Toyotas ran very prudently at the start of the race, tackling the 24-hour race as a real endurance event, and taking no part in the scramble for pole position. The tactics paid off for Lees-Ogawa-Sekiya, who finished a good sixth close behind the Nissan. The other TOM's Team Toyota car, number 37 driven by Suzuki, Ravaglia and Dumfries, was eliminated in a collision with another Nissan in the braking area for the Dunlop corner on Saturday.

Mazda's honour was saved at Le Mans by the victory of Terada, Katayama and Hoshino in the IMSA category. The 787 (202) driven by Gachot, Herbert and Weidler, the most durable of the new cars, retired at 6 am on Sunday morning, having never been higher than 30th. Given the changes in the rules, it seems unlikely that a rotary engine will ever win the 24 Hours.

By pairing Jochen Mass with a number of young German drivers, Mercedes apparently designated Schlesser and Baldi (below) as favourites for the 1990 championship. But they had to wait until the Montreal race, before they could be certain of the title.

mula Mercedes produced a completely new chassis which, as the team hoped, gave enough forward momentum to maintain the advantage over rivals.

Tom Walkinshaw Racing improved the XJR-11 substantially, but again lost reliability when it really mattered; Nissan developed a new chassis, from Lola, but the Nissan Motorsports Europe organisation was split from top to bottom by Japanese politics, and suffered accordingly; and Toyota developed the existing chassis and engine, but were let down by Denso who failed to improve the engine management system.

The first sighting of the new Mercedes C11 was at Suzuka, the opening round of the 1990 series in April, but it didn't last long. World Champion Schlesser tried too hard, too soon to capture the pole position from Geoff Lees' Toyota, and crashed the C11 as spots of rain threatened the final qualifying session. The fact that the new chassis was made of composite materials, and was twice as strong as the old C9, probably protected Schlesser in the accident.

The Japanese race developed like a thriller article. Schlesser's old C9 was taken off the grid with a fuel leak, and started the 480 kilometre event 60 seconds, or half a lap, after the others. Jochen Mass touched another car and spun his C9 in the second corner, losing 30 seconds, so it really seemed that rivals could make some ground.

Soon the two 'Silver Arrows' were scything through the field, up to fourth and fifth places when the first pit stops were due (just 18 sec and 25 sec behind the leading Silk Cut Jaguars, it was easily noted), and the rest was a formality. Karl Wendlinger, one of Mercedes' 21-year-old 'apprentice' drivers, handled the C9 with maturity in the middle stint and took the lead on the 32nd lap, of 80, with Baldi in close pursuit.

Both Jaguars succumbed to oil pump failures after making a very good start to the race, and the Nissan of Masahiro Hasemi and Anders Olofsson narrowly beat the Tom's Toyota of Lees and Hitoshi Ogawa to third place, one lap behind the Mercedes which finished in 1-2 formation.

For reasons never properly understood, the Toyotas were not able to repeat this form. In fact their next race, at Monza, was an absolute disaster as both cars were crashed during qualifying and again in the race, so the Tom's team had to take three wrecks back to their European base in Norfolk, England.

Throughout qualifying the monitor screens read

A TASTE OF SPICES

"Spices will form half the grids in 1991. We will be replacing Porsche!" Jeff Hazell, managing director of Spice Engineering Limited, has good reason to be optimistic as his company's order book for Group C and IMSA cars is bulging. There have been some good results since Gordon Spice and Hazell formed the company, at Silverstone, in 1985. There have been five World Championships in the WS-PC Group C2 class and three IMSA Camel Lights titles in America.

In 1990 the tasks became considerably more difficult as the 'works' team and its customers tackled the top groups. In America there have been a pole position, a couple of races led, but no elusive victory. The closest to that came in May at Elkhart Lake, where Chevrolet VS powered Spices finished second and third to the winning Jaguar XJR-10.

The World Championship has yielded third places overall in the two British rounds, at Silverstone and Donington, and fourth at Spa. Spice's points tally of 13 is fourth only to Mercedes, Jaguar and Nissan... and equals the combined scores of the two top Porsche teams, Joest Racing and Kremer.

In September Spice tested a new car powered by Lamborghini's V12 GP engine, which was under consideration by the team for the '91 season.

Spice Engineering had previously limited its efforts to winning in the C2 category, but after a "learning" season in the senior division, the British cars were more than just competitive. At Silverstone (above) Giacomelli and Velez finished on the podium, as did Harvey and Euser later at Donington.

Of the three young newcomers paired with the veteran Jochen Mass, Karl Wendlinger was the star, winning at Spa and twice finishing second, but they all produced excellent results. Schumacher was disqualified at Silverstone, but came back at Dijon (left) where the No 2 Mercedes was only a few seconds behind the leading C11, repeating the performance at the Nürburgring. Frentzen's only appearance with the team, at Donington, also saw him on the podium with a second place.

Toyota was a surprise force in the 1990 IMSA series this year with three victories, at Topeka, Sear's Point and San Antonio. Using the tactics which had been so successful for Nissan, the rival Japanese manufacturer gave an American organisation complete responsibility for developing the GTP, with Dan Gurney in overall charge of the project.

Geoff Brabham, son of Sir Jack, took his third successive IMSA title, and has scored 24 victories in the series, all for Nissan. His loyalty to the company must have helped his achievement, but titles in SuperVee (1979) and Can Am (1981) and his frequent appearances in CART races show his versa-

tility. He also surprised some European drivers at Le Mans by taking pole position on Wednesday and leading the race until the early hours of Sunday morning.

Jaguar started the season well with victory at Daytona. But the subsequent results of Davy Jones, Price Cobb and John Nielsen were irregular, as here at Miami where neither of the two XJR10s finished well. Wins did come at Lime Rock and Portland, but were inadequate compensation for a poor season.

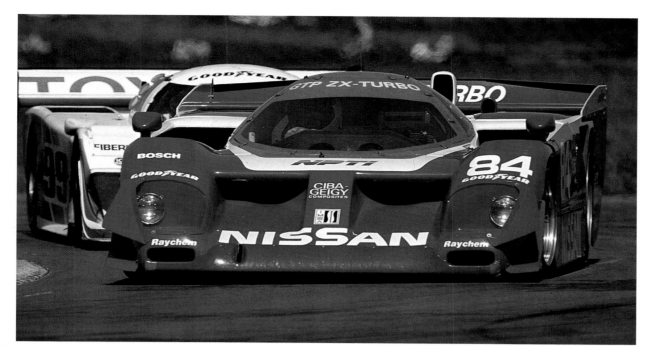

The IMSA 1990 season was notable for the duel between Nissan and Toyota, with Jaguar as the strong outsider, but the series suffered from the withdrawal of the private Porsche teams, which were not inclined to enter cars that would be beaten as much by the rules as by the opposition.

NISSAN'S THIRD IMSA

A change of ownership has done the Nissan team no harm in the IMSA Camel GT Championship. For two years Don Devendorf enjoyed the successes of his Electramotive team, having mortgaged himself to the hilt to reach the top, and in 1990 the third successive titles came the way of Nissan and Geoff Brabham.

Now, though, Nissan owns the Californian team which is renamed Nissan Performance Technology Inc (NPTI), removing financial worries from Devendorf's shoulders. There is a new car to keep the momentum going, the NPT-90 designed by Trevor Harris, and the next project is a 3,5-litre sports car chassis that will serve both Nissan's IMSA and World Championship teams in 1992.

It is not all plain sailing for Nissan in America. Competition is mounting, from Toyota as well as from Jaguar, and the days when Brabham could reel off eight successive victories (as he did in 1988) have gone. NPTI did amply well to keep the titles, but did not win as many races as they did in 1989. Jaguar's Castrol backed IMSA team, managed by Tony Dowe, started the season well with a heartening 1-2 in the Daytona 24-Hours. The cars were the trusty V12 models, now XJR-12, and as happened in 1988 the Daytona victory was a good omen for Le Mans. Jaguar found it more difficult to win with the turbocharged XJR-10, having to wait for Lime Rock in May, and Portland in July, for the next sightings of the chequered flag.

Nissan soon settled into the winning routine, outclassing the field in the 'prestige' races at Miami, Sebring, Road Atlanta and West Palm Beach. That streak, it turned out, was enough to claim the championship before the season was over, but the high season was marked by three victories for Juan Manuel Fangio II, nephew of the former five-times World Champion, driving an All-American Racers Toyota Eagle built by Dan Gurney in America. The Toyota is powered by a 2.1-litre single-turbo engine, and enjoys a 90-pound weight advantage which allows it to qualify and race on softer compound tyres.

In July the Porsches, almost extinct, were allowed a 200 pound advantage (from 2100 pounds, the same as the Nissans and Jaguars, to 1900 pounds), and this is expected to encourage at least three professional teams to run the Weissach cars in 1991. As if to beckon them, James Weaver won the important Tampa race in Rob Dyson's Porsche on the last day of September.

A number of problems beset the IMSA championship, most in common with the world series... high costs of competing, low sponsorship returns, consequently small grids, and inadequate television exposure. It may be that this series had its hey-day in the 1980s.

The 1990 season was the second in GTP for Juan Manuel Fangio II, whose record was hardly impressive as it opened — one second place and a number of lesser results meant he was better known for his prestigious name than for his track success. But during the season, the Argentine became an international star to his countrymen and the idol of many South Americans living in the United States.

Louis Descartes was the only constructor entered in C2 in 1989 who took up the challenge of moving into C1 in 1990, had a difficult year. Lack of time and budget meant that he could not build a new chassis, and could do little more than graft a 3.3-litre Cosworth V8 in place of the previous six-cylinder BMW engine. The best efforts of François Migault were only just enough to get the car onto a grid.

'1-2-3-4', the numbers of the Mercedes and Jaguar teams, and it was a tale repeated often during the season, Mercedes took a pair of new C11s to Monza and fairly dominated the proceedings, though Martin Brundle and Jan Lammers made the V6 powered Jaguar XJR-11s look very respectable, in contrast to the difficult learning season in 1989.

For the second time Mass had an early setback, tangling with Lammers in the first chicane only seconds after the start, and both cars were badly delayed. It was a measure of their performances that Mass and Wendlinger were able to get back to second place at the finish, 17 seconds behind Schlesser and Baldi, while Lammers and Andy Wallace were able to finish fourth, behind Brundle and Alain Ferté.

The exclusion of the Mass/Schumacher Mercedes at Silverstone, after a very minor breach of regulations, was a travesty of the sport and a punishment not only to the team but to the spectators and the organisation. The Silk Cut Jaguar team was delighted to finish first and second, of course, following the retirement of the Schlesser/Baldi Mercedes, but it was not such a satisfactory achievement as the team's previous three Silverstone victories.

Mercedes did not lose another race. Mass and Wendlinger won at Spa, actually putting the young Austrian into the joint lead of the World Championship, with Mass, and fully justifying Neerpasch's policy of encouraging three young drivers. Brundle retired from the Belgian event when leading, and Schlesser/Baldi dropped back with an elusive ignition fault which robbed them of points.

The Spanish round, at Jarama, was cancelled in controversial circumstances, and there was a long wait after Le Mans before the next race at Dijon-Prenois, in intense heat. There, in Burgundy, the two Mercedes romped away from the Jaguars, the British cars overheating their tyres, and the Nissan R90C driven by Julian Bailey and Mark Blundell moved up to a worthy third place.

The pattern was repeated at the Nürburgring, where an uninspiring race produced the result Mercedes 1-2, Jaguar 3-4 one lap behind. One more success, at Donington in September, was enough to secure for Sauber Mercedes the Teams Championship for the second year in succession.

Fortunately for our recollections of the season, the last two races were lively and memorable. Both were won by

Mercedes, but not with the Swiss-German team's usual ease. Brundle led in Montreal, then Bailey in the Nissan, and it was only two laps before the red flag was shown that Baldi took the Mercedes into the lead. The race was stopped prematurely when a manhole cover was sucked from the roadway, causing extensive damage to several cars, especially the Brun Motorsport Porsche of Jesus Pareja, which crashed in flames.

The suitability of the circuit for Group C racing was inevitably called into question, and there are doubts too about the excrutiatingly bumpy track in Mexico City. Again Brundle, the World Champion driver in 1988, led the race in his Silk Cut Jaguar but again the two Mercedes 'Silver Arrows' asserted their dominance, Michael Schumacher proving to be another young star in his handling of the C11 declared the winner.

Certainly, the post-race controversy (which could have been avoided with a regulation allowing for the amount of fuel remaining in the cars' tanks to be considered) marred recollections of Group C racing. The shine on Mercedes' illustrious star was not tarnished by the episode — all credit to Mercedes and Peter Sauber for operating the most dominant team of the 1989-90 period.

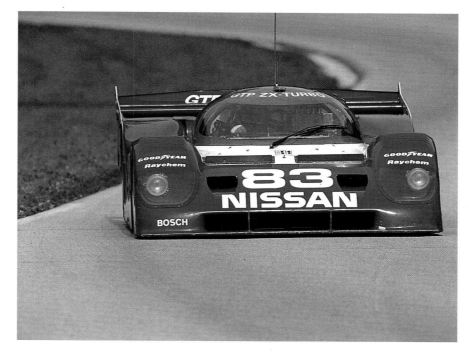

After somewhat difficult development period, the carburation of the new Nissan NPT 90 (above) was sorted out in time to win at Mid-Ohio, Watkins Glen and Road America.

The Ferrari France team made two sorties to measure its potential and then returned to IMSA determined to be fully competitive. It was partially successful, with a highlight being the second place scored by Jean-Pierre Jabouille at Elkhart Lake (left).

The new Nissan 300 ZX turbos (below) surprisingly won on four occasions, giving Steve Millen (75) the chance of fighting for the title right to the finish.

191

Despite major progress, the Jaguar XJR11s were never really able to challenge the Mercedes. A psychologically important success at Silverstone and a stirring end to the season saved the championship from becoming monotonous. But Tom Walkinshaw (below, congratulating his opposite number, Max Welti, at Donington) certainly expected better results from his excellent organisation.

Jean Todt (on the right) naturally had confidence in the Peugeot 905, in Jean-Pierre Jabouille (at left) and lead driver Keke Rosberg. The Finn qualified the new car in mid-grid for its debut race, at Montreal, and ran as high as tenth before retiring with a minor fault. Its performance confirmed the promise of this handsome car.

CENTRE OF ATTRACTION

Keke Rosberg, Formula 1 World Champion in 1982, ground out his Marlboro and donned his helmet. This was the moment, in Montreal, that everyone had been waiting for: the first laps in anger for the Peugeot 905.

Jean-Pierre Jabouille warmed the Peugeot up and gave the seat to Rosberg deferentially. The Finn, who retired at the end of 1986, returned with his reputation for press-on driving as high as ever, and soon had the V10 engine wailing. 'Whee... whee... whee... whee...'. Down went Rosberg through the six-speed gearbox, braking savagely as he took three lumbering Porsches on the approach to Turn 1.

And then we recalled how sports cars should sound, used to sound before the age of turbochargers, and before the fuel economy formula seized Group C in an unwelcome embrace. Not since the last Matra V12 wailed into a museum had we heard such a sports car noise, and that was back in 1974! Peugeot's 905 was individually styled, and owed nothing to the Porsche look-a-like school: white, pretty, pristine, and bearing allegiance to Esso, Michelin and the chassis constructor, Dassault aerospace, the Peugeot was bound to be the centre of attraction at the eighth round of the World Sports-Prototype Championship, in Canada.

That the Peugeot had a good debut was a bonus. Jean Todt, the company's sport director, made it clear that the last two races of the 1990 season were to start the learning curve. The team learned that 'bottoming' on the bumpy track loosened the aerodynamic undertray, but the 905 covered 45 laps in the first session with no great problems, and qualified for twelfth place on the grid in the afternoon.

Up against the turbocharged cars, "150 to 200bhp more powerful" as Peugeot's release made clear, without disclosing their own figure, it was evidently not going to get among the leaders, and Saturday's qualifying was slowed by rain.

The 905 is designed to run with four-wheel steering, but not yet. Todt let a cat out of the bag when he disclosed that the T-car (spare test-bed) had stopped with a steering pump hydraulic leak, which is unusual to say the least with a racing car, and furthermore it was leaking onto the exhaust pipes! So the 4-ws system, when it is used, will be hydraulically operated.

Rosberg drove a conservative race, around 10th place, until the fuel pressure dropped and stalled him on the outside of a slow corner while the pace car was circulating. Peugeot's 905 raced again, in Mexico two weeks later, in preparation for the new formula in 1991. In Mexico there were handling problems in practice (Rosberg qualified it 11th) and time was lost in the pits during the race, when Rosberg and Jabouille brought it through to finish 13th.

THE LOST ERA OF ECONOMY

MICHAEL COTTON

Reflections on nine years of sports-prototype racing, on lessons learned and opportunities lost under rules dominated by fuel consumption aspects. A formula that did not stretch development engineers, often failed to please competitors and spectators, sometimes provided memorable events.

Turbocharged Porsches, Jaguars and Nissans will continue to race in the 1991 World Sports Car Championship, but they will be so handicapped as to run behind the new breed of 3.5-litre sports cars. The fuel economy controlled Group C formula, introduced in 1982, has now effectively been terminated and we can reflect on the efficacy of a formula that often infuriated the drivers, bemused the spectators but pleased the engineers.

The verdict? Group C did *not* bring about any technical advances for production cars that would not have happened anyway. It did succeed in equating the power from different engine configurations, but not as successfully as the air restrictors introduced by the IMSA organisation in America. Admirable though the cars may have been, the Group C economy rules will pass without lament.

The Porsche company provided the sport with a common theme where consumption controlled racing is concerned, having been involved in Group C racing from 1982 through to the end of the 1990 season, and in Grand Prix racing — through the TAG engine connection — between 1983 and 1987 when fuel efficiency was of prime importance.

"Group C has been interesting, but for us the development of the 1.5-litre turbo engine was more important" declares Dipl. Ing. Hans Mezger, head of Porsche's race engine development team. "To summarise, we learned a lot about general engine efficiency... reducing friction, improving combustion chamber design, the optimisation of engine management. We had already been working on Group C for two years but we did not have strong opposition; Formula 1 is much more competitive and we had to work harder.

"Management is a most important aspect of engine design nowadays because we look to control very accurately the fuel and ignition at all points in the range. If you use one per cent too little fuel you burn the pistons; one per cent too much wastes fuel and makes the engine less efficient. *The management system enables you to run the engine as efficiently as the design allows. If it is not a good design it will not be efficient.*"

Asked if any racing developments been transferred to production cars, Ing. Norbert Singer, Porsche's senior race engineer, has to answer 'no'. "There is nothing I can point to on a 911, for instance, and say that it was developed on a 962. We improved the oil system in the racing engine, and in the 911 but these were parallel developments. For the race engine we chose a sophisticated and expensive solution which was not really suitable for the volume car.

"The production engineers can always see what we are doing. They talk to us, but they always find that our solutions are too expensive, or won't work on the production line. So they do something in a different way that has similar results."

Between colleagues there are shades of opinion, but agreement that the collaboration with the Robert Bosch company and development of the Motronic engine management system has been the single most important factor in improving engine efficiency.

In 1982 the original Porsche 956 was equipped with the relatively inefficient Bosch mechanical injection system, a carry-over from the 1981. It was good enough to win every Group C race in which it appeared, with a crushing 1-2-3 victory at Le Mans, but it wasn't good enough for engineers Mezger, Peter Falk (then competitions director) and Singer.

"The Motronic 1.2 system was clearly more efficient than the mechanical system, but we were already working on something better for the TAG Formula 1 engine" says Mezger. "In Formula 1 we needed a more sophisticated system from the start, but we kept the MP1.2 system on the Group C cars until 1988, at Le Mans." In fact TAG (Techniques d'Avant Garde) is reputed to have paid for the development of the Bosch system that evolved into the 1.7 when it became available to other teams, and it kept the Marlboro-McLaren-TAG-Porsche combination at the F1 forefront between 1984 and 1986, winning titles in each season.

Group C racing, by contrast, did not stretch Porsche's design staff in any way. Production model 956 cars were

Fuel was strictly 'rationed' in Group C racing, the allocation from 1985 being 51 litres per 100 kilometres. That may sound generous, but 700 horsepower engines are thirsty. So teams had to balance speed and consumption very carefully — if the judgment was absolutely right a car should run out of fuel just past the flag...

Porsche customers took delivery of the 2.65 litre, 620bhp, 956 from 1983, as the season opened the Joest team beat the works team at Monza. At Brands Hatch, where the Ickx-Mass Rothmans Porsche is taking a tight line inside the Canon Porsche driven by Palmer and Lammers, the works cars were again beaten, by the Fitzpatrick 956 driven by Derek Warwick and John Fitzpatrick. Once customer teams started running Porsche 956s in 1983, the marque completely dominated the Le Mans 24-hour Race — in 1982 the Rothmans Porsches took the top three places, and in the folowing yeasr the works cars placed first and second were followed by six independent Porsches.

In Group C from 1982 refuelling was metered. It was assumed that a car started with 100 litres, the full system capacity, on board, and 410 litres could be taken on during a 1000km race. Even the rate of refuelling was controlled, at 60 litres per minute from 1986. Curiously though, the authorities never bothered to check the amount of fuel in the pipeline, although this could be as much as 20 litres.

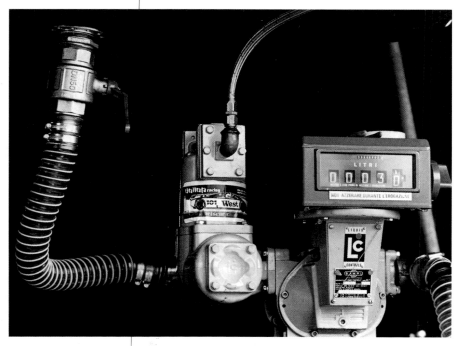

GROUP C RULES

The intention of the Group C sports car regulations introduced in 1982 was simple: to regulate power through fuel consumption, 60 litres/100km, reduced to 51 litres in 1985. Minimum weights were 800kg, then 850kg in 1985 and 900kg in 1989, and throughout the formula maximum dimensions were 4800mm long, 2000mm wide, and height not more than 1100mm or less than 1000mm. Fuel tank capacity could not be more than 99 litres — allowing 1 litre more for fuel in the system — and fuel was metered in at 50 litres/min, rising to 60 litres/min in 1986.

To encourage smaller teams, FISA ran a Group C Junior class from 1983, renamed Group C2 in 1985, and abandoned at the end of 1989 after five years of domination by Spice Engineering and its customers. The cars weighed a minimum of 700kg and were allowed 33 litres per 100km, rising to 36.3 litres/100km in 1988.

In 1982 Porsche quoted 620bhp for the 2.65 litre twin turbocharged flat six engine. The claimed figure (always conservative, according to rivals) rose to 640bhp for the 3-litre version in 1986, and eventually to 670bhp for the 3.2-litre version in 1990.

released to teams in 1983, though still with mechanical injection. The Reinhold Joest, Erwin and Manfred Kremer, John Fitzpatrick and Richard Lloyd teams, ran the works cars close on occasions (Joest's actually beat the Rothmans-Porsche team at Monza) and dealt with the under-developed works Lancias as well.

Politics came to the fore in 1984. FISA had intended to reduce the fuel allocation by 15 per cent, from 600 litres to 510 litres, in keeping with an overall objective to 'raise the bar' continually and stretch manufacturers in the quest for improving economy. Porsche had spent a considerable amount of money with Bosch, and Lancia with Weber-Marelli, before Jean-Marie Balestre returned from Daytona with the makings on an agreement with IMSA. Rigorous economy would be scrapped, he said. Another way would be found to limit the power output — Bishop proposed that air restrictors made more sense than fuel restrictors — and the two bodies would align their regulations in 1985.

It was, unfortunately, pie in the sky. IMSA didn't want a 'marriage' nearly as much as Balestre did; Porsche's management exploded with rage and withdrew the team from Le Mans as a protest. (Reinhold Joest's team won

the race handsomely, and Porsches filled the top seven places, rather than the top eight the year before.)

FISA's decision was overturned, as IMSA did not reciprocated the goodwill gestures and the World Championship for Group C cars developed as originally planned. The fuel allocation was reduced to 51 litres/100km in 1985, and curiously the Porsche factory had more difficulty in coming to grips with the tighter allocation than the customers.

Rothmans-Porsche was almost humiliated at Mugello, Monza, Silverstone and Le Mans, but won the first and the third rounds simply by being a better organised team. Somehow the delicate equation of power and economy had gone wrong. Porsche chose to restrict the power to suit the fuel allocation, while without notable exception the customers chose power. They felt it was better to run a fast race and slow down towards the end if necessary, reasoning that it might rain, or more likely, a course car would slow everyone's space and bring them back to the fuel targets.

"We did reduce the power, certainly" Singer agrees. "We made our calculations on the basis of the drivers using all the power available without exceeding the economy.

Top: The works Porsche team has always had its share of fine drivers and 'characters'. The most popular in the 1980s was Hans Stuck, photographed in his 'office' during the Hockenheim 1000km race in 1985. Stuck was joint World Sportscar Champion that year, sharing the title with co-driver Derek Bell.

Above: Prof. Helmut Bott, Porsche's director of research and development (right) with competitions director Peter Falk (left).

196

Our customers chose what we call a power overshoot, and they trusted their drivers more. At Le Mans we had to do the same, and our team then took its place at the front again."

With Motronics, Singer explains, there is no straight power: economy line but a 'map' with thousands of variables. "With digital ignition you can change so many things... at 0.5 bar boost, and three-quarters throttle, you can adjust the fuel setting at 5,126rpm if you like! We cut back on the fuel, cut back some more and the drivers could cope, but we made the car more difficult to drive and eventually our drivers were using *more* fuel again. It took us a while to understand the problem."

It was a surplus of fuel in the wrong place, the reservoir, that caused a frightening pits-lane fireball at Hockenheim and put Singer into hospital with burns, but a happier aspect of the race was that Rothmans-Porsche looked like a winning team again, and performed well enough in the latter half of the season to make Hans Stuck and Derek Bell the World Champion drivers.

The challenge from Jaguar, with a heavy but efficient V12 engine, looked serious in 1986 and the maiden victory came early, at Silverstone. Reliability problems, usually on a random basis, prevented the team from taking any titles that season but in 1987 Silk Cut Jaguar swept to the Teams and Drivers championships with eight victories in ten races.

Porsche was, by this time, devoting more resources to the development of the Indycar and actually withdrew from the World Championship series, though it sold the water-cooled engines to the customer teams and stepped up the support service. A year later the advanced Motronic 1.7 system was introduced at Le Mans, where Porsche did run a team, and was made available to customers afterwards.

The full 3-litre engine used by the Porsche factory from 1986 onwards was significant because it was fully water-cooled (the customer engines were equipped with water-cooled cylinder heads), and therefore represented the final break with the company's tradition.

"A water-cooled engine is a little more efficient because it runs cooler" Singer explains. "An air-cooled engine has hot spots, we always knew that, but the Group C regulations forced us to use water cooling. With more efficient cooling we could run the engines leaner, and use a little more boost. Gradually we eliminated the hot spots and made the engine more efficient."

The use of PDK semi-automatic transmission was a blind alley, the system being heavier and generally less reliable. It was company policy to enter every race with some new development on test, a delight for some engineers but an anathema to the real racing men! PDK was a complex electro-hydraulic system of gearchanging which equipped Hans Stuck's Porsche when he won the 1987 German Supercup series but never succeeded in a full-length World Championship race... and ironically the system has now been shelved, succeeded by the Tiptronic automatic box for production cars.

It is difficult to quantify the gains in efficiency obtained in nine seasons of Group C sports car racing. The circuits have changed, engines have improved and so have aerodynamics and tyres. Whether the teams have 60 litres of fuel, or 51 litres, per 100 kilometres the objective is the same, to cross the line with a litre in the tank!

We *can* say with certainty that the overall gains in efficiency are significant. To take one example, at Spa in 1983 Stefan Bellof claimed pole position at 2 min 10.19 sec in his Rothmans-Porsche 956, and set a new Group C race lap record at 2 min 14.11 sec, a speed of 186.536kmh/115.913mph; the average speed of the race, won by Ickx

---

IMSA – VIVE LA DIFFERENCE!

The very successful IMSA organisation was far from happy about FISA's proposal for Group C in 1982. The Europeans set out a technical challenge for automotive engineers — the best of whom would build the most successful racing cars — the Americans wanted close and varied racing, and were prepared to tune the regulations to see that no marque or team became too dominant.

In 1981 IMSA announced that it would prepare separate regulations, and that the Daytona 24-hour race would no longer be part of the World Championship. Car weights were on a sliding scale related to engines, so that a car powered by a 3-litre racing engine (eg, Cosworth DFV) would weigh 900kg, while with a 3.9-litre DFL it would have to weigh 1000kg.

Porsche's 3-litre type 935 single turbo engine, with air cooling and two valves per cylinder, carried a weight of 900kg rising to 1000kg for the 3.5-litre version, but the water-cooled 4-valve engine was ruled out by top limit of 2-litres, rescinded in 1988 when air restrictors were introduced as a further method of equalising performances.

Fuel tank capacities were restricted to 120 litres, and all four road wheels had to be of the same diameter.

THE COMPETITION

Ford Cosworth DFV/DFL (3.3, 3.5 and 3.9-litre) V8 engines were used by several teams in 1982 but were made to look obsolete when Porsche's 956 with the twin-turbocharged flat-six engine of 2.65-litres appeared in May. At the end of the year Ford's C-100 racing car programme was cancelled and the Cosworth engine development programme that had seemed promising was halted.

Lancia became the main challenger in 1983 with the Martini sponsored LC2, but the car rarely finished ahead of Porsche's customer teams, never mind the factory's Rothmans-Porsche outfit. Lancia beat Rothmans-Porsche only once, at Spa in 1985 when the ill-fated race was stopped early following the death of Stefan Bellof.

Peter Sauber's Mercedes powered C8 made its fleeting debut at Le Mans in June 1985, while Jaguar's XJR-6 V12s appeared for the first time at Mosport two months later. Lancia departed the fray after two races in 1986, and these two marques became more competitive. Jaguar won at Silverstone, Mercedes at the Nürburgring, and they took the laurels from Porsche in each successive year... but never without a fight, which peaked at Le Mans.

One of the most successful partnerships in endurance racing was between Jacky Ickx, Belgium's seven-times Le Mans winner, and Norbert Singer, technical manager of the Porsche sports-racing car programme from 1973 (above).

Right: According to engine designer Hans Mezger, development of the TAG-backed Formula 1 engine in 1982-86 was more beneficial to product research than the Group C programme. The PDK semi-automatic twin-clutch transmission system was developed in 1984-87, and was highly regarded by Hans Stuck, who used it successfully in German Championship races. But it was never used over a full 1000km distance.

and Mass, was 174.82kmh/108.63mph. In 1989 the Joest Racing Porsche 962C driven by Bob Wollek qualified on a damp track at 2 min 08.94 sec and set a fastest race lap of 2 min 11.72 sec, a speed of 189.672kmh/117.86mph. The Porsche's average speed was 180.43kmh/112.12mph, but it finished 2 min 16 sec behind the winning Sauber Mercedes.

An increase of 5.61kmh/3.49mph may not suggest a great improvement in seven years, but in a race lasting five hours it would represent 28 kilometres. And these improvements have been found despite the 15 per cent reduction in fuel allocation (1985), and despite an 11 per cent increase in car weight (from a minimum of 815kg, when the regulations allowed 800kg, to 905kg, just above the 900kg minimum). The underfloor venturi have been halved in height, reducing the so-called ground effect, and the specification of the fuel is now strictly controlled with a minimum of 97 octane.

Limitation of power, through fuel consumption, fairly equated the outputs of such disparate engines as the 7-litre Jaguar V12, the 5-litre Mercedes twin-turbo V8, Porsche's 3-litre twin-turbo flat-six, and race-designed V8 engines from Toyota and Nissan. In that sense Group C has been a success, because where manufacturers see a technical challenge and believe they can succeed, they will enter the arena.

To ration fuel was an arbitrary decision which had certain drawbacks, and two criteria decided that it was not really successful: neither the drivers nor the public enjoyed or appreciated 'economy racing', so it was never well supported in the grandstands, while engineers were divided on the technical merit. Had IMSA's proposal to limit the amount of *air* going through the engine been adopted, we might have been able to enjoy a very much more vigorous and popular form of racing.

The introduction of the 3 1/2 litre 'free' formula in 1991 is likely to mark the start of new controversies. Two seasons of normally aspirated Grand Prix racing have been a mixed blessing as Honda, Renault and Ferrari now explore the realms of 200 horsepower per litre, a level not even imagined less than ten years ago.

Already, powerful voices are calling for reason, among them that of top designer John Barnard who was responsible for the world championship winning McLaren-TAG cars of 1984-86. He argues that the level of development is now similar to that which went on in the turbo era, and that adding cylinders, and simply burning more fuel, is not the path we should be taking. The quest for better efficiency would help racing in two ways, Barnard says: "It would help in equalising the competition, to some degree, and reduce the differences between the bigger and smaller teams. And, it is very important in these times when environmental considerations are so important, that racing makes an effort to be more efficient and responsible."

Dr. Ulrich Bez, Porsche's director of research and development, believes that the Group C economy formula has served its purpose but entertains deep reservations about the future of sports car racing, now developing along the same lines as Formula 1. "We believe that the future of sports car racing should include the development of technology which can be brought to series production cars. We have shown that small displacement turbocharged engines can be more economical than high revving, normally aspirated engines, and we believe that they should have a future in racing."

Turbochargers, though, are liable to blow holes in any legislation, as was demonstrated by Honda in Grand Prix racing in 1988, a performance that will never be forgotten by FISA's rule makers. There can never be a simple solution which will keep everyone happy.

WORLD RALLY CHAMPIONSHIP

ON THE BRINK

PETER FOUBISTER

World Championship rallying enters a new decade full of excitement and promise. Peter Foubister, Editor of *Autosport*, looks at the season and new stars ready to take over.

International rallying has enjoyed highs and lows since it emerged as a major sport in the sixties. The cancellation of the supercar era in the mid-eighties, however, caused a terrible trough with but one team enjoying the necessary commitment to chase the world titles.

But as the sport enters the nineties a new peak is approaching, with Lancia — masters since the advent of the production car regulations — resisting ever-greater pressures from the Japanese manufacturers.

The breakthrough came in 1989 on the 1000 Lakes when Swedish coming-man Mikael Ericsson scooped outright honours for Mitsubishi, although in truth it had been Toyota Team Europe which had been leading the eastern attack.

For 1990, that Toyota determination was strengthened with Ove Andersson's Cologne headquarters prepared for a world-wide campaign against the official Martini Lancia team. But typically, it appeared that the Italians had stolen the initiative when they lured from Andersson Finnish driver Juha Kankkunen, offering him equal billing with reigning World Champion, Miki Biasion and their own tip for the top, Didier Auriol.

Kankkunen, himself a double World Champion, had found life with TTE frustrating — he had come so close to victory so often that the promise of a reliable Lancia, under the eye of an experienced team was too much to resist. On paper, therefore it was all going the Italian way, until the battle was joined in the mountains above Monte Carlo, and Toyota's Carlos Sainz wasted no time in showing that he intended to put his stamp on the 1990 World Rally Championship.

Suddenly, the old fire which had been such a hallmark of Toyota Team Europe through its African campaign of the mid-eighties, was burning again, led by the commitment and star-quality which Carlos enjoyed. He did not just have natural flair behind the wheel, a warm personality and ambition. There was leadership, so that mechanics, tyre fitters and tea ladies again believed in themselves.

Of course, it was not quite that simple — team boss Andersson had a better structure within the team, recruiting the experienced Maurice Guaslard from Michelin to lead affairs on-event and delegating specific responsibilities to his senior engineers, Karl-Heinz Goldstein (testing and development) and Gerd Pfeiffer (rally engineer).

And the new squad stole an important psychological advantage on that opening event. Instead of the familiar snow and ice which usually makes up a 'Monte', there was sunshine and dry roads, the team service crews equipped with Formula 1-style tyre warmers to ensure that the rubber was already at its optimum temperature from the start line of each stage. It could not work every time — any lengthy delay at a stage start meant the benefit was lost — but for once in their lives, the Lancia hierarchy was not on the offensive, instead sending troops home to counter the move by borrowing similar equipment from the Alfa Romeo race team.

So the challengers looked more complete than ever before, this commitment yet further demonstrated at the

The battle between Carlos Sainz in a Toyota (right) and Didier Auriol (Lancia) on the uncharacteristically dry roads of the Monte Carlo Rally was a Clash of the Titans. The two men swapped the lead repeatedly, and were equal leaders on no fewer than five occasions. That was the situation at the end of the 22nd of the 28 special stages when the battle, so hard fought until then, ended abruptly in circumstances that appeared questionable: to the great surprise of the Spanish driver, the Lancia's performance seemed to improve as Auriol headed for victory during the final night.

event finish where Andersson took the unusual step of protesting the winning Lancia. Sour grapes said some, but the Toyota boss denied this, highlighting Didier Auriol's remarkable times in the final stages of the competition. Sainz had suddenly found himself unable to compete after having swapped second for second with the Frenchman since the start.

At the heart of the controversy was FISA's inability to implement new technical regulations which demanded turbocharged cars to be fitted with an air restrictor designed to limit outright performance. Had the FISA officials prepared correctly (the regulations had been due for introduction one full year earlier), then a watertight system of policing turbo repairs or replacements would have been established. But they had not, and with the World Rally Championship offering manufacturers important marketing benefits, it was no surprise that trouble flared.

Ultimately FISA ruled that Lancia had no case to answer on Monte Carlo, Didier Auriol therefore snatching a slender points advantage over Sainz. If TTE boss Andersson was publicly upset, perhaps privately he knew that some ground rules had been set for the battle ahead.

In theory the next qualifier should have been a Drivers-only event in Sweden but when unseasonally warm temperatures left Scandinavia denuded of snow and ice, the event organisers had little option but to cancel the rally. That reduced the full series to a 12 round competition. Team managers were, perhaps, not so sad about the loss: for years they have campaigned for a slimline World Championship. At the heart of such motives is the belief that the series could assume greater status if FISA adopted certain rules already in force in Formula 1 and World Sports-Prototype Championship racing, such as

the requirement for competitors to start every event. As it was, Sainz and the rest of the circus moved directly to Portugal, inevitably one of the season's most interesting confrontations, decided over both asphalt and gravel roads. Not only that, but some of the gravel is rough, taking a heavy toll on cars. Only a few years ago — in the heyday of the Group B supercars — Group A production based cars used to struggle to survive a hard Portuguese Rally. Even if we are already into the second or third generation of Group A cars, it is testament to the expertise of the works engineers that current cars not only survive, they often set times which compare very favourably with those Group B dinosaurs.

Engine power for all vehicles in international rallying is officially limited to 300bhp by a FISA rule which has never been heavily policed. Most front-running cars are considered now to have in excess of that figure, but the greatest efforts are no longer directed towards chasing outright power, rather better and better torque figures which will give a driver the best possible throttle response. So although the cars have shed the wild wings and spoilers which featured on the supercars, they represent a much more sophisticated generation of competition machine.

The greatest advances have obviously come in the evolution of four-wheel drive systems. Original equipment in the mid-eighties was perhaps restricted to a fixed 50-50 torque split between axles, whereas a contemporary rally car will boast torque sensing systems which redirect drive to the wheel with the greatest slip at any one moment. Similarly, the systems are now also influenced by sensor readings constantly monitoring throttle position and other parameters so that a modern 'intelligent' four-wheel drive system is working with the driver all the time.

Didier Auriol (below) would have been better pleased if his victory at Monte Carlo had not been overshadowed by doubts raised by "missing" turbocharger seals. The incident did serve a purpose, however, as it showed up a flaw in the new regulations which came into force at the start of 1990. The 40mm restrictor called for on turbocharged engines will not be sensible unless all possibility of cheating can be eliminated.

Cornering speeds have consequently increased dramatically in recent years, especially on asphalt where tyre technology has complimented the 4WD advances to place drivers and co-drivers under considerable G-forces. The cockpit of Juha Kankkunen's Lancia in 1990 underlined the problems, the driver's legs restrained by padded bars which left Kankkunen with a tunnel into which he could slide his legs — racing car style.

His Lancia Delta Integrale 16V cannot any more be considered as the most sophisticated car on the market. The basic Delta floorplan is now over 10 years old, even if the Italians have churned out a succession of quick-build Deltas in batches of 5000 to qualify for rallying.

The Toyota Celica GT-Four, Mitsubishi's Galant VR-4, Mazda 323 4WD GTX, and the Subaru Legacy RS all feature newer chassis and as a consequence are generally considered to offer better inherent balance. Whereas the Deltas still understeer, and are often described by drivers as "nervous", those in Japanese machinery talk of the stability and neutral handling which helps them through the stages.

Such was the pace of change through 1990, that picking an outstanding car of the year is impossible. Toyota's

Competing under the colours of Lancia France, Bruno Saby should have been a contender for victory in the Monte Carlo Rally. But on one of the stages he knew best, on his home ground in the Grenoble area and where he had practised many times, he hit a kerb (which he said had not been present during reconnaissance). It cost him any chance of victory in his 15th Monte.

GT-Four would probably win a vote — power is considered to be almost as good as the Lancia, its chassis significantly better. But on the Acropolis, Prodrive introduced its Subaru with a flat four engine and lots of potential while on the 1000 Lakes there were new cars from Mazda and Ford. In fact, both the update from Achim Warmbold's Mazda workshops in Brussels and the Boreham headquarters of Ford were acknowledged as interim cars.

The 323 has always won marks in handling competitions, but both the regular drivers, Hannu Mikkola and Timo Salonen, have acknowledged that a capacity disadvantage compared with rivals was too much. Even this new car runs only a 1.8-litre turbo engine (the rest have 2.0-litre turbos) so for 1991 it still looks as if the drivers are going to have to compensate for a power deficiency. Ford meanwhile, have the Cosworth Sierra 4x4 (debuted on the 'Finnish Grand Prix' by Pentti Airikkala, Malcolm Wilson and Franco Cunico) featuring a unique seven-speed gearbox and intended for competition work until a four-wheel drive Cosworth Escort is homologated. Officially, that may still be 1992, but Ford executives were quick to capitalise on a debut win for the prototype

The drivers of the Mazda 323 4WD cars entered by Achim Warmbold's team needed real winter conditions if they were to stay with the leaders. The lack of snow meant they could only play supporting roles. Hannu Mikkola was forced to retire because of a transmission failure and Timo Salonon had to fight hard to retain eighth place — he managed by just 12 seconds — against attacks of the Peugeot 309 GTi driven by François Delecour, who did not have the aid of a turbo or four-wheel drive.

Between his reconnaissance and the start of the Monte Carlo Rally, Ari Vatanen competed in the Paris-Dakar, and so he was faced with a major problem of re-acclimatisation. After victories scored by Mikael Ericsson in the 1000 Lakes and Penti Airikkala in the RAC in 1989, the Mitsubishi Galant VR4s had a reputation to uphold. But Vatanen, like his team mate Kenneth Eriksson, was led down by his engine.

As was the case in the 1000 Lakes, the San Remo Rally, the 1989 RAC and again in the 1990 Monte Carlo, Carlos Sainz led the Portuguese Rally, taking over from his team mate Armin Schwarz, the victim of an "off". But reliability was again a problem, and Sainz had to retire only a few kilometres from the finish, transmission failure costing Toyota precious championship points.

Clearly off form in the Monte Carlo Rally, Miki Biasion regained all his motivation to score a brilliant win in the Portuguese Rally, for the third consecutive year. Didier Auriol (right) and Juha Kankkunen (opposite, top) completed a Lancia works team monopoly of the podium. The Integrales of Dario Cerrato and the local driver Carlos Bica completed an astonishing achievement for the Italian marque — for the first time one manufacturer took the top five places in a round of the World Championship.

Opposite, centre: Belgian driver Marc Duez drove with his customary verve in a Ford Sierra Cosworth in Portugal, finishing eighth and first in the (unofficial) two-wheel drive category.

The winner of the FIA Cup for drivers of production cars in 1989, and winner of the Ivory Coast Rally (the first win by a Group N car in a Championship round) Alain Oreille (opposite, bottom) had a fuller programme in 1990. Second in class in the Monte, he could not better fifth in Portugal.

on a Spanish Championship event in September, rushing the car back overnight to place it on desplay at the British Motor Show.

There were others as well: Volkswagen took some hesitant but positive steps with the supercharged Rallye Golf G60 on a few events, and while Nissan may not have quite made it into battle in 1990, they had so many 'casual' observers on later events that pundits are already talking of the little Pulsar GTiR (under development with former World Champion, Stig Blomqvist) as a car for the future.

Back in the spring of 1990, however, experience was bringing dividends, and further heightening the tension within the World series. Lancia's incredible team knowledge helped them dominate in Portugal, while Toyota success on the Marlboro Safari Rally at Easter was in no small way due to the efforts of veteran Björn Waldegård.

Lancia's win was awesome in many ways: apart from the driver's expertise there was a major contribution, too, from Michelin's remarkable ATS (run-flat) tyres which allow a driver to take incredible liberties with his car on rough, stoney ground.

Miki Biasion won the event, but Lancias filled the top five places with Martini team mates Didier Auriol and Juha Kankkunen second and third, followed by Dario Cerrato and Carlos Bica. Hannu Mikkola took sixth for Mazda and Toyota stumbled, youngster Armin Schwarz crashing out and Carlos Sainz eliminated by transmission problems in the later stages.

The Spaniard was not entered on the Safari, most considering it impossible to give 100 per cent to the cluster of European special stage rallies which are grouped around Kenya's Easter classic. So while Sainz departed Portugal and concentrated on the Tour de Corse, Ove Andersson renewed friendships with Bjorn Waldegard and Fred Gallagher, the partnership which was at the centre of TTE during its African campaigns some five years earlier.

The brief was to win, and while Lancia confidence was on a high — Miki Biasion aiming for his hat-trick and Lancia flew out hosts of guests to witness the occasion — the rainy season was about to throw its wild card into proceedings. For the first time in recent history, rally supremo Mike Doughty (who would resign his position later in the year) had cars in mudholes, cars stuck in ruts and competitors really struggling to avoid being time-barred.

It was a real Safari and it demanded cunning, an understanding of this wild country and luck. Lancia director Claudio Lombardi found it too much to believe that the lead Toyota had escaped one particular mudhole while his men had sunk up to their axles. With advisors at the ready, he prepared to protest the route used by Waldegard & Co to skirt the trouble spot, but ultimately he withdrew and Toyota was back in the championship hunt.

For Waldegard this was a quite special moment. The

Mission accomplished for Kenjiro Shinozuka, whose Mitsubishi Galant VR4 finished the Safari in fifth place.

A last-minute entry, Carlos Sainz (above) was on his first Safari. His fourth place was meritorious and brought him ten points towards the World Drivers' Championship, which Toyota saw as possible goal. All three Toyota Celica GT4s, entered for the first time in an African rally, finished.

Didier Auriol will always remember the Tour de Corse as a happy event: in 1989, his son Robin was born, and in 1990, for the third consecutive time, he won the rally. With wins in two rounds, plus a second place in Portugal, he could look towards the 1990 title.

Victory for Didier Auriol (top right) came only after another tough battle with Carlos Sainz, and could have slipped away in the final stages. But he was well served by his mechanics, and luck was with him rather than with Sainz.

THE LADIES TAKE THE STAGE

Michele Mouton's impact on international rallying was considerable. The French star notched up the first victory for the Quattro on a Manufacturers round of the World series and came so close to winning the 1982 World Championship with Audi.

When she retired there was a void until the formation of the FIA Ladies Cup for 1990, and a couple of pretenders to Michele's crown emerged on stage.

The two — Paola de Martini from Italy and Louise Aitken-Walker from Scotland — had clashed a year earlier in the European series and essentially the squabble for the World title was a re-run of that contest: de Martini in a private Audi Quattro versus Aitken-Walker in a works run Vauxhall Astra GTE.

The Astra/Kadett obviously had a highly professional team in attendance — essentially preparing the groundwork for the future should their four-wheel drive car receive the go-ahead — but it was only front-wheel drive. The Italians had four-wheel drive and Italian enthusiasm on their side as the ladies prepared for Monte-Carlo — where both would open their bids. Blue skies over the Maritime Alps meant de Martini's team had reason to curse because the dry tarmac roads favoured the Vauxhall, Aitken-Walker capitalising on her previous experience of the event to scoop another Coupe des Dames with an impressive 11th position overall.

If that left the Scots girl — who grew up on a farm in the border country near the town of Duns where both Jim Clark and Andrew Cowan were born — on a high, then the Portuguese qualifier underlined the dangers involved.

Squally showers were breaking out in the early moments of the Rally of Portugal when the Vauxhall skidded off the tarmac, down an enormous drop into deep water. Remarkably, both driver and co-driver, Christina Thorner, swam to the surface but it was a lucky escape and hardly ideal preparation for the duo's next event, Corsica where the drops are even bigger.

De Martini was into the best part of her year — maximum points in Portugal and Corsica (where her rival failed to score due to mechanical failure). But then the pendulum swung against her just as it had done one year earlier when she lost the Euro title in the closing months. Retirement in Greece, a disastrous Argentine outing, a finish outside the all-important top 20 on the 1000 Lakes and another failure in Australia left her an uphill battle to face in the final rounds. Aitken-Walker, meanwhile, notched up maximum scores in both New Zealand and Australia, to approach San Remo and the Lombard RAC with confidence. But whether either girl can truly claim to be the equal of Mouton, only time will tell.

Dominating the French Rally Championship, François Chatriot (BMW M3) was among the favourite for the Tour de Corse. But Chatriot, seen here in the fabulous Calanche de Piana, could not repeat his 1989 winning exploit and had to settle for third place. At least he was ahead of his national rival, Bruno Saby.

In Corsica, Carlos Sainz was still seeking his first victory in the World Championship. Five times in the seven years he has competed in the event he had led it, but each time he has had to settle for a place finish.

inaugural World Rally Champion (back in 1979), his future was effectively with the Peugeot/Citroen Rally Raid programme and he took great satisfaction from this one-off appearance which saw him notch up win number 16 in his own personal World Championship career.

Another interesting aspect of this success was that — prior to the San Remo Rally — it was the only such success by a member of the old guard in the whole of the World Championship campaign. Messrs Mikkola, Salonen, Vatanen and Blomqvist — the names so dominant through the eighties — had at last been forced to make way for the new generation. Kankkunen (31 years old) and Biasion (32) are both established World title holders, but interestingly the title fight approaching the fifth round of the 1990 series was between two uncrowned heroes: Auriol and Sainz.

The next stop was Corsica, where the regular stars were again ready for the fray. More than any other event, the all-tarmac Tour de Corse has in recent years found itself heavily criticised from a safety point of view. The deaths of Attilio Bettega and Henri Toivonen plus Sergio Cresto have forever left their mark, and teams know only too well the dangers of racing speeds on a mountainous Mediterranean island.

It is probably the most specialised event in the series and for those in two-wheel drive cars it remains the only truly competitive arena left in which they can even dream of success. Bernard Beguin and Auriol won respectively with a BMW M3 and a Ford Sierra Cosworth in 1986 and 1987 but in truth Francois Chatriot — the lead man for Prodrive's BMW team — knew he was on a hiding to nothing.

So it proved, with Auriol notching up his hat-trick but only after a nerve-racking duel with Sainz and surviving

In the Acropolis Rally, the Ralliart-Europe Mitsubishi Galants had their third outing of the season. Once again, the efforts of the team managed by Andrew Cowan were unsuccessful, Kenneth Eriksson being let down by his turbo and Ari Vatanen (below) going off the road.

After many disappointments, Carlos Sainz finally triumphed in Greece (left). In a rally which tested suspensions and engines to the limit, the Spanish driver was worried until the final moments, but this time there were no small problems to delay him, as has been so often the case in the past. His talent and the qualities of the Toyota Celica finally came together in a long-overdue victory.

After Didier Auriol's retirement and the problems encountered by Massimo Biasion, Juha Kankkunen (below) was the only driver in the Lancia team able to trouble Carlos Sainz. He tried everything he knew, but in vain.

a late differential failure. Behind the scenes there was much more to it however. Of course, there was the tyre war, Michelin and Lancia believing that they had the slightest edge over their Pirelli rivals on the Toyota, and there was a potential horrific moment which left Sainz and co-driver Luis Moya with the fright of their life. At high speed they had to avoid a local car which was on the road, mid-stage.

Bearing in mind the rally's record and the fact that the Corsican roads offer absolutely no room for error, it was hardly surprising that the Spaniard's commitment took a bit of a shaking. The last time such an incident occurred to a lead driver was in New Zealand in 1986, when Markku Alen (in a Lancia) met a local pick-up head-on and was lucky to escape The rally lost its status in the Manufacturers championship.

When Sainz spoke about his problem after the event, the President of the FIA, M Jean-Marie Balestre, slammed him for being unsporting!

No one cancelled the stage, the affair was apparently pushed to one side, and rallying seemed to have escaped a major tragedy without really caring.

Many were discussing the potential consequences of that

Opposite: The VW Rallye Golf G60 made its second appearance in the World Championship in the Rally of New Zealand. In the hands of Erwin Weber it showed potential, but also the need for further development, notably in the transmission. Nevertheless, third place in the rally, won for the second successive time by Carlos Sainz, was encouraging for VW.

212

Jorge Recalde turned away from the FIA Cup for drivers of production cars to drive a car capable of an outright win at home in the Argentine Rally. His lack of experience with the Toyota Celica GT4 was the probable reason for a spectacular "off", happily without injuries. Recalde attempted to continue but the time lost and the state of the car meant that this effort was pointless.

Corsican near-miss when the circus re-grouped a couple of weeks later on the Greek coastline, with the Acropolis Rally in prospect. As with the Safari, this was one which the Italians must have approached with confidence but as in Kenya, Toyota would win the day with Pirelli's tyres proving more than capable of enduring those rough Greek tracks which have broken so many hopes over the years.

In many ways the mid-season Greek qualifier proved the turning point in the Drivers contest. Because while Sainz returned victorious, the man who pursued him to the finish for Lancia was not Auriol, but Juha Kankkunen. The Finn had at last cleaned out the cobwebs and strung together an impressive attack free of incident and mechanical failure.

Auriol, meanwhile, was contemplating an engine failure which left him on the retirement list. There is no question that Lancia reliability through 1990 did not match that achieved in earlier seasons, a consequence of the need to up the pace against the increased Eastern threat. Another technical problem would keep him behind Sainz in Argentina and then an accident at a time of high pressure in Finland effectively brought to an end his title

hopes for the season. So good on asphalt, he is more susceptible on loose surfaces — Lancia's mechanics have rebuilt a few shells for the Frenchman in recent years. Sainz, in contrast, kept adding up the points and benefitted from the TTE push in the Drivers series — historically the half of the World Championship which has stubbornly been ignored by the Italians over the years.

Effectively, New Zealand offered a very easy 20 points — no one else of particular note was present — and while it may have been a fairly expensive round-the-world trip for TTE, Sainz came back with a healthy championship advantage (although Lancia retained the advantage in the Manufacturers series, no points available for the Makes contenders in New Zealand).

And Sainz must soon have been very glad that the cash had been spent on that trip. His Argentine outing proved difficult with an atypical accident ultimately attributed to-co-driver Luis Moya turning over two pages of pace notes at once and sending the Toyota into a corner far too fast.

The Spaniards still finished and then headed non-stop to Finland for the rally which tests a driver's bravery like no

Miki Biasion again showed his tactical skill in winning the South American round of the championship. His knowledge of the route was an advantage, which allowed him to use his favourite tactic of attacking where he knew he could gain time, and then spare his car in the more difficult sections. The win was a boost for Lancia's hopes for the manufacturers' title, while with second place Sainz took a step towards the drivers' crown.

other. This was, perhaps, the scene of Sainz's greatest achievement, becoming the first non-Scandinavian ever to beat the assembled might of the Finns on home ground.

Predictably, the early opposition came from Kankkunen's Lancia which set the pace but was then delayed by a stuck throttle spring. It was a trivial failure, but a heart-breaking one as Juha has yet to win in front of his home crowds. However, further evidence of his own return to form came in September when he turned the tables on Sainz and Toyota by winning Rally Australia after a determined performance.

Headquartered in Perth, and contested around Western Australia the gravel roads comprise very small pellet-type stones so that handling is at a premium. Observers believed that the Finn actually held an advantage having driven on such roads before but irrespective of that fact this was a fine performance — which actually pushed him back into a mathematical chance of stealing the overall Driver's crown.

Of the others who must have hoped to be in that position at the start of the year, Miki Biasion — outgoing World Champion — only really dropped out of contention

Greatly delayed early in the event by a turbo failure, Didier Auriol (opposite) owed an unexpected third place finish to the immense superiority of his car over the local Renault 18 GTX and Fiat Regattas. After this seventh round, the Frenchman was the best placed Lancia driver in the title race.

The six Finns with a realistic chance of victory in the 1000 Lakes had recorded a total of 108 starts and 17 victories between them — but the event fell to Spanish driver Sainz, who won at his third try. Bad luck — a broken accelerator cable in his Lancia — hit Juha Kankkunen (right) and dropped him back to fifth. After 10 attempts, the double World Champion has still not won his home classic. Ari Vatanen (below) finished an excellent second for Mitsubishi. Timo Salonen (bottom), who finished sixth, and Hannu Mikkola were at last able to fight on equal terms with their rivals in the new and more powerful Mazda 323.

Despite customary bad weather, the 1000 Lakes produces remarkable photographs, such as the picture (left) of the Group N Lancia driven by Argentine Ernesto Soto. The rally's timing means that it can accept newly homologated cars to enrich an entry list which is always one of the best in the Championship, and its innumerable "yumps" make the event highly spectacular. Apart from the Mazda, the Ford Sierra Cosworth 4x4 (below, Malcolm Wilson's car) made its first appearance in Finland, but the debut was disappointing for none of the three cars finished.

Second place in Rally Australia virtually assured Carlos Sainz (opposite) of the World Championship. The title was a fitting reward for his excellent season, and recompense for earlier performances dogged by bad luck.

Although the new 1840cc Mazda 323 had been newly homologated, the team used the older version in Australia, brought directly from the Rally of New Zealand. Ingvar Carlsson (top) finished fifth, while Grégoire de Mevius, sixth, was handicapped by communications problems with his Swedish navigator Arne Hertz, Hannu Mikkola's usual co-driver — this meant he did not drive to his limits.

Juha Kankkunen was a winner again in Australia at the wheel of the Lancia Delta Integrale. The double World Champion had not wasted champagne since the previous Rally Australia, which he won with Toyota. The result gave him a slim mathematical chance of beating Sainz, had Lancia not made the Constructor's title their priority. The Finn had to win all the last three events, including the Ivory Coast Rally which counted only for the Driver's title and was not included in Lancia's programme.

when a slipped disc demanded treatment in late summer, forcing him to miss the 1000 Lakes and Australia. Alex Fiorio was never a fancied runner in the overall competition, and had a disappointing season with the Jolly Club semi-official Lancia.

Under the Toyota flag, Armin Schwarz showed promise on his occasional outings and is tipped for greater things in the nineties, but Swede Mikael Ericsson had a number of upsetting runs. Perhaps his troubles only served to underline the immense talent which Sainz obviously has, but he wanted to establish himself against the Spaniard in 1990.

Mitsubishi scored a couple of major wins a year earlier — on the 1000 Lakes and the RAC Rally — but it was the second half of 1990 before they looked complete. Ari Vatanen and Kenneth Eriksson are at opposite ends of their careers and sometimes it showed, although when it all came together in Finland there was an indication of what they are capable of. Vatanen, more motivated than for years, finished only 19 seconds behind Sainz while Eriksson was third, the young Swede's first result of the season.

Mazda had another slimline programme, with former World Champions Timo Salonen and Hannu Mikkola doing most of the work, but with Ingvar Carlsson and young Belgian Gregoire de Mevius playing supporting roles. The new car in Finland helped Salonen to fifth place and while the squad is obviously much-improved, the technical specification of the car still leaves it with a horsepower deficiency.

Subaru represents an interesting addition to the Championship cast, and while the Legacy RS appeared fairly frequently it is too early to measure the impact it will have on future competitions. By mid-1990 Subaru had wound up its Formula 1 connections and committed itself to the Prodrive operation run by former World Champion co-driver, David Richards, who had hired Markku Alen to drive. There is no questioning the expertise within Prodrive's HQ, Richards could well turn the compact outfit into a world-beater.

It is also difficult to fully assess the potential of Volkswagen's Rallye G60 which the talented Erwin Weber used on a few occasions. This was a toe-in-the-water exercise for the Germans through 1990, but the super-charged Golf will need an intense development programme thrown at it if the promise is to be turned into a Lancia-beating reality.

SAINZ – MAKING HISTORY

With the Spanish flag draping their Toyota Celica GT-Four on the winner's rostrum, Carlos Sainz and Luis Moya could afford to smile. Because this was no ordinary victory, this was the podium of the 1000 Lakes Rally — the event which demands the greatest commitment, the greatest speed. Never before had a non-Scandinavian won and at the winner's press conference, Sainz spoke about his feelings.

"When I was young, I watched television and saw drivers like Ari (Vatanen) and really wanted to be able to drive like a Finn," he explained. "Years have passed and now we are here, no one can understand what that means to us." Yet the Finns did understand and they saluted the victor.

That in itself was a tribute to the man's character for he had won admiration not only for that aggressive, spectacular style behind the wheel, but for his enthusiasm for the competition, the country, the sport.

In a couple of short years he has taken rallying by storm, learning lessons quickly to emerge as the hottest property on the driver market, bar none. It is an achievement which has hardly surprised his family, Carlos — now 28 — and a sports freak from the start moved into motor sports just as soon as he could. The rally debut was in 1980 and the progress was swift, perhaps first making an impression at the wheel of a Ford Sierra RS Cosworth in Portugal.

Then came the move to Toyota for 1988, a bundle of promise in 1989, and that first major victory on the Acropolis Rally in 1990 while under immense pressure from Juha Kankkunen — the man who fondly nicknamed him 'Matador'. Carlos also won in New Zealand and then took that historical victory in Finland so that Toyota Team Europe boss, Ove Andersson, started to smile.

Second place in Australia put the 1990 World Drivers Championship almost beyond doubt, and Andersson must have reflected on the events of exactly one year earlier when Juha Kankkunen severed his long-standing Toyota links to sign for Lancia in 1990. It was at a time when Andersson was desperately trying to turn TTE into a winning outfit and the last thing he needed was a vote of no confidence from his lead driver. Then Sainz gave him hope, starring on San Remo, almost winning the RAC Rally and recharging Andersson's batteries so much that the team boss commented: "You never know, perhaps Lancia got the wrong man..."

Those words, one year on, have been justified perhaps even beyond Andersson's wildest dreams. His Spanish star has not only won events, but been the driving force behind the whole team, restoring to TTE its spirit and that all-important will to win, so ensuring that Toyota can look forward to a strong rallying future.

Tyres are as decisive in rallying as in Formula 1, and nowadays are also pre-heated. In Australia, Michelin coped with the unique terrain, sand covered by small pebbles, by removing some of the tyre tread, allowing the pebbles to become embedded in the tyres. Experience surprisingly showed that contact between the pebbles in the tyres and those on the road gave the best grip, and Michelin won its 90th World Rally Championship victory, as its withdrawal came nearer.

For the first time since 1983, the World Rally Championship was decided at the San Remo Rally. Didier Auriol (opposite) scored a stylish victory to give the Lancia Delta its fourth consecutive title.

Toyota now is clearly on equal terms with Lancia. After a brilliant and hard-fought season, Carlos Sainz (below) finished third in the San Remo to clinch the title of World Champion Rally Driver. Mikael Ericsson (opposite, bottom) and the rising star Armin Schwarz also showed in Italy that they could be among the main contenders in 1991.

Under Howard Marsden in Milton Keynes, a Nissan operation is rapidly taking shape. If homologation proceeds as planned the Pulsar could be run in a two-car four-event programme in 1991, and a massive attack on the World titles for the following year.

That commitment for the future only really became evident after FISA reaffirmed its intention to stick with Group A. Renault, which had hoped for a return to prototype rallying, looked certain to stay on the fringes of the sport as a consequence. Recent years have seen the marque in the production car — Group N — category and 1990 was no exception, with Alain Oreille one of the stars of a second division series.

The rules are basically as those for the main series, and it largely attracted young bloods. Support came from South America — Gustavo Trelles, Ernesto Soto and Jorge Recalde all running Lancias and up against Oreille's Renault 5 GT Turbo. Later, Tommi Makinen (no relation to the Finnish star of the sixties and seventies) emerged, teamed with former World Champion co-driver Seppo Harjanne, and took his Mitsubishi Galant VR-4 to a string of successes.

There is no question that for such young men there will be many more opportunities to make their mark in the nineties. Cesare Fiorio, for so long the driving force behind Martini Lancia, once remarked that with the supercars it was impossible to risk using an unknown driver, but with Group A a manager could gamble a bit. The four years since that switch towards Group A have, indeed, seen a whole new breed of young drivers emerge — a trend which has added an exciting new dimension to rallying and, hopefully, other Scandinavians will follow Makinen's example — it is somehow quite unthinkable to consider a World Rally Championship without the next generation of Swedes and Finns.

The International Rally Championship, later the World Rally Championship for Manufacturers, seriously undermined the European Championship, which had enjoyed great prestige from its introduction in 1953. The later creation of a drivers' title further eroded the importance of the European series, and as the 1990s opened this occupied an uneasy position between national and World championships.

Since 1980 Robert Droogmans' name has appeared regularly in the top placings of the European Championship, but he had to wait until 1990 to take the title. After driving Fords (Escort, RS200 and Sierra) and Porsches, he opted for Lancia. It had to be the right choice, given that the Italian car had dominated the championship since 1983.

EUROPEAN RALLY CHAMPIONSHIP

IN THE SHADOWS

ANDRÉ MARZOLI

Rallying was a natural sporting activity for the owners of early automobiles, and while there may be some controversy about its origins as an organized motor sport the first of all motor sport events, the 1894 Paris-Rouen, had more in common with a rally than the race which historians tend to call it — indeed, it was proclaimed as a regularity trial more associated with travel or tourism than with competition. The early city-to-city races also had features that placed them nearer to rallying in the modern sense than to racing — interval starts, riding mechanics, routes on public highways with neutralized sections, and so on.

Then came the 1904-06 Herkomer Trophies, which were unquestionably rallies, and the subsequent Prince Henry and Austrian Alpine Trials which were the direct forerunners of modern rallies — the Alpine event included tests on mountain passes. Both attracted works teams from companies such as Austro-Daimler — their 1910 Prince Henry cars were prepared by the redoubtable Ferdinand Porsche — and even Rolls-Royce, whose team did well in the 1913 Alpenfahrt.

By that time the rally that was to become the most famous of all had been run for the first time, although it has to be admitted that the Monte Carlo Rally was created in 1911 to attract tourists, away from its rival and neighbour Nice, and in the off season. It was a leisurely affair, with its only tests at Monte Carlo and the outcome being decided on 'comfort marks'. There were only 20 starters, and after the 1912 event it was dropped until 1924. In the Edwardian period it was a run for gentlemen, sometimes driven by their chauffeurs, and there was no question of manufacturers' teams running in it... that was to change completely, while the great events of that first era of rallying were to fade away.

There were great rallies in the 1930s, the Austrian Alpine and the Marathon de la Route among them, but the Monte Carlo increasingly caught the public imagination. But in terms of length, difficulty and challenges to stamina the Liege-Rome-Liege, once the Marathon de la Route and destined to end in 1964 as the Liege-Sofia-Liege, springs to mind as the toughest. When it was at its peak in the 1950s and early 1960s the number of rallies was increasing rapidly, and organizers competed to make their events more difficult, with speed tending to overshadow thoughts of regularity. Manufacturers responded, too, as rallying generated increased interest at a time when the automobile was really becoming the means of mass transport in Europe.

But at the same time, the first difficulties with obaining permission to use roads essential to rallies were developing and the use of special stages on closed public roads was developed. This period saw the introduction of some of the events that are now regarded as classics, the heart of rallying: the Swedish Rally in 1950, the 1000 Lakes and the RAC Rally — which had been a national event from 1932 to 1939 — the following year, the Acropolis in 1952, the Safari Rally in 1953 and the Tour of Corsica in 1956. Over most of Europe rallying flourished and it became increasingly evident that a

formal championship structure was needed. Thus, three years after the introduction of the Formula 1 World Championship, the first European Rally Championship was created.

In that year, 1953, ten events formed the first European Champonship series, the title being only for the drivers, as it was to be until 1967. The development of the championship was not without its problems. If events like the Monte Carlo, Liege-Rome-Liege or the Coupe des Alpes were well established and well run, the organizers of others still had to prove that their events were worthy (and the changing nature of the sport and everyday motoring meant that some disappeared). Another preoccupation was to enable cars of all types and of performance capabilites to compete in the same event. Each rally had its own method. It was not until 1965 that the idea of an outright winner was generally adopted. In 1968 the European Championship for Makes was introduced, and this was the forerunner of the International Championship, established two years later and becoming the World Championship in 1973.

Since the 1970s, the European Championship has thus had to find new attractions in order to survive in the

shadow of the World series, in which interest developed rapidly. The exploits of Germany's Helmut Polenski, the first European Champion at the wheel of a Porsche, were long in the past. While the drivers had been the title winners in Europe, manufacturers won the glory in the International and then World competitions. From 1970 to 1976, until the creation of the FIA Drivers' Cup, the forerunner of the World Championship for Drivers, the European series was the place for drivers to make names for themselves. It was the era which saw the rise of stars such as Jean-Claude Andruet, Rafaele Pinto, Sandro Munari, Walter Rohrl, Maurizio Verini and Bernard Darniche, who succeeded the generation led by the likes of Gunnar Andersson, Tom Trana, Rauno Aaltonen, Pauli Toivonen and Harry Kallstrom.

The increasing number of events led the sporting authorities to apply coefficients from 1975, according to the status of the event. The oldest rallies got the maximum coefficient (4) while those created more recently got a coefficient of 1. This procedure remained in effect until 1987 with the number of events peaking at 50 between 1984 and 1986, run in some 20 countries, and with only eight having the 'right' to coefficient 4 (compe-

titors could count only their eight best results at the end of the season). That system invited rivalry among organisers and led them to improve their events. Thus the Garrigues Rally which became a European Championship event in 1982 'rose through the ranks' to achieve coefficient 4 in 1986.

But it was becoming increasingly clear that interest in the European Championship was declining steadily, with only a handful of competitors seriously going after the title. The 1983 season really showed this up.

Massimo Biasion was then building his reputation and after two seasons with Opel, he had joined the Jolly Club team. Six wins and a second place, driving the Lancia 037 in seven high-coefficient events, virtually sealed his European Championship with 16 rallies still on the calendar. His domination was such that he was entered for the final rounds of the Italian championship, which he also won. None of his rivals were really interested in the European title. Guy Frequelin finished second to Biasion only because of points scored in French Championship events which also counted in the European series, like Spain's Antonio Zanini, who placed third, and competed basically in his own national events, though he

Droogmans' only obvious opponent early in the season was his fellow Belgian Patrick Snijers (below, in the Costa Smeralda Rally) but he was quickly soon out of the running. Eventually only two other Lancia drivers, Tabaton and Cerrato, were possible challengers to the Jolly Club driver.

ventured out once to win the Golden Sands Rally in Bulgaria.

Only once in 45 events counting for the championship did the top three, and Jimmy McRae, who placed fourth, all compete in the same rally, the Halkidikis in Greece — ironically, all four retired. For Biasion, however, the European Championship did prove a real springboard to the World Championship series.

The following years saw a Lancia monopoly develop while the domination by Italian drivers, which had started in 1981, continued unchecked with the 037 (Carlo Capone in 1984, Dario Cerrato in 1985) and then the Delta S4 (Fabrizio Tabaton in 1986) and the Delta HF 4WD (Dario Cerrato again, in 1987).

With the laudable objective of strengthening the interest in a declining championship, FISA instituted a new system of coefficients in 1988. The effect was simply to increase the interest in the ten leading rounds of the series, which were given coefficients of 20. It may have been good for the leading rallies, which entry lists burgeoning, but it certainly was not for the other events which were mostly reduced to the level of national rounds. Driving the Lancia Delta Integrale and thanks to

a considerable number of good place finishes, Tabaton won the title again despite not scoring a single victory; the runner-up, Belgian Patrick Snijers, won twice. The two men were on almost equal terms, Snijers with 1380 points and Tabaton with 1340, before the last coefficient 20 event. If the BMW M3 driver had not retired from the Cyprus Rally, they would both have had to take part in the final (low coefficient) events to decide the title.

So the rules were changed again for 1989, with the coefficients fixed henceforth be 20, 10, 5 and 2. As in 1988, it was a two-horse race, this time with Yves Loubet entered to defend Lancia's colours. But what was an apprenticeship for Biasion looked more like relegation for the Corsican driver, his only opponent being the Belgian, Robert Droogmans. The result of the duel between the Lancia and the Ford Sierra Cosworth was indecisive for much of the year, but ended in anti-climax. Droogmans retired from the Manx Rally and decided not to compete in Cyprus, the final coefficient 20 event. Loubet, whose parallel efforts in the World Championship had proved fruitless, was crowned Champion of Europe to near-general indifference.

On the ground, the drivers had fought hard and well in

The creation of the World Championship for Constructors in 1979 took much of the prestige away from the European competition. With only two victories (in the Boucles de Spa and the Halkidikis Rally), Jochi Kleint (below) became the first champion of this "new era" when he beat Spain's Antonio Zanini, who was to take the title in 1980.

With some 50 rounds of the championship taking place throughout the year, all types of terrain and weather conditions can be encountered. There has even been snow on the Costa Brava Rally in February, as shown by this shot of Carlos Sainz' Renault Maxi 5 Turbo in 1986.

The special regulations of the Belgian Championship, permitting competitors to score points abroad, allowed Marc Duez (right, in the 1986 24 Heures d'Ypres with the MG Metro 6R4) to contest some of the most prestigious rounds of the European Championship.

Twice World Champion, Massimo Biasion forged his reputation in the European Championship. With a Lancia 037 of the Jolly Club, the team which he had just joined (here in the San Marino Rally), he won the title handsomely in 1983 with seven victories. Several of them were far from easy, but the overall lack of competition during the season detracted from the excellent performances by the rising Italian star.

Riding the wave of his victories in the 1985 RAC and the 1986 Monte, Henri Toivonen won the 1986 Costa Smeralda Rally (above). The Lancia-Martini team sends one of its drivers to compete in Sardinia each year, even if he is not in contention for the title. With the Rallye Catalunya-Costa Brava, this Italian island event is one of the landmark rallies of the season because of the impressive entry list.

The Championship even brought an American driver to measure himself against the Europeans. John Buffum finished tenth in the Hunsrück Rally in Germany.

Winner in 1986 and 1988 with the Lancia Delta S4, second in 1985 and fourth in 1989, Fabrizio Tabaton (below) is an old hand in the European Championship, always with Lancia. While sporting director of the Grifone team, running Piero Liatti in the Italian Championship, he still drove in several rounds in 1990 (right, in the Rallye Catalunya-Costa Brava) and again achieved a top-three finish.

Droogmans this year entered all the maximum coefficeint rounds and scored points on every outing, building a strong lead over the whole field. (Right, centre: Droogmans in the Rallye des Garrigues, the French round run entirely on tarmac).

European Championship events are often ideal testing grounds for a new car before it is entered in World-ranking rallies. Thus when the VW Rallye Golf G60 was run in the Rallye Costa Smeralda in 1990 (opposite) it was up against a quality field.

TWENTY NATIONS

The European Rally Championship extends over 20 nations (21 if Italy and San Marino are considered separately) at a time when the 12-nation European Community, the 'independent' countries and those of Eastern Europe are moving closer together. The 11 nations which have a coefficient 20 round — a prime event in the series — are: Spain, France, Italy, Bulgaria, Belgium, Poland, Germany, Portugal, Greece, Britain and Cyprus, with Western Europe naturally hosting the majority of the rounds, reflecting the healthy state of motor sport. Italy alone organises six — which partly explains the domination of the series by Italians cars and drivers — Spain, France and Belgium have five, Germany four, and Britain and Portugal three each. Less favoured countries are the Netherlands, Norway and Austria (when there is one coefficient 2 rally), and Switzerland, Sweden and Turkey (one coefficient 5 event). The last six of the 48 events on the 1990 calendar were split between Yugoslavia, Finland and Czechoslovakia.

All kinds of routes are represented: asphalt, gravel and snow-covered roads, but in any event, only the rounds with the highest coefficient interest the rare contenders for the title. In certain countries, notably Belgium, the regulations for the national championship allow the inclusion of results achieved in foreign events. Those who can afford it or whose sponsors seek the exposure, thus contest chosen European events in which they can hope for a good result, and sometimes almost unintentionally gain an honourable placing in the European Championship.

The events which have most consistently retained the maximum coefficient are the Golden Sands Rally in Bulgaria, which has held it for nine years, and the Costa Smeralda in Sardinia which has been a top event for eight years. All eight rounds that had coefficient 4 status in 1987 were promoted to coefficient 20 under the new system and have maintained that status. The Rally Deutschland and the 24 Hours of Ypres were promoted to the top rank in 1988, as was the Polish Rally from 1989.

The record of victories is held by Lancia drivers, who have won the European Championship 14 times, against six for Porsche and four for Mercedes-Benz drivers. One driver won three times, Zasada (1966 in a Group 2 Steyr Puch, 1967 in a Group 1 Porsche, 1971 in a BMW), and five drivers won twice: Schock (1957 and 1960, Mercedes), Gunnar Andersson (1958 and 1964, Volvo), Darniche (1976 and 1977, Lancia), Cerrato (1985 and 1987, Lancia), and Tabaton (1986 and 1988, Lancia).

what was often a stirring battle which was reported only sparsely in the most specialised press. Was 1990 to prove a better vintage? At the start of the season only two drivers sought the title, both Belgians, Droogmans in a Lancia and Snijers in a Toyota. The latter, second in the championship in 1986, 1987 and 1988, saw his chances evaporate in a series of retirements and after eight of the 11 coefficient 20 rounds, Droogmans was already sure of taking the title.

It appeared at one time as if Cerrato, Droogmans, Jolly Club team mate, might try for the title after winning the Catalunya-Costa Brava Rally (one of the best organised rounds of the championship, which is aiming to become a World Championship round) and then the Costa Smeralda in Sardinia. But though he was continually a front runner, he could never seriously challenge Droogmans. Dutchman John Bosch in a BMW M3 also had designs on the title but could not match the pace of the Lancias which, for the eighth consecutive year, were the class cars. Once again, drivers like Mark Duez or Francois Chatriot, who were competing in their national championships, found themselves well placed in the European series, quite unintentionally. Only Duez competed in several rounds outside his home country, because the specific regulations of the Belgian Championship allowed the inclusion of points scored in the European Championship.

The lack of media exposure does little to encourage manufacturers to become consistently interested in the European series as a whole, their appearances being sporadic and confined to rounds with a high coefficient. Despite that, every weekend drivers battle against the clock from the first special stage to the last, indifferent to the general indifference. Even if the stars are professionals, paid for their efforts, they would undoubtedly like to see their achievements recognised.

The small number of drivers vying for the European title in recent years often allowed drivers competing in their national championship to record top finishes in the European series. Guy Fréquelin was second in 1983, as was François Chatriot (here on the Rallye des Garrigues in a BMW M3) in 1990.

Breaking the monopoly of Italian drivers which had lasted since 1981, Yves Loubet was Champion of Europe in 1989 at the wheel of a Team Grifone Lancia Integrale. Unhappily for the Corsican driver (shown here in the Rallye Catalunya-Costa Brava where he ran in works team colours), media attention did not match his achievements.

The US Secretary of Health and Human Services' proposal to ban tobacco advertising from sports struck a $100 million dollar nerve in the country's racing community. That is the amount tobacco companies are estimated to spend each year on motor sports in the USA. The timing of the announcement, while numerous racing series are in flux and just beginning to enjoy a prominence they have long sought, could not have been worse. As US sanctioning bodies seek new and larger markets outside national boundaries and others attempt to contain them within territorial limits, a multi-front war loomed ahead of the American racing industry. There is a growing demand for racing in the USA, though it is hardly indiscriminate, as F1 difficulties attest. The contrasting success of CART's new Denver and Vancouver street races suggests a regionalism that ignores the fact most of the series' hardware is made elsewhere. There are no US-built chassis, though Truesports plans one for 1991. A few American "stock-block" engines compete, primarily at Indianapolis where USAC rules allow them ten extra inches of boost. Early in 1990, CART, which sanctions the other 15 races, refused more.

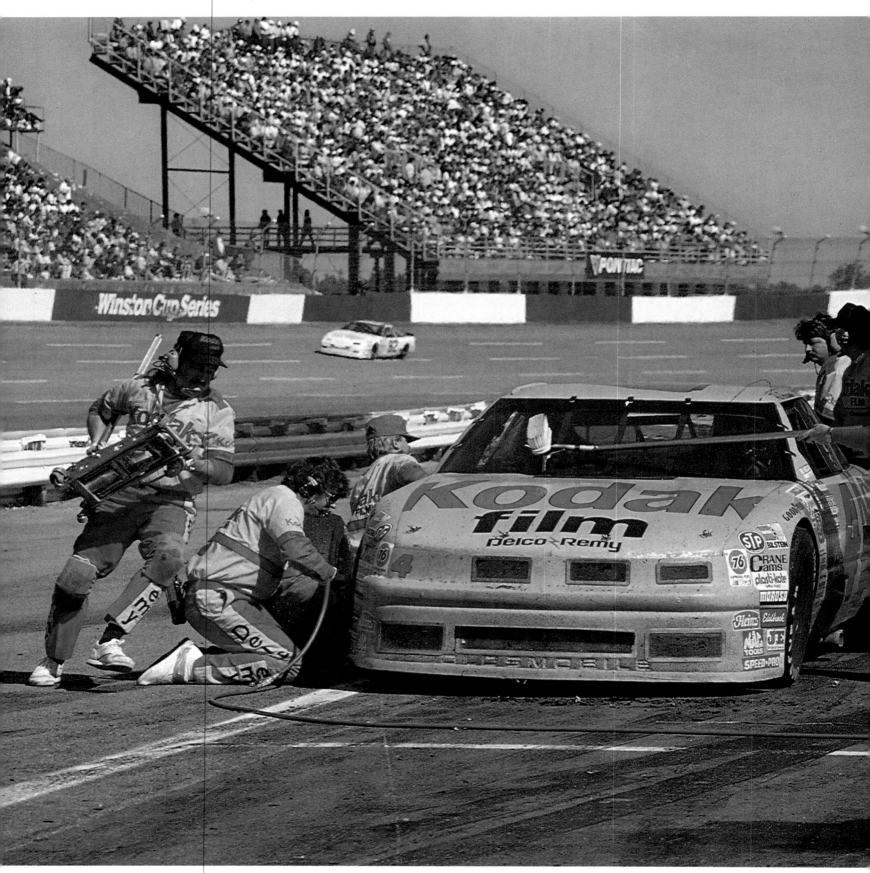

PRESSURE FROM WITHIN, PRESSURE FROM WITHOUT

RICK MILLER

England is the source of most of the machines and expertise. Without March, Lola, Cosworth ("Ford") and Ilmor ("Chevrolet"), CART would look very different indeed. Even Penske and newly-merged Galles-Kraco have English bases, while both Patrick and Ganassi Racing are preparing them. The presence of Porsche and Alfa Romeo proclaims CART's global status and with other world-class companies expected, the business cycle is typical of international trade: CART assembles its product from suppliers abroad, struggling to market it in the lands from which the parts come.

CART's Achilles' heel is a seeming inability to convince major US corporations of its importance. Porsche's difficulty in securing prime sponsorship after Moneytron's disappearance, coupled with their ultimate choice of Australian Foster's Lager, underscored the problem. A mid-field CART budget is about $6 million — two to three times that of a NASCAR contender, though CART has only about half as many races. Even if its TV ratings and attendance matched NASCAR's, which they do not, that is less value for the sponsors' money. Also, NASCAR telecasts are frequently twice as long as CART's. Predictably, most CART sponsors are auto industry-related.

Except for the Indianapolis 500, sanctioned by USAC, races receive little local or national news coverage. In the USA, pro sports is a buyer's market and sixteen events are too few for recurring programming and too many for individual significance. Numerous sports leagues with overlapping seasons and local appeal fill the time available. CART has responded to this with an innovative approach using cable television, which claims over 50 per cent of US households. In addition to time trial broadcasts, a three-year contract entails the airing of three separate 26-episode, half-hour TV series about CART.

The irony may be that to succeed in the USA, CART may first have to succeed abroad. Clearly, the international interest in racing, which existing series do not begin to satisfy, suggests that this is a real need for CART to have an international presence.

The FIA will reject that approach, but the extent of its authority remains to be seen. CART owes its existence to stubborn team owners who revolted against a similarly-domineering USAC, and is unlikely to be bullied, but the keys may be elsewhere.

CART's continuing vitality and determination, if occasionally misguided or unfocused, was demonstrated before the 1990 season when the more numerous smaller teams asserted themselves over previously dominant larger ones. CART's Board of Directors was enlarged from 11 members to 22 owners, and two new top administrators were hired. Since they will go head to head with the FIA over CART's expansion, the selection process was a crucial one. Only time will tell if new CEO A. William Stokkan, of Playboy Enterprises, and President John Capels, a former driver and team owner, are the men needed.

It will be difficult for even the strongest US sanctioning

227

Arie Luyendyk's popular Indianapolis 500 victory was worth $1.1 million, more than some top CART drivers won in the remaining 15 events combined. It was the first European victory since Jim Clark and Graham Hill won back-to-back 25 years ago, and Luyendyk found the success that eluded even Jackie Stewart.

Opposite: Numerous pit stops (and the lead changes that frequently result from them) add to NASCAR's appeal. The success of its Winston Cup division has heavily influenced other US racing series like IMSA GTO/GTU and SCCA Trans Am. Here, Phil Parson's Oldsmobile gets tyres and fuel at Rockingham.

Rick Mears in the Penske-Chevy 90, known outside the US as the PC19. After dominating the opening Phoenix race, Mears experienced a long dry spell that crippled his Championship hopes. One of the great oval track racers, he has proved he can win on any type of circuit, given a car up to the task.

Opposite, bottom: John Andretti, the son of Mario's twin brother Aldo, acquitted himself well in his season with the Porsche Motorsport team. He proved a worthy partner to Fabi, posting several top-five finishes and scoring more championship points. (Aldo was a noted driver before a racing accident shortened his career.)

body to achieve international status alone. Conversely, a partnership between CART, USAC, IMSA and NASCAR (supplying all forms of racing the FIA does and one it does not, NASCAR) could hardly fail. Playing a pivotal role in any outcome will be Indianapolis Motor Speedway President Tony Hulman George. Disenchanted with both CART and USAC, George's mid-year meeting with FIA heads caused speculation about his desire for growth beyond licensing the forthcoming Japanese 500-mile event to an international oval-track series.

The CART season

CART took a step toward safety by imposing regulation changes (to be in force through 1991) to reduce downforce and cornering speeds by reducing wing size and tunnel height. New chassis dimensions placed the driver further back, as in F1 earlier, but came too late for Scott Pruett. The young driver seriously injured his feet and back while testing an older car and missed the entire season, replaced by Raul Boesel.

While designers successfully incorporated the rule

changes into faster 1990 cars, teams with older chassis struggled to keep pace, and numerous wrecks resulted. The cars' balance had been altered, and previous data was useless. Under-financed teams were ill-equipped to deal with unknown cars, but a request to "run as designed" was denied by both CART and USAC.

Porsche, too, suffered. With rules prohibiting full carbon fibre tubs lapsing, March constructed one for them, but at a late date CART arbitrarily banned the proven method. Awaiting replacement chassis, Porsche raced modified 1989 cars, then developed its radical 1990 car (gearbox ahead of rear wheels, turbo ahead of engine) in competition. Engine compartment heat and excess weight from the substitute tub caused problems better discovered in testing. The resulting season raised doubts about Porsche's return, even as an engine supplier, borne out in September. Alfa Romeo, using separately-designed and built March chassis, purchased Lolas when results did not come. Guerrero immediately took fifth at Michigan, but a suspension failure led team mate Al Unser Sr. to have his worst-ever crash, breaking a leg, collarbone and three ribs.

Quick work prevented fires (from invisibly burning

Top: Michael Andretti showed a precision and speed that left many hungering to see him compete in Formula 1. That same anticipation which gives the younger Andretti a skill in traffic unmatched in CART will, however, prevent his leaving the US series unless assured of a competitive ride.

Above: The Lola-Chevrolet of Mario Andretti. Repeated mechanical failures again ruined his season. Once the most agressive of drivers, the champion now drives with a smooth, economical style belying his pace. Given a car capable of winning, he still charges, showing the change is from choice, not necessity.

methanol) involving Didier Theys and Al Unser Jr. from becoming disasters. Theys' occurred at Detroit, his sprained ankle exiting the car the main injury. Unser's came as he led Cleveland. He and four crew members were taken to hospital with minor burns. CART blamed human error and improper equipment maintenance.

The other fuel issue, consumption, brought criticism from drivers and critics alike. CART has long required engines to achieve 1.8mpg, allotting fuel on that basis. In qualifying, Chevrolet engines may give only 1.4mpg, necessitating "short-shifting" and lean mixtures during some races. Efficiency, even compared to NASCAR where cars sometimes achieve nearly 5mpg, is not the question. Fuel is power: whatever the limit, engines will use all of it.

Fully ten drivers had Chevrolet engines and the new Gen-III (Generation Three) management system developed in last year's Trans Am Berettas, from Indianapolis 500 "Rookie of the Year" Eddie Cheever to the renowned A.J. Foyt. Cheever, impressive in Fittipaldi's 1989 title-winning car, became a contender when Ganassi Racing bought him a new Lola. Foyt's driving ability remained, but lack of testing prevented results. Another legendary Texan, Jim Hall, whose Chaparrals won so many races for Chevrolet in the 1960s and 1970s returns with a 1991 Lola-Chevrolet.

Purchasing a Chevrolet engine and Gen-III software and coupling it to a new Lola with Pi data acquisition is not unlike buying a McLaren-Honda for Formula 1. Information obtained by sensors and accelerometers can be displayed on the digital dash and easily off-loaded, obviating investments in the telemetry Penske and Porsche use.

At the Phoenix opening race, the surprise was not that a Penske-Chevy 90 won — it had been testing six weeks longer than the rest — but that the Lola T90s were so competitive. The victory could have been due to Rick Mears' driving skill — it was his second in a row there and the next three cars were Lolas. Al Unser Jr. (T90) won the next race, his third in a row at Long Beach. While the Nigel Bennett designed Penske looked to be his best yet for CART's combination of oval, street and road circuits, it was a difficult car off slow corners and the Bruce Ashmore-designed Lola took five straight wins before Sullivan interrupted the streak at Cleveland.

The Penske "superteam" of Fittipaldi, Sullivan and Mears struggled through the season, qualifying poorly (for them) and racing inconsistently. Testing improved qualifying performance, but a race set-up proved elusive. The Lola-Chevrolets of Galles-Kraco (Al Unser Jr. and Bobby Rahal) and Newman-Haas (Michael and Mario Andretti) fully matched them.

The surprise, then, was not that a Lola-Chevrolet won the Indianapolis 500 (though it was Lola's first win there since 1978), it was that the driver was Dutchman Arie Luyendyk. Throughout May, while others fluctuated between 220mph and 228mph, he ran 224mph consistently. In the race, it was the same. Others used tyre pressures intended for qualifying and blistered, but Luyendyk ran flawlessly. Capable of 222mph laps on demand, he passed Rahal with 32 laps to go, and posted a convincing victory.

An extra Michael Andretti fuel stop gave Milwaukee to Al Unser Jr., but Michael fought back, winning Detroit, Portland and the Meadowlands amid rumors that he and Unser might go to F1. Unser chose three more years at Galles-Kraco, but Andretti remained a question mark despite having a season left on his contract. The importance of Unser's continuing presence was underscored by his record-breaking mid-season win streak, building a commanding points lead while others faltered.

When Alfa-Romeo struggled in the early season, the Patrick team was unable to tell where its problems lay because both the engine and March chassis were unique. Purchasing a 1990 Lola to use as a baseline, the team skipped Toronto to test it and arrived at Michigan with two of the cars in "speedway" trim. Early in the meeting, one of the cars, driven by Al Unser Sr., crashed heavily, apparently due to the high g-forces and rough 18-degree banking collapsing a front pushrod. Lola advised teams with similar cars to reinforce the parts as a precautionary measure and no similar problems occurred. In the race, Roberto Guerrero (shown here) took fifth place with the older long-stroke engine. The team persevered, looking forward to the arrival of the promising five-valve engine. Guerrero's talent, equalled only by his bad luck, showed through as he out-qualified and outran several Lola-Chevrolets.

Fierce determination and persistence

Worldwide, no series enjoys the diverse sponsorship NASCAR does. The presence of laundry detergents, beauty products, and health care money reflects research showing 40-50 per cent of its tremendously loyal fans are women. Originally concentrated in the south eastern States, professional NASCAR fans now cover the country. One wonders how a comprehensive agreement to televise the series globally via satellite would fare, but, ironically, no such "package" exists, each promoter

acting independently. The sale of Atlanta International Raceway to Bruton Smith, board chairman of Charlotte Motor Speedway, may lead to one.

Just as it is only a matter of time until NASCAR moves outside the USA, it is inevitable that non-US manufacturers will invade NASCAR. Although the rules call for cars to be US-built, many international companies have production capability in the States for trade reasons. NASCAR has said they may compete if they make a pushrod V8 engine, but it is unlikely the firms commonly mentioned (Honda, Nissan, Toyota) would take that backward step.

Should NASCAR adopt smaller V6 engines, however, which the car makers have and which NASCAR's junior Grand National circuit uses, the move would also address the problem of excessively high speeds. The influence of such manufacturers, who typically compete in other categories and would look to races in their home countries, would be invaluable to a series expanding internationally.

It is difficult to imagine a more competitive environment than NASCAR. Although severe technological restrictions result in the cars being somewhat dated with respect to component design, that is not to say they are ineffective. Except for two road course events, the series' banked tracks and smooth surfaces by and large eliminate the need for sophisticated suspensions and suspension geometry to control tyre movement, leaving only the questions of car balance and tyre usage to be explored. Over time, teams have made this a science. Their data logs, though sometimes hand-written instead of printed out by computer, are no less comprehensive than teams in other series. The strong, reliable engines produce more than enough power (it is equality, not supremacy, NASCAR seeks) and it is a team sport in every sense. Frequent pit stops and long races produce an environment where crew members take an active part in winning, or losing, races. The season, too, is long. At 29 races, with most tracks visited twice, there are two ways to view the battle: over the entire year the best-prepared team with the best drivers will win, or, with evenly-matched entrants, luck will decide the result. Typically, point of view varies with finishing position...

As the speeds go up, so does the cost of doing business, particularly that of insurance. Consequently, at super-speedways, NASCAR mandates use of four-hole "res-

forcing NASCAR to mandate rear spoiler angles be increased to at least 30 degrees at mid-year. The change was particularly damaging to Ford and Pontiac since Luminas already used higher settings.

NASCAR's year

Against the backdrop of the filming of *Days of Thunder*, partially based on the careers of former NASCAR driver Tim Richmond and crew chief Harry Hyde, Chevrolet's Lumina quickly became dominant. NASCAR is a "silhouette" series, however, so while the multi-decalled, hand-built aluminum bodies resemble their production counterparts, there the similarity ends: tubular frames and special engines are part of the package. Ernie Irvan's Bristol-winning Lumina, for example, began the year as an Oldsmobile.

A debris-induced tyre failure one-half mile from the end of the Daytona 500 robbed Dale Earnhardt of victory in a race he dominated. Another Lumina — Derrike Cope's — won, Cope proving it was no fluke by winning later at Dover. As the season progressed, Earnhardt, racing's all-time earnings leader (over $11 million) demonstrated

Goodyear continued to introduce radial tyres into Winston Cup racing on a track-by-track basis. The heaviest of any major series' machines, the stock cars are also devoid of aerodynamic assistance, their weight and slippage creating challenges markedly different from that of winged open-wheelers. The construction method's advantages are obvious, but the tyres require a different driving style. Not heating up as quickly as bias-ply tyres, for example, they cannot be driven hard as soon. In early races, low ambient temperatures caused frequent spins after restarts as drivers explored the differences.

trictor plates" between the huge four-barrel carburettors and intake manifolds. Already smaller than last year, the holes shrank again during the season. Reducing horse-power from an unrestricted 650bhp to below 450bhp, they threaten the competition for which the series is famous. Less power, coupled with the fact the cars are more aerodynamic in trains of three or four, means that a driver pulling out of line to pass is as likely to go backward as forward. Superspeedway passing attempts are now, therefore, calculated risks. Hand signals between drivers and agreements between crew chiefs result in impromptu (and short-lived) alliances for the purpose of mutually-benefitting enchanced aerodynamics and competitiveness.

The withdrawal for economic reasons of Hoosier Tire — after 11 wins in 2 years — meant that one decision, which tyre to use, was made for the competitors. Hoosier is working on a radial tyre, reportedly using a new material, and is expected to return in 1991. Goodyear, the sole supplier, continued introducing radial tyres, but the heavy stock cars were adapted far less easily than open-wheelers. Improved performance, however, partially offset restrictor plate reductions,

that unique talent could still make a difference. Despite mechanical problems and bad luck, strong performances, particularly on the superspeedways, kept him in the points chase. After losing last year's title by 12 points (in more than 4000), the team resolved to keep him on the track at all costs, several times returning him after problems that would have sidelined others.

Like Roger Penske's CART effort, Rick Hendrick's three-car Lumina "superteam" — for Ken Schrader, Ricky Rudd and Darrell Waltrip — was impressive in pre-season testing, but failed to achieve the results expected of it. Schrader won the pole at Daytona, starting 39th after a pre-race crash. In the race, he ran in the top five until his motor blew, and it foreshadowed his season. He drove well, but engine failures (a Hendrick rarity) kept him out of title contention. Ricky Rudd, Rusty Wallace's main competition on road courses, won at Watkins Glen, but had a disappointing season overall. At mid-season, Hendrick diversified to a fourth team, co-owned by actor Paul Newman (who also co-owns CART's Newman-Haas team), for primary *Days of Thunder* driver Greg Sacks. In their initial race, Sacks finished second to Earnhardt at Talladega and ran competitively thereafter. Three-time

Winston Cup Champion Waltrip, who bought his team at mid-year, sustained a concussion, broken thigh and elbow in the worst crash of his career, practising for the Pepsi 400, and was out of racing for two months.

Neil Bonnett suffered a concussion and memory loss after a Darlington accident and withdrew for an entire year, with Dale Jarrett (son of former NASCAR star and TV commentator, Ned) taking over from him. The injuries to Bonnett and Waltrip, sustained in devastating multi-car wrecks reminiscent of the *Days of Thunder* crash, proved the cars were not fully up to protecting the drivers in the close racing.

Of the Ford Thunderbird runners, Mark Martin was the most consistent, frequently leading the "tortoise and hare" title fight, but winning few races compared to Earnhardt. Martin's Richmond-winning car received NASCAR's largest-ever fine, $40 000 for running an illegal carburettor spacer, after Roush Racing's appeal was denied. The sanction, amid allegations of other violations, also cost Martin a much-needed 46 of his win's 180 points. Bill Elliott had another disappointing season, but should be a threat in 1991. Davey Allison followed in his father Bobby's tyre tracks, winning at Bristol for the first

INVESTING IN THE FUTURE

CART's Australian ties, prominent Foster's sponsorship and the points-paying Queensland race scheduled to open its 1991 season, are obvious. NASCAR's, potentially even more extensive, are less apparent. Australia's presence in NASCAR increased this year, largely courtesy of Bob Jane (owner of the country's Calder Park Thunderdome), and probably foreshadows further ties between the two nations' racers and sanctioning bodies. Jane took a number of Australian drivers to the US to experience NASCAR competition, as well as two NASCAR-specification cars (a Holden Commodore and Ford Falcon) to stage a demonstration run. Even more significantly, a US base from which Australian teams may operate is being established, and the hope is that the experience and knowledge gained while competing will later be returned home, to the benefit of all involved. Jane's far-sighted, long-run thinking is a rarity in the sport at any level.

Australian Touring Car Champion Dick Johnson once again commuted between the countries to drive in NASCAR, but experienced a lack of results belying his talent; improved sponsorship could change that. Other visiting drivers included Robin Best, Terry Byers, Kim Jane and Terri Sawyer.

NASCAR's stock cars are neither truly "stock," as the name suggests, nor high-tech, but somewhere in between. Tube frames, analog gauges and 6-litre V8 engines comprise the rolling chassis onto which a hand-built aluminum body is painstakingly assembled. This is Bill Elliott's Thunderbird. NASCAR typifies the struggle in some US series against advancing technology. IMSA GTO/U and SCCA Trans Am have limited data gathering and data processing in hopes of imitating NASCAR's success. Enhanced competition and improved cost control are the ultimate aims of the movement.

Opposite, top: Racing for the first time with team owner Roger Penske, 1989 Championship winner Emerson Fittipaldi seemed likely to repeat his success. But the PC19 chassis proved difficult to balance over race distance, though, and the few times it was absolutely right, generally on oval tracks, mechanical failures let him down.

Belgian Didier Theys was impressive on road circuits and at Indianapolis where his Buick engine was more on terms with the competition. His 1988 Lola, when altered to CART's revised tunnel specifications, generated less downforce than new cars, but even so he often finished in the top ten.

Bottom: Arie Luyendyk's Shierson Team chose to concentrate early season effort on Indianapolis, forsaking road course testing. He won there, but found life difficult for several races afterward as the team sorted out its sensitive new Lola. His fourth place at Meadowlands marked their return to competitiveness.

Opposite, bottom: Vince Granatelli, owner of Theys' car, was in the center of major battles over allowing pre-'90 chassis to run as designed and permitting additional inches of boost for stock-block engines. USAC continued to grant extra boost at Indianapolis, but denied the chassis request. CART refused both pleas. Granatelli's voice was that of the smaller owner seeking to preserve the less commercial form of the sport. Admittedly, he had a vested interest in the result, but so did everyone else. His plight demonstrated the way CART is becoming manufacturer-based, leaving non-allied teams uncompetitive.

NASCAR's reputation for excitement was further enhanced by its closest-ever Championship fight, with the Thunderbird of Mark Martin leading most of the season. A patient, consistent racer, Martin frequently worked his way up from mid-field starting spots to top-five finishes.

Trans Am driving champion Tommy Kendall (here in his Chevrolet Beretta) is progressing steadily to the higher formulae. After clinching his SCCA title early, Kendall then tried NASCAR, but found the going difficult. One of the US' most promising young drivers, the 24 year-old's next stop is uncertain.

BALANCING ACT: SILHOUETTE WARS

NASCAR's success has heavily influenced both SCCA Trans Am and IMSA GTO.

The two nearly-identical silhouette series have struggled as entrants switched between them, seeking rules advantages. In the 1990 season, Trans Am, with fields matching the total of IMSA GTO/U competitors, moved closer yet to becoming a NASCAR clone. Unlike IMSA, which claims its mid-season changes introduce next year's rules early, Trans Am officials make no pretence about their interventions. Every race, seemingly, brings adjustments: weight added or removed, components legalized or banned. Restrictions on technology increased markedly in 1990 and more are on the way. Telemetry, chassis monitoring, data acquisition, even digital dashes, have been prohibited: only engine management systems remain, but seem doomed. Fuel injection is suspect.

In this environment, winning has little meaning beyond the driving competition. Manufacturers, on whom sanctioning bodies depend, cannot use such racing for research and development — some of their road cars are more sophisticated. Thus, one of the two incentives to participate is removed; with continual rule changes, it almost becomes a question of who is allowed to win. That removes their other reason to race: to demonstrate

engineering prowess.

In 1990, V6 engines dominated. It was not that the previously successful V8s or their drivers were suddenly inferior, they were simply at a regulatory disadvantage. The Chevy Beretta team of Tommy Kendall and Chris Kneifel kept ahead of both competitors and administrators and found success. Kendall brought the team its first win in Cleveland, beginning a string of six victories only interrupted by Kneifel. Trans Am has been a training ground for new talent, but, unfortunately, both drivers are not only matched in ability, but in height, Kendall the shorter at 6ft 4in. In the absence of mandatory cockpit dimensions, there seems little hope of his progression to open-wheeled competition.

The V8 Mustang of Finland's Robert Lappalainen won the first race, but the Berettas' real opposition came from the V6 Oldsmobile Cutlasses of Darin Brassfield, Scott Sharp and Irv Hoerr — each different mechanically and cosmetically. The racing was exciting, providing the spectators with great entertainment. At this stage, however, spectators are not paying the bills and the rulemakers' constant intrusions may scare off manufacturer money needed for growth beyond support-series status. Ironically, the main factor operating in the SCCA's favour may be that IMSA has also frequently re-regulated competitors.

In recent years, Dale Earnhardt has dominated NASCAR in the same way Ayrton Senna has ruled Formula One. Championships have sometimes eluded him, but he has always been the man to beat. Again this year he won the most races, but found Mark Martin a relentless opponent. Shown here at Watkins Glen, Earnhardt's road course skill has not gone unappreciated by others, including Trans Am Champion Kendall. Although either Rusty Wallace or Ricky Rudd has won every NASCAR road event since Tim Richmond's 1987 Watkins Glen victory, Earnhardt can never be counted out.

The Porsche engine. A 90-degree V8 of 2.649 litres. Bore and stroke: 88.2mm x 54.2mm. Double overhead camshafts and four valves per cylinder. Claimed to produce 725bhp at 12000rmp and 343lb/ft of torque at 8500rpm. Compression ratio: 12 to 1. Bosch Motronic engine management. Used exclusively by Teo Fabi and John Andretti, first in modified 89P chassis and from Indianapolis on in the new 90P. This engine is in an 89P which has been modified to comply with CART's 1990 rule changes which revised tunnel height, wing dimensions and wing placement specifications. In September Porsche announced its withdrawal from Indycar racing.

The Judd engine. A 90-degree V8 of 2638 litres. (Bore and stroke not available). Double overhead camshafts and four valves per cylinder. Zytek engine management system. Claimed to produce 710bhp at 12000rpm. Used by Raul Boesel, Scott Goodyear, Jon Beekhuis (his '88 Lola is pictured), and Willy T. Ribbs. Truepower, the engine division of the Truesports team in which Boesel replaced the injured Scott Pruett, has taken over development of the venerable engine. They have increased power and rpm capability and claim 50 per cent of the engine's components are now US-made.

238

The Chevrolet-Ilmor engine. A 90-degree V8 of 2.647 litres. Bore and stroke: 88mm×54.4mm. Double overhead camshafts and four valves per cylinder. Compression ratio: 11 to 1. Power (estimated): 730bph at 12200rpm. Chevrolet GEN-III (Generation III) engine management system. Used by the Galles-Kraco, Newman-Haas and Penske teams as well as Eddie Cheever, A.J. Foyt and Arie Luyendyk (his '90 Lola is pictured). The winner of every race in 1990. Next year, Chevrolet will add the teams of Tony Bettenhausen, Jim Hall and Dick Simon to its list of users, making a total of 13 cars racing the powerplant.

time and bringing the family total to five. Geoff Bodine, always a top contender, fought through a season of bad luck, but still finished well up in the standings.

His brother Brett's Buick Regal won at North Wilkesboro, and when Geoff won at Martinsville, they became only the fourth set of brothers to win consecutive Winston Cup races on consecutive weekends. Brett's controversial victory followed an apparent NASCAR scoring mistake (NASCAR uses a manual system, and is only now investigating F1-style methods) allowing him to pit and restart ahead of non-pitting competitors.

Pontiac Grand Prix driver Kyle Petty (son of all-time great, Richard), won NASCAR's record $294 450 purse at Rockingham ($66 450 plus a $228 000 bonus for winning from pole position accumulated over one year). The most successful Pontiac driver, though, was 1989 Winston Cup champion Rusty Wallace, but championship duties interfered with his defence. A reduction of personal appearances meant competitiveness returned.

AT 50 years of age, Harry Gant became the oldest driver (by 65 days, over Bobby Allison) to win a 500-mile race, nursing his oil-starved Oldsmobile home in the Round 13 race at Pocono. It was the make's only victory.

Al Unser Jr. The 1990 PPG Indy Car World Series Champion. His CART record-setting string of four victories at Toronto, Michigan, Denver and Vancouver propelled the 28 year-old driver to his first National Championship. Winning on long ovals, short ovals, and road courses (both wet and dry), he demonstrated a complete mastery of the series' unique challenges. The son of three-time National Champion Al Unser (who edged Al Jr. for his third title by one point in 1985), Al Jr. signed a new three-year contract with Galles-Kraco racing at mid-season, ending rumors that he might try Formula 1.

The Alfa Romeo engine. A 90-degree V8 of 2.648 litres. Bore & stroke: 86mm×57mm. Double overhead camshafts and four valves per cylinder. Compression ratio: 11 to 1. Magneti Marelli IAW electronic indirect injection. Claimed to produce 700bhp at 11 500rpm. A short-stroke version appeared at Michigan. Used exclusively by Roberto Guerrero and, at Indianapolis and Michigan, by Al Unser Sr. Run initially in a purpose-built March 90CA chassis, the team switched to Lola T90s at Michigan. CART rules limit engines to 8 cylinders, but do not address valve configuration and a five-valve variant will appear.

239

The Buick engine. Used by Didier Theys, Randy Lewis (his '88 Penske is pictured), Tony Bettenhausen and, at Indianapolis, Jim Crawford. The last of the "stock block" engines racing in CART. At Toronto, a 75-pound lighter aluminum block was introduced. In addition to racing engines of 2.65 litres, CART permits production-derived non-overhead camshaft engines with pushrod operated valves of 3.43 litres, but gives them no additional boost over that of the 45 inches (1.5 bar) granted racing engines. More than 10 000 units per year must be produced and stock camshafts and crankshafts must function in the blocks.

After a decade in F1, Eddie Cheever was "Rockie of the Year" not only in CART, but at the Indianapolis 500. Initially racing a 1989 Penske PC18, Cheever finished a strong third in Detroit (above). From Meadowlands on, except for Michigan, he used a Lola T90, but could not improve on the placing.

With Penske fielding only a two-car team in 1991 (for Emerson Fittipaldi and Rick Mears), Danny Sullivan was temporarily without a ride. As the season drew to a close, the 1988 CART champion was frequently the fastest of the three drivers and headed the shopping lists of several driverless teams.

ACCORDING TO PLAN

MARK GALLAGHER

This was the first time that the pre-season favourite walked away with the championship crown, for F3000 is so competitive, and the margins so slim, that surprise winners are commonplace. In 1985 Christian Danner won when we all expected Mike Thackwell to do so. The following season Ivan Capelli's Genoa Racing March defeated the might of ORECA, Onyx and Pavesi. Then Stefano Modena came along and brought the dominant Ralt team to its knees in 1987, while in 1988 it was Roberto Moreno in the unfancied Bromley Reynard who produced the goods.

After Alesi's success in 1989 the cream of the F3000 field was carefully scooped up by the Formula 1 gurus. Grand Prix racing was able to claim Martin Donnelly, Eric Bernard, JJ Lehto and even Claudio Langes. That left F3000 with a young, and much less experienced driver line-up in 1990, and there was no one who doubted that Comas would come to the fore.

He had finished 1989 on equal points with Alesi, but with only two wins to Alesi's three, the 26 year old from Romans was forced to accept the runner-up spot. "I wanted to come back and win the championship," admitted Comas, "because it is only when I win the F3000 title that I will feel happy about going for Formula 1. I've only been out of F3 for one season — I need another year."

Such maturity is rare among the fragile egos of so-called rising stars, but Comas has always had the look of a man who is going places. In 1989 he won twice — at Le Mans and Dijon — overshadowing team mate Eric Bernard in the process. He opted to stay with DAMS this year, and he had the benefit of the large publicity machine provided by Marlboro. His Lola T90/50 ran in full red and white livery alongside the identical car of team mate Allan McNish, and from day one it was obvious that DAMS

(Driot Arnoux Motor Sports) would be the team to beat. Comas started the year with a superb performance at Donington Park, starting from the front row of the grid and benefitting from some slick team work when it came to switching from wet to dry tyres. He had picked up where he had left off in 1989 — winning races — and the die was cast for the 1990 championship. A strong second place behind McNish at Silverstone was followed by an accident in Pau and two dominant victories in Jerez and Monza. With five races gone he had scored no less than 33 championship points — only six short of his total for the ten race 1989 series...

"I cannot afford to relax," he said after Monza, "because it is too easy for me to have some bad races and other drivers to win. Perhaps I can drive for points now, and maybe be happy to finish on the podium."

At the time his words sounded much too negative, but he turned out to be right. The next four rounds of the championship brought a single fourth place and three desperately disapointing retirements. At Enna he crashed, while at Brands Hatch and Birmingham there were mechanical problems. All in all, Coman's mid-season malaise was a disaster which could so easily have lost him the championship. Except that no one was able to string together the consistent results which were needed to catch him. As a result he went to the tenth round in Le Mans-Bugatti with a 10 point lead over McNish. The young Scot fell by the wayside, while Comas's other rivals such as Apicella, Van de Poele and Morbidelli were in trouble. The title was his, and the relief on Erik's face was a joy to see. He deserved his Crown.

"Suddenly it's over, and I am very very happy today," he said afterwards. "After such a bad summer, I expected to work hard in order to win the championship, and I think I have been a little lucky that the others did not take more

F3000 was the final launch for Jean Alesi, Martin Donnelly and Eric Bernard, so the 1990 F3000 season attracted much interest. Erik Comas started as clear favourite, and he obliged by winning three races during the first half of the season and tied up the title with another at the end. This continued Comas' record of winning every championship he has entered.

Being the favourite in F3000 has never been easy — indeed, it has often seemed to be a lightning conductor attracting every imaginable problem. But the supposed jinx never seemed to affect the determined and calm approach of Eric Comas, who justified his position as favourite throughout the season. In the Autumn he signed a two-year F1 contract with Ligier.

The French DAMS Motorsport team demonstrated remarkable efficiency and consistency in 1990, giving Eric Comas (26) and his team mate Allan McNish every opportunity to exploit their Mugen-engined Lola T90/50s (left).

advantage of my problems. But, my car has been good enough to win four races so far, and it has been fantastic to have a team like DAMS and a team mate like Allan behind me."

For his part, McNish continued to prove that he has a special all-round talent which could certainly make him into a World Championship one day. At only 20 years of age he came into F3000 with an enviable reputation. Second in the 1989 British F3 Championship, the former karting ace moved into the DAMS team with typical confidence, and early fears that he might find it difficult to integrate into a French team were soon quashed. His engineer was Paul Crosby, the man who helped Alesi to success in 1989, while he was at Eddie Jordan Racing. The Crosby-McNish combination worked exceedingly well. As the works Lola team, DAMS also had the full attention of designer Mark Williams, and McNish also established an excellent rapport with team mate Comas and engineer Alain Rouy.

The French press were amazed to discover that McNish could speak their language — a rare ability among British drivers — and the totally professional and commited way in which he approached the season impressed everyone.

It is not surprising that he is being guided by Ron Dennis, because McNish was born to race for McLaren.

Having made his F3000 debut in the final round of the 1989 series at Dijon, where he drove for Pacific Racing, McNish came to the first round in Donington full of confidence. He qualified fifth, but stalled at the start of the parade lap and had to dive into the pit lane. He changed to slick tyres, and began to charge back through the field. Sadly, his superb performance ended when his car collided with Emanuele Naspetti's Reynard. The Marlboro Lola somersaulted over the barriers approaching Donington's chicane, and flying debris caused the death of a spectator.

It was a traumatic start to the season for him, and although he was unhurt, no one would have been surprised if McNish had taken a few races to get back in the groove. This was not the case. After an arduous test at Croix-en-Ternois in France, McNish came to the second round at Silverstone. He claimed pole position and won the race after Damon Hill's Middlebridge Lola had retired with electrical problems. It was a superb victory, and a few months later he notched up his second win when he drove a disciplined race to score nine points at Brands Hatch. He finished second at Enna, and was unlucky not to achieve the same result in Hockenheim and Le Mans, but mechanical failures intervened. Richly talented, McNish is already a McLaren test driver, and he now has the 1991 F3000 Championship title firmly in his sights.

Eddie Irvine recovered from a poor start to the season and produced a string of strong performances during the latter half of the year in order to salvage some glory for EJR — the reigning Champions. Difficulties with the sensitive Reynard 90D caused handling and balance problems early on, but Irvine and engineer Trevor Foster patiently worked towards a competitive set-up.

A close second place to Comas at Monza gave the first indication of Irvine's resurgence. The Northern Ireland driver then produced a stunning display in front of the Formula 1 teams to win the Grand Prix supporting race at Hockenheim, while third places at Brands Hatch and Le Mans gave him the opportunity to battle over second place in the championship with McNish although eventually Van de Poele pushed them down to third and fourth on the table.

Irvine has a few sharp edges, both on and off the track, but he is gradually being moulded into a more mature and complete driver who could easily put together a

More mature and better organised in 1989, F3000 became even more professional in 1990 — the equipment may have lacked variety but it was usually impeccable, the teams were generally better structured and the entry lists were more balanced. This was true from the opening race at Donington (left), which saw the first win for Comas (26). But costs soared alarmingly, and will have to be contained if the formula is to remain healthy at the European level.

As the springboard to Formula One, tomorrow's stars gain experience in each race and sometimes benefit from the advice of veterans. Young Allan McNish (below, at Silverstone in his second race where his success demonstrated his talent) had counsel from former World Champion James Hunt, a firm supporter of F3000 (opposite, bottom).

A new generation of German drivers has appeared in F3000, although they achieved little in 1990. Among them was Heinz-Harald Frentzen (opposite), who drove for the Eddie Jordan Racing team with modest results, and was a member of the "Mercedes Junior Team" in World Sports Car racing.

championship win in 1991. The same cannot be said of his team mates in 1990, for neither Emanuele Naspetti or Heinz Harald Frentzen showed any sign of producing the combination of speed and consistency which is the hallmark of a winner.

Italy's Marco Apicella should have been Comas' closest rivals, but as the season progressed it became increasingly clear that luck was not on his side. By the time Comas had clinched the title, Apicella had yet to win an F3000 race — after four years of trying. He had three finishes in the top three, a pole at Birmingham and three fastest laps, but victory eluded him. Adding insult to injury, his FIRST Racing Reynard was disqualified at Brands Hatch for using illegal fuel in qualifying, and as a result he had third place and fastest lap taken away.

He should have won in Pau, but made a critical error of judgement and crashed while leading comfortably. At Birmingham Apicella again dominated, but a punctured radiator ended his run.

On both these occasions the man to benefit was Belgium's Eric Van de Poele, and his two street-racing victories were extremely popular. Van de Poele is one of racing's nice guys, and although he may ultimately lack the outright speed of a Comas or Apicella, he has shown sufficient ability to be given a crack at Grand Prix racing. His GA Motorsport Reynard was at the forefront of the Ford Cosworth's battle against the Mugen V8, and he was ably supported in this by Gianni Morbidelli and Damon Hill. Morbidelli's Forti Racing Lola failed to display any winning potential until it qualified second in Monza and finished fourth in the race. Enna brought a fortuitous victory, the Ferrari F1 test driver making the most of the disgraceful track conditions as his rivals fell the wayside. From then on he was always quick, and sometimes a little too aggressive, but he deserved his opportunity to join

Gianni Morbidelli (right), the Italian Formula 3 champion in 1989, started racing in Formula 1 before he tackled F3000! He was called in by Dallara at short notice to replace Emanuele Pirro, who was out for action for the Phoenix GP. He was already a test driver for Ferrari, when he won the Enna F3000 race, and before the end of the season he had a 1991 F1 contract with Minardi.

TECHNICAL ASIDES

On the chassis front, the Lola T90/50 was superior to the Reynard 90D, and the Huntingdon-based company deserved to win the title. Designer Mark Williams produced a visibly different car this year, with Benetton F1-style sidepods and a totally new monocoque with new aerodynamic styling, construction and improved driver comfort. The Reynard was similar to the 89D, but had more forward weight distribution, a stiffer chassis and revised suspension geometry. Once again the long wheelbase Reynard suited fast, more open tracks, while the Lola was particularly good on the twisty circuits. By the time Comas had tied up the championship at Le Mans, Lola had seven pole positions and seven wins out of ten races, with five fastest laps. The Reynard was good, but not quite there.

Leyton House Engineering had a new chassis, the 90B, and the Peter Vennik designed car proved difficult on most occasions, but very quick on others. The works team ran Andreas Gilbert-Scott until Hockenheim, and then signed up Paul Warwick and Philippe Favre. The drivers found the car unbalanced and lacking in grip, and the highlight of the year came in the opening round when Gilbert-Scott made it up to second after starting on slick tyres. Sadly, he then suffered a puncture.

Leyton House was forced to produce a much revised chassis mid-season, with long wheelbase versions available, but even this vast effort by the factory did not change their fortunes. There was one customer car, and this was driven by Fabrizio Barbazza for Crypton Engineering. This new team is owned by Patrizio Cantu, formerly with the Dallara F1 team, and during the year Barbazza produced several memorable performances, including a superb drive through to fourth in Jerez. He could have finished third in Birmingham had his incredible performance not been brought to a dramatic end when he collided with Irvine's Reynard and somersaulted into a run-off area.

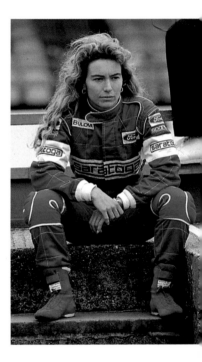

The Italian girl Giovanna Amati represented the so-called "weaker sex" in a discipline where the aggressive temperament of the rising young stars leaves little room for courtesy. She at least showed that she can look after herself in a race, but in terms of achievement did not have a good 1990 season, often complaining that her car was inferior to those of her male opponents.

the Minardi F1 team. Meanwhile Van de Poele snatched the runner-up spot in the championship with a well-timed victory at Nogaro.

Damon Hill only scored points at Brands Hatch, but he was devastating during qualifying in Monza, Enna and Hockenheim. His hat trick of pole positions was one of the highlights of the season, and he not only led the races in question, but also the second round at Silverstone where he started third on the grid. Electrical problems and accidents perhaps robbed him of a win, but after years of scratching the surface, Hill finally broke through as a top line driver.

His Tickford Cosworth engine was the subject of cynical scrutiny, but although it appeared to have bags of top end power and slow-corner torque, it is doubtful that there was any advantage over the other Cosworths or Mugens. The 9000rpm limit keeps a tight rein on the best engines producing some 470bhp.

Aside from being a difficult name to pronounce, Mansell Madgwick Motorsport made good progress this season with Italian Andrea Montermini and Frenchman Jean-Marc Gounon as drivers. Their Reynards were often highly competitive, but both men suffered lapses.

To stay with the leaders in the highly competitive world of F3000, a driver must always be on the limit, like Austrian Karl Wendlinger (above), even if that leads to inevitable incidents which leave scars on the bodywork, as on Canadian Stéphane Proulx' Lola T90/50.

246

Two solid members of the F3000 family are Belgian Eric van de Poele and Swiss Andrea Chiesa. Van de Poele won two prestigious victories on the streets circuits of Pau (below) and Birmingham and a third at Nogaro. Chiesa (opposite) was often among the leaders and distinguished himself twice in Britain, placing second at Donington and Birmingham.

Gounon had a slow start to the year while Montermini made a remarkable debut by claiming pole position at Donington. From then on Montermini was expected to show well, but he hit a mid-season bad patch before bouncing back with a strong second in Le Mans. Gounon's third in Hockenheim was followed soon after by fourths in Birmingham and Le Mans, underlining the ability which brought him the French F3 title in 1989.

Paul Stewart Racing had an indifferent first season. There were two high points: Donington, where Chiesa and Jones finished second and third on the team's debut, and Birmingham when Chiesa was second again. Over the balance of the year Chiesa again proved that he is underrated, while Jones proved little. PSR will become a top team, for the money is there, but it needs greater engineering strength. Others to show good form on occasions were former World Kart Champion Fabrizio Giovanardi and reigning British F3000 Champion Gary Brabham. Giovanardi drove several steady points-scoring races, and even qualified on the front row at Pau by virtue of an unfair Group A & B qualifying system. Brabham was on the podium in Monza and Enna, producing solid drives in both races.

As team leader for the Italian team FIRST Racing, and driving a Reynard 90D/Mugen (like half of an F3000 field), Marco Apicella was heralded as a title contendor in 1990. But fate was not always with him: with a little luck he might have won at least two races, but in championship points terms he actually finished the year out of touch with the leaders.

The Leyton House team was still in a transition phase in 1990, Swiss driver Philippe Favre (13) and his team mate Paul Warwick (12), brother of the F1 driver, finding life difficult among the Lolas and Reynards.

A famous name and a distinctive helmet: Damon Hill (right), son of the late World Champion Graham Hill, is continuing the family tradition. His excellent practice performances (including three pole positions) in 1990 deserved a better reward than one second place, at Brands Hatch.

Date: 19-23 November 1989
Total distance: 2458 km/1527 miles
Liaison sections: 1858 km/1154 miles
55 special stages: 600 km/373 miles
188 starters, 83 finishers

	Driver/Co-driver	No	Car	Group	Result
1	P. Airikkala-R. McNamee*	19	Mitsubishi Galant VR4	T	6.19′22″
2	C. Sainz-L. Moya	3	Toyota Celica GT4	T	6.20′50″
3	J. Kankkunen-J. Piironen	1	Toyota Celica GT4	T	6.23′11″
4	K. Eriksson-S. Parmander	5	Toyota Celica GT4	T	6.25′30″
5	A. Vatanen-B. Berglund	2	Mitsubishi Galant VR4	T	6.27′44″
6	T. Salonen-V. Silander	4	Mazda 323 4WD	T	6.30′09″
7	M. Sundström-J. Repo	23	Mazda 323 4WD	T	6.30′56″
8	I. Carlsson-P. Carlsson	9	Mazda 323 Turbo 4WD	T	6.32′54″
9	H. Mikkola-A. Hertz	6	Mazda 323 4WD	T	6.35′52″
10	M. Wilson-I. Grindrod	7	Opel Kadett GSi	T	6.40′11″
	.../...				
18	L. Aitken-Walker-E. Morgan**	17	Vauxhall Astra GTE 16v	T	6.55′49″
19	G. de Mevius-W. Lux*	30	Mazda 323 4WD	P	7.05′52″

* Group winners **Ladies' Prize

Principal retirements

Driver/Co-driver	No	Car	Reason	Stages completed
F. Skoghag-C. Thörner	50	Lancia Delta Integrale	gearbox	3
A. Schwarz-K. Wicha	22	Audi 200 Quattro	accident	5
H. Eriksson-J. Johansson	29	Peugeot 309 GTi	accident	8
R. Brookes-N. Wilson	33	Ford Sierra Cosworth	engine	14
J. Haider-M. Nicholson	10	Opel Kadett GSi 16s	withdrew	23
G. Trelles-D. Muzio	28	Lancia Delta Integrale	engine	26
D. Llewellin-P. Short	20	Toyota Celica GT4	drive shaft	27
F. Dunico-T. Harryman	25	Ford Sierra Cosworth	accident	31
C. McRae-D. Ringer	27	Ford Sierra Cosworth	accident	31
S. Lincholm-S. Harjanne	24	Lancia Delta Integrale	gearbox	32
P. Eklund-B. Cederberg	11	Lancia Delta Integrale	OTL	55

Successive leaders:

1st stage: Sainz; 2nd stage: Llewellin; 3rd to 8th stages: Kankkunen; 9th stage: Kankkunen and Eriksson; 10th stage: Eriksson; 11th to 15th stages: Kankkunen; 16th to 19th stages: Sainz; 20th to 31st stages: Kankkunen; 32nd to 52nd stages: Sainz; 53rd to 55th stages: Airikkala.

Date: 19-25 January 1990
Total distance: 3806 km/2365 miles
Liaison sections: 3249 km/2019 miles
26 special stages: 557 km/346 miles
178 starters, 80 finishers

	Driver/Co-driver	No	Car	Group	Result
1	D. Auriol-B. Occelli*	7	Lancia Delta Integrale 16v	T	5.56′52″
2	C. Sainz-L. Moya	2	Toyota Celica GT4	T	5.57′44″
3	M. Biasion-T. Siviero	1	Lancia Delta Integrale 16v	T	6.00′31″
4	D. Cerrato-G. Cerri	10	Lancia Delta Integrale 16v	T	6.04′43″
5	A. Schwarz-K. Wicha	12	Toyota Celica GT4	T	6.06′04″
6	B. Saby-D. Grataloup	8	Lancia Delta Integrale 16v	T	6.10′09″
7	M. Ericsson-C. Billstam	5	Toyota Celica GT4	T	6.16′33″
8	T. Salonen-V. Silander	3	Mazda 323 Turbo 4WD	T	6.18′33″
9	F. Delecour-"Tilber"	20	Peugeot 309 GTi	T	6.18′45″
10	B. Balas-E. Laine*	21	Lancia Delta Integrale 16v	P	6.38′52″
11	L. Aitken-Walker-C. Thorner**	17	Vauxhall Astra GTE	T	6.39′10″

* Group winners **Ladies' Prize

Principal retirements

Driver/Co-driver	No	Car	Reason	Stages completed
J. Kleint-W. Schleicher	18	Lancia Delta Integrale	accident	3
J. Kankkunen-J. Piironen	4	Lancia Delta Integrale 16v	accident	4
K. Eriksson-S. Parmander	9	Mitsubishi Galant VR4	engine	8
P. de Martini-U. Gibellini	15	Audi 90 Quattro	electrics	10
P. Roux-P. Corthay	24	Lancia Delta Integrale	gearbox	13
P. Bernardini-P. Dran	23	Lancia Delta Integrale 16v	gearbox	14
H. Mikkola-A. Hertz	6	Mazda 323 Turbo 4WD	transmission	17
A. Vatanen-B. Berglund	14	Mitsubishi Galant VR4	withdrawn	17

Successive leaders:

1st stage: Auriol, Saby and Sainz; 2nd stage: Sainz; 3rd and 4th stages: Auriol; 5th stage: Auriol and Sainz; 6th stage: Auriol; 7th and 9th stages (8th stage cancelled): Auriol and Sainz; 10th to 16th stages: Auriol; 17th stage: Sainz; 18th stage: Auriol; 19th stage cancelled; 20th and 21st stages: Sainz; 22nd stage: Auriol and Sainz; 23rd to 28th stages: Auriol.

Date: 6-10 March 1990
Total distance: 2060 km/1280 miles
Liaison sections: 1510 km/938 miles
38 special stages: 550 km/342 miles
100 starters, 34 finishers

	Driver/Co-driver	No	Car	Group	Result
1	M. Biasion-T. Siviero*	1	Lancia Delta Integrale 16v	T	6.17′57″
2	D. Auriol-B. Occelli	4	Lancia Delta Integrale 16v	T	6.20′33″
3	J. Kankkunen-J. Piironen	6	Lancia Delta Integrale 16v	T	6.23′08″
4	D. Cerrato-G. Cerri	9	Lancia Delta Integrale 16v	T	6.34′23″
5	C. Bica-F. Prata	11	Lancia Delta Integrale 16v	T	6.45′24″
6	H. Mikkola-A. Hertz	8	Mazda 323 4WD	T	6.48′21″
7	J. Recalde-M. Christie*	12	Lancia Delta Integrale 16v	P	6.53′01″
8	M. Duez-A. Lopes	16	Ford Sierra Cosworth	T	6.54′11″
9	J. Santos-M. Oliveira	17	Ford Sierra Cosworth	T	6.55′14″
10	R. Holzer-K. Wendel	24	Lancia Delta Integrale 16v	T	6.59′57″
11	P. de Martini-U. Gibellini**	20	Audi 90 Quattro	T	7.11′41″

* Group winners **Ladies' Prize

Principal retirements

Driver/Co-driver	No	Car	Reason	Stages completed
T. Salonen-V. Silander	5	Mazda 323 4WD	engine	1
L. Aitken-Walker-C. Thorner	18	Opel Kadett GSi	accident	3
G. de Mevius-L. Manset	10	Mazda 323 4WD	clutch	5
A. Schwarz-K. Wicha	15	Toyota Celica GT4	accident	10
R. Baumschlager-R. Zeltner	21	VW Golf GTi	accident	10
A. Vatanen-B. Berglund	3	Mitsubishi Galant VR4	accident	17
K. Eriksson-S. Parmander	7	Mitsubishi Galant VR4	transmission	21
G. Fischer-T. Zeltner	22	Audi 200 Quattro	engine	31
C. Sainz-L. Moya	2	Toyota Celica GT4	transmission	33

Successive leaders:

1st stage: Biasion; 2nd stage: Schwarz; 3rd stage: Biasion; 4th to 7th stages: Vatanen; 8th to 10th stages: Schwarz; 11th stage cancelled; 12th to 17th stages: Sainz; 18th to 39th stages: Biasion.

Date: 6-9 April 1990
Total distance: 1397 km/868 miles
Liaison sections: 795 km/494 miles
30 special stages: 602 km/374 miles
94 starters, 48 finishers

	Driver/Co-driver	No	Car	Group	Result
1	D. Auriol-B. Occelli*	1	Lancia Delta Integrale 16v	T	6.45′16″
2	C. Sainz-L. Moya	2	Toyota Celica GT4	T	6.45′52″
3	F. Chatriot-M. Perin	3	BMW M3	T	6.49′05″
4	B. Saby-D. Grataloup	6	Lancia Delta Integrale 16v	T	6.51′12″
5	R. Baumschlager-R. Zeltner	11	Volkswagen Golf GTi 16v	T	7.21′26″
6	L. Poggi-E. Buresi	25	Citroën AX Sport	T	7.23′30″
7	C. Balesi-J.-P. Cirindini*	21	Renault 5 GT Turbo	P	7.24′05″
8	A. Oreille-M. Roissard	7	Renault 5 GT Turbo	P	7.25′37″
9	P. de Martini-U. Gibellini**	10	Audi 90 Quattro	T	7.31′20″
10	S. Polo-H. Sauvage	19	Renault 5 GT Turbo	P	7.31′56″

* Group winners **Ladies' Prize

Principal retirements

Driver/Co-driver	No	Car	Reason	Stages completed
J. Ragnotti-G. Thimonier	14	Renault 5 GT Turbo	engine	5
F. Delecour-"Tilber"	15	Peugeot 309 GTi	engine	10
A. Schwarz-K. Wicha	9	Toyota Celica GT4	transmission	12
M. Duez-A. Lopes	8	Ford Sierra Cosworth	engine	16
Y. Loubet-J.-P. Chiaroni	5	Lancia Delta Integrale 16v	transmission	17
C. Driano-M.-C. Lallement	17	Citroën AX Sport	suspension	18
F. Serpaggi-J.-B. Serpaggi	33	Ford Sierra Cosworth	engine	18
L. Aitken-Walker-C. Thorner	12	Opel Kadett GSi 16v	engine	22
A. Albertini-A. Pasquali	20	Alfa Romeo 75 Turbo	suspension	23
P. Bernardini-P. Dran	22	Lancia Delta Integrale 16v	transmission	27

Successive leaders:

1st stage: Loubet and Sainz; 2nd stage: Loubet; 3rd and 4th stages: Sainz; 5th to 30th stages: Auriol.

Marlboro 4 EPSON Safari Rally Kenya

Date: 11-16 April 1990
Total distance: 4086 km/2539 miles
80 time controls
1 special stage: 4.8 km/2.98 miles
59 starters, 10 finishers

	Driver/Co-driver	No	Car	Group	Result
1	B. Waldegård-F. Gallagher*	3	Toyota Celica GT4	T	8.39'11"
2	J. Kankkunen-J. Piironen	5	Lancia Delta Integrale 16v	T	9.17'23"
3	M. Ericsson-C. Billstam	6	Toyota Celica GT4	T	11.26'58"
4	C. Sainz-L. Moya	67	Toyota Celica GT4	T	12.58'42"
5	K. Shinozuka-J. Meadows	12	Mitsubishi Galant VR4	T	15.11'31"
6	J. Heather-Hayes-A. Levitan	17	Subaru Legacy	T	15.12'40"
7	R. Stohl-R. Kaufmann	14	Audi 90 Quattro	T	17.49'58"
8	P. Njiru-D. Williamson*	18	Subaru Legacy	P	18.04'51"
9	A. Pattni-B. Khan	62	Daihatsu Charade	T	28.54'51"
10	S. Anthony-P. Valentine	31	Daihatsu Charade	T	30.49'30"

* Group winners

Principal retirements

Driver/Co-driver	No	Car	Reason	Controls passed
M. Alén-I. Kivimaki	1	Subaru Legacy	overheating	8
P. Bourne-R. Freeth	9	Subaru Legacy	engine	9
I. Duncan-I. Munro	10	Subaru Legacy	engine	15
G. Colsoul-A. Khan	68	Mitsubishi Galant VR4	suspension	19
V. Preston Jr.-J. Lyall	11	Nissan 200 SX	suspension	30
M. Kirkland-S. Thattni	7	Subaru Legacy	engine	32
A. Fiorio-L. Pirollo	4	Lancia Delta Integrale 16v	engine	38
M. Biasion-T. Siviero	2	Lancia Delta Integrale 16v	engine	61

successive leaders:

special stage and controls 2 to 5: Alen; controls 6 to 51: Waldegård; controls 52 to 54: Biasion; controls 55 to 83: Waldegård.

5 ΕΛΠΑ 37 ΡΑΛΛΥ ΑΚΡΟΠΟΛΙΣ

Date: 3-6 June 1990
Total distance: 2035 km/1265 miles
Liaison sections: 1441 km/895 miles
46 special stages: 593 km/370 miles
97 starters, 34 finishers

	Driver/Co-driver	No	Car	Group	Result
1	C. Sainz-L. Moya*	2	Toyota Celica GT4	T	7.34'44"
2	J. Kankkunen-J. Piironen	4	Lancia Delta Integrale 16v	T	7.35'30"
3	M. Biasion-T. Siviero	1	Lancia Delta Integrale 16v	T	7.37'42"
4	M. Ericsson-C. Billstam	6	Toyota Celica GT4	T	7.49'40"
5	A. Fiorio-L. Pirollo	9	Lancia Delta Integrale 16v	T	8.02'07"
6	M. Rayneri-L. Roggia	25	Lancia Delta Integrale	T	8.22'08"
7	"Jigger"-K. Stefanis	14	Lancia Delta Integrale 16v	T	8.36'57"
8	I. Duncan-Y. Mehta*	24	Subaru Legacy RS	P	8.52'39"
9	G. Trelles-D. Muzio	11	Lancia Delta Integrale	P	8.59'10"
10	P. Moschoutis-E. Sassalos	27	Nissan 200 SX	T	9.02'05"

* Group winners

Principal retirements

Driver/Co-driver	No	Car	Reason	Stages completed
P. Gaban-L. Lejeune	17	Audi 90 Quattro	engine	3
M. Bin Sulayem-R. Morgan	20	Toyota Celica GT4	steering	3
E. Soto-J. del Buono	22	Lancia Delta Integrale	suspension	3
R. Holzer-K. Wendel	19	Lancia Delta Integrale 16v	suspension	8
J. Recalde-M. Christie	11	Lancia Delta Integrale 16v	accident	18
E. Weber-M. Feltz	15	VW Rallye Golf G60	suspension	18
R. Stohl-E. Rohringer	16	Audi 90 Quattro	suspension	20
K. Eriksson-S. Parmander	8	Mitsubishi Galant VR4	turbo	21
P. de Martini-U. Gibellini	18	Audi 90 Quattro	oil pump	28
D. Auriol-B. Occelli	7	Lancia Delta Integrale 16v	engine	29
A. Vatanen-B. Berglund	3	Mitsubishi Galant VR4	accident	32
M. Alen-I. Kivimaki	5	Subaru Legacy RS	engine	38

Successive leaders:

1st stage: Alen, Ericsson and Erkisson; 2nd and 3rd stages: Ericsson; 4th stage: Sainz; 5th to 8th stages (stage 6 cancelled): Ericsson; 9th to 19th stages (stage 15 cancelled): Sainz; 20th stage: Kankkunen; 21st to 48th stages: Sainz.

Rothmans RALLY NEW ZEALAND 1990

Date: 30 June-3 July 1990
Total distance: 2113 km/1313 miles
Liaison sections: 1506 km/936 miles
43 special stages: 607 km/377 miles
65 starters, 41 finishers

	Driver/Co-driver	No	Car	Group	Result
1	C. Sainz-L. Moya*	2	Toyota Celica GT4	T	6.48'26"
2	I. Carlsson-P. Carlsson	1	Mazda 323 4WD	T	6.49'57"
3	E. Weber-M. Feltz	8	VW Golf Rallye G60	T	6.56'24"
4	R. Dunkerton-F. Gocentas	12	Mitsubishi Galant VR4	T	7.00'28"
5	P. Bourne-R. Freeth	11	Subaru Legacy	T	7.05'48"
6	T. Makinen-S. Harjanne*	21	Mitsubishi Galant VR4	P	7.09'13"
7	G. Trelles-D. Muzio	6	Lancia Delta Integrale 16v	P	7.11'14"
8	J. Recalde-M. Christie	5	Lancia Delta Integrale 16v	P	7.17'17"
9	G. Pianezzola-L. Baggio	22	Toyota Celica GT4	P	7.23'58"
10	A. Oreille-M. Roissard	7	Renault 5 GT Turbo	P	7.25'35"
11	L. Aitken Walker-C. Thörner**	10	Opel Kadett GSi 16v	T	7.27'38"

* Group winners   ** Ladies' prize

Principal retirements

Driver/Co-driver	No	Car	Reason	Stages completed
M. Kirkland-S. Thatthi	4	Subaru Legacy	accident	12
R. Millen-T. Sircombe	3	Mazda 323 4WD	turbo	23
E. Soto-J. del Buono	17	Lancia Delta Integrale 16v	engine	23
M. Rayneri-L. Roggia	19	Lancia Delta Integrale 16v	accident	29
G. Carr-I. Stewart	9	Lancia Delta Integrale 16v	accident	37

Successive leaders:

1st to 3rd stages: Carlsson; 4th stage: Millen; 5th stage: Carlsson; 6th and 7th stages: Sainz; 8th stage: Carlsson; 9th to 12th stages: Sainz; 13th to 23rd stages: Carlsson; 24th to 43rd stages: Sainz.

10 Rally Argentina '90 — Marlboro

Date: 24-28 July 1990
Total distance: 2119 km/1317 miles
Liaison sections: 1555 km/966 miles
30 special stages: 564 km/351 miles
83 starters (plus 13 in Group S), 26 finishers (plus 3 in Groupe S)

	Driver/Co-driver	No	Car	Group	Result
1	M. Biasion-T. Siviero*	3	Lancia Delta Integrale 16v	T	6.51'27"
2	C. Sainz-L. Moya	1	Toyota Celica GT4	T	6.59'29"
3	D. Auriol-B. Occelli	5	Lancia Delta Integrale 16v	T	7.26'22"
4	R. Stohl-R. Kaufmann	9	Audi 90 Quattro	T	7.50'48"
5	E. Soto-J. del Buono	11	Lancia Delta Integrale 16v	P	7.53'19"
6	A. Oreille-M. Roissard	6	Renault 5 GT Turbo	P	7.56'35"
7	M. Raies-J. Gonzalez	67	Renault 18 GTX	T	8.33'10"
8	G. Martin-J. Volta	38	Fiat Regatta 85	T	8.39'23"
9	O. Maccari-C. Ostaschinsky	50	Renault 18 GTX	T	8.43'16"
10	F. Marino-R. Ghilini	57	Fiat Regatta 85	T	9.04'12"
.../...					
	J. Fossat-V. Roca*	98	Fiat 128 SE 1.5	S	9.24'10"

* Group winners

Principal retirements

Driver/Co-driver	No	Car	Reason	Stages completed
P. de Martini-U. Gibbelini	10	Lancia Delta Integrale 16v	withdrawn	1
J. Recalde-M. Christie	4	Toyota Celica GT4	accident damage	4
G. Trelles-D. Muzio	7	Lancia Delta Integrale 16v	gearbox	10
J. Kankkunen-J. Piironen	2	Lancia Delta Integrale 16v	gearbox	12
G. Raies-R. Campana	15	Renault 18 GTX	suspension	17
C. Mennem Jr-V. Zuchini	14	Lancia Delta Integrale 16v	transmission	10

Successive leaders:

1st and 2nd stages: Kankkunen; 3rd to 6th stages: Biasion; 7th stage: Biasion and Sainz; 8th to 30th stages: Biasion.

Date: 23-26 August 1990
Total distance: 1604 km/997 miles
Liaison sections: 1076 km/687 miles
42 special stages: 528 km/310 miles
186 starters, 92 finishers

	Driver/Co-driver	No	Car	Group	Result
1	C. Sainz-L. Moya*	4	Toyota Celica GT4	T	4.40'55"
2	A. Vatanen-B. Berglund	6	Mitsubishi Galant VR4	T	4.41'14"
3	K. Eriksson-S. Parmander	9	Mitsubishi Galant VR4	T	4.45'53"
4	M. Alen-I. Kivimäki	3	Subaru Legacy	T	4.46'47"
5	J. Kankkunen-J. Piironen	2	Lancia Delta Integrale 16v	T	4.47'10"
6	T. Salonen-V. Silander	5	Mazda 323 4WD	T	4.49'02"
7	L. Lampi-P. Kuukkala	25	Mitsubishi Galant VR4	T	4.50'14"
8	S. Lindholm-T. Hantunen	17	Lancia Delta Integrale 16v	T	4.50'51"
9	E. Saarenpää-O. Männistö	24	Audi 200 Quattro	T	5.04'26"
10	R. Buri-J. Stenroos	29	Audi 90 Quattro	T	5.05'06"
11	T. Mäkinen-S. Harjanne*	18	Mitsubishi Galant VR4	P	5.06'46"
.../...					
32	P. de Martini-U. Gibellini**	22	Audi 90 Quattro	T	5.37'57"

* Group winners   ** Ladies' Prize

Principal retirements

Driver/Co-driver	No	Car	Reason	Stages completed
P. Airikkala-R. McNamee	8	Ford Sierra Cosworth 4x4	gearbox	3
M. Wilson-N. Grist	12	Ford Sierra Cosworth 4x4	withdrawn (gearbox problems)	18
F. Cunico-S. Evangelisti	20	Ford Sierra Cosworth 4x4	accident	20
H. Mikkola-A. Hertz	11	Mazda 323 4WD	engine	21
M. Ericsson-C. Billstram	1	Toyota Celica GT4	accident	21
P. Eklund-J.-O. Bohlin	13	Lancia Delta Integrale 16v	turbo	23
M. Sundström-J. Repo	16	Mazda 323 4WD	turbo	25
D. Auriol-B. Occelli	7	Lancia Delta Integrale 16v	accident	27
A. Fiorio-L. Pirollo	10	Lancia Delta Integrale 16v	gearbox	32

Successive leaders:
1st stage: Kankkunen; 2nd stage: Ericsson; 3rd stage: Sainz; 4th-9th stages: Kankkunen; 10th-42nd stages: Sainz.

Date: 20-23 September 1990
Total distance: 2042 km/1269 miles
Liaison sections: 1472 km/915 miles
35 special stages: 571 km/354 miles
62 starters, 38 finishers

	Driver/Co-driver	No	Car	Group	Result
1	J. Kankkunen-J. Piironen*	1	Lancia Delta Integrale 16v	T	5.43'48"
2	C. Sainz-L. Moya	2	Toyota Celica GT4	T	5.45'28"
3	A. Fiorio-L. Pirollo	9	Lancia Delta Integrale 16v	T	5.49'28"
4	P. Bourne-R. Freeth	19	Subaru Legacy	T	5.57'45"
5	I. Carlsson-P. Carlsson	5	Mazda 323 4WD	T	6.00'49"
6	G. de Mevius-A. Hertz	8	Mazda 323 4WD	T	6.04'57"
7	T. Mäkinen-S. Harjanne*	22	Mitsubishi Galant VR4	P	6.09'44"
8	G. Trelles-D. Muzio	13	Lancia Delta Integrale 16v	P	6.16'26"
9	K. Inoue-S. Hayashi	23	Mitsubishi Galant VR4	P	6.20'00"
10	E. Ordynski-J. Browne	21	Mitsubishi Galant VR4	P	6.20'31"
.../...					
13	L. Aitken Walker-C. Thorner**	15	Opel Kadett GSi	T	6.36'19"

* Group winners   ** Ladies' Prize

Principal retirements

Driver/Co-driver	No	Car	Reason	Stages completed
A. Oreille-M. Roissard	14	Renault 5 GT Turbo	accident	1
D. Auriol-B. Occelli	7	Lancia Delta Integrale 16v	engine	2
M. Ericsson-C. Billstam	6	Toyota Celica GT4	transmission	2
R. Millen-T. Sircombe	11	Mazda 323 4WD	withdrawn	4
K. Eriksson-S. Parmander	3	Mitsubishi Galant VR4	clutch	9
M. Rayneri-L. Roggia	17	Lancia Delta Integrale 16v	wheel	13
P. de Martini-U. Gibellini	16	Audi 90 Quattro	engine	15
E. Weber-M. Feltz	10	VW Rallye Golf G60	excluded	27
R. Dunkerton-S. McKimmie	18	Mitsubishi Galant VR4	accident	29

Successive leaders:
1st stage: Kankkunen; 2nd to 6th stages: Eriksson; 7th to 35th stages: Kankkunen.

Date: 14-18 October 1990
Total distance: 2237 km/1398 miles
Liaison sections: 1622 km/1013 miles
35 special stages: 615 km/384 miles
104 starters, 47 finishers

	Driver/Co-driver	No	Car	Group	Result
1	D. Auriol-B. Occelli*	11	Lancia Delta Integrale 16v	T	7.30'39"
2	J. Kankkunen-J. Piironen	6	Lancia Delta Integrale 16v	T	7.31'23"
3	C. Sainz-L. Moya	2	Toyota Celica GT4	T	7.32'23"
4	D. Cerrato-G. Cerri	4	Lancia Delta Integrale 16v	T	7.33'25"
5	P. Liatti-L. Tedeschini	21	Lancia Delta Integrale 16v	T	7.36'52"
6	M. Ericsson-C. Billstam	7	Toyota Celica GT4	T	7.37'12"
7	P.-G. Deila-P.-A. Scalvini	27	Lancia Delta Integrale 16v	T	7.37'49"
8	A. Fiorio-L. Pirollo	8	Lancia Delta Integrale 16v	T	7.38'23"
9	G. Grossi-A. Mari	22	Lancia Delta Integrale 16v	T	7.56'57"
10	A. Fassina-M. Chiapponi*	30	Ford Sierra Cosworth 4x4	P	7.58'13"
.../...					
18	L. Aitken Walker-C. Thorner**	24	Opel Kadett GSi	T	8.20'41"

* Group winners   ** Ladies' Prize

Principal retirements

Driver/Co-driver	No	Car	Reason	Stages completed
P. de Martini-U. Gibellini	23	Audi 90 Quattro	alternator	1
F. Cunico-S. Evangelisti	20	Ford Sierra Cosworth 4x4	throttle cable	3
M. Alén-I. Kivimaki	3	Subaru Legacy	clutch	4
G. de Mevius-W. Lux	14	Mazda 323 4WD	accident	4
F. Chatriot-M. Perin	9	Subaru Legacy	outside time limit (clutch)	11
M. Wilson-N. Grist	10	Ford Sierra Cosworth 4x4	suspension	24
M. Biasion-T. Siviero	1	Lancia Delta Integrale 16v	accident	26
A. Schwarz-K. Wicha	19	Toyota Celica GT4	accident	32
P. Alessandrini-A. Alessandrini	29	Lancia Delta Integrale 16v	turbo	32

Successive leaders:
1st stage: Cunico, Kankkunen, Sainz, Schwarz and Wilson; 2nd to 13th stages: Biasion; 14th to 26th stages: Sainz; 27th to 35th stages: Auriol.

EUROPEAN

CLASSIFICATION*		1	2	3	4	5	6	7	8	9	10	11
1	R. Droogmans	—	200	—	—	—	300	—	—	—	—	—
2	D. Cerrato	—	400	—	—	—	—	—	—	—	—	—
3	F. Tabaton	—	240	—	—	—	—	—	—	—	—	—
4	J. Bosch	—	60	—	—	—	200	—	—	—	—	—
5	C. McRae	—	—	—	—	—	400	—	—	—	—	100
	F. Chatriot	—	—	—	—	—	400	—	—	—	—	100
7	M. Sundstrom	—	—	—	—	200	—	—	—	—	—	—
	R. Holzer	—	—	—	60	—	—	—	—	—	—	—
9	M. Duez	—	—	50	—	—	—	—	100	—	—	—
10	B. Thiry	—	—	—	—	—	—	—	—	—	—	—
11	Y. Loubet	—	300	—	—	—	—	—	—	—	—	—
12	R. Brookes	—	—	—	—	—	—	—	—	—	—	—
13	P. Liatti	—	—	—	—	—	—	100	—	—	—	—
	J. Haider	—	—	100	—	—	—	—	—	—	—	—
15	P. Snijers	—	—	—	—	—	—	—	—	—	—	—
16	H. Demuth	—	—	—	—	—	—	—	—	—	—	—
17	M. Rayneri	—	—	—	—	—	—	—	—	—	—	—
	. Mavropoulos	—	—	—	—	—	—	—	—	—	—	—
	F. Delecour	—	—	—	—	—	240	—	—	—	—	40
20	M. Jonsson	—	—	—	—	—	—	—	—	—	—	—
21	P.-G. Deila	—	—	—	—	—	—	—	—	—	—	—
22	G. de Mevius	—	—	60	—	—	—	—	75	—	—
23	S. Aljasov	—	—	—	—	—	—	—	—	—	—	—
24	B. Saby	—	—	100	—	—	—	—	—	—	—	60
25	C. Baroni	—	—	—	—	—	—	—	—	—	—	75
26	D. Llewellin	—	—	—	—	—	—	—	—	—	—	—
	K. Apostolou	—	—	—	—	—	—	—	—	—	—	—
	B. Fisher	—	—	—	—	—	—	—	—	—	—	—
	. Terzian	—	—	—	—	—	—	—	—	—	—	—
	. Coutinho	—	—	—	—	—	—	—	—	—	—	—
31	J. Bassas	—	—	—	—	—	—	—	—	20	—	—
32	M. Soulet	—	—	10	—	—	—	—	—	—	—	—
33	L. Attakan	—	—	—	—	—	—	—	—	—	—	—
34	J. Ragnotti	—	—	—	—	—	160	—	—	—	20	
35	R. Verreydt	—	—	75	—	—	—	—	60	—	—	
36	F. Arletti	—	—	—	—	—	—	—	—	—	—	—
	T. Kalemtzakis	—	—	—	—	—	—	—	—	—	—	—
	J. Cullen	—	—	—	—	—	—	—	—	—	—	—
	. Artemenko	—	—	—	—	—	—	—	—	—	—	—
40	I. Carlsson	—	—	—	75	—	—	—	—	—	—	—
41	G. Petrov	—	—	—	—	—	—	—	—	—	—	—
	E. Doctor	—	—	—	—	—	—	—	—	50	—	
	A. Aghini	—	—	—	—	—	—	75	—	—	—	
44	C. Bica	—	—	—	—	—	—	—	—	—	—	—
	. Tsouloftas	—	—	—	—	—	—	—	—	—	—	—
46	J.-M. Bardolet	—	160	—	—	—	—	—	—	—	30	
	G. Middleton	—	—	—	—	—	—	—	—	—	—	—
48	E. Saarenpaa	75	—	—	—	100	—	—	—	—	—	
	. Santos	—	—	—	—	—	—	—	—	—	—	—
		1	2	3	4	5	6	7	8	9	10	11

VIKING 11 Rallye COTE D'IVOIRE - BANDAMA 1990

Date: 28 October-1 November 1990
Total distance: 3110 km/1943 miles
86 time controls
32 starters, 14 finishers

	Driver/Co-driver	No	Car	Group	Time
1	P. Tauziac-C. Papin*	1	Mitsubishi Galant VR4	T	4.54'
2	R. Stohl-E. Rohringer	10	Audi 90 Quattro	T	5.56'
3	A. Oreille-M. Roissard*	4	Renault 5 GT Turbo	P	6.52'
4	A. Ambrosino-D. Le Saux	2	Nissan March Turbo	T	8.09'
5	P. Servant-D. Charbonnel	6	Toyota Corolla 16V	T	8.25'
6	M. Molinie-P. Lemarie	8	Toyota Corolla 16V	T	9.35'
7	J. P. Bernier-Y. Malus	19	Toyota Corolla 16V	T	10.35'
8	V. Evina-N. Chastagnol**	25	Toyota Corolla 16V	P	11.27'
9	J. M. Dionneau-T. Brion	21	Toyota Celica GT4	T	11.53'
10	A. Choteau-J.-P. Claverie	3	Toyota Corolla 16V	T	12.42'

* Group winners   ** Ladies' Prize

Principal retirements

Driver/Co-driver	No	Car	Reason	Time controls
G. Trelles-D. Muzio	12	Lancia Delta Integrale	accident	2
K. Shinozuka-J. Meadows	9	Mitsubishi Galant VR4	accident	47
S. Assep-C. Konan	11	Toyota Celica GT4	gave up	35
B. Antoine-C. Raymond	15	Peugeot 205 GTi	engine	53

Successive leaders:
Controls 1 to 5: Tauziac; controls 6 to 15: Shinozuka; controls 16 to 36: Tauziac; controls 37 to 47: Shinozuka; controls 48 to 86: Tauziac.

EUROPEAN RALLY CHAMPIONSHIP FOR DRIVERS

* With six rallies still to go.

1: Arctic Rally, SF; 2: Rally Catalunya Costa Brava, E; 3: Finnskog Vinterrally, N; 4: Boucles de Spa, B; 5: Sachs Winterrallye, D; 6: Hankiralli, SF; 7: Rallye des Garrigues, F; 8: Rallye 1000 Miglia, I; 9: Circuit des Ardennes, B; 10: Rallye Sierra Morena, E; 11: Rallye Alpin-Behra, F; 12: Rallye Costa Smeralda, I; 13: Circuit of Ireland, GB; 14: Hellendoorn Rally, NL; 15: Rally Volta a Portugal, P; 16: Targa Florio, I; 17: Rallye Zlatni Piassatzi, BG; 18: Rallye Saturnus, YU; 19: Haspengouw Rally, B; 20: South Swedish Rally, S; 21: Scottish Rally, GB; 22: Rally Hessen, D; 23: Barum Rally, CS; 24: Rally Hebros, BG; 25: Rally of Turkey, TR; 26: 24 Heures d'Ypres, B; 27: Hunsruck Rally, D; 28: Rallye de Pologne, PL; 29: Rallye Deutschland, D; 30: Rallye della Lana, I; 31: Rallye Vinho da Madeira, P; 32: Rallye Elpa Halkidikis, GR; 33: Rallye Piancavallo, I; 34: Rallye du Mont-Blanc, F; 35: Rallye Principe de Asturias, E; 36: Manx International Rally, GB; 37: Yu Rally, YU; 38: Cyprus Rally, CY; 39: Rallye d'Antibes, F; 40: Rallye do Algarve, P; 41: Rallye el Corte Ingles, E; 42: Rallye du Valais, CH; 43: Rallye San Marino, RSM; 44: Rallye Bohemia, CS; 45: Semperit Rally, A; 46: Rallye du Condroz, B; 47: Rallye Valeo, E; 48: Rallye du Var, F.

RALLY CHAMPIONSHIP FOR DRIVERS

12	13	14	15	16	17	18	19	20	21	22	23	24	25	26	27	28	29	30	31	32	33	34	35	36	37	38	39	40	41	42	43	44	45	46	47	48	TOTAL
40	—	—	—	—	300	—	—	—	—	—	—	—	—	400	—	400	400	—	300	—	—	—	—	—	—	—	—	—	—	—	—	—	—	—	—	—	2340
400	—	—	—	60	—	—	—	—	—	—	—	—	—	300	—	—	—	100	—	—	200	—	—	—	—	—	—	—	—	—	—	—	—	—	—	—	1460
—	—	—	—	—	400	—	—	—	—	—	—	—	—	—	—	—	—	—	400	—	—	—	—	—	—	—	—	—	—	—	—	—	—	—	—	—	1040
—	—	30	—	—	—	—	—	—	—	150	—	—	—	—	—	240	—	—	—	—	—	—	—	240	—	—	—	—	—	—	—	—	—	—	—	—	680
—	60	—	—	—	—	—	—	—	150	—	—	—	—	200	—	—	—	—	—	—	—	—	—	—	—	150	—	—	—	—	—	—	—	—	—	—	650
—	—	—	—	—	—	—	—	—	—	—	200	—	—	—	—	160	—	—	—	—	—	—	—	—	—	—	—	—	—	—	—	—	—	—	—	—	650
—	—	—	—	—	—	—	—	—	100	—	—	—	—	—	200	—	200	—	—	—	—	—	—	—	—	—	—	—	—	—	—	—	—	—	—	—	560
—	—	—	—	—	—	100	—	—	—	—	—	—	—	—	—	300	—	—	—	—	—	—	—	—	—	—	—	—	—	—	—	—	—	—	—	—	550
—	—	—	—	200	—	75	—	—	—	—	—	—	—	60	—	200	—	—	—	—	—	—	—	—	—	—	—	—	—	—	—	—	—	—	—	—	535
200	—	—	—	—	—	—	—	—	—	—	—	—	—	—	—	—	—	—	—	—	—	16	—	—	—	—	10	—	—	—	—	—	—	—	—	—	526
—	—	—	—	—	—	—	—	120	—	—	—	—	—	—	—	—	—	—	—	—	—	—	400	—	—	—	—	—	—	—	—	—	—	—	—	—	520
300	—	—	—	100	—	—	—	—	—	60	—	—	—	—	—	120	—	—	—	—	—	—	120	—	—	—	—	—	100	—	—	—	—	—	—	500
240	—	—	—	240	—	—	—	—	75	—	—	—	—	80	—	300	—	—	—	—	—	—	—	—	—	—	—	—	—	—	—	—	—	—	—	—	480
—	—	—	—	—	—	—	—	—	—	—	—	—	—	—	—	—	—	—	—	400	—	—	—	—	—	—	—	—	—	—	—	—	—	—	—	455
—	—	—	—	—	—	—	—	—	—	—	—	—	—	—	—	—	—	—	—	—	20	—	—	400	—	—	—	—	—	—	—	—	—	—	—	400
—	—	—	—	—	—	—	100	—	50	—	—	—	—	—	240	—	—	—	—	—	—	—	—	—	100	—	—	—	—	—	—	—	—	—	400
160	—	—	—	75	—	—	—	—	—	—	—	—	—	—	—	—	—	—	150	—	—	—	—	—	—	—	—	—	—	—	—	—	—	—	—	385
—	—	—	—	—	80	—	—	—	—	—	240	—	—	—	—	—	—	—	—	—	—	—	—	—	—	—	—	—	—	—	—	—	—	—	—	375
—	—	—	—	—	—	—	—	—	—	—	—	—	—	—	—	—	—	—	—	120	—	—	—	160	—	—	—	—	—	—	—	—	—	—	360
—	—	—	—	—	—	—	—	—	—	—	—	—	—	—	—	—	—	—	—	—	40	—	—	—	120	—	—	—	—	—	—	—	—	—	320
—	—	—	—	—	—	—	—	—	—	—	—	—	—	—	—	—	—	—	—	—	30	—	—	—	200	—	—	—	—	—	—	—	—	—	305
—	100	—	—	—	—	—	200	—	—	—	—	—	—	—	—	—	—	—	—	—	—	—	—	—	—	—	—	—	—	—	—	—	—	—	300
—	—	—	—	—	—	—	—	—	—	—	—	—	—	—	—	—	—	300	—	—	—	—	—	—	—	—	—	—	—	—	—	—	—	—	300
—	—	—	—	—	—	—	—	—	—	—	—	—	—	—	—	—	—	—	—	—	—	300	—	—	—	—	—	—	—	—	—	—	—	—	300
—	—	—	—	—	—	—	—	—	—	—	—	—	—	—	—	—	—	—	—	—	—	—	300	—	—	—	—	—	—	—	—	—	—	—	300
—	—	200	—	—	—	—	—	—	—	—	—	—	—	—	—	—	—	—	—	—	—	—	—	—	—	—	100	—	—	—	—	—	—	—	300
—	—	16	—	—	120	—	—	—	—	—	—	—	—	20	—	120	—	—	—	—	—	—	—	—	—	—	—	200	—	—	—	—	—	—	295
—	—	—	—	—	—	—	—	—	—	—	75	—	—	—	—	—	—	—	—	200	—	—	—	—	—	—	—	—	—	—	—	—	—	—	286
—	—	—	—	—	—	—	—	—	—	—	—	—	—	—	—	—	—	—	—	—	12	—	—	—	80	—	—	—	—	—	—	—	—	—	272
—	—	—	—	—	—	—	—	—	—	120	—	—	—	—	—	—	—	—	—	—	—	—	—	—	—	—	—	—	—	—	—	—	—	—	255
—	—	—	—	—	—	—	—	—	—	—	—	—	—	—	—	—	240	—	—	—	—	—	—	—	—	—	—	—	—	—	—	—	—	—	240
—	—	—	—	—	—	—	—	—	—	—	—	—	—	—	—	—	—	—	240	—	—	—	—	—	—	—	—	—	—	—	—	—	—	—	240
—	—	—	—	—	—	—	—	—	—	—	—	—	—	—	—	—	—	—	—	—	—	200	—	—	—	—	—	—	—	—	—	—	—	—	240
—	—	—	—	—	—	—	—	—	—	—	—	—	—	—	—	—	—	—	—	—	—	—	—	240	—	—	—	—	—	—	—	—	—	—	240
—	—	—	—	—	—	—	—	—	—	—	—	—	—	—	—	160	—	—	—	—	—	—	—	—	—	—	—	—	—	—	—	—	—	—	235
—	—	—	—	160	—	—	—	—	—	50	—	—	—	—	—	—	—	—	—	—	—	—	—	—	—	—	—	—	—	—	—	—	—	—	210
—	40	—	—	—	—	—	—	—	—	—	—	40	—	80	—	—	—	—	—	—	—	—	—	—	—	—	—	—	—	—	—	—	—	210
—	—	—	—	—	—	—	—	—	—	—	—	—	—	—	—	—	75	—	—	—	—	—	—	—	—	—	60	—	—	—	—	—	—	—	210
—	—	—	—	—	—	—	—	—	—	—	—	—	—	—	—	—	—	200	—	—	—	—	—	200	—	—	—	—	—	—	—	—	—	—	200
—	30	—	—	—	—	—	—	—	—	—	—	—	—	—	—	—	—	—	—	—	—	—	160	—	—	—	—	—	—	—	—	—	—	—	190
—	—	—	—	—	—	—	—	—	—	—	—	—	—	—	—	—	—	—	—	—	—	—	—	—	160	—	—	—	—	—	—	—	—	—	190
—	—	—	—	—	100	—	—	—	—	—	—	—	—	—	—	—	—	—	—	—	—	—	—	—	—	—	75	—	—	—	—	—	—	—	175
—	—	—	—	—	—	—	—	—	—	—	—	—	—	—	—	—	—	—	—	—	—	—	—	—	—	—	75	—	—	—	—	—	—	—	175

| 12 | 13 | 14 | 15 | 16 | 17 | 18 | 19 | 20 | 21 | 22 | 23 | 24 | 25 | 26 | 27 | 28 | 29 | 30 | 31 | 32 | 33 | 34 | 35 | 36 | 37 | 38 | 39 | 40 | 41 | 42 | 43 | 44 | 45 | 46 | 47 | 48 | TOTAL |

WORLD RALLY CHAMPIONSHIP

	FINAL CLASSIFICATION*	Monte-Carlo	Portugal	Safari	Corsica	Acropolis	Argentina	1000 Lakes	Australia	Italy	RAC	Total
1	Lancia	20	20	(17)	20	17	20	(10)	20	20		
2	Toyota	17	—	20	17	20	17	20	12	(14)		
3	Subaru	—	—	8	—	11	—	12	12	—		
4	Mitsubishi	—	—	10	—	—	—	17	12	10		
5	Mazda	4	8	—	—	—	—	—	8	—		
6	Renault	—	—	—	12	—	12	—	—	—		
	Audi	—	—	6	4	—	12	2	—	—		
7	BMW	—	—	—	14	—	—	—	—	9		
	Ford	—	5	—	—	—	—	—	—	—		
8	Volkswagen	—	—	—	10	—	—	—	—	—		
9	Citroën	—	—	—	8	—	—	—	—	—		
	Renault RA	—	—	—	—	—	8	—	—	—		
10	Fiat RA	—	—	—	—	—	6	—	—	—		
11	Daihatsu	—	—	3	—	—	—	1	—	—		
12	Peugeot	2	—	—	—	—	—	—	—	—		
13	Nissan	—	—	—	—	—	2	—	—	—		

* At the time of going to press, the RAC had not yet taken place. The results will be given in the next edition of *Automobile Year*, but a column has been provided fo readers to complete the results table, while points scores can be inserted in the "total" column.

WORLD RALLY CHAMPIONSHIP FOR DRIVERS

	FINAL CLASSIFICATION*	Monte-Carlo	Portugal	Safari	Corsica	Acropolis	New Zealand	Argentina	1000 Lakes	Australia	Italy	Ivory Coast	RAC	Total
1	C. Sainz	15	+	(10)	15	20	20	15	20	15	12	—		
2	D. Auriol	20	15	—	20	+	—	12	+	+	20	—		
3	J. Kankkunen	+	12	15	—	15	—	+	8	20	15	—		
4	M. Biasion	12	20	+	—	12	—	20	—	F	+	—		
5	M. Ericsson	4	—	12	—	10	—	—	+	+	6	—		
6	D. Cerrato	10	10	—	—	—	—	—	—	—	10	—		
7	R. Stohl	—	—	4	—	+	—	10	—	—	—	15		
8	I. Carlsson	—	—	—	—	—	15	—	—	8	—	—		
	A. Fiorio	—	—	+	—	8	—	—	+	12	3	—		
9	A. Oreille	**	**	—	3	**	1	6	—	+	**	12		
10	B. Waldegård	—	—	20	—	—	—	—	—	—	—	20		
	P. Tauziac	—	—	—	—	—	—	—	—	—	—	20		
11	P. Bourne	—	—	+	—	—	8	—	—	10	—	—		
12	B. Saby	6	—	—	10	—	—	—	—	—	—	—		
13	A. Vatanen	+	+	—	—	+	—	—	15	—	+	—		
14	F. Chatriot	—	—	—	12	—	—	—	—	—	+	—		
	E. Weber	—	—	—	—	+	12	—	—	+	—	—		
	K. Eriksson	+	+	—	—	+	—	—	12	+	—	—		
15	R. Dunkerton	—	—	—	—	—	10	—	—	+	—	—		
	M. Alén	—	—	+	—	+	—	—	10	—	+	—		
	T. Mäkinen	—	—	—	—	—	6	—	**	4	**	—		
	A. Ambrosino	—	—	—	—	—	—	—	—	—	—	10		
16	T. Salonen	3	+	—	—	—	—	—	6	—	—	—		
	G. Trelles	—	**	—	—	2	4	+	**	3	**	+		
17	A. Schwarz	8	+	—	+	—	—	—	—	—	+	—		
	C. Bica	—	8	—	—	—	—	—	—	—	—	—		
	K. Shinozuka	—	—	8	—	—	—	—	—	—	—	—		
	R. Baumschlager	—	+	—	8	—	—	—	—	—	—	—		
	E. Soto	—	**	—	—	+	+	8	**	+	—	—		
	P. Liatti	—	—	—	—	—	—	—	—	—	8	—		
	P. Servant	—	—	—	—	—	—	—	—	—	—	8		
18	J. Recalde	—	4	—	—	+	3	+	**	**	F	—		
19	H. Mikkola	+	6	—	—	—	—	—	+	—	—	—		
	J. Heather-Hayes	—	—	6	—	—	—	—	—	—	—	—		
	L. Poggi	—	—	—	6	—	—	—	—	—	—	—		
	M. Rayneri	—	—	—	—	6	+	—	—	+	—	F		
	G. de Mevius	—	—	—	—	—	—	—	—	6	+	—		
	M. Molinie	—	—	—	—	—	—	—	—	—	—	6		

* At the time of going to press, the RAC had not yet taken place. The results will be given in the next edition of *Automobile Year*, but a column has been provided for readers to complete the results table, while points scores can be inserted in the "total" column.
+ Retired   ** Not classified among first 10 finishers   — Did not participate   F = Did not start.

FIA CUP FOR PRODUCTION CARS' DRIVERS

	FINAL CLASSIFICATION*	Monte-Carlo	Portugal	Safari	Corsica	Acropolis	New Zealand	Argentina	1000 Lakes	Australia	Italy	Ivory Coast	RAC	Total
1	A. Oreille	10	4	—	10	5	4	10	—	+	(3)	13		
2	G. Trelles	—	10	—	—	10	10	+	7	10	5	+		
3	T. Mäkinen	—	—	—	—	—	13	—	13	13	7	—		
4	J. Recalde	—	13	—	—	+	7	—	2	4	—	—		
5	E. Soto	—	7	—	—	+	+	13	5	+	—	—		
6	G. Pianezzola	—	5	—	—	+	5	—	—	+	4	—		
7	P. Njiru	—	—	13	—	—	—	—	—	—	—	—		
8	V. Evina	—	—	—	—	—	—	—	—	—	—	11		
9	C. Vella	—	—	—	—	—	—	—	—	—	—	8		
	A. Oudit	—	—	—	—	—	—	—	—	—	—	8		
10	K. Inoue	—	—	—	—	—	—	—	—	7	—	—		
11	S. Mafall	—	—	—	—	—	—	—	—	—	—	6		
12	E. Ordynski	—	—	—	—	—	—	—	—	5	—	—		
13	R. Meekings	—	—	—	—	—	3	—	—	—	—	—		
	T. Challis	—	—	—	—	—	—	—	—	—	3	—		
14	J. McAndrew	—	—	—	—	—	2	—	—	—	2	—		
	R. Cremen	—	—	—	—	—	—	—	—	2	—	—		
15	T. Teesdale	—	—	—	—	—	1	—	—	—	—	—		
	S. Ashton	—	—	—	—	—	—	—	—	1	—	—		

* At the time of going to press, the RAC had not yet taken place. The results will be given in the next edition of *Automobile Year*, but a column has been provided for readers to complete the results table, while points scores can be inserted in the "total" column.
+ Retired   ** Not classified among first 10 finishers   — Did not participate   F = Did not start.

INTERNATIONAL F3000 CHAMPIONSHIP

DONINGTON

Date: 22 April 1990. **Distance:** 50 laps of the Donington circuit = 201.17 km/125.00 miles. **Weather:** cloudy, track drying at start.

Result:

Driver	Car	Laps	Time	Speed
1 Comas	Lola T90/50-Mugen	50	1.12′15″3	167.04 kmh/
2 Chiesa	Lola T90/50-Mugen	50	+ 25″8	103.79 mph
3 Jones	Lola T90/50-Mugen	50	+ 26″8	
4 Tamburini	Reynard 90D-Cosworth	50	+ 27″4	
5 Dean	Reynard 90D-Mugen	50	+ 38″9	
6 van de Poele	Reynard 90D-Cosworth	50	+ 1′03″6	
7 Delétraz	Reynard 90D-Cosworth	50	+ 1′09″5	
8 Morbidelli	Lola T90/50-Cosworth	50	+ 1′09″6	
9 Gache	Reynard 90D-Cosworth	50	+ 1′13″3	
10 Bonanno	Lola T90/50-Mugen	50	+ 1′15″	
11 Bartels	Reynard 90D-Mugen	49		
12 Proulx	Lola T90/50-Mugen	49		

Fastest lap: Proulx, Lola T90/50-Mugen, 1′22″29 = 176.0 kmh/ 109.36 mph (record).

Retirements:

Driver	Car	Laps	Reason
Giovanardi	Reynard 90D-Mugen	0	spun
Aloï	Reynard 90D-Cosworth	0	spun
McNish	Lola T90/50-Mugen	2	accident
Naspetti	Reynard 90D-Mugen	2	accident
Barbazza	Leyton-House 90B-Cosworth	5	electrics
Belmondo	Reynard 90D-Mugen	11	gearbox
Montermini	Reynard 90D-Mugen	11	stub axle failure
Irvine	Reynard 90D-Mugen	12	gearbox, spun
Amati	Reynard 90D-Cosworth	23	spun, collision
Gounon	Reynard 90D-Mugen	29	collision
Frentzen	Reynard 90D-Mugen	35	spun
Gilbert-Scott	Leyton-House 90B-Cosworth	42	puncture, spun
Andrews	Reynard 90D-Mugen	45	collision (classified)
Apicella	Reynard 90D-Mugen	45	out of fuel (classified)

SILVERSTONE

Date: 19 May 1990. **Distance:** 41 laps of the Silverstone GP circuit = 195.98 km/121.77 miles. **Weather:** sunny.

Result:

Driver	Car	Laps	Time	Speed
1 McNish	Lola T90/50-Mugen	41	54′23″2	216.19 kmh/
2 Comas	Lola T90/50-Mugen	41	+ 2″0	134.338mph
3 Apicella	Reynard 90D-Mugen	41	+ 10″8	
4 Montermini	Reynard 90D-Mugen	41	+ 28″3	
5 van de Poele	Reynard 90D-Cosworth	41	+ 29″3	
6 Irvine	Reynard 90D-Mugen	41	+ 29″8	
7 Dean	Reynard 90D-Mugen	41	+ 44″6	
8 Bonanno	Lola T90/50-Mugen	41	+ 51″7	
9 Tamburini	Reynard 90D-Cosworth	41	+ 1′04″1	
10 Naspetti	Reynard 90D-Mugen	41	+ 1′08″8	
11 Jones	Lola T90/50-Mugen	41	+ 1′18″8	
12 Gilbert-Scott	Leyton-House 90B-Cosworth	41	+ 1′19″3	
13 Gounon	Reynard 90D-Mugen	40		
14 Wendlinger	Lola T90/50-Cosworth	40		
15 Aloï	Reynard 90D-Cosworth	40		
16 Giovanardi*	Reynard 90D-Mugen	36		

* Classified, not running at end.

Fastest lap: McNish, Lola T90/50-Mugen, 1′18″31 = 219.722 kmh/ 136.533 mph.

Retirements:

Driver	Car	Laps	Reason
Proulx	Lola T90/50-Mugen	2	accident
Artzet	Reynard 90D-Cosworth	3	gearbox
Brabham	Lola T90/50-Cosworth	7	puncture, left track
Bartels	Reynard 90D-Mugen	11	gearbox
Andrews	Reynard 90D-Mugen	13	engine
Frentzen	Reynard 90D-Mugen	13	puncture, spun
Hill	Lola T90/50-Cosworth	16	electrics
Morbidelli	Lola T90/50-Cosworth	21	accident
Barbazza	Leyton-House 90B-Cosworth	23	engine
Chiesa	Lola T90/50-Mugen	33	fuel pick-up

PAU

Date: 4 June 1990. **Distance:** 69 laps of the Pau street circuit = 192 km/116.7 miles. **Weather:** overcast.

Result:

Driver	Car	Laps	Time	Speed
1 van de Poele	Reynard 90D-Cosworth	69	1.24′18″7	135.86 kmh/
2 Giovanardi	Reynard 90D-Mugen	69	+ 20″3	83.97 mph
3 Morbidelli	Lola T90/50-Cosworth	69	+ 34″8	
4 Jones	Lola T90/50-Mugen	69	+ 1′03″4	
5 Fréon	Lola T89/50-Cosworth	65	not running at end	
6 McNish	Lola T90/50-Mugen	65	not running at end	

Fastest lap: Apicella, Reynard 90D-Mugen, 1′11″71 = 138.55 kmh/ 86.04 mph.

Retirements:

Driver	Car	Laps	Reason
Bartels	Reynard 90D-Mugen	0	disqualified
Frentzen	Reynard 90D-Mugen	3	accident
Irvine	Reynard 90D-Mugen	7	accident
Barbazza	Leyton-House 90B-Cosworth	7	accident
Naspetti	Reynard 90D-Mugen	8	accident
Artzet	Reynard 90D-Cosworth	16	accident
Hill	Lola T90/50-Cosworth	19	fuel pump
Delétraz	Reynard 90D-Cosworth	21	accident
Dean	Reynard 90D-Mugen	24	accident
Gache	Reynard 90D-Cosworth	25	engine
Chiesa	Lola T90/50-Mugen	27	accident
Tamburini	Reynard 90D-Cosworth	32	battery
Proulx	Lola T90/50-Mugen	36	accident
Apicella	Reynard 90D-Mugen	40	accident
Montermini	Reynard 90D-Mugen	54	fuel leak

JEREZ

Date: 17 June 1990. **Distance:** 48 laps of the Jerez circuit = 202.0 km/ 125.52 miles. **Weather:** fine, hot.

Result:

Driver	Car	Laps	Time	Speed
1 Comas	Lola T90/50-Mugen	48	1.18′07″	155.508 kmh/
2 Apicella	Reynard 90D-Mugen	48	+ 1″3	96.63 mph
3 Montermini	Reynard 90D-Mugen	48	+ 31″1	
4 Barbazza	Leyton-House 90B-Cosworth	48	+ 54″8	
5 Chiesa	Lola T90/50-Mugen	48	+ 1′00″4	
6 Giovanardi	Reynard 90D-Mugen	48	+ 1′02″2	
7 Hill	Lola T90/50-Cosworth	48	+ 1′05″1	
8 Sospiri	Reynard 90D-Mugen	48	+ 1′10″3	
9 van de Poele	Reynard 90D-Cosworth	47		
10 Gilbert-Scott	Leyton-House 90B-Cosworth	47		
11 Artzet	Reynard 90D-Cosworth	47		
12 Brabham	Lola T90/50-Cosworth	47		
13 Tamburini	Reynard 90D-Cosworth	47		
14 Gache	Reynard 90D-Cosworth	47		
15 Aloï	Reynard 90D-Cosworth	47		
16 McNish	Lola T90/50-Mugen	47		
17 Frentzen	Reynard 90D-Mugen	47		

Fastest lap: Apicella, Reynard 90D-Mugen, 1′35″22 = 159.471 kmh/ 99.09 mph.

Retirements:

Driver	Car	Laps	Reason
Morbidelli	Lola T90/50-Cosworth	0	accident
Jones	Lola T90/50-Mugen	7	accident
Gounon	Reynard 90D-Mugen	8	accident
Bonnano	Lola T90/50-Mugen	8	accident
Dean	Reynard 90D-Mugen	11	gearbox
Belmondo	Reynard 90D-Mugen	13	suspension damage
Bartels	Reynard 90D-Mugen	31	accident
Proulx	Lola T90/50-Mugen	38	accident

MONZA

Date: 24 June 1990. **Distance:** 34 laps of the Monza circuit = 197.2 km/ 122.54 miles. **Weather:** fine, hot.

Result:

Driver	Car	Laps	Time	Speed
1 Comas	Lola T90/50-Mugen	34	55′19″12	213.88 kmh/
2 Irvine	Reynard 90D-Mugen	34	+ 1″7	132.90 mph
3 Brabham	Lola T90/50-Cosworth	34	+ 3″1	
4 Morbidelli	Lola T90/50-Cosworth	34	+ 4″6	
5 Apicella	Reynard 90D-Mugen	34	+ 7″4	
6 McNish	Lola T90/50-Mugen	34	+ 9″2	
7 Chiesa	Lola T90/50-Mugen	34	+ 14″0	
8 Tamburini	Reynard 90D-Cosworth	34	+ 21″4	
9 van de Poele	Reynard 90D-Cosworth	34	+ 26″5	
10 Giovanardi	Reynard 90D-Mugen	34	+ 1′01″3	
11 Hill	Lola T90/50-Cosworth	33		

Fastest lap: Hill, Lola T90/50-Cosworth, 1′35″66 = 218.27 kmh/ 135.63 mph.

Retirements:

Driver	Car	Laps	Reason
Artzet	Reynard 90D-Cosworth	0	accident
Delétraz	Reynard 90D-Cosworth	1	accident
Dean	Reynard 90D-Mugen	1	accident damage
Montermini	Reynard 90D-Mugen	2	accident
Naspetti	Reynard 90D-Mugen	3	battery
Barbazza	Leyton-House 90B-Cosworth	4	accident
Bartels	Reynard 90D-Mugen	4	puncture
Proulx	Lola T90/50-Mugen	7	accident damage
Gounon	Reynard 90D-Mugen	8	accident
Frentzen	Reynard 90D-Mugen	10	accident damage
Belmondo	Reynard 90D-Mugen	10	suspension damage
Gache	Reynard 90D-Cosworth	16	accident
Gilbert-Scott	Leyton-House 90B-Cosworth	16	engine
Wendlinger	Lola T90/50-Cosworth	23	engine electrics
Jones	Lola T90/50-Mugen	28	cv joint

ENNA

Date: 22 July 1990. **Distance:** 36 laps of the Enna-Pergusa circuit = 178.27 km/110.72 miles. **Weather:** very hot.

Result:

Driver	Car	Laps	Time	Speed
1 Morbidelli	Lola T90/50-Cosworth	36	55′27″21	192.809 kmh/
2 McNish	Lola T90/50-Mugen	36	+ 46″86	119.809 mph
3 Brabham	Lola T90/50-Cosworth	36	+ 1′13″1	
4 Irvine	Reynard 90D-Mugen	36	+ 1′13″9	
5 Frentzen	Reynard 90D-Mugen	36	+ 1′17″5	
6 Giovanardi	Reynard 90D-Mugen	36	+ 1′46″6	
Gounon*	Reynard 90D-Mugen	36		
7 Bartels	Reynard 90D-Mugen	34		
8 Tamburini	Reynard 90D-Cosworth	33		

* Black flagged, excluded for outside assistance after spin.

Fastest lap: Hill (Lola T90/50-Cosworth) 1′29″42 = 199.277 kmh/ 123.828 mph.

Retirements:

Driver	Car	Laps	Reason
Chiesa	Lola T90/50-Mugen	0	accident
Montermini	Reynard 90D-Mugen	0	accident
Gilbert-Scott	Leyton House 90B-Cosworth	1	throttle stuck, accident
Greco	Reynard 90D-Cosworth	1	accident
Gache	Reynard 90D-Cosworth	1	accident
Barbazza	Leyton House 90B-Cosworth	2	fuel pump
Naspetti	Reynard 90D-Mugen	4	spin
Wendliger	Lola T90/50-Cosworth	6	spin
Andrews	Reynard 90D-Mugen	7	spin
Jones	Lola T90/50-Mugen	7	spin
Gitto	Lola T90/50-Mugen	9	spin, push start, excluded
Comas	Lola T90/50-Mugen	10	spin
Apicella	Reynard 90D-Mugen	11	spin
van de Poele	Reynard 90D-Cosworth	14	accident
Artzet	Reynard 90D-Cosworth	20	accident
Proulx	Lola T90/50-Mugen	28	accident
Hill	Lola T90/50-Cosworth	29	fuel pump

HOCKENHEIM

Date: 28 July 1990. **Distance:** 29 laps of the Hockenheim circuit = 197.11 km/122.407 miles. **Weather:** fine, hot.

Result:

Driver	Car	Laps	Time	Speed
1 Irvine	Reynard 90D-Mugen	29	58′14″6	203.058 kmh/
2 Apicella	Reynard 90D-Mugen	29	+ 4″83	126.109 mph
3 Gounon	Reynard 90D-Mugen	29	+ 32″79	
4 Comas	Lola T90/50-Mugen	29	+ 39″55	
5 Wendlinger	Lola T90/50-Cosworth	29	+ 53″57	
6 Frentzen	Reynard 90D-Mugen	29	+ 54″80	
7 Giovanardi	Reynard 90D-Mugen	29	+ 55″73	
8 Artzet	Reynard 90D-Cosworth	29	+ 1′11″57	
9 Barbazza	Leyton House 90B-Cosworth	29	+ 1′23″46	
10 Proulx	Lola T90/50-Mugen	29	+ 1′33″42	
11 Belmondo	Reynard 90D-Mugen	29	+ 1′52″62	
12 Andrews	Reynard 90D-Mugen	29	+ 1′56″45	
13 Brabham*	Lola T90/50-Mugen	28		
14 Amati	Reynard 90D-Mugen	28		

* Classified, not running at end.

Fastest lap: Apicella (Reynard 90D-Mugen) 1′59″35 = 204.940 kmh/ 127.267 mph.

Retirements:

Driver	Car	Laps	Reason
Hill	Lola T90/50-Cosworth	1	accident
Montermini	Reynard 90D-Mugen	2	spin
Bartels	Reynard 90D-Mugen	8	differential
McNish	Lola T90/50-Mugen	10	electrics
van de Poele	Reynard 90D-Cosworth	11	front suspension
Gache	Reynard 90D-Cosworth	12	engine
Gitto	Lola T90/50-Mugen	13	engine
delle Piane	Reynard 90D-Cosworth	16	spin
Chiesa	Lola T90/50-Mugen	19	gearbox
Morbidelli	Lola T90/50-Cosworth	20	stuck throttle, off road
Naspetti	Reynard 90D-Mugen	21	spin
Brabham	Lola T90/50-Cosworth	28	battery

INTERNATIONAL F3000 CHAMPIONSHIP

BRANDS HATCH

Date: 19 August 1990. **Distance:** 48 laps of the Brands Hatch Grand Prix circuit = 200.85 km/124.81 miles. **Weather:** wet at start, track drying during race.

Result:

	Driver	Car	Laps	Time	Speed
1	McNish	Lola T90/50-Mugen	49	1.09'09"6	174,22 kmh/
2	Hill	Lola T90/50-Cosworth	49	+ 10"2	108.26 mph
3	Apicella	Reynard 90D-Mugen	49	+ 20"4	
4	Irvine	Reynard 90D-Mugen	49	+ 22"4	
5	Chaves	Reynard 90D-Mugen	49	+ 36"2	
6	Chiesa	Lola T90/50-Mugen	49	+ 42"8	
7	Gounon	Reynard 90D-Mugen	49	+ 58"5	
8	Frentzen	Reynard 90D-Mugen	49	+ 1'09"1	
9	Brabham	Lola T90/50-Mugen	48		
10	Bonanno	Lola T90/50-Mugen	48		
11	Gilbert-Scott	Reynard 90D-Cosworth	48		
12	Bartels	Reynard 90D-Mugen	46		
13	Favre	Leyton House 90B-Cosworth	44		

Fastest lap: Bartels, Reynard 90D-Mugen, 1'15"56 = 199.35 kmh/123.87 mph.

Retirements:

Driver	Car	Laps	Reason
Barbazza	Leyton House 90B-Cosworth	7	accident
Montermini	Reynard 90D-Mugen	10	spin
della Piane	Reynard 90D-Cosworth	13	misfire
Proulx	Lola T90/50-Mugen	14	gearbox
Warwick	Leyton House 90B-Cosworth	23	electrics
Naspetti	Reynard 90D-Mugen	24	gearbox
Comas	Lola T90/50-Mugen	26	oil pressure
Tamburini	Reynard 90D-Cosworth	26	engine
Giovanardi	Reynard 90D-Mugen	27	spin
Andrews	Reynard 90D-Mugen	28	accident
van de Poele	Reynard 90D-Cosworth	38	fuel pick-up
Morbidelli	Lola T90/50-Cosworth	38	accident
Belmondo	Reynard 90D-Mugen	43	battery loose

BIRMINGHAM

Date: 27 August 1990. **Distance:** 51 laps of the Birmingham street circuit = 202.73 km/125.97 miles. **Weather:** fine, overcast.

Result:

	Driver	Car	Laps	Time	Speed
1	van de Poele	Reynard 90D-Cosworth	51	1.11'47"	171,64 kmh/
2	Chiesa	Lola T90/50-Mugen	51	+ 18"9	106.65 mph
3	Artzet	Reynard 90D-Cosworth	51	+ 19"6	
4	Gounon	Reynard 90D-Mugen	51	+ 20"4	
5	Giovanardi	Reynard 90D-Mugen	51	+ 33"1	
6	Naspetti	Reynard 90D-Mugen	51	+ 43"4	
7	Gilbert-Scott	Reynard 90D-Cosworth	50		

8	Warwick	Leyton House 90B-Cosworth	50
9	Montermini	Reynard 90D-Mugen	50
10	Wendlinger	Lola T90/50-Cosworth	50
11	Jones	Lola T90/50-Mugen	49

Fastest lap: Apicella (Reynard 90D-Mugen) 1'22"93 = 172.55 kmh/107.22 mph.

Retirements:

Driver	Car	Laps	Reason
Chaves	Reynard 90D-Mugen	6	gearbox
Hill	Lola T90/50-Cosworth	9	brakes/handling
McNish	Lola T90/50-Mugen	17	gearbox
Apicella	Reynard 90D-Mugen	19	holed radiator
Andrews	Reynard 90D-Mugen	20	accident
Morbidelli	Lola T90/50-Cosworth	23	hand injured
Frentzen	Reynard 90D-Mugen	30	accident
Tamburini	Reynard 90D-Cosworth	33	suspension
Proulx	Lola T90/50-Mugen	34	accident
Comas	Lola T90/50-Mugen	34	brakes
Belmondo	Reynard 90D-Mugen	35	gearbox
Bartels	Reynard 90D-Mugen	35	engine
Barbazza	Leyton House 90B-Cosworth	38	accident
Irvine	Reynard 90D-Mugen	38	accident

LE MANS

Date: 23 September 1990. **Distance:** 45 laps of the Le Mans Bugatti circuit = 199.35 km/123.75 miles. **Weather:** sunny.

Result:

	Driver	Car	Laps	Time	Speed
1	Comas	Lola T90/50-Mugen	45	1.11'41"6	166,83 kmh/
2	Montermini	Reynard 90D-Mugen	45	+ 11"1	103.67 mph
3	Irvine	Reynard 90D-Mugen	45	+ 16"9	
4	Gounon	Reynard 90D-Mugen	45	+ 17"1	
5	Chiesa	Lola T90/50-Mugen	45	+ 18"3	
6	Belmondo	Reynard 90D-Mugen	45	+ 18"8	
7	Morbidelli	Lola T90/50-Cosworth	45	+ 19"5	
8	Brabham	Lola T90/50-Cosworth	45	+ 26"3	
9	Jones	Lola T90/50-Mugen	45	+ 35"4	
10	van de Poele	Reynard 90D-Cosworth	45	+ 49"1	
11	Gilbert-Scott	Reynard 90D-Cosworth	45	+ 53"9	
12	Andrews	Reynard 90D-Mugen	45	+ 54"5	
13	Bartels	Reynard 90D-Mugen	45	+ 1'05"6	
14	Fréon	Reynard 90D-Cosworth	45	+ 1'17"4	
15	Favre	Leyton House 90B-Cosworth	44		
16	Tamburini	Reynard 90D-Cosworth	42		
17	Delubac	Reynard 90D-Cosworth	42		
18	Apicella*	Reynard 90D-Mugen	40		
19	Proulx*	Lola T90/50-Mugen	40		

* Not running at end (accident).

Fastest lap: Gache, Lola T90/50-Cosworth, 1'33"21 = 171.097 kmh/106.32 mph (record).

Retirements:

Driver	Car	Laps	Reason
Warwick	Leyton House 90B-Cosworth	0	DNS (wheel nut)
Barbazza	Leyton House 90B-Cosworth	2	CV joint
Gache	Lola T89/50-Cosworth	8	electronics
Frentzen	Reynard 90D-Mugen	11	accident
McNish	Lola T90/50-Mugen	25	electrics
Giovanardi	Reynard 90D-Mugen	30	engine
Hill	Lola T90/50-Cosworth	35	broken exhaust

NOGARO

Date: 7 October 1990. **Distance:** 55 laps of the Nogaro circuit = 199.98 km/124.98 miles. **Weather:** cool and rainy.

Result:

	Driver	Car	Laps	Time	Speed
1	van de Poele	Reynard 90D-Cosworth	55	1.20'27"8	149.12 kmh/
2	Comas	Lola T90/50-Mugen	55	+ 11"0	93.2 mph
3	Morbidelli	Lola T90/50-Mugen	55	+ 26"3	
4	Tamburini	Reynard 90D-Cosworth	55	+ 46"0	
5	Apicella	Reynard 90D-Mugen	55	+ 46"4	
6	Bartels	Reynard 90D-Mugen	55	+ 48"2	
7	Proulx	Lola T90/50-Mugen	55	+ 48"8	
8	McNish	Lola T90/50-Mugen	55	+ 51"2	
9	Wendlinger	Lola T90/50-Cosworth	54		
10	Hill	Lola T90/50-Cosworth	54		
11	Brabham	Lola T90/50-Cosworth	54		
12	Menu	Reynard 90D-Mugen	54		
13	Gilbert-Scott	Reynard 90D-Cosworth	54		
14	Chaves	Reynard 90D-Cosworth	54		
15	Warwick	Leyton House 90B-Cosworth	54		
16	Fréon	Reynard 90D-Cosworth	54		
17	Delubac	Reynard 90D-Cosworth	54		
18	Barbazza	Leyton House 90B-Cosworth	54		
19	Andrews	Reynard 90D-Mugen	54		

Fastest lap: Comas (Lola T90/50-Mugen) 1'20"30 = 163.00 kmh/101.87 mph.

Retirements:

Driver	Car	Laps	Reason
Belmondo	Reynard 90D-Mugen	1	accident
Gounon	Reynard 90D-Mugen	2	spun
Irvine	Reynard 90D-Mugen	5	accident
Chiesa	Lola T90/50-Mugen	11	gearbox
Gache	Lola T89/50-Cosworth	19	ignition
Giovanardi	Reynard 90D-Mugen	39	accident
Montermini	Reynard 90D-Mugen	47	accident

	FINAL CLASSIFICATION		Doning-ton	Silver-stone	Pau	Jerez	Monza	Enna	Hocken-heim	Brands Hatch	Birming-ham	Bugatti-Le Mans	Nogaro	Total
1	E. COMAS (F)	Lola T90/50-Mugen	9	6	—	9	9	—	3	—	—	9	6	51
2	E. VAN DE POELE (B)	Reynard 90D-Cosworth	1	2	9	—	—	—	—	—	9	—	9	30
3	E. IRVINE (GB)	Reynard 90D-Mugen	—	1	—	—	6	3	9	4	—	4	—	27
4	A. McNISH (GB)	Lola T90/50-Mugen	—	9	1	—	1	6	—	9	—	—	—	26
5	G. MORBIDELLI (I)	Lola T90/50-Cosworth	—	—	4	—	3	9	—	—	—	—	4	20
	M. APICELLA (I)	Reynard 90D-Mugen	—	4	—	6	2	—	6	—	—	—	2	20
6	A. CHIESA (CH)	Lola T90/50-Mugen	6	—	—	2	—	—	—	2	6	2	—	18
7	A. MONTERMINI (I)	Reynard 90D-Mugen	—	3	—	4	—	—	—	—	6	—	13
8	J.-M. GOUNON (F)	Reynard 90D-Mugen	—	—	—	—	—	—	4	1	3	3	—	11
9	F. GIOVANARDI (I)	Reynard 90D-Mugen	—	—	6	1	—	1	—	—	2	—	—	10
10	G. BRABHAM (AUS)	Lola T90/50-Cosworth	—	—	—	—	4	4	—	—	—	—	—	8
11	J. JONES (CDN)	Lola T90/50-Cosworth	4	—	3	—	—	—	—	—	—	—	—	7
12	D. HILL (GB)	Lola T90/50-Cosworth	—	—	—	—	—	—	—	6	—	—	—	6
	A. TAMBURINI (I)	Reynard 90D-Cosworth	3	—	—	—	—	—	—	—	—	—	3	6
13	D. ARTZET (F)	Reynard 90D-Cosworth	—	—	—	—	—	—	—	—	4	—	—	4
14	F. BARBAZZA (I)	Leyton House 90B-Cosworth	—	—	—	—	3	—	—	—	—	—	—	3
	H.-H. FRENTZEN (A)	Reynard 90D-Mugen	—	—	—	—	—	2	1	—	—	—	—	3
	P. CHAVES (F)	Reynard 90D-Cosworth	—	—	—	—	—	—	—	3	—	—	—	3
15	K. WENDLINGER (D)	Lola T90/50-Cosworth	—	—	—	—	—	—	2	—	—	—	—	2
	R. DEAN (GB)	Reynard 90D-Mugen	2	—	—	—	—	—	—	—	—	—	—	2
	F. FREON (F)	Lola T89/50-Cosworth	—	—	2	—	—	—	—	—	—	—	—	2
		Reynard 90D-Cosworth												
16	E. NASPETTI (I)	Reynard 90D-Mugen	—	—	—	—	—	—	—	—	1	—	—	1
	P. BELMONDO (F)	Reynard 90D-Mugen	—	—	—	—	—	—	—	—	1	—	—	1
	M. BARTELS (D)	Reynard 90D-Mugen	—	—	—	—	—	—	—	—	—	—	1	1

WORLD SPORTS-PROTOTYPE CHAMPIONSHIP

SUZUKA

Date: 9 April 1990. **Distance:** 82 laps of the 5.859 km/3.641 mile Suzuka circuit = 480.470 km/298.564 miles. **Weather:** dull, track damp at start.

Result:

	Drivers	No	Car	Laps	Time	Speed
1	Schlesser-Baldi	1	Sauber C9-Mercedes	82	2.43'45"	176,031 kmh/
2	Mass-Wendlinger	2	Sauber C9-Mercedes	82	+42"	109.385 mph
3	Hasemi-Olofsson	24	Nissan R 90 CP	81		
4	Lees-Ogawa	36	Toyota 90 C-V	81		
5	Takahashi-Mogi	11	Porsche 962 C	80		
6	Huysman-Larrauri	15	Porsche 962 C	80		
7	Andskar-Fouché	17	Porsche 962 GTI	80		
8	Needell-Bell	34	Porsche 962 C	80		
9	Schuppan-Elgh	19	Porsche 962 C	79		
10	Weidler-Nakaya	39	Porsche 962 C	79		
11	Palmer-Pescarolo	8	Porsche 962 C	78		
12	Fabre-Robert	13	Cougar C24S-Porsche	78		
13	Lässig-Altenbach	27	Porsche 962 C	77		
14	Schneider-Okada	10	Porsche 962 C	77		
15	Takahashi-Hoy	12	Cougar C24S-Porsche	77		
16	Reuter-Perez Sala	14	Porsche 962 GTI	77		
17	"Winter"-Dickens	9	Porsche 962 C	76		
18	Lee Davey-Ricci	20	Porsche 962 C	76		
19	Jourdain-Salazar	21	Spice SE90C-Cosworth	75		
20	Konrad-Ricci	32	Porsche 962 C	75		
21	Suzuki-Dumfries	37	Toyota 90 C-V	73		
22	Hobbs-de Henning*	30	Spice SE90C-Cosworth	60		

* Classified, but not running at end.

Fastest lap: Brundle, Jaguar XJR 12, 1'53"732 = 185.40 kmh/115.20 mph.

Retirements:

Drivers	No	Car	Laps	Reason
Asai-Yoneyama	29	TOM's 86C-Cosworth	13	accident
Randaccio-Stingbrace	40	Spice SE90C-Cosworth	14	accident
Wollek-Jelinski	10	Porsche 962 C	23	pits fire
Harvey-Giacomelli	22	Spice SE90C-Cosworth	28	fuel filler
Migault	35	ALD C 289-Cosworth	36	accident
Lammers-Wallace	4	Jaguar XJR 12	44	engine
Acheson-Wada	25	Nissan R 89 C	45	accident
Grohs	26	Porsche 962 C	39	electrics
Hoshino-Gilbert-Scott	23	Nissan R 90 CP	65	accident
Pareja-Brun	16	Porsche 962 C	74	driveshaft
Brundle-Ferté	3	Jaguar XJR 12	77	engine
Ratzenberger-Raphanel	38	Toyota 90 C-V	79	out of fuel

MONZA

Date: 29 April 1990. **Distance:** 83 laps of the 5.8 km/3.6 mile Monza circuit = 481.400 km/299.13 miles. **Weather:** fine.

Result:

	Drivers	No	Car	Laps	Time	Speed
1	Schlesser-Baldi	1	Mercedes C 11	83	2.17'11"	210.532 kmh/
2	Mass-Wendlinger	2	Mercedes C 11	83	+17"	130.824 mph
3	Brundle-Ferté	3	Jaguar XJR 11	83	+26"	
4	Lammers-Wallace	6	Jaguar XJR 11	82		
5	Wollek-Jelinski	7	Porsche 962 C	82		
6	Taylor-van de Poele	22	Spice SE90C-Cosworth	81		
7	Bailey-Acheson	23	Nissan R 90 CK	81		
8	Palmer-Needell	8	Porsche 962 C	81		
9	Schneider-van de Merwe	10	Porsche CK 6	80		
10	Olofsson-Reid	11	Porsche CK 6	79		
11	Jourdain-Velez	21	Spice SE90C-Cosworth	79		
12	Sigala-Elgh	17	Porsche 962 C	79		
13	Fabre-Gabbiani	13	Cougar C24 S-Porsche	79		
14	Ricci-Pescarolo	6	Porsche 962 C	78		
15	Grohs-Oppermann**	26	Porsche 962 C	77		
16	Salamin-Taverna	39	Porsche 962 C	76		
	Ballabio-Giacomelli*	20	Porsche 962 C	76		
17	Reuter-Weaver	14	Porsche 962 C	70		

** Classified, but not running at end.
* Disqualified.

Fastest lap: Mass, Mercedes C 11, 1'33"426 = 223.492 kmh/138.878 mph.

Retirements:

Drivers	No	Car	Laps	Reason
Lees-Suzuki	36	Toyota 90 C-V	4	accident
Migault-Morin	35	ALD C289-Cosworth	5	electrics
Konrad-Coppelli	32	Porsche 962 C	7	transmission
Lässig-Altenbach	27	Porsche 962 C	11	accident
de Henning-Hoy	30	Spice SE90C-Cosworth	14	engine
Larrauri-Huysmans	15	Porsche 962 C	20	engine
Euser	29	Spice SE90C-Cosworth	20	accident
Randaccio-Barberio	40	Spice SE90C-Cosworth	50	brakes, spun
Ravaglia-Dumfries	37	Toyota 90 C-V	56	accident
Pareja-Brun	16	Porsche 962 C	63	disqualified
Boesel	33	Porsche 962 C	65	engine
"Winter"-Dickens	9	Porsche 962 C	77	out of fuel
Blundell-Brancatelli	24	Nissan R 90 CK	79	out of fuel

SILVERSTONE

Date: 20 May 1990. **Distance:** 101 laps of the 4.78 km/2.97 mile Silverstone GP circuit = 482.760 km/299.97 miles. **Weather:** fine.

Result:

	Drivers	No	Car	Laps	Time	Speed
1	Brundle-Ferté	3	Jaguar XJR 11	101	2.19'39"46	207,413 kmh/
2	Lammers-Wallace	4	Jaguar XJR 11	100		128.886 mph
3	Velez-Giacomelli	21	Spice SE90C-Cosworth	100		
4	Wollek-Jelinski	7	Porsche 962 C	99		
	Blundell-Brancatelli*	24	Nissan R 90 C	99		
5	Schneider-Anskar	10	Porsche 962 CK 6	98		
6	Larrauri-Huysman	15	Porsche 962 C	97		
7	Pareja-Brun	16	Porsche 962 C	97		
8	Sigala-Santal	17	Porsche 962 C	96		
9	Elgh-Reid	11	Porsche 962 CK 6	96		
10	Grohs-Oppermann	26	Porsche 962 C	96		
11	Weaver-Reuter	14	Porsche 962 CTI	96		
12	Lees-Watson	36	Toyota 89 C-V	95		
13	Lavaggi-Lee Davey	20	Porsche 962 C	95		
	Scott-Toledano*	20	Porsche 962 C	94		
14	Konrad-Toivonen	32	Porsche 962 C	93		
15	Trollé-Fabre	13	Cougar C24 S-Porsche	92		
16	Los-Thuner	12	Cougar C24 S-Porsche	92		
17	Adams-Piper	29	Spice SE90C-Cosworth	90		
18	Lässig-Altenbach	27	Porsche 962 CTI	88		
19	"Stingbrace"-Randaccio	40	Spice SE90C-Cosworth	87		
20	Migault-Morin	35	ALD C 289-Cosworth	78		

* Took flag but unclassified as last lap took too long.

Fastest lap: Schlesser, Mercedes C11, 1'16"649 = 224.504 kmh/139.49 mph.

Retirements:

Drivers	No	Car	Laps	Reason
"Winter"-Dickens	9	Porsche 962 C	3	accident
Wood-Barberio	31	Spice SE87C-Cosworth	16	electrics
Euser-Nytten	28	Spice SE89C-Cosworth	32	suspension
Nurminen-de Henning	30	Spice SE90C-Cosworth	35	electrics
Schlesser-Baldi	1	Mercedes C 11	40	engine
Palmer-Needell	8	Porsche 962 C	70	transmission
Taylor-Harvey	22	Spice SE90C-Cosworth	70	engine
Bailey-Acheson	23	Nissan R 90 C	92	suspension
Ogawa-Dumfries	37	Toyota 90 C-V	92	disqualified

SPA-FRANCORCHAMPS

Date: 3 June 1990. **Distance:** 70 laps of the 6.94 km/4.312 mile Spa-Francorchamps circuit = 485.760 km/301.85 miles. **Weather:** wet at start, track drying.

Result:

	Drivers	No	Car	Laps	Time	Speed
1	Mass-Wendlinger	2	Mercedes C 11	70	2.42'54"8	178.916 kmh/
2	Lammers-Wallace	4	Jaguar XJR 11	70	+ 1'30"7	111.176 mph
3	Bailey-Acheson	23	Nissan R 90 CP	70	+ 1'36"2	
4	Velez-Harvey	21	Spice SE90C-Cosworth	69		
5	Larrauri-Huysman	15	Porsche 962 C	69		
6	Andskar-Reuter	14	Porsche 962 GTI	69		
7	Wollek-Jelinski	7	Porsche 962 C	69		
8	Schlesser-Baldi	1	Mercedes C 11	68		
9	Schneider-van der Merwe	10	Porsche 962 CK6	68		
10	Blundell-Brancatelli	24	Nissan R 90 CP	67		
11	Lässig-Altenbach	27	Porsche 962 C	67		
12	Reid-Olofsson	11	Porsche 962 C	66		
13	Konrad-Toivonen	32	Porsche 962 C	65		
14	Sigala-Santal	17	Porsche 962 C	65		
15	Ricci-Pescarolo	6	Porsche 962 C	65		
16	"Winter"-Dickens	9	Porsche 962 C	65		
17	Lavaggi-Lee Davey	19	Porsche 962 C	65		
18	Dumfries-Watson	36	Toyota 90 C-V	63		
19	Euser-Hytten	28	Spice SE90C-Cosworth	63		
20	Los-Thuner	12	Cougar C24 S-Porsche	62		
21	Salamin-Taverna	39	Porsche 962 C	60		
22	Almeras-Almeras	34	Porsche 962 C	58		
23	"Stingbrace"-Randaccio	40	Spice SE90C-Cosworth	58		
24	Nurminen-Bovy	30	Spice SE90C-Cosworth	56		
25	Migault-Morin	35	ALD C 289-Cosworth	56		

Fastest lap: Baldi, Mercedes C 11, 2'06"211 = 197.954 kmh/123.006 mph.

Retirements:

Drivers	No	Car	Laps	Reason
Grohs-Oppermann	26	Porsche 962 C	17	accident
Palmer-Bell	8	Porsche 962 C	27	accident
Fabre-Trollé	13	Cougar C24 S-Porsche	28	engine
Adams-Hausmann	29	Spice SE90C-Cosworth	40	gearbox
Brundle-Ferté	3	Jaguar XJR 11	46	electrical fire
Pareja-Brun	16	Porsche 962 C	62	engine

LES 24 HEURES DU MANS

Date:	June 16-17 1990
Weather:	Fine
Circuit:	13.6 km/8.45 miles
Starters:	49
Finishers:	29
Winners:	NIELSEN-COBB-SALAZAR, Jaguar XJR 12, 4882.4 km/3033.87 miles at 204.03 kmh/126.78 mph
Winners in 1989:	MASS-REUTER-DICKENS, Sauber C9-Mercedes, 5265.115 km/3271.74 miles at 199.661 kmh/124.066 mph
Fastest lap:	BOB EARLE, Nissan R 90 CK, 3'40"03 = 222.515 kmh/138.268 mph (record for revised circuit).

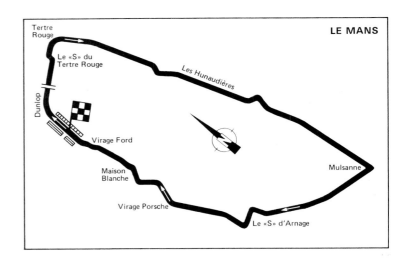

LE MANS

RESULT

	No	Drivers	Car	Group	Laps	Speed
1	3	NIELSEN-COBB-BRUNDLE*	Jaguar XJR 12	C1	359	204.03 kmh/
2	2	LAMMERS-WALLACE-KONRAD	Jaguar XJR 12	C1	355	126.78 mph
3	45	NEEDELL-SEARS-REID	Porsche 962 C	C1	352	
4	7	STUCK-BELL-JELINSKI	Porsche 962 C	C1	350	
5	23	HASEMI-HOSHINO-SUZUKI	Nissan R 90 CP	C1	348	
6	36	LEES-SEKIYA-OGAWA	Toyota 90 C-V	C1	347	
7	13	FABRE-TROLLÉ-ROBERT	Cougar C24 S-Porsche	C1	347	
8	9	"WINTER"-DICKENS-WOLLEK	Porsche 962 C	C1	346	
9	27	LÄSSIG-YVER-ALTENBACH	Porsche 962 C	C1	341	
10	15	HUYSMAN-SIGALA-SANTAL	Porsche 962 C	C1	335	
11	44	WATSON-GIACOMELLI-BERG	Porsche 962 C	C1	335	
12	33	HAYWOOD-TAYLOR-RYDELL	Porsche 962 C	C1	332	
13	63	FOUCHÉ-ANDSKAR-HASUYA	Porsche 962 C	C1	330	
14	6	RICCI-PESCAROLO-LAFFITE	Porsche 962 C	C1	328	
15	55	ELGH-DANIELSSON-MEZERA	Porsche 962 C	C1	326	
16	11	GONIN-ALLIOT-DE DRYVER	Porsche 962 C	C1	319	
17	84	EARL-ROE-MILLEN	Nissan R 90 CK	C1	311	
18	21	HARVEY-HODGETTS-VELEZ	Spice SE90C-Cosworth	C1	308	
19	19	COHEN OLIVAR-LAVAGGI	Porsche 962 C	C1	306	
20	203	KATAYAMA-YORINO-TERADA**	Mazda 767 B	IMSA GTP	304	
21	116	PIPER-IACOBELLI-YOULES***	Spice SE89C-Cosworth	C2	304	
22	82	REGOUT-CUDINI-LOS	Nissan R 89 C	C1	300	
23	102	GRAND-MAISONNEUVE-LAPEYRE	Spice C002-Cosworth	C2	290	
24	10	TAKAHASHI-VAN DER MERWE	Porsche 962 C	C1	291	
25	103	SHEAD-STIRLING-HYETT	Spice SE88C-Cosworth	C2	274	
26	20	ITEKANI-LEE DAVEY	Porsche 962 C	C1	260	
27	131	WOOD-JONES-HYNES	Spice SE87C-Cosworth	C2	259	
28	128	HAUSMANN-DONOVAN-DE HENNING	Spice SE87C-Cosworth	C2	254	
29	132	FENWICK-SIMMISS-POSTAN	Tiga GC 288-Cosworth	C2	254	

* Group C1 winner   ** IMSA GTP winner   *** Group C2 winner

RETIREMENTS

No	Drivers	Car	Hour	Reason
24	Acheson-Donnelly-Grouillard	Nissan R 90 CK	1st	transmission
113	Farjon-Messaoudi	Cougar C20 B-Porsche	3rd	accident
37	Suzuki-Dumfries-Ravaglia	Toyota 90 C-V	4th	accident
106	Migault-Heuclin-Tremblay	ALD C289-Cosworth	5th	transmission
25	Bailey-Blundell-Brancatelli	Nissan R 90 CK	7th	gearbox
54	Monti-Magnani	Lancia-Ferrari	7th	accident
230	Moretti-Adams-Gebhardt	Porsche 962 C	10th	gearbox
26	Oppermann-Grohs-Duez	Porsche 962 C	10th	gearbox
201	Johansson-Kennedy-Dieudonné	Mazda 787	12th	oil leak
43	Reuter-Weaver-Lehto	Porsche 962 C	14th	fire

No	Drivers	Car	Hour	Reason
202	Gachot-Herbert-Weidler	Mazda 787	15th	electrics
105	Harrower-Mahony-Sheldon	ADA-Cosworth	15th	suspension
85	Wada-Olofsson-Sala	Nissan 89 C	15th	ignition
107	Lombardi-Morin-de Lesseps	Spice SE87C-Cosworth	16th	accident
1	Brundle-Ferté-Leslie	Jaguar XJR 12	16th	engine
83	Brabham-Robinson-Daly	Nissan R 90 CK	19th	fuel leak
38	Raphanel-Ratzenberger-Nagasaka	Toyota 90 C-V	19th	accident
4	Jones-Perez Sala-Ferté	Jaguar XJR 12	20th	overheating
16	Larrauri-Pareja-Brun	Porsche 962 C	24th	engine

POSITIONS HOUR BY HOUR

No	Team	Car	Gr.	Pos.	1	2	3	4	5	6	7	8	9	10	11	12	13	14	15	16	17	18	19	20	21	22	23	24	Class.
24	BAILEY-BLUNDELL-BRANCATELLI	Nissan R 90 CK	C1	1	16	24	24	1	83	1	16	83	83	83	3	3	3	3	3	3	3	3	3	3	3	3	3	3	3
16	LARRAURI-PAREJA-BRUN	Porsche 962 C	C1	2	24	1	1	3	1	16	4	3	16	3	83	83	83	83	83	16	16	16	16	16	16	16	2	2	2
23	HASEMI-HOSHINO-SUZUKI	Nissan R 90 CP	C1	3	1	16	83	24	3	83	2	16	3	16	16	2	16	16	16	83	83	7	7	2	2	2	2	45	45
83	BRABHAM-ROBINSON-DALY	Nissan R 90 CK	C1	4	3	83	16	4	16	4	3	2	2	2	16	2	23	23	7	7	2	2	2	2	45	45	7	7	7
25	ACHESON-DONNELLY-GROUILLARD	Nissan R 90 CK	C1	5	83	3	2	23	4	3	83	4	23	23	23	23	23	1	1	2	2	45	23	45	23	23	23	23	23
7	STUCK-BELL-JELINSKI	Porsche 962 C	C1	6	2	2	4	83	24	2	24	24	7	7	4	4	1	7	7	45	23	23	45	23	7	7	7	36	36
4	JONES-PEREZ SALA-M. FERTÉ	Jaguar XJR 12	C1	7	4	4	16	16	2	24	23	23	45	4	1	1	7	2	2	9	45	9	9	36	36	36	36	13	13
1	BRUNDLE-A. FERTÉ-LESLIE	Jaguar XJR 12	C1	8	23	23	2	45	7	45	45	4	1	7	7	45	45	45	23	9	13	36	9	9	13	13	9	9	9
3	NIELSEN-COBB-SALAZAR	Jaguar XJR 12	C1	9	9	9	45	9	7	23	7	7	9	45	45	45	9	9	9	4	4	36	13	13	13	9	9	27	27
36	LEES-SEKIYA-OGAWA	Toyota 90 C-V	C1	10	43	45	9	45	23	45	9	9	1	9	9	9	4	4	4	36	36	27	27	27	27	27	27	15	15
63	FOUCHÉ-ANDSKAR-HASUYA	Porsche 962 C	C1	11	36	43	10	7	9	6	6	1	24	33	33	36	36	36	36	13	13	15	4	4	15	15	15	44	44
10	TAKAHASHI-VAN DER MERWE-OKADA	Porsche 962 C	C1	12	37	10	43	36	33	9	1	6	6	36	36	13	33	13	13	27	27	4	15	15	44	44	44	33	33
43	REUTER-WEAVER-LEHTO	Porsche 962 C	C1	13	10	44	7	6	13	13	13	33	33	6	13	33	13	6	27	15	15	83	44	44	33	33	33	63	63
37	SUZUKI-DUMFRIES-RAVAGLIA	Toyota 90 C-V	C1	14	44	7	6	13	55	27	33	13	13	13	6	6	6	27	15	11	44	44	11	11	63	63	63	6	6
26	OPPERMANN-GROHS-DUEZ	Porsche 962 C	C1	15	45	82	36	55	6	33	27	27	36	27	27	27	27	15	63	44	11	11	33	33	6	6	6	55	55
38	RAPHANEL-RATZENBERGER-NAGASAKA	Toyota 90 C-V	C1	16	7	37	33	33	43	36	36	36	27	24	43	43	43	44	63	63	63	63	63	63	55	55	55	11	11
2	LAMMERS-WALLACE-KONRAD	Jaguar XJR 12	C1	17	33	33	13	43	36	43	43	43	43	26	15	15	15	63	6	82	38	33	6	6	11	11	11	84	84
9	«WINTER»-DICKENS-WOLLEK	Porsche 962 C	C1	18	6	6	55	36	27	203	203	26	26	43	63	55	55	44	11	38	33	6	55	55	10	84	84	21	21
11	GONIN-ALLIOT-DE DRYVER	Porsche 962 C	C1	19	85	13	37	21	230	230	26	15	230	15	38	63	63	38	38	33	82	38	83	10	84	21	21	20	20
45	NEEDELL-SEARS-REID	Porsche 962 C	C1	20	26	56	203	201	203	11	15	230	203	230	55	38	44	11	82	6	6	82	10	84	20	116	116	203	203
44	WATSON-GIACOMELLI-BERG	Porsche 962 C	C1	21	84	15	26	26	11	85	85	203	15	201	201	44	38	82	33	55	55	55	84	20	21	20	20	116	116
202	GACHOT-HERBERT-WEIDLER	Mazda 787	GTP	22	82	21	21	27	201	26	82	85	201	21	44	85	85	203	203	203	10	10	20	116	116	10	203	82	82
201	JOHANSSON-KENNEDY-DIEUDONNÉ	Mazda 787	GTP	23	11	11	201	203	82	82	203	82	85	63	85	11	11	85	55	10	21	84	82	21	203	203	82	102	102
85	WADA-OLOFSSON-SALA	Nissan 89 C	C1	24	13	36	27	230	85	15	201	201	21	38	11	82	82	55	116	116	84	20	21	128	82	82	102	10	10
84	EARL-ROE-MILLER	Nissan 90 CK	C1	25	15	203	230	82	26	201	11	21	63	44	82	203	203	116	10	21	20	21	116	82	128	102	10	103	103
13	FABRE-TROLLÉ-ROBERT	Cougar C24S-Porsche	C1	26	55	202	44	11	15	107	21	63	55	55	203	116	116	10	21	84	116	116	128	203	102	103	103	19	19
33	HAYWOOD-TAYLOR-RYDELL	Porsche 962 C	C1	27	203	26	12	12	21	102	63	44	44	85	24	20	10	21	84	20	128	128	203	102	103	128	128	131	131
27	LÄSSIG-YVER-ALTENBACH	Porsche 962 C	C1	28	21	230	82	44	107	21	116	55	38	11	128	10	21	20	20	128	203	203	102	103	19	19	19	128	128
82	REGOUT-CUDINI-LOS	Nissan 89 C	C1	29	202	27	84	84	102	44	44	116	82	203	116	128	20	84	128	102	102	102	103	19	132	131	131	132	132
6	RICCI-PESCAROLO-LAFFITE	Porsche 962 C	C1	30	63	201	11	15	116	116	55	38	11	82	21	105	84	128	102	103	103	103	19	131	131	132	132		
55	ELGH-DANIELSSON-MEZERA	Porsche 962 C	C1	31	201	12	107	107	63	63	107	11	116	116	20	21	128	107	103	19	19	19	132	132					
21	HARVEY-HODGETTS-VELEZ	Spice SE90C-Cosworth	C1	32	230	107	102	102	44	20	10	128	202	84	107	105	107	132	132	132	131	132	131						
15	HUYSMAN-SIGALA-SANTAL	Porsche 962 C	C1	33	107	128	116	116	105	55	38	128	202	202	10	26	105	103	19	131	131	131							
203	KATAYAMA-YORINO-TERADA	Mazda 767 B	GTP	34	20	84	105	105	128	38	10	202	20	20	105	107	19	102	132										
230	MORETTI-ADAMS-GEBHARDT	Porsche 962 C	GTP	35	128	102	15	85	20	10	102	20	105	105	84	202	103	19	131										
103	SHEAD-STIRLING-HYETT	Spice SE88C-Cosworth	C2	36	27	131	20	63	37	202	128	105	103	10	107	19	102	202											
54	MONTI-MAGNANI	Lancia-Ferrari	C1	37	12	116	128	202	38	105	202	103	10	107	19	103	202	131											
107	LOMBARDI-MORIN-DE LESSEPS	Spice SE87C-Cosworth	C2	38	102	20	85	128	10	128	103	107	107	84	103	102	131	132											
102	GRAND-MAISONNEUVE-LAPEYRE	Spice SE C002-Cosworth	C2	39	116	19	113	20	202	103	105	102	84	103	102	131	132												
12	THUNER-IANETTA-PESSIOT	Cougar C24S-Porsche	C1	40	131	63	202	10	103	54	54	84	19	19	131	132													
19	IKETANI-COHEN OLIVAR	Porsche 962 C	C1	41	38	113	63	38	12	131	19	19	131	102	132														
113	FARJON-MESSAOUDI	Cougar C20 B-Porsche	C2	42	113	105	38	103	54	132	84	54	102	131	54														
131	WOOD-JONES-HYNES	Spice SE87C-Cosworth	C2	43	105	85	103	113	131	19	131	132	132	132															
106	MIGAULT-HEUCLIN-TREMBLAY	ALD C289-Cosworth	C2	44	106	106	131	54	84	84	132	131	54	54															
128	HAUSMANN-DONOVAN-DE HENNING	Spice SE87C-Cosworth	C2	45	54	103	132	132	132																				
116	PIPER-IACOBELLI-YOULES	Spice SE89C-Cosworth	C2	46	19	38	19	131	19																				
132	FENWICK-SIMMISS-POSTAN	Tiga GC 288-Cosworth	C2	47	103	132	54	106	113																				
105	HARROWER-MAHONY-SHELDON	ADA-Cosworth	C2	48	132	54	106	19	106																				

DIJON

Date: 22 July 1990. **Distance:** 127 laps of the 3.8 km/2.36 mile Dijon-Prenois circuit = 480.60 km/299.72 miles. **Weather:** fine, hot.

Result:

	Drivers	No	Car	Laps	Time	Speed
1	Schlesser-Baldi	1	Mercedes C 11	127	2.39'03"6	182,044 kmh/
2	Mass-Schumacher	2	Mercedes C 11	127	+ 3"4	113.120 mph
3	Bailey-Blundell	23	Nissan R 90 CK	126		
4	Lammers-Wallace	4	Jaguar XJR 11	125		
5	Brundle-Ferté	3	Jaguar XJR 11	125		
6	Taylor-Salazar	22	Spice SE90C-Cosworth	124		
7	Wollek-Jelinski	7	Porsche 962 C	124		
8	Palmer-Hobbs	8	Porsche 962 C	122		
9	Ricci-Pescarolo	6	Porsche 962 C	121		
10	Fabre-Robert	13	Cougar C24 S-Porsche	121		
11	Pareja-Brun	16	Porsche 962 C	121		
12	Larrauri-Huysman	15	Porsche 962 C	121		
13	Nurminen-Gabbiani	30	Spice SE90C-Cosworth	120		
14	Adams-Hausmann	28	Spice SE90C-Cosworth	120		
15	Dauer-Unser	33	Porsche 962 C	120		
16	Santal	17	Porsche 962 C	118		
17	Altenbach-Yver	27	Porsche 962 C	117		
18	Reid-Barth	19	Porsche 962 C	117		
19	Trollé-Thuner	12	Cougar C24 S-Porsche	117		
20	Konrad-Toivonen	32	Porsche 962 C	116		
21	Acheson-Brancatelli	24	Nissan R 90 CK	116		
22	Salamin-Taverna	39	Porsche 962 C	115		
23	Almeras-Almeras	34	Porsche 962 C	115		
24	van der Merw	10	Porsche 962 C	114		
25	"Stingbrace"-Randaccio	40	Spice SE90C-Cosworth	106		
26	Migault-Tremblay	35	ALD C 289-Cosworth	88		

Fastest lap: Schlesser, Mercedes C 11, 1'08"973 = 198.338 kmh/123.247 mph.

Retirements:

Drivers	No	Car	Laps	Reason
Dumfries-Ravaglia	36	Toyota 90 C-V	7	engine
Lees-Watson	37	Toyota 90 C-V	9	engine
Winter-Dickens	9	Porsche 962 C	57	door
Lee Davey-Smith	20	Porsche 962 C	80	engine
Williams-de Henning	29	Spice SE90C-Cosworth	89	excluded
Velez-Euser	21	Spice SE90C-Cosworth	117	engine

NÜRBURGRING

Date: 19 August 1990. **Distance:** 106 laps of the 4.542 km/2.822 mile Nürburgring circuit = 481.452 km/299.17 miles. **Weather:** fine.

Result:

	Drivers	No	Car	Laps	Time	Speed
1	Schlesser-Baldi	1	Mercedes C 11	106	2.39'15"913	181.377 kmh/
2	Mass-Schumacher	2	Mercedes C 11	106	+ 22"562	112.706 mph
3	Brundle-Ferté	3	Jaguar XJR 11	105		
4	Lammers-Wallace	4	Jaguar XJR 11	105		
5	Blundell	23	Nissan R 90 CP	103		
6	Wollek-Jelinski	7	Porsche 962 C	103		
7	Los-Euser	21	Spice SE90C-Cosworth	102		
8	Huysman-Larrauri	15	Porsche 962 C	102		
9	Acheson-Brancatelli	24	Nissan R 90 CP	102		
10	Fabre-Robert	13	Cougar C24 S-Porsche	101		
11	Boesel	33	Porsche 962 C	101		
12	Winter-Dickens	9	Porsche 962 C	100		
13	Rensing-Santal	17	Porsche 962 C	100		
14	Konrad-Toivonen	32	Porsche 962 C	100		
15	Trollé-Thuner	12	Cougar C24 S-Porsche	99		
16	Lässig-Altenbach	27	Porsche 962 C	99		
17	Grohs-Oppermann	26	Porsche 962 C	98		
18	Schneider-van der Merwe	10	Porsche 962 C	98		
19	Almeras-Almeras	34	Porsche 962 C	97		
20	Salamin-Cohen-Olivar	39	Porsche 962 C	96		
21	Migault-Wettling	35	ALD C 289-Cosworth	86		

Fastest lap: Schlesser, Mercedes C 11, 1'26"092 = 189.927 kmh/118.020 mph.

Retirements:

Drivers	No	Car	Laps	Reason
Palmer	8	Porsche 962 C	16	engine
Randaccio-Barberio	40	Spice SE90C-Cosworth	49	engine and bodywork
Dumfries-Ravaglia	50	Toyota 90 C-V	50	engine
Adams-Hausmann	28	Spice SE89C-Cosworth	65	out of fuel
Reuter-Anskar	14	Porsche 962 C	71	suspension, brakes
Reid-Elgh	11	Porsche 962 C	72	suspension damage
Pareja-Brun	16	Porsche 962 C	90	clutch
Lees-Ogawa	37	Toyota 90 C-V	96	out of fuel

DONINGTON

Date: 2 September 1990. **Distance:** 120 laps of the 4.02 km/2.5 mile Donington Park circuit = 482.4 km/300.00 miles. **Weather:** fine.

Result:

	Drivers	No	Car	Laps	Time	Speed
1	Schlesser-Baldi	1	Mercedes C 11	120	2.53'40"919	166,649 kmh/
2	Mass-Frentzen	2	Mercedes C 11	120	+ 1'22"215	103.55 mph
3	Harvey-Euser	22	Spice SE90C-Cosworth	118		
4	Acheson-Brancatelli	24	Nissan R 90 CP	117		
5	Giacomelli-van de Poele	21	Spice SE90C-Cosworth	117		
6	Bailey-Blundell	23	Nissan R 90 CP	117		
7	Wollek-Jelinski	7	Porsche 962 C	116		
8	Olofsson-Reid	11	Porsche 962 C	116		
9	Schneider-van der Merwe	10	Porsche 962 C	115		
10	Palmer-Bartels	8	Porsche 962 C	115		
11	Reuter-Anskar	14	Porsche 962 C	114		
12	Pareja-Brun	16	Porsche 962 C	113		
13	Grohs-Altenbach	26	Porsche 962 C	113		
14	Winter-Pescarolo	9	Porsche 962 C	113		
15	Santal	17	Porsche 962 C	113		
16	Konrad-Toivonen	32	Porsche 962 C	112		
17	Musetti-Lavaggi	20	Porsche 962 C	111		
18	Stirling-Thuner	29	Spice SE90C-Cosworth	108		
19	Salamin-Cohen-Olivar	39	Porsche 962 C	107		
20	Migault-Wettling	35	ALD C 289-Cosworth	97		

Fastest lap: Baldi, Mercedes C 11, 1'23"597 = 173.116 kmh/107.65 mph.

Retirements:

Drivers	No	Car	Laps	Reason
Altenbach	27	Porsche 962 C	1	accident
Hoy	28	Spice SE89C-Cosworth	7	transmission damage
Nurminen-Gabbiani	30	Spice SE90C-Cosworth	35	spun off
Piper	31	Spice SE90C-Cosworth	35	electrics
Randaccio-"Stingbrace"	40	Spice SE90C-Cosworth	45	electrics
Trollé-Fabre	13	Cougar C24 S-Porsche	54	exhaust
Dumfries-Ravaglia	36	Toyota 90 C-V	99	out of fuel
Lees-Watson	37	Toyota 90 C-V	112	out of fuel
Huysman-Larrauri	15	Porsche 962 C	116	out of fuel

Jaguar XJR 11s No 3 (Brundle) and No 4 (Lammers-Wallace) finished third and seventh on the road but were excluded from the results for refuelling infringement.

MONTREAL

Date: 23 September 1990. **Distance:** 61 laps of the 4.39 km/2.73 mile Circuit Gilles Villeneuve, Montreal = 266.96 km/165.92 miles. **Weather:** cloudy.

Result:

	Drivers	No	Car	Laps	Time	Speed
1	Schlesser-Baldi	1	Mercedes C 11	61*	1.44'42"012	163.461 kmh/
2	Blundell-Bailey	23	Nissan R 90 CP	61	+ 6"448	101.665 mph
3	Reuter-Anskar	14	Porsche 962 C	61	+ 1'23"564	
4	Schneider	10	Porsche 962 C	61	+ 1'24"141	
5	Acheson-Brancatelli	24	Nissan R 90 CP	61	+ 1'51"315	
6	Wollek-Jelinski	7	Porsche 962 C	61	+ 1'52"373	
7	Lees-Watson	37	Toyota 90 C-V	60		
8	Palmer-Stuck	8	Porsche 962 C	60		
9	Mass-Wendlinger	2	Mercedes C 11	60		
10	Larrauri-Huysman	15	Porsche 962 C	59		
11	Grohs	26	Porsche 962 C	59		
12	Piper	29	Spice SE89C-Cosworth	59		
13	Winter-Pescarolo	9	Porsche 962 C	59		
14	Dumfries-Ravaglia	36	Toyota 90 C-V	59		
15	Brundle-Lammers	3	Jaguar XJR 11	58		
16	Santal-Pareja	17	Porsche 962 C	58		
17	Altenbach-Lässig	27	Porsche 962 C	58		
18	Almeras-Almeras	34	Porsche 962 C	57		
19	Thuner-Morin	12	Cougar C24 S-Porsche	56		
20	Salamin-Cohen Olivar	39	Porsche 962 C	56		
21	Taylor-Velez	22	Spice SE90C-Cosworth	55		
22	Konrad-Toivonen	32	Porsche 962 C	52		
23	Fabre-Trollé**	13	Cougar C24 S-Porsche	46		

* Race stopped at 61 of scheduled 110 laps after accident involving cars 12, 15 and 17. All competitors who completed 60 per cent of distance classified, including 12, 15, 17.
** Not running at end.

Fastest lap: Baldi, Mercedes C 11, 1'28"725 = 178.123 kmh/110.68 mph.

Retirements:

Drivers	No	Car	Laps	Reason
Migault-Taverna	33	ALD C 289-Cosworth	3	accident
Francia	41	Alba CSAI-Buick	8	electrics
Pareja-Brun	16	Porsche 962 C	22	accident
Rosberg-Jabouille	44	Peugeot 905	22	fuel pressure
Hepworth-Gabbiani	30	Spice SE90C-Cosworth	23	electrical fire
Lee Davey	20	Porsche 962 C	30	suspension AR
Jones-Wallace	4	Jaguar XJR 11	37	driveshaft

MEXICO

Date: 7 October 1990. **Distance:** 109 laps of the 4.42 km/2.747 mile Circuit Hermanos Rodriguez = 481.78 km/299.37 miles. **Weather:** hot, rain during race.

Result:

	Drivers	No	Car	Laps	Time	Speed
1	Mass-Schumacher	2	Mercedes C 11	109	2.47'54"9	172.190 kmh/
2	Bailey-Blundell	23	Nissan R 90 CK	107		106.99 mph
3	Wallace-Jones	4	Jaguar XJR 11	107		
4	Acheson-Brancatelli	24	Nissan R 90 CK	106		
5	Palmer-Stuck	8	Porsche 962 C	106		
6	Wollek-Jelinski	7	Porsche 962 C	105		
7	Schneider-Lopez Rocha	10	Porsche 962 C	105		
8	Winter-Pescarolo	9	Porsche 962 C	103		
9	Grohs-Altenbach	27	Porsche 962 C	103		
10	Salazar-Velez	21	Spice SE90C-Cosworth	103		
11	Fabre-Trollé	13	Cougar C24 S-Porsche	102		
12	Konrad-Toivonen	32	Porsche 962 C	102		
13	Rosberg-Jabouille	44	Peugeot 905	101		
14	Hessert-Contreras	30	Spice SE90C-Cosworth	91		

15	Jourdain-Jourdain	20	Porsche 962 C	88
16	Francia-Migault	41	Alba CSAI-Buick	85

Fastest lap: Schumacher, Mercedes C 11, 1'23"250 = 191.178 kmh/118.796 mph.

Retirements:

Drivers	No	Car	Laps	Reason
"Stingbrace"	40	Spice SE90C-Cosworth	0	transmission
Lees	37	Toyota 90 C-V	15	oil pressure
Hausmann	29	Spice SE90C-Cosworth	23	electrics
Reuter	14	Porsche 962 C	42	engine
Brundle-Lammers	3	Jaguar XJR 11	46	alternator
Salamin-Cohen Olivar	39	Porsche 962 C	52	gearbox
Pareja-Brun	16	Porsche 962 C	56	suspension/accident
Larrauri	15	Porsche 962 C	65	oil leak
Dumfries-Ravaglia	36	Toyota 90 C-V	70	gearbox
Almeras-Almeras	34	Porsche 962 C	75	engine
Baldi-Schlesser	1	Mercedes C 11	109	excluded (fuel infringement)

WORLD SPORTS-PROTOTYPE CHAMPIONSHIP

FINAL CLASSIFICATION **DRIVERS**	Suzuka	Monza	Silverstone	Spa-Francorchamps	Dijon	Nürburgring	Doningвton	Montréal	Mexico	Total
1 BALDI	9	9	—	—	9	9	9	4.5	—	49.5
SCHLESSER	9	9	—	—	9	9	9	4.5	—	49.5
3 MASS	6	6	—	9	6	6	6	—	9	48
4 WALLACE	—	3	6	6	3	3	—	—	4	25
5 WENDLINGER	6	6	—	9	—	—	—	—	—	21
SCHUMACHER	—	—	—	—	6	6	—	—	9	21
7 LAMMERS	—	3	6	6	3	3	—	—	—	21
8 BRUNDLE	—	4	9	—	2	4	—	—	—	19
9 BAILEY	—	—	—	4	4	—	1	3	6	18
10 BLUNDELL	—	—	—	—	4	2	1	3	6	16
11 ACHESON	—	—	—	4	—	—	3	1	3	11
12 FERTÉ	—	4	—	—	2	4	—	—	—	10
13 JELINSKI	—	2	3	—	—	1	—	0.5	1	7.5
WOLLEK	—	2	3	—	—	1	—	0.5	1	7.5
15 HARVEY	—	—	—	3	—	—	4	—	—	7
VELEZ	—	—	4	3	—	—	—	—	—	7
17 FRENTZEN	—	—	—	—	—	6	—	—	—	6
18 GIACOMELLI	—	—	4	—	—	2	—	—	—	6
19 BRANCATELLI	—	—	—	—	—	—	3	—	3	6
20 OLOFSSON	4	—	—	—	—	—	—	—	—	4
HASEMI	4	—	—	—	—	—	—	—	—	4
EUSER	—	—	—	—	—	—	4	—	—	4
JONES	—	—	—	—	—	—	—	—	4	4
24 LARRAURI	1	—	1	2	—	—	—	—	—	4
25 SCHNEIDER	—	—	2	—	—	—	—	1.5	—	3.5
26 REUTER	—	—	—	1	—	—	—	2	—	3
27 OGAWA	3	—	—	—	—	—	—	—	—	3
LEES	3	—	—	—	—	—	—	—	—	3
29 VAN DE POELE	—	1	—	—	—	—	2	—	—	3
ANSKAR	—	—	2	1	—	—	—	—	—	3
31 TAKAHASHI	2	—	—	—	—	—	—	—	—	2
MOGI	2	—	—	—	—	—	—	—	—	2
STUCK	—	—	—	—	—	—	—	—	2	2
PALMER	—	—	—	—	—	—	—	—	2	2
35 TAYLOR	—	1	—	—	1	—	—	—	—	2
36 SALAZAR	—	—	—	—	1	—	—	—	—	1
HUYSMAN	1	—	—	—	—	—	—	—	—	1

FINAL CLASSIFICATION **TEAMS**	Suzuka	Monza	Silverstone	Spa-Francorchamps	Dijon	Nürburgring	Doningвton	Montréal	Mexico	Total
1 Sauber Mercedes	9	9	—	9	9	9	9	4.5	9	67.5
2 Silk Cut Jaguar	—	4	9	6	3	4	—	—	4	30
3 Nissan Motorsport	4	—	—	4	4	2	3	3	6	26
4 Spice Engineering	—	1	4	3	1	—	4	—	—	13
5 Joest Porsche	—	2	3	—	—	1	—	0.5	2	7.5
6 Porsche Kremer	2	—	2	—	—	—	—	1.5	—	5.5
7 Brun Motorsport	1	—	1	2	—	—	—	—	—	4
8 Richard Lloyd Racing	—	—	—	1	—	—	—	2	—	3
9 Toyota Team Tom's	3	—	—	—	—	—	—	—	—	3

UNITED STATES GRAND PRIX

Date:	11 March 1990
Venue and distance:	Phoenix street circuit. 72 laps of the 3.8 km/2.36 mile circuit, 273.6 km/169.92 miles
Weather:	overcast, cool
Attendance:	approx. 25 000 spectators
Previous winner:	Alain Prost, McLaren MP4/5, at 140.578 kmh/87.370 mph (1989)
Existing lap record:	Ayrton Senna, McLaren MP4/5, 1'33"696 = 145.474 kmh/90.413 mph (1989)

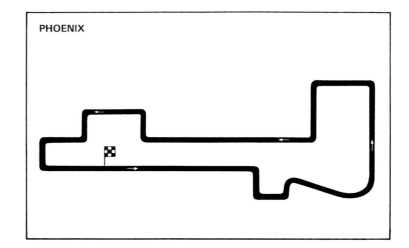

PHOENIX

STARTING GRID

23. MARTINI 1'28"731
Minardi M189-Ford DFR V8

28. BERGER 1'28"664
McLaren MP4/5B-Honda V10

4. ALESI 1'29"408
Tyrrell 018-Ford DFR V8

21. DE CESARIS 1'29"019
Dallara BMS 190-Ford DFR V8

19. PIQUET 1'29"862
Benetton B189-Ford F1 V8

27. SENNA 1'29"431
McLaren MP4/5B-Honda V10

14. GROUILLARD 1'29"947
Osella FA1M90-Ford DFR V8

1. PROST 1'29"910
Ferrari 641-Ferrari V12

7. MODENA 1'30"127
Brabham BT58-Judd V8

5. BOUTSEN 1'30"059
Williams FW13/B-Renault V10

6. PATRESE 1'30"213
Williams FW13/B-Renault V10

3. NAKAJIMA 1'30"130
Tyrrell 018-Ford DFR V8

24. BARILLA 1'31"194
Minardi M189B-Ford DFR V8

25. LARINI 1'30"424
Ligier JS33/B-Ford DFR V8

33. MORENO 1'31"247
EuroBrun ER189B-Judd V8

29. BERNARD 1'31"226
Lola LC89/90-Lamborghini V12

30. SUZUKI 1'31"414
Lola LC89/90-Lamborghini V12

2. MANSELL 1'31"363
Ferrari 641-Ferrari V12

10. SCHNEIDER 1'31"892
Arrows A11/B-Ford DFR V8

12. DONNELLY 1'31"650
Lotus 102-Lamborghini V12

20. NANNINI 1'31"984
Benetton B189-Ford F1 V8

9. ALBORETO 1'31"948
Arrows A11/B-Ford DFR V8

11. WARWICK 1'32"400
Lotus 102-Lamborghini V12

8. FOITEK 1'32"398
Brabham BT58-Judd V8

14. CAPELLI 1'33"044
Leyton House CG901-Judd V8

15. GUGELMIN 1'32"904
Leyton House CG901-Judd V8

Failed to pre-qualify:

17. TARQUINI (AGS JH24-Ford DFR V8) 1'35"240
18. DALMAS (AGS JH24-Ford DFR V8) 1'35"481
34. LANGES (EuroBrun ER189B-Judd V8) 1'37"399
39. BRABHAM (Life 190-Rocchi W12) 2'07"147
31. GACHOT (Coloni C3-Subaru 12 boxer) 5'15"010

Did not qualify:

35. JOHANSSON (Onyx ORE 01-Ford DFR V8) 1'33"468
22. MORBIDELLI (Dallara BMS 190-Ford DFR V8) 1'34"292
26. ALLIOT (Ligier JS33/B-Ford DFR V8) disqualified
36. LEHTO (Onyx ORE 01-Ford DFR V8) no time

All grid times set in first qualifying session.

RESULT

	Driver	Car	Laps	Time	Fastest lap
1	SENNA	McLaren	72	1.52'32"829	1'32"178
2	ALESI	Tyrrell	72	+ 8"685	1'32"221
3	BOUTSEN	Williams	72	+ 54"080	1'32"915
4	PIQUET	Benetton	72	+ 1'08"358	1'32"685
5	MODENA	Brabham	72	+ 1'09"503	1'33"147
6	NAKAJIMA	Tyrrell	71		1'32"707
7	MARTINI	Minardi	71		1'51"568
8	BERNARD	Lola	71		1'32"681
9	PATRESE	Williams	71		1'32"222
10	ALBORETO	Arrows	70		1'34"517
11	NANNINI	Benetton	70		1'32"694
12	SCHNEIDER	Arrows	70		1'33"573
13	MORENO	EuroBrun	65		1'35"446
14	GUGELMIN	Leyton House	64		1'37"058

Winner's speed: 145.75 kmh/90.586 mph.

Fastest lap: BERGER, McLaren, 1'31"050 = 150.14 kmh/93.311 mph (record).

RETIREMENTS

Driver	Laps	Reason	Fastest lap
DONNELLY	0	Starter (DNS)	
LARINI	5	throttle	1'36"971
WARWICK	7	rear suspension	1'35"396
CAPELLI	21	electrics	1'35"598
PROST	22	gearbox	1'33"170
DE CESARIS	26	engine	1'34"067
FOITEK	40	accident	1'34"156
GROUILLARD	40	accident	1'35"350
BERGER	45	clutch	1'31"050
MANSELL	50	engine	1'32"814
SUZUKI	54	brakes	1'33"819
BARILLA	55	driver fatigue	1'34"265

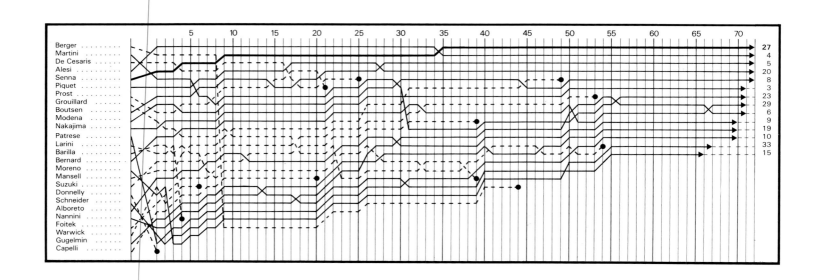

GRANDE PRÊMIO DO BRASIL

Date:	25 March 1990
Venue and distance:	Interlagos. 71 laps of the 4.325 km/2.687 mile circuit, 307.075 km/190.777 miles
Weather:	fine
Attendance:	approx. 75 000 spectators
Previous winner:	Nigel Mansell, Ferrari 640, at 186.034 kmh/ 115.527 mph (race run at Jacarepagua)
Lap record:	to be established (new circuit)

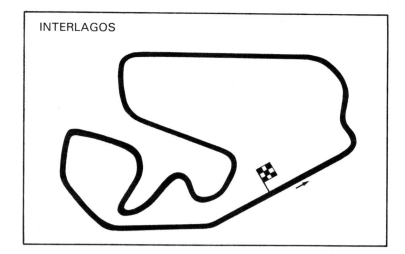
INTERLAGOS

STARTING GRID

27. SENNA 1'17"277 [2]
McLaren MP4/5B-Honda V10

28. BERGER 1'18"504 [1]
McLaren MP4/5B-Honda V10

5. BOUTSEN 1'18"150 [2]
Williams FW13/B-Renault V10

6. PATRESE 1'18"288 [2]
Williams FW13/B-Renault V10

2. MANSELL 1'18"509 [1]
Ferrari 641-Ferrari V12

1. PROST 1'18"631 [1]
Ferrari 641-Ferrari V12

4. ALESI 1'18"923 [2]
Tyrrell 018-Ford DFR V8

23. MARTINI 1'19"039 [1]
Minardi M189B-Ford DFR V8

21. DE CESARIS 1'19"125 [1]
Dallara BMS 190-Ford DFR V8

26. ALLIOT 1'19"309 [1]
Ligier JS33/B-Ford DFR V8

29. BERNARD 1'19"406 [1]
Lola LC89/90-Lamborghini V12

7. MODENA 1'19"425 [1]
Brabham BT58-Judd V8

19. PIQUET 1'19"629 [1]
Benetton B189-Ford F1 V8

12. DONNELLY 1'20"032 [1]
Lotus 102-Lamborghini V12

20. NANNINI 1'20"055 [1]
Benetton B189-Ford F1 V8

22. MORBIDELLI 1'20"164 [1]
Dallara BMS 190-Ford DFR V8

24. BARILLA 1'20"282 [1]
Minardi M189B-Ford DFR V8

30. SUZUKI 1'20"557 [1]
Lola LC89/90-Lamborghini V12

3. NAKAJIMA 1'20"568 [1]
Tyrrell 018-Ford DFR V8

25. LARINI 1'20"650 [1]
Ligier JS33/B-Ford DFR V8

16. GROUILLARD 1'20"884 [2]
Osella FA1M90-Ford DFR V8

8. FOITEK 1'20"902 [2]
Brabham BT58-Judd V8

9. ALBORETO 1'20"920 [1]
Arrows A11/B-Ford DFR V8

11. WARWICK 1'20"998 [2]
Lotus 102-Lamborghini V12

10. CAFFI 1'21"065 [1]
Arrows A11/B-Ford DFR V8

18. DALMAS 1'21"087 [2]
AGS JH24-Ford DFR V8

Failed to pre-qualify: 17. TARQUINI (AGS JH24-Ford DFR V8) 1'24"265
7. MORENO (EuroBrun ER189B-Judd V8) 1'25"763
31. GACHOT (Coloni C3-Subaru 12 boxer) 1'34"046
34. LANGES (EuroBrun ER189B-Judd V8) 1'39"188
39. BRABHAM (Life 190-Rocchi W12) no time

Did not qualify: 35. JOHANSSON (Monteverdi-Onyx ORE 01-Ford DFR V8) 1'21"241 [1]
36. LEHTO (Monteverdi-Onyx ORE 01-Ford DFR V8) 1'21"323 [1]
14. CAPELLI (Leyton House CG901-Judd V8) 1'21"383 [2]
15. GUGELMIN (Leyton House CG901-Judd V8) 1'21"616 [1]

[1] Times set in first qualifying session.
[2] Times set in second qualifying session.

RESULT

	Driver	Car	Laps	Time	Fastest lap
1	PROST	Ferrari	71	1.37'21"258	1'20"010
2	BERGER	McLaren	71	+ 13"564	1'19"899
3	SENNA	McLaren	71	+ 37"722	1'20"067
4	MANSELL	Ferrari	71	+ 47"266	1'20"389
5	BOUTSEN	Williams	70		1'20"089
6	PIQUET	Benetton	70		1'20"650
7	ALESI	Tyrrell	70		1'22"536
8	NAKAJIMA	Tyrrell	70		1'22"398
9	MARTINI	Minardi	69		1'21"799
10	NANNINI*	Benetton	68		1'21"820
11	LARINI	Ligier	68		1'22"649
12	ALLIOT	Ligier	68		1'23"115
13	PATRESE*	Williams	65		1'20"132
14	MORBIDELLI	Dallara	64		1'22"987

* Not running at end, but classified.

Winner's speed: 189.252 kmh/117.525 mph.

Fastest lap: BERGER, McLaren, 1'19"899 = 194.871 kmh/121.087 mph (establishes record).

RETIREMENTS

Driver	Laps	Reason	Fastest lap
DE CESARIS	0	accident	
GROUILLARD	8	accident damage	1'25"308
BERNARD	13	gearbox	1'24"658
FOITEK	14	gear selector	1'24"922
SUZUKI	24	suspension	1'23"491
ALBORETO	24	shock absorber	1'23"292
WARWICK	25	electrics	1'23"390
DALMAS	27	suspension	1'22"948
BARILLA	37	engine	1'24"177
MODENA	39	spun off	1'23"255
DONNELLY	43	spun off	1'22"899
CAFFI	49	driver fatigue	1'23"671
PATRESE	64	oil cooler	1'20"132
NANNINI	68	tread looseness	1'21"820

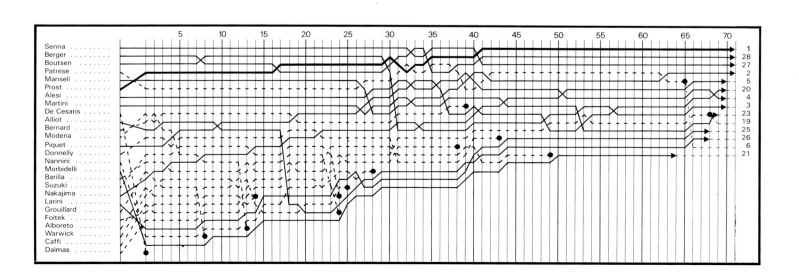

Gran Premio di San Marino

Date:	13 May 1990
Venue and distance:	Imola. 61 laps of the 5.04 km/3.13 mile circuit, 307.44 km/190.93 miles
Weather:	sunny, warm
Attendance:	approx. 150 000 spectators
Previous winner:	Ayrton Senna, McLaren MP4/5, at 201.939 kmh/125.485 mph (1989)
Existing lap record:	Alain Prost, McLaren MP4/5, 1'26"795 = 209.044 kmh/129.89 mph (1989)

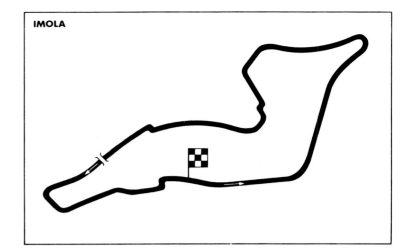

IMOLA

STARTING GRID

27. SENNA 1'23"220	28. BERGER 1'23"781
McLaren MP4/5 B5-Honda V10	McLaren MP4/5 B5-Honda V10
6. PATRESE 1'24"444	5. BOUTSEN 1'25"039
Williams FW13/B-Renault V10	Williams FW13/B-Renault V10
2. MANSELL 1'25"095	1. PROST 1'25"761
Ferrari 641/2-Ferrari V12	Ferrari 641-Ferrari V12
4. ALESI 1'25"230	19. PIQUET 1'25"761
Tyrrell 019-Ford DFR V8	Benetton B190-Ford F1 V8
20. NANNINI 1'26"042	11. WARWICK 1'26"682
Benetton B190-Ford F1 V8	Lotus 102-Lamborghini V12
12. DONNELLY 1'26"714	15. GUGELMIN 1'26"836
Lotus 102-Lamborghini V12	Leyton House CG901-Judd V8
29. BERNARD 1'26"838	8. MODENA 1'27"008
Lola LC89/90-Lamborghini V12	Brabham BT59-Judd V8
30. SUZUKI 1'27"068	26. ALLIOT 1'27"214
Lola LC89/90-Lamborghini V12	Ligier JS33/B-Ford DFR V8
21. DE CESARIS 1'27"217	14 CAPELLI 1'27"521
Dallara BMS 190-Ford DFR V8	Leyton House CG901-Judd V8
3. NAKAJIMA 1'27"532	25. LARINI 1'27"564
Tyrrell 019-Ford DFR V8	Ligier JS33/B-Ford DFR V8
22. PIRRO 1'27"613	16. GROUILLARD 1'28"009
Dallara BMS 190-Ford DFR V8	Osella FA1M90-Ford DFR V8
35. FOITEK 1'28"111	33. MORENO 1'28"603
Onyx ORE 01-Ford DFR V8	EuroBrun ER189B-Judd V8
36. LEHTO 1'28"625	24. BARILLA 1'28"667
Onyx ORE 01-Ford DFR V8	Minardi M190-Ford DFR V8

Failed to pre-qualify:	31. GACHOT (Coloni C3-Subaru 12 boxer) 1'33"554
	34. LANGES (EuroBrun ER189B-Judd V8) 1'34"292
	39. GIACOMELLI (Life-Rocchi W12) 7'16"212
	17. TARQUINI (AGS JH24-Ford DFR V8) no time
Did not qualify:	10. CAFFI (Dallara BMS 190-Ford DFR V8) 1'28"699
	9. ALBORETO (Arrows A11/B-Ford DFR V8) 1'28"797
	7. BRABHAM (Brabham BT58-Judd V8) 1'28"927
	23. MARTINI (Minardi M190-Ford DFR V8) 1'26"466

All fastest times set in second qualifying session, except TARQUINI, MORENO, FOITEK, LEHTO and MARTINI.

RESULT

	Driver	Car	Laps	Time		Fastest lap
1	PATRESE	Williams	61	1.30'55"478		1'27"475
2	BERGER	McLaren	61	+	5"117	1'27"636
3	NANNINI	Benetton	61	+	6"240	1'27"156
4	PROST	Ferrari	61	+	6"843	1'27"164
5	PIQUET	Benetton	61	+	53"112	1'28"558
6	ALESI	Tyrrell	60			1'29"144
7	WARWICK	Lotus	60			1'29"229
8	DONNELLY	Lotus	60			1'29"527
9	ALLIOT	Ligier	60			1'29"813
10	LARINI	Ligier	59			1'30"461
11	BARILLA	Minardi	59			1'30"848
12	LEHTO	Onyx	59			1'31"374
13	BERNARD*	Larrousse	56			1'29"731

* Not running but classified.

Winner's speed: 202.876 kmh/126.067 mph.

Fastest lap: NANNINI, Benetton, 1'27"156 = 208.178 kmh/129.362 mph.

RETIREMENTS

Driver	Laps	Reason	Fastest lap
NAKAJIMA	0	accident	
CAPELLI	0	accident	
MORENO	0	blocked throttle slides	
PIRRO	2	spun off	1'34"866
SENNA	3	broken rear wheel	1'30"615
SUZUKI	17	clutch	1'31"136
BOUTSEN	17	gearbox	1'28"840
GUGELMIN	24	misfire	1'32"547
DE CESARIS	29	wheel hub	1'32"125
MODENA	31	brakes	1'31"661
FOITEK	35	engine	1'31"944
MANSELL	38	engine	1'27"626
GROUILLARD	52	wheel bearing	1'32"011
BERNARD	56	gearbox	1'29"731

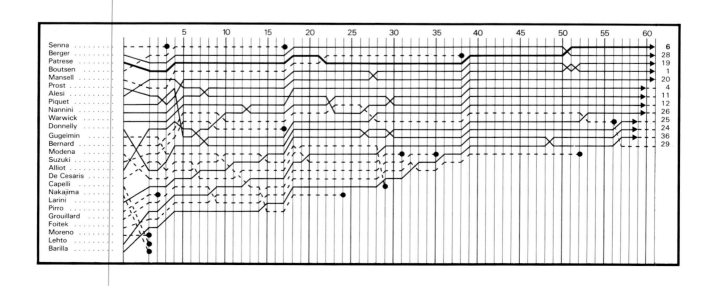

Grand Prix de Monaco

Date:	27 May 1990
Venue and distance:	Monaco street circuit. 78 laps of the 3.328 km/ 2.068 mile circuit, 259.584 km/161.304 miles
Weather:	overcast, warm
Attendance:	approx. 100 000 spectators
Previous winner:	Ayrton Senna, McLaren MP4/5, at 135.401 kmh/84.13 mph (1989)
Existing lap record:	Alain Prost, McLaren MP4/5, 1'25"501 = 140.125 kmh/87.069 mph (1989)

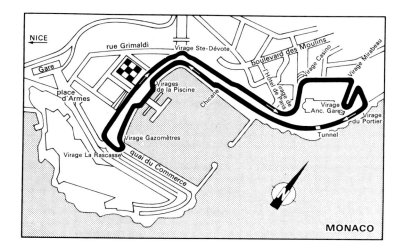

MONACO

STARTING GRID

1. PROST 1'21"776 Ferrari 641/2-Ferrari V12	**27. SENNA 1'21"314** **McLaren MP4/5B-Honda V10**
6. PATRESE 1'22"026 Williams FW13/B-Renault V10	4. ALESI 1'21"801 Tyrrell 019-Ford DFR V8
5. BOUTSEN 1'22"691 Williams FW13/B-Renault V10	28. BERGER 1'22"682 McLaren MP4/5B-Honda V10
23. MARTINI 1'23"149 Minardi M190-Ford DFR V8	2. MANSELL 1'22"733 Ferrari 641/2-Ferrari V12
19. PIQUET 1'23"586 Benetton B190-Ford F1 V8	21. PIRRO 1'23"494* Dallara BMS 190-Ford DFR V8
22. DE CESARIS 1'23"613 Dallara BMS 190-Ford DFR V8	12. DONNELLY 1'23"600 Lotus 102-Lamborghini V12
8. MODENA 1'23"920 Brabham BT59-Judd V8	11. WARWICK 1'23"656 Lotus 102-Lamborghini V12
20. NANNINI 1'24"139 Benetton B190-Ford F1 V8	30. SUZUKI 1'24"023 Lola L90-Lamborghini V12
26. ALLIOT 1'24"294 Ligier JS33/B-Ford DFR V8	25. LARINI 1'24"206 Ligier JS33/B-Ford DFR V8
35. FOITEK 1'24"367 Onyx ORE 1B-Ford DFR V8	24. BARILLA 1'24"334 Minardi M190-Ford DFR V8
10. CAFFI 1'25"000 Arrows A11/B-Ford DFR V8	3. NAKAJIMA 1'24"371 Tyrrell 019-Ford DFR V8
29. BERNARD 1'25"398 Lola L90-Lamborghini V12	14. CAPELLI 1'25"020 Leyton House CG901-Judd V8
36. LEHTO 1'25"508 Onyx ORE 1B-Ford DFR V8	7. BRABHAM 1'25"420 Brabham BT59-Judd V8

Failed to pre-qualify:
17. TARQUINI (AGS JH24-Ford DFR V8) 1'28"677
18. DALMAS (AGS JH24-Ford DFR V8) 1'30"511
34. LANGES (EuroBrun ER189B-Judd V8) 1'33"195
31. GACHOT (Coloni C3-Subaru 12 boxer) 1'39"295
39. GIACOMELLI (Life-Rocchi W12) 1'41"187

Did not qualify:
9. ALBORETO (Arrows A11/B-Ford DFR V8) 1'25"622
16. GROUILLARD (Osella FA1M90-Ford DFR V8) 1'25"785
15. GUGELMIN (Leyton House CG901-Judd V8) 1'26"192
33. MORENO (EuroBrun ER189B-Judd V8) 1'26"604

* Engine failed to start on second grid, pushed away.

All grid times except BERNARD, GROUILLARD, LARINI and MORENO set in second qualifying session.

RESULT

	Driver	Car	Laps	Time	Fastest lap
1	SENNA	McLaren	78	1.52'46"982	1'24"468
2	ALESI	Tyrrell	78	+ 1"087	1'25"353
3	BERGER	McLaren	78	+ 2'037	1'25"021
4	BOUTSEN	Williams	77		1'26"366
5	CAFFI	Arrows	76		1'26"421
6	BERNARD	Lola	76		1'26"635
7	FOITEK*	Onyx	72		1'27"296

* Classified, not running at end.

Winner's speed: 138.097 kmh/85.75 mph.

Fastest lap: SENNA, McLaren, 1'24"468 = 141.838 kmh/88.08 mph (record).

RETIREMENTS

Driver	Laps	Reason	Fastest lap
MODENA	2	transmission	1'32"072
DONNELLY	5	gearbox	1'28"366
MARTINI	6	electrics	1'28"700
SUZUKI	10	ignition	1'28"872
LARINI	11	transmission	1'29"165
CAPELLI	12	brakes	1'29"374
BRABHAM	15	transmission	1'31"639
NANNINI	19	oil pressure	1'27"542
PROST	29	battery failed	1'25"888
PIQUET	35	disqualified	1'26"055
NAKAJIMA	35	suspension	1'27"557
DE CESARIS	37	throttle linkage	1'26"931
PATRESE	40	electrics	1'26"255
ALLIOT	46	gearbox	1'28"265
LEHTO	51	gearbox	1'28"587
BARILLA	51	gearbox	1'27"539
MANSELL	62	battery	1'24"971
WARWICK	65	spun, stalled	1'27"339
FOITEK	72	collision, spun, stalled	1'27"298

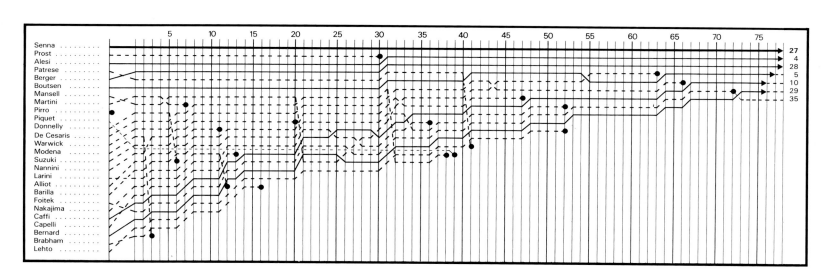

Canadian Grand Prix

Date:	10 June 1990
Venue and distance:	Circuit Gilles Villeneuve, Montreal. 70 laps of the 4.41 km/2.73 mile circuit, 308.07 km/191.10 miles
Weather:	drying (track wet at start)
Attendance:	107,000 spectators (practice and race days)
Previous winner:	Thierry Boutsen, Williams FW12C, at 149.707 kmh/92.960 mph (1989)
Existing lap record:	Ayrton Senna, McLaren MP4/4, 1'24"973 = 185.988 kmh/115.567 mph (1988)

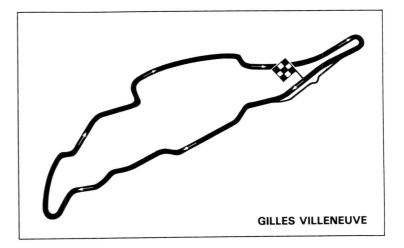

GILLES VILLENEUVE

STARTING GRID

28. BERGER 1'20"465
McLaren MP4/5B-Honda V10

27. SENNA 1'20"399
McLaren MP4/5B-Honda V10

19. NANNINI 1'21"302
Benetton B190-Ford F1 V8

1. PROST 1'20"826
Ferrari 641/2-Ferrari V12

5. BOUTSEN 1'21"599
Williams FW13/B-Renault V10

20. PIQUET 1'21"568
Benetton B190-Ford F1 V8

4. ALESI 1'21"748
Tyrrell 019-Ford DFR V8

2. MANSELL 1'21"641
Ferrari 641/2-Ferrari V12

8. MODENA 1'22"660
Brabham BT59-Judd V8

6. PATRESE 1'22"018
Williams FW13/B-Renault V10

12. DONNELLY 1'22"703
Lotus 102-Lamborghini V12

11. WARWICK 1'22"673
Lotus 102-Lamborghini V12

9. ALBORETO 1'23"744
Arrows A11/B-Ford DFR V8

3. NAKAJIMA 1'23"605
Tyrrell 019-Ford DFR V8

23. MARTINI 1'23"795
Minardi M190-Ford DFR V8

14. GROUILLARD 1'23"779
Osella FA1M90-Ford DFR V8

30. SUZUKI 1'23"915
Lola L90-Lamborghini V12

26. ALLIOT 1'23"899
Ligier JS33/B-Ford DFR V8

25. LARINI 1'24"285
Ligier JS33/B-Ford DFR V8

22. PIRRO 1'24"269
Dallara BMS 190-Ford DFR V8

36. LEHTO 1'24"425
Onyx ORE 1B-Ford DFR V8

35. FOITEK 1'24"397
Onyx ORE 1B-Ford DFR V8

14. CAPELLI 1'24"554
Leyton House CG901-Judd V8

29. BERNARD 1'24"451
Lola L90-Lamborghini V12

10. CAFFI 1'25"113
Arrows A11/B-Ford DFR V8

22. DE CESARIS 1'24"621
Dallara BMS 190-Ford DFR V8

Failed to pre-qualify: 17. TARQUINI (AGS JH24-Ford DFR V89) 1'29"855
18. DALMAS (AGS JH24-Ford DFR V8) 1'30"460
31. GACHOT (Coloni C3-Subaru 12 boxer) 1'44"185
34. LANGES (EuroBrun ER189B-Judd V8) 1'47"118
39. GIACOMELLI (Life-Rocchi FH190/1 W12) 1'50"253

Did not qualify: 33. MORENO (EuroBrun ER189B-Judd V8) 1'25"172
15. GUGELMIN (Leyton House CG901-Judd V8) 1'25"712
24. BARILLA (Minardi M190-Ford DFR V8) 1'25"951
7. BRABHAM (Brabham BT59-Judd V8) 1'26"771

All grid times set in first qualifying session.

RESULT

	Driver	Car	Laps	Time	Fastest lap
1	SENNA	McLaren	70	1.42'56"400	1'23"375
2	PIQUET	Benetton	70	+ 10"497	1'22"854
3	MANSELL	Ferrari	70	+ 13"385	1'22"839
4	BERGER*	McLaren	70	+ 14"854	1'22"077
5	PROST	Ferrari	70	+ 15"820	1'23"078
6	WARWICK	Lotus	69		1'24"948
7	MODENA	Brabham	69		1'25"693
8	CAFFI	Arrows	69		1'24"770
9	BERNARD	Lola	68		1'25"571
10	CAPELLI	March	68		1'25"846
11	NAKAJIMA	Tyrrell	68		1'26"703
12	SUZUKI	Lola	66		1'24"678
13	GROUILLARD	Osella	65		1'28"108

* Penalized one minute for jumped start.

Winner's speed: 179.114 kmh/111.296 mph.

Fastest lap: BERGER, McLaren, 1'22"077 = 192,551 kmh/119.645 mph (record).

RETIREMENTS

Driver	Laps	Reason	Fastest lap
MARTINI	0	spun out	
PIRRO	11	accident	1'40"699
ALBORETO	11	accident	1'39"464
LARINI	18	accident	1'34"545
BOUTSEN	19	accident	1'26"486
NANNINI	21	accident	1'25"545
ALESI	26	accident	1'24"781
PATRESE	44	brakes	1'25"566
LEHTO	46	engine	1'29"032
DE CESARIS	50	transmission	1'26"158
FOITEK	53	engine	1'26"177
DONNELLY	57	engine	1'25"430

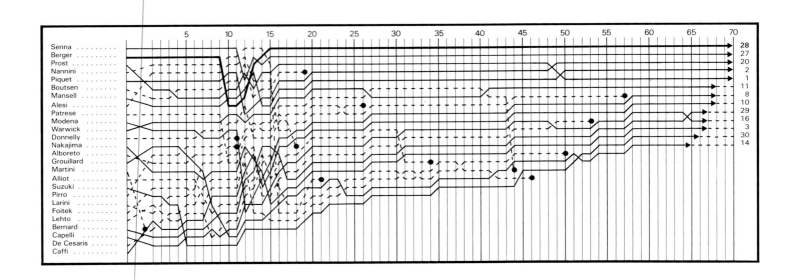

GRAN PREMIO DE MEXICO

Date:	24 June 1990
Venue and distance:	Hermanos Rodriguez circuit, Mexico City. 69 laps of the 4.042 km/2.51 mile circuit, 278.89 km/173.29 miles
Weather:	overcast, cool
Attendance:	approx. 65,000 spectators
Previous winner:	Ayrton Senna, McLaren, MP4/5, at 191,941 kmh/119.20 mph (1989)
Existing lap record:	Alain Prost, McLaren MP4/4, 1'18"608 = 202.468 kmh/125.811 mph (1988)

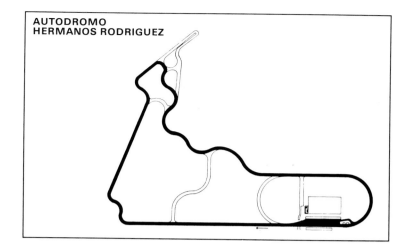

AUTODROMO
HERMANOS RODRIGUEZ

STARTING GRID

6. PATRESE 1'17"498[1]
Williams FW13/B-Renault V10

**28. BERGER 1'17"227[1]
McLaren MP4/5B-Honda V10**

2. MANSELL 1'17"732[2]
Ferrari 641/2-Ferrari V12

27. SENNA 1'17"670[2]
McLaren MP4/5B-Honda V10

4. ALESI 1'18"982[2]
Tyrrell 019-Ford DFR V8

5. BOUTSEN 1'17"883[2]
Williams FW13/B-Renault V10

20. PIQUET 1'18"561[2]
Benetton B190-Ford F1 V8

23. MARTINI 1'18"526[1]
Minardi M190-Ford DFR V8

8. MODENA 1'18"592[1]
Brabham BT59-Judd V8

3. NAKAJIMA 1'18"575[2]
Tyrrell 019-Ford DFR V8

12. DONNELLY 1'18"994[2]
Lotus 102-Lamborghini V12

11. WARWICK 1'18"951[2]
Lotus 102-Lamborghini V12

19. NANNINI 1'19"227[2]
Benetton B190-Ford F1 V8

1. PROST 1'19"026[2]
Ferrari 641/2-Ferrari V12

24. BARILLA 1'19"897[1]
Minardi M190-Ford DFR V8

22. DE CESARIS 1'19"865[2]
Dallara BMS 190-Ford DFR V8

21. PIRRO 1'20"044[2]
Dallara BMS 190-Ford DFR V8

9. ALBORETO 1'19"941[2]
Arrows A11/B-Ford DFR V8

14. GROUILLARD 1'20"274[1]
Osella FA1M90-Ford DFR V8

30. SUZUKI 1'20"268[2]
Lola L90-Lamborghini V12

26. ALLIOT 1'20"657[2]
Ligier JS33/B-Ford DFR V8

7. BRABHAM 1'20"447[1]
Brabham BT59-Judd V8

26. LARINI 1'21"116[2]
Ligier JS33/B-Ford DFR V8

35. FOITEK 1'21"012[1]
Onyx ORE 1B-Ford DFR V8

36. LEHTO 1'21"519[1]
Onyx ORE 1B-Ford DFR V8

29. BERNARD 1'21"273[1]
Lola L90-Lamborghini V12

Failed to pre-qualify:
18. DALMAS (AGS JH24-Ford DFR V8) 1'27"830
17. TARQUINI (AGS JH24-Ford DFR V8) 1'28"499
31. GACHOT (Coloni C3-Subaru 12 boxer) 1'28"805
34. LANGES (EuroBrun ER189B-Judd V8) 1'40"414
39. GIACOMELLI (Life-Rocchi W12) 4'07"475
33. MORENO (EuroBrun ER189B-Judd V8) disqualified

Did not qualify:
16. CAPELLI (Leyton House CG901-Judd V89) 1'21"544[2]
15. GUGELMIN (Leyton House CG901-Judd V8) 1'21"665[2]
10. CAFFI (Arrows A11/B-Ford DFR V8) 1'22"154[2]

[1] Grid times set in first qualifying session.
[2] Grid times set in second qualifying session.

RESULT

	Driver	Car	Laps	Time	Fastest lap
1	PROST	Ferrari	69	1.32'35"783	1'17"958
2	MANSELL	Ferrari	69	+ 25"531	1'18"487
3	BERGER	McLaren	69	+ 25"530	1'18"223
4	NANNINI	Benetton	69	+ 41"099	1'19"378
5	BOUTSEN	Williams	69	+ 46"669	1'19"525
6	PIQUET	Benetton	69	+ 46"943	1'18"365
7	ALESI	Tyrrell	69	+ 49"077	1'19"474
8	DONNELLY	Lotus	69	+ 1'06"142	1'19"508
9	PATRESE	Williams	69	+ 1'09"918	1'18"653
10	WARWICK	Lotus	68		1'19"932
11	MODENA	Brabham	68		1'20"355
12	MARTINI	Minardi	68		1'20"230
13	DE CESARIS	Dallara	68		1'20"601
14	BARILLA	Minardi	67		1'20"789
15	FOITEK	Onyx	67		1'21"408
16	LARINI	Ligier	67		1'21"235
17	ALBORETO	Arrows	66		1'22"082
18	ALLIOT	Ligier	66		1'21"467
19	GROUILLARD	Osella	65		1'22"779
20	SENNA*	McLaren	63		1'19"062

*Not running at end.

Winner's speed: 197.664 kmh/122.82 mph.

Fastest lap: PROST, Ferrari, 1'17"958 = 204.156 kmh/126.85 mph (record).

RETIREMENTS

Driver	Laps	Reason	Fastest lap
PIRRO	10	engine	1'23"476
BRABHAM	11	electrics	1'26"487
NAKAJIMA	11	accident	1'21"736
SUZUKI	11	accident	1'22"936
BERNARD	12	brakes	1'22"636
LEHTO	26	engine	1'23"816
SENNA	63	puncture	1'19"062

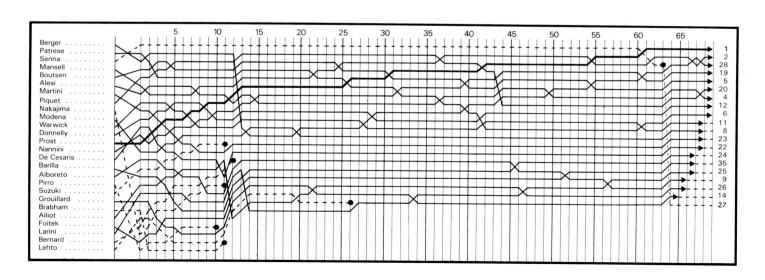

GRAND PRIX DE FRANCE

Date:	8 July 1990
Venue and distance:	Paul Ricard Circuit. 80 laps of the 3.813 km/2.369 mile circuit, 350.04 km/189.543 miles
Weather:	Sunny, hot
Attendance:	approx. 85,000 spectators
Previous winner:	Alain Prost, McLaren MP4/5, at 185.830 kmh/115.400 mph (1989)
Existing lap record:	Nelson Piquet, Williams FW11B, 1'09"548 = 197.372 kmh/122.811 mph (1987)

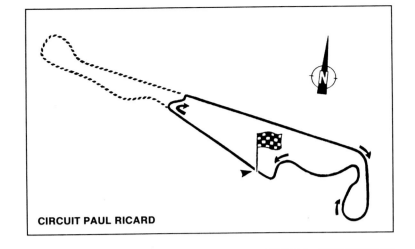

CIRCUIT PAUL RICARD

STARTING GRID

28. BERGER 1'04"512 [2]
McLaren MP4/5B-Honda V10

2. MANSELL 1'04"402 [1]
Ferrari 641/2-Ferrari V12

1. PROST 1'04"781 [2]
Ferrari 641/2-Ferrari V12

27. SENNA 1'04"549 [1]
McLaren MP4/5B-Honda V10

6. PATRESE 1'05"059 [1]
Williams FW13/B-Renault V10

19. NANNINI 1'05"009 [2]
Benetton B190-Ford F1 V8

5. BOUTSEN 1'05"446 [1]
Williams FW13/B-Renault V10

16. CAPELLI 1'05"369 [2]
March CG901-Judd V8

15. GUGELMIN 1'05"818 [1]
March CG901-Judd V8

20. PIQUET 1'05"640 [1]
Benetton B190-Ford F1 V8

26. ALLIOT 1'05"986 [1]
Ligier JS33/B-Ford DFR V8

29. BERNARD 1'05"852 [2]
Lola L90-Lamborghini V12

30. SUZUKI 1'06"100 [1]
Lola L90-Lamborghini V12

4. ALESI 1'06"084 [1]
Tyrrell 019-Ford DFR V8

11. WARWICK 1'06"624 [1]
Lotus 102-Lamborghini V12

3. NAKAJIMA 1'06"563 [2]
Tyrrell 019-Ford DFR V8

9. ALBORETO 1'06"847 [1]
Arrows A11/B-Ford DFR V8

12. DONNELLY 1'06"647 [1]
Lotus 102-Lamborghini V12

8. MODENA 1'06"937 [1]
Brabham BT59-Judd V8

25. LARINI 1'06"856 [2]
Ligier JS33/B-Ford DFR V8

10. CAFFI 1'07"207 [2]
Arrows A11/B-Ford DFR V8

22. DE CESARIS 1'07"137 [2]
Dallara BMS 190-Ford DFR V8

21. PIRRO 1'07"687 [1]
Dallara BMS 190-Ford DFR V8

23. MARTINI 1'07"315 [1]
Minardi M190-Ford DFR V8

18. DALMAS 1'07"926 [2]
AGS JH24-Ford DFR V8

7. BRABHAM 1'07"733 [1]
Brabham BT59-Judd V8

Failed to pre-qualify: 14. GROUILLARD (Osella FA1M90-Ford DFR V8) 1'08"219
33. MORENO (EuroBrun ER189B-Judd V8) 1'09"885
34. LANGES (EuroBrun ER189B-Judd V8) 1'10"368
31. GACHOT (Coloni C3-Subaru 12 boxer) 14'02"465
39. GIACOMELLI (Life-Rocchi W12) no time

Did not qualify: 24. BARILLA (Minardi M190-Ford DFR V8) 1'08"008 [1]
17. TARQUINI (AGS JH24-Ford DFR V8) 1'08"147 [2]
35. FOITEK (Onyx ORE 1B-Ford DFR V8) 1'08"232 [2]
36. LEHTO (Onyx ORE 1B-Ford DFR V8) 1'08"487 [2]

[1] Times set in first qualifying session.
[2] Times set in second qualifying session.

268

RESULT

	Driver	Car	Laps	Time	Fastest lap
1	PROST	Ferrari	80	1.33'29"606	1'08"212
2	CAPELLI	March	80	+ 8"626	1'08"373
3	SENNA	McLaren	80	+ 11"606	1'08"573
4	PIQUET	Benetton	80	+ 41"207	1'09"135
5	BERGER	McLaren	80	+ 42"219	1'09"206
6	PATRESE	Williams	80	+ 1'09"351	1'08"922
7	SUZUKI	Lola	79		1'09"720
8	BERNARD	Lola	79		1'09"895
9	ALLIOT	Ligier	79		1'09"752
10	ALBORETO	Arrows	79		1'09"134
11	WARWICK	Lotus	79		1'08"882
12	DONNELLY	Lotus	79		1'08"023
13	MODENA	Brabham	78		1'09"934
14	LARINI	Ligier	78		1'10"374
	DE CESARIS**	Dallara	78		
15	BRABHAM	Brabham	77		1'11"110
16	NANNINI	Benetton	75		1'08"214
17	DALMAS	AGS	75		1'09"877
18	MANSELL*	Ferrari	72		1'08"012

* Not running at end, but classified.

** Disqualified (under weight).

Winner's speed: 195.761 kmh/121.644 mph.

Fastest lap: MANSELL, Ferrari, 1'08"012 201.829 kmh/125.41 mph (record).

RETIREMENTS

Driver	Laps	Reason	Fastest lap
PIRRO	7	brake disc	1'12"275
BOUTSEN	8	engine	1'10"837
CAFFI	22	rear suspension	1'11"242
ALESI	23	differential	1'10"265
MARTINI	40	electrics	1'11"406
GUGELMIN	58	engine	1'08"983
NAKAJIMA	63	gear linkage	1'08"916
MANSELL	72	engine	1'08"012
NANNINI	75	electrics	1'08"214

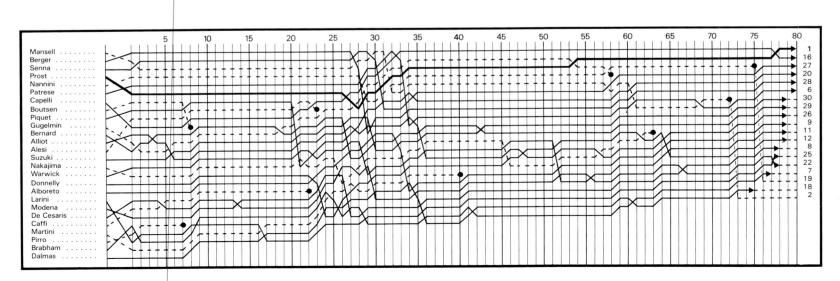

BRITISH GRAND PRIX

Date:	15 July 1990
Venue and distance:	Silverstone. 64 laps of the 4.778 km/2.969 mile circuit, 305.792 km/190.08 miles
Weather:	sunny, hot
Attendance:	approx. 100 000 spectators (race day)
Previous winner:	Alain Prost, McLaren MP4/5, at 231.203 kmh/143.694 mph (1989)
Existing lap record:	Nigel Mansell, Williams FW11, 1'09"832 = 243.324 kmh/153.059 mph (1987)

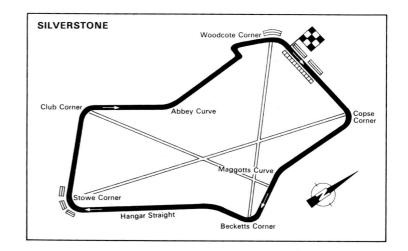

STARTING GRID

27. SENNA 1'08"071 [1]
McLaren MP4/5B-Honda V10

2. MANSELL 1'07"428 [2]
Ferrari 641/2-Ferrari V12

5. BOUTSEN 1'08"291 [2]
Williams FW13/B-Renault V10

28. BERGER 1'08"246 [1]
McLaren MP4/5B-Honda V10

4. ALESI 1'08"370 [2]
Tyrrell 019-Ford DFR V8

1. PROST 1 08"336 [2]
Ferrari 641/2-Ferrari V12

29. BERNARD 1'09"003 [2]
Lola L90-Lamborghini V12

6. PATRESE 1'08"677 [1]
Williams FW13/B-Renault V10

16. CAPELLI 1'09"308 [2]
March CG901-Judd V8

30. SUZUKI 1'09"243 [1]
Lola L90-Lamborghini V12

3. NAKAJIMA 1'09"608 [2]
Tyrrell 019-Ford DFR V8

20. PIQUET 1'09"407 [2]
Lotus 102-Lamborghini V12

12. DONNELLY 1'09"741 [2]
Lotus 102-Lamborghini V12

19. NANNINI 1'09"641 [2]
Benetton B190-Ford F1 V8

11. WARWICK 1'10"092 [2]
Lotus 102-Lamborghini V12

15. GUGELMIN 1$10"044 [2]
March CG901-Judd V8

23. MARTINI 1'10"303 [2]
Minardi M190-Ford DFR V8

10. CAFFI 1'10"110 [2]
Arrows A11/B-Ford DFR V8

8. MODENA 1'11"070 [1]
Brabham BT59-Judd V8

21. PIRRO 1'10"847 [2]
Dallara BMS 190-Ford DFR V8

26. ALLIOT 1'11"215 [2]
Ligier JS33/B-Ford DFR V8

25. LARINI 1'11"180 [2]
Ligier JS33/B-Ford DFR V8

24. BARILLA 1'11"387 [2]
Minardi M190-Ford DFR V8

22. DE CESARIS 1'11"234 [2]
Dallara BMS 190-Ford DFR V8

17. TARQUINI 1'11"681 [2]
AGS JH24-Ford DFR V8

9. ALBORETO 1'11"562 [1]
Arrows A11/B-Ford DFR V8

Failed to pre-qualify:
33. MORENO (EuroBrun ER189B-Judd V8) 1'12"544
18. DALMAS (AGS JH24-Ford DFR V8) 1'12"653
34. LANGES (EuroBrun ER189B-Judd V8) 1'15"059
31. GACHOT (Coloni C3-Subaru 12 boxer) 1'19"230
39. GIACOMELLI (Life-Rocchi W12) 1'25"947

Did not qualify:
14. GROUILLARD (Osella FA1M90-Ford DFR V8) 1'11"710 [2]
7. BRABHAM (Brabham BT59-Judd V8) 1'11"741 [1]
36. LEHTO (Onyx ORE 1B-Ford DFR V8) 1'12"631 [2]
35. FOITEK (Onyx ORE 1B-Ford DFR V8) 1'13"271 [2]

[1] Grid times set in first qualifying session.
[2] Grid times set in second qualifying session.

RESULT

	Driver	Car	Laps	Time	Fastest lap
1	PROST	Ferrari	64	1.18'30"999	1'11"526
2	BOUTSEN	Williams	64	+ 39"092	1'12"879
3	SENNA	McLaren	64	+ 42"088	1'12"250
4	BERNARD	Lola	64	+ 1'15"302	1'13"088
5	PIQUET	Benetton	64	+ 1'24"003	1'12"723
6	SUZUKI	Lola	63		1'12"227
7	CAFFI	Arrows	63		1'13"573
8	ALESI	Tyrrell	63		1'12"639
9	MODENA	Brabham	62		1'13"338
10	LARINI	Ligier	62		1'14"953
11	PIRRO	Dallara	61		1'13"731
12	BARILLA	Minardi	61		1'15"607
13	ALLIOT	Ligier	61		1'14"848
14	BERGER*	McLaren	60		1'12"393

*Classified, but not running at end.

Winner's speed: 233.775 kmh/145.253 mph.

Fastest lap: MANSELL, Ferrari, 1'11"291 = 241.377 kmh/149.977 mph.

RETIREMENTS

Driver	Laps	Reason	Fastest lap
GUGELMIN	0	fuel pump (DNS)	
MARTINI	2	alternator	1'17"827
DE CESARIS	12	gearbox	1'16"039
NANNINI	15	accident	1'13"405
NAKAJIMA	20	electrics	1'15"192
PATRESE	26	accident damage	1'14"130
ALBORETO	37	electrics	1'13"932
TARQUINI	41	engine	1'15"889
WARWICK	46	engine	1'14"416
DONNELLY	48	engine	1'13"204
CAPELLI	48	fuel system	1'11"712
MANSELL	55	gearbox	1'11"291
BERGER	60	throttle	1'12"393

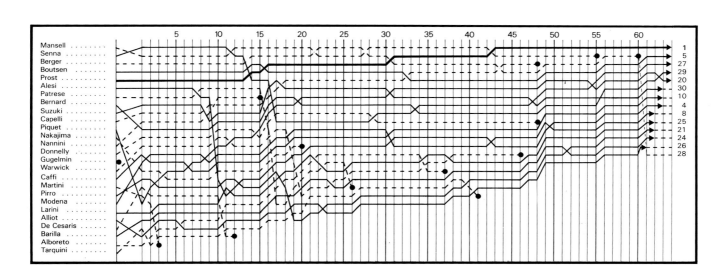

GROSSER PREIS VON DEUTSCHLAND

Date:	29 July 1990
Venue and distance:	Hockenheim. 45 laps of the 6.797 km/4.226 mile circuit, 305.86 km/190.17 miles
Weather:	hot, humid
Attendance:	approx. 100 000 spectators
Previous winner:	Ayrton Senna, McLaren MP4/5, at 224.566 kmh/139.455 mph (1989)
Existing lap record:	Nigel Mansell, Williams FW11B, 1′45″716 = 231.462 kmh/143.864 mph (1987)

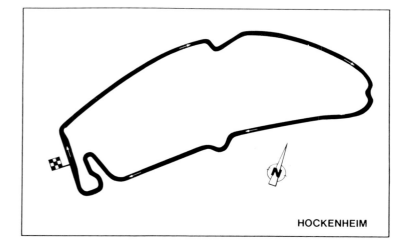

HOCKENHEIM

STARTING GRID

27. SENNA 1′40″198 [1]
McLaren MP4/5B-Honda V10

28. BERGER 1′40″434 [1]
McLaren MP4/5B-Honda V10

1. PROST 1′41″732 [1]
Ferrari 641/2-Ferrari V12

2. MANSELL 1′42″057 [2]
Ferrari 641/2-Ferrari V12

6. PATRESE 1′42″195 [2]
Williams FW13/B-Renault V10

5. BOUTSEN 1′42″380 [2]
Williams FW13/B-Renault V10

20. PIQUET 1′42′P′872 [2]
Benetton B190-Ford F1 V8

4. ALESI 1′43″255 [1]
Tyrrell 019-Ford DFR V8

19. NANNINI 1′43″594 [1]
Benetton B190-Ford F1 V8

16. CAPELLI 1′44″349 [2]
Leyton House CG901-Judd V8

30. SUZUKI 1′44″363 [2]
Lola L90-Lamborghini V12

29. BERNARD 1′44″496 [2]
Lola L90-Lamborghini V12

3. NAKAJIMA 1′44″650 [2]
Tyrrell 019-Ford DFR V8

15. GUGELMIN 1′45″193 [2]
Leyton House CG901-Judd V8

23. MARTINI 1′45″237 [2]
Minardi M190-Ford DFR V8

11. WARWICK 1′45″244 [2]
Lotus 102-Lamborghini V12

8. MODENA 1′45″5476 [1]
Brabham BT59-Judd V8

10. CAFFI 1′45″604 [2]
Arrows A11/B-Ford DFR V8

9. ALBORETO 1′45″751 [2]
Arrows A11/B-Ford DFR V8

12. DONNELLY 1′45″790 [2]
Lotus 102-Lamborghini V12

7. BRABHAM 1′46″110 [1]
Brabham BT59-Judd V8

25. LARINI 1′46″187 [2]
Ligier JS33/B-Ford DFR V8

21. PIRRO 1′46″506 [2]
Dallara BMS 190-Ford DFR V8

26. ALLIOT 1′46″596 [1]
Ligier JS33/B-Ford DFR V8

36. LEHTO 1′46″857 [2]
Monteverdi ORE 1B-Ford DFR V8

35. FOITEK 1′47″209 [1]
Monteverdi ORE 1B-Ford DFR V8

Failed to pre-qualify: 17. TARQUINI (AGS JH24-Ford DFR V8) 1′48″127 [1]
33. MORENO (EuroBrun ER189B-Judd V8) 1′48″983 [1]
31. GACHOT (Coloni C3-Subaru 12 boxer) 1′50″460 [1]
34. LANGES (EuroBrun ER189B-Judd V8) 1′50″897 [2]

Did not qualify: 14. GROUILLARD (Osella FA1M90-Ford DFR V8) 1′47″429 [1]
24. BARILLA (Minardi M190-Ford DFR V8) 1′47″747 [1]
18. DALMAS (AGS JH24-Ford DFR V8) 1′47″789 [1]
22. DE CESARIS (Dallara BMS 190-Ford DFR V8) 1′48″032 [2]

[1] Grid times set in first qualifying session.
[2] Grid times set in second qualifying session.

270

RESULT

	Driver	Car	Laps	Time	Fastest lap
1	SENNA	McLaren	45	1.20′47″164	1′45″711
2	NANNINI	Benetton	45	+ 6″520	1′46″146
3	BERGER	McLaren	45	+ 8″553	1′46″098
4	PROST	Ferrari	45	+ 45″270	1′46″839
5	PATRESE	Williams	45	+ 48″028	1′46″891
6	BOUTSEN	Williams	45	+ 1′21″491	1′45″602
7	CAPELLI	Leyton House	44		1′48″799
8	WARWICK	Lotus	44		1′48″547
9	CAFFI	Arrows	44		1′49″054
10	LARINI	Ligier	43		1′48″502
11	ALESI*	Tyrrell	40		1′48″421

* Classified, not running at end.

Winner's speed: 227.334 kmh/141.154 mph.

Fastest lap: BOUTSEN, Williams, 1′45″602 = 231.882 kmh/143.978 mph (record).

RETIREMENTS

Driver	Laps	Reason	Fastest lap
PIRRO	0	accident	
MODENA	0	clutch	
DONNELLY	0	clutch	
ALBORETO	10	engine	1′52″041
GUGELMIN	11	engine	1′50″255
BRABHAM	12	engine	1′52″018
MANSELL	15	undertray damaged	1′47″268
FOITEK	19	accident	1′51″456
MARTINI	20	engine	1′51″326
PIQUET	23	engine	1′46″949
NAKAJIMA	24	engine	1′49″896
SUZUKI	33	clutch	1′49″128
BERNARD	35	fuel pressure	1′49″071
ALESI	40	engine	1′48″421

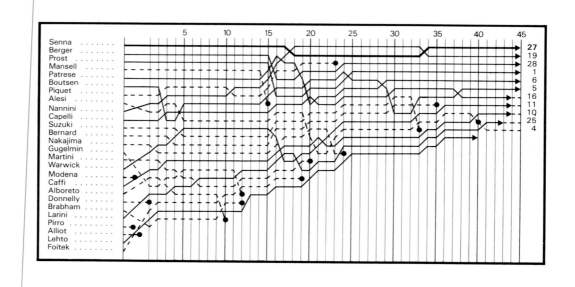

Hungarian Grand Prix

Date:	12 August 1990
Venue and distance:	Hungaroring. 77 laps of the 3.968 km/ 2.461 mile circuit, 305.53 km/189.497 miles
Weather:	hot and sunny
Attendance:	approx. 130 000 spectators
Previous winner:	Nigel Mansell, Ferrari 640, at 167.197 kmh/103.821 mph (1989)
Existing lap record:	Nigel Mansell, Ferrari 640, 1'22"637 = 172.862 kmh/107.411 mph (1989)

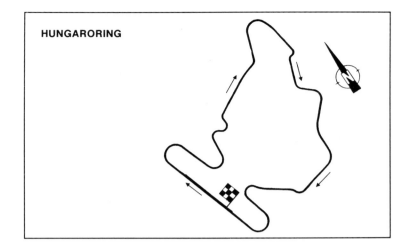

HUNGARORING

STARTING GRID

5. BOUTSEN 1'17"919[2]
Williams FW13/B-Renault V10

6. PATRESE 1'17'955[2]
Williams FW13/B-Renault V10

28. BERGER 1'18"127[1]
McLaren MP4/5B-Honda V10

27. SENNA 1'18"162[2]
McLaren MP4/5B-Honda V10

2. MANSELL 1'18"719[2]
Ferrari 641/2-Ferrari V12

6. ALESI 1'18"726[2]
Tyrrell 019-Ford DFR V8

19. NANNINI 1'18"901[2]
Benetton B190-Ford F1 V8

1. PROST 1'19"029[2]
Ferrari 641/2-Ferrari V12

20. PIQUET 1'19"453[2]
Benetton B190-Ford F1 V8

22. DE CESARIS 1'19"675[2]
Dallara BMS 190-Ford DFR V8

11. WARWICK 1'19"839[2]
Lotus 102-Lamborghini V12

29. BERNARD 1'19"963[2]
Lola L90-Lamborghini V12

21. PIRRO 1'19"970[2]
Dallara BMS 190-Ford DFR V8

23. MARTINI 1'20"197[2]
Minardi M190-Ford DFR V8

3. NAKAJIMA 1'20"202[2]
Tyrrell 019-Ford DFR V8

16. CAPELLI 1'20"385[2]
Leyton House CG901-Judd V8

15. GUGELMIN 1'20"397[2]
Leyton House CG901-Judd V8

12. DONNELLY 1'20"602[2]
Lotus 102-Lamborghini V12

30. SUZUKI 1'20"619[2]
Lola L90-Lamborghini V12

8. MODENA 1'20"715[2]
Brabham BT59-Judd V8

26. ALLIOT 1'21"003[2]
Ligier JS33/B-Ford DFR V8

9. ALBORETO 1'21"758[2]
Arrows A11/B-Ford DFR V8

24. BARILLA 1'21"849[2]
Minardi M190-Ford DFR V8

17. TARQUINI 1'21"964[2]
AGS JH24-Ford DFR V8

25. LARINI 1'22"078[2]
Ligier JS33/B-Ford DFR V8

10. CAFFI 1'22"126[2]
Arrows A11/B-Ford DFR V8

Failed to pre-qualify: 14. GROUILLARD (Osella FA1M90-Ford DFR V8) 1'23"582
31. GACHOT (Coloni C3-Subaru 12 boxer) 1'23"670
33. MORENO (EuroBrun ER189B-Judd V8) 1'24"386
34. LANGES (EuroBrun ER189B-Judd V8) 1'26"514
39. GIACOMELLI (Life-Rocchi W12) 1'41"431

Did not qualify: 18. DALMAS (AGS JH24-Ford DFR V8) 1'22"263[2]
7. BRABHAM (Brabham BT59-Judd V8) 1'22"488[2]
36. LEHTO (Monteverdi ORE 1B-Ford DFR V8) 1'22"647[2]
35. FOITEK (Monteverdi ORE 1B-Ford DFR V8) 1'24"361[1]

[1] Grid times set in first qualifying session.
[2] Grid times set in second qualifying session.

RESULT

	Driver	Car	Laps	Time	Fastest lap
1	BOUTSEN	Williams	77	1.49'30"597	1'23"934
2	SENNA	McLaren	77	+ 0"238	1'22"577
3	PIQUET	Benetton	77	+ 27"893	1'23"164
4	PATRESE	Williams	77	+ 31"833	1'22"058
5	WARWICK	Lotus	77	+ 1'14"244	1'24"140
6	BERNARD	Lola	77	+ 1'24"308	1'23"864
7	DONNELLY	Lotus	76		1'22"561
8	GUGELMIN	Leyton House	76		1'24"062
9	CAFFI	Arrows	76		1'24"388
10	PIRRO	Dallara	76		1'24"765
11	LARINI	Ligier	76		1'23"147
12	ALBORETO	Arrows	75		1'24"418
13	TARQUINI	AGS	74		1'24"921
14	ALLIOT	Ligier	74		1'24"073
15	BARILLA	Minardi	74		1'25"710
16	BERGER*	McLaren	72		1'22"122
17	MANSELL*	Ferrari	71		1'22"235

* Classified, not running at end.

Winner's speed: 167.402 kmh/104.018 mph.

Fastest lap: PATRESE, Williams, 1'22"058 = 174.082 kmh/108.173 mph (record).

RETIREMENTS

Driver	Laps	Reason	Fastest lap
NAKAJIMA	0	accident	1'27"900
DE CESARIS	22	engine	1'25"523
MARTINI	35	accident	1'25"930
MODENA	35	engine	1'26"474
ALESI	36	accident	1'24"414
PROST	36	gearbox, spun	1'24"214
SUZUKI	37	engine	1'25"209
CAPELLI	56	gearbox	1'24"245
NANNINI	64	accident	1'22"639
MANSELL	71	accident	1'22"235
BERGER	72	accident damage	1'22"122

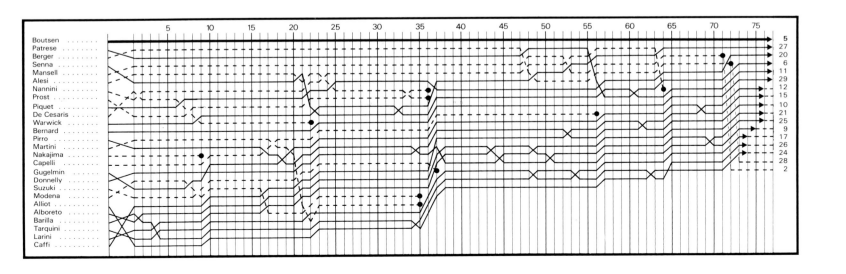

GRAND PRIX DE BELGIQUE

Date:	26 August 1990
Venue and distance:	Spa-Francorchamps. 44 laps of the 6.94 km/ 4.312 mile circuit, 305.360 km/189.741 miles
Weather:	cloudy, humid
Attendance:	approx. 50 000 spectators
Previous winner:	Ayrton Senna, McLaren MP4/5, at 181.576 kmh/112.758 mph (1989)
Existing lap record:	Alain Prost, McLaren MP4/3, 1′57″153 = 213.260 kmh/132.513 mph (1987)

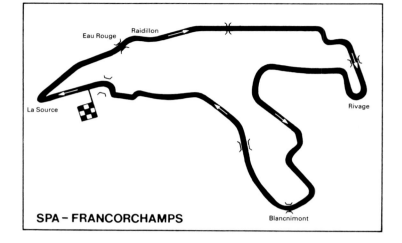

SPA – FRANCORCHAMPS

STARTING GRID

28. BERGER 1′50″948
McLaren MP4/5B-Honda V10

27. SENNA 1′50″365
McLaren MP4/5B-Honda V10

5. BOUTSEN 1′51″902
Williams FW13/B-Renault V10

1. PROST 1′51″043
Ferrari 641/2-Ferrari V12

19. NANNINI 1′52″648
Benetton B190-Ford F1 V8

2. MANSELL 1′52″267
Ferrari 641/2-Ferrari V12

20. PIQUET 1′52″853
Benetton B190-Ford F1 V8

6. PATRESE 1′52″703
Williams FW13/B-Renault V10

3. NAKAJIMA 1′53″468
Tyrrell 019-Ford DFR V8

4. ALESI 1′52″885
Tyrrell 019-Ford DFR V8

16. CAPELLI 1′53″783
Leyton House CG901-Judd V8

30. SUZUKI 1′53″523
Lola L90-Lamborghini V12

15. GUGELMIN 1′54″120
Leyton House CG901-Judd V8

8. MODENA 1′53″916
Brabham BT59-Judd V8

23. MARTINI 1′54″312
Minardi M190-Ford DFR V8

29. BERNARD 1′54″251
Lola L90-Lamborghini V12

11. WARWICK 1′55″068
Lotus 102-Lamborghini V12

21. PIRRO 1′54″595
Dallara BMS 190-Ford DFR V8

22. DE CESARIS 1′55″261
Dallara BMS 190-Ford DFR V8

10. CAFFI 1′55″199
Arrows A11/B-Ford DFR V8

12. DONNELLY 1′55″304
Lotus 102-Lamborghini V12

25. LARINI 1′55″278
Ligier JS33/B-Ford DFR V8

7. BRABHAM 1′55″668
Brabham BT59-Judd V8

14. GROUILLARD 1′55″334
Osella FA1M90-Ford DFR V8

9. ALBORETO 1′56″055
Arrows A11/B-Ford DFR V8

24. BARILLA 1′55″859
Minardi M190-Ford DFR V8

Failed to pre-qualify:
33. MORENO (EuroBrun ER189B-Judd V8) 2′00″270
34. LANGES (EuroBrun ER189B-Judd V8) 2′01″405
39. GIACOMELLI (Life-Rocchi W12) 2′19″445

272

Did not qualify:
26. ALLIOT (Ligier JS33/B-Ford DFR V8) 1′56″118
17. TARQUINI (AGS JH24-Ford DFR V8) 1′57″566
18. DALMAS (AGS JH24-Ford DFR V8) 1′57″704
31. GACHOT (Coloni C3-Ford DFR V8) 1′58″520

All grid times set in second qualifying session.

RESULT

	Driver	Car	Laps	Time	Fastest lap
1	SENNA	McLaren	44	1.26′31″997	1′55″132
2	PROST	Ferrari	44	+ 3″550	1′55″087
3	BERGER	McLaren	44	+ 28″462	1′55″531
4	NANNINI	Benetton	44	+ 49″337	1′55″650
5	PIQUET	Benetton	44	+ 1′29″650	1′57″036
6	GUGELMIN	Leyton House	44	+ 1′48″851	1′58″163
7	CAPELLI	Leyton House	43		1′58″351
8	ALESI	Tyrrell	43		1′58″531
9	BERNARD	Lola	43		1′56″531
10	CAFFI	Arrows	43		2′00″610
11	WARWICK	Lotus	43		1′59″081
12	DONNELLY	Lotus	43		1′58″330
13	ALBORETO	Arrows	43		2′00″671
14	LARINI	Ligier	42		1′59″956
15	MARTINI	Minardi	42		2′00″157
16	GROUILLARD	Osella	42		2′00″886
17	MODENA*	Brabham	39		1′59″415

* Classified, not running at end.

Winner's speed: 211.729 kmh/131.562 mph.

Fastest lap: PROST, Ferrari, 1′55″087 = 217.088 kmh/134.891 mph (record).

RETIREMENTS

Driver	Laps	Reason	Fastest lap
SUZUKI	0	accident (DNS, second start)	
BARILLA	0	accident (DNS, third start)	
NAKAJIMA	4	misfire	2′14″599
PIRRO	5	water leak	2′03″152
PATRESE	18	gearbox	1′58″666
MANSELL	19	handling, abandoned	1′59″767
BOUTSEN	21	transmission	1′58″199
DE CESARIS	27	engine	2′02″225
BRABHAM	36	electrics	2′01″959
MODENA	39	engine	1′59″415

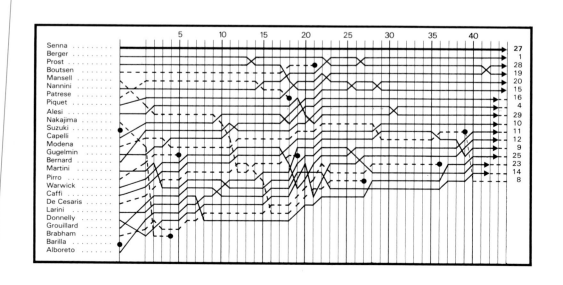

GRAN PREMIO D'ITALIA

Date:	9 September 1990
Venue and distance:	Monza, 53 laps of the 5.8 km/3.6 mile circuit, 307.4 km/191.01 miles
Weather:	hot, sunny
Attendance:	approx. 150 000 spectators
Previous winner:	Alain Prost, McLaren MP4/5, at 232.119 kmh/144.145 mph (1989)
Existing lap record:	Ayrton Senna, Lotus 99T, 1'26"796 = 240.564 kmh/149.479 mph (1987)

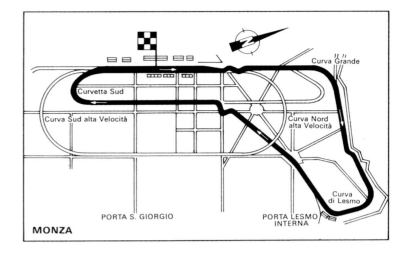

MONZA

STARTING GRID

27. SENNA 1'22"533 [2]
McLaren MP4/5B-Honda V10

1. PROST 1'22"935 [2]
Ferrari 641/2-Ferrari V12

28. BERGER 1'22"936 [2]
McLaren MP4/5B-Honda V10

2. MANSELL 1'23"141 [1]
Ferrari 641/2-Ferrari V12

4. ALESI 1'23"526 [1]
Tyrrell 019-Ford DFR V8

5. BOUTSEN 1'23"984 [2]
Williams FW13/B-Renault V10

6. PATRESE 1'24"253 [1]
Williams FW13/B-Renault V10

19. NANNINI 1'24"583 [2]
Benetton B190-Ford F1 V8

20. PIQUET 1'24"699 [1]
Benetton B190-Ford F1 V8

15. GUGELMIN 1'25"556 [2]
Leyton House CG901-Judd V8

12. DONNELLY 1'25"626 [2]
Lotus 102-Lamborghini V12

11. WARWICK 1'25"677 [2]
Lotus 102-Lamborghini V12

29. BERNARD 1'25"927 [1]
Lola L90-Lamborghini V12

3. NAKAJIMA 1'26"081 [2]
Tyrrell 019-Ford DFR V8

23. MARTINI 1'26"330 [1]
Minardi M190-Ford DFR V8

16. CAPELLI 1'26"712 [1]
Leyton House CG901-Judd V8

8. MODENA 1'26"950 [1]
Brabham BT59-Judd V8

30. SUZUKI 1'26"962 [2]
Lola L90-Lamborghini V12

21. PIRRO 1'26"964 [2]
Dallara BMS 190-Ford DFR V8

26. ALLIOT 1'27"043 [2]
Ligier JS33/B-Ford DFR V8

10. CAFFI 1'27"410 [2]
Dallara BMS 190-Ford DFR V8

9. ALBORETO 1'27"448 [2]
Arrows A11/B-Ford DFR V8

14. GROUILLARD 1'27"541 [1]
Osella FA1M90-Ford DFR V8

18. DALMAS 1'27"673 [2]
AGS JH24-Ford DFR V8

22. DE CESARIS 1'27"772 [1]
Dallara BMS 190-Ford DFR V8

25. LARINI 1'27"937 [2]
Ligier JS33/B-Ford DFR V8

Failed to pre-qualify:
33. MORENO (EuroBrun ER189B-Judd V8) 1'28"703
34. LANGES (EuroBrun ER189B-Judd V8) 1'35"061
39. GIACOMELLI (Life-Rocchi W12) 1'55"244

Did not qualify:
17. TARQUINI (AGS JH24-Ford DFR V8) 1'28"107 [1]
24. BARILLA (Minardi M190-Ford DFR V8) 1'28"258 [1]
7. BRABHAM (Brabham BT59-Judd V8) 1'28"382 [1]
31. GACHOT (Coloni C3-Ford DFR V8) 1'28"952 [1]

[1] Times set in first qualifying session.
[2] Times set in second qualifying session.

RESULT

	Driver	Car	Laps	Time	Fastest lap
1	SENNA	McLaren	53	1.17'57"878	1'26"254
2	PROST	Ferrari	53	+ 6"054	1'26"376
3	BERGER	McLaren	53	+ 7"404	1'26"650
4	MANSELL	Ferrari	53	+ 56"219	1'27"776
5	PATRESE	Williams	53	+ 1'25"274	1'28"608
6	NAKAJIMA	Tyrrell	52		1'28"777
7	PIQUET	Benetton	52		1'27"882
8	NANNINI	Benetton	52		1'28"483
9	CAFFI	Dallara	51		1'29"820
10	DE CESARIS	Dallara	51		1'29"750
11	LARINI	Ligier	51		1'30"640
12	ALBORETO*	Arrows	50		1'30"348
13	ALLIOT	Ligier	50		1'32"881
14	DALMAS	AGS	45		1'29"868

* Classified, not running at end.

Winner's speed: 236.569 kmh/146.996 mph.

Fastest lap: SENNA, McLaren, 1'26"254 = 242.076 kmh/150.418 mph (record).

273

RETIREMENTS

Driver	Laps	Reason	Fastest lap
ALESI	4	spun off	1'29"386
MARTINI	7	suspension failure	1'31"740
BERNARD	10	clutch	1'29"949
DONNELLY	13	engine	1'29"876
PIRRO	14	spun	1'31"668
WARWICK	15	gearbox	1'30"521
BOUTSEN	18	suspension failure	1'28"672
MODENA	21	engine	1'32"025
GUGELMIN	24	engine	1'29"298
CAPELLI	36	engine	1'29"112
SUZUKI	36	electrics	1'29"138
ALBORETO	50	spun	1'30"348

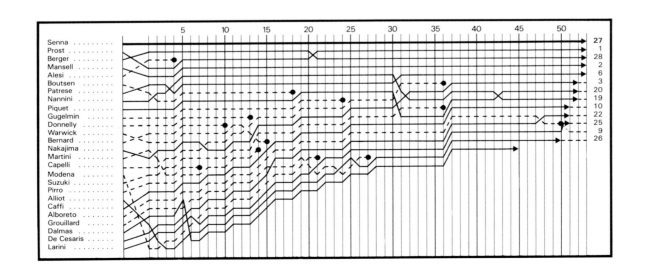

GRANDE PRÊMIO DE PORTUGAL

Date:	23 September 1990
Venue and distance:	61 laps of the 4.35 km/2.703 mile circuit, 265.35 km/164.885 miles
Weather:	warm, cloudy
Attendance:	approx. 72 000 spectators
Previous winner:	Gerhard Berger, Ferrari 640, at 191.418 kmh/118.945 mph
Existing lap record:	Gerhard Berger, Ferrari 640, 1'18"986 = 198.263 kmh/123.195 mph (1989)

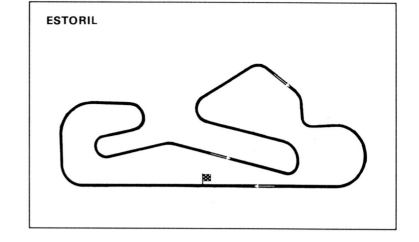

ESTORIL

STARTING GRID

2. MANSELL 1'13"557
Ferrari 641/2-Ferrari V12

1. PROST 1'13"595
Ferrari 641/2-Ferrari V12

27. SENNA 1'13"601
McLaren MP4/5B-Honda V10

28. BERGER 1'14"292
McLaren MP4/5B-Honda V10

6. PATRESE 1'14"723
Williams FW13/B-Renault V10

20. PIQUET 1'14"728
Benetton B190-Ford F1 V8

5. BOUTSEN 1'14"934
Williams FW13/B-Renault V10

4. ALESI 1'15"122
Tyrrell 019-Ford DFR V8

19. NANNINI 1'15"411
Benetton B190-Ford F1 V8

29. BERNARD 1'15"673
Lola L90-Lamborghini V12

30. SUZUKI 1'16"012
Lola L90-Lamborghini V12

16. CAPELLI 1'16"284
Leyton House CG901-Judd V8

21. PIRRO 1'16"290
Dallara BMS 190-Ford DFR V8

15. GUGELMIN 1'16"296
Leyton House CG901-Judd V8

12. DONNELLY 1'16"762
Lotus 102-Lamborghini V12

23. MARTINI 1'16"795
Minardi M190-Ford DFR V8

10. CAFFI 1'16"946
Arrows A11/B-Ford DFR V8

22. DE CESARIS 1'17"066
Dallara BMS 190-Ford DFR V8

9. ALBORETO 1'17"081
Arrows A11/B-Ford DFR V8

3. NAKAJIMA* 1'17"097
Tyrrell 019-Ford DFR V8

26. ALLIOT 1'17"120
Ligier JS33/B-Ford DFR V8

11. WARWICK 1'17"259
Lotus 102-Lamborghini V12

25. LARINI 1'17"269
Ligier JS33/B-Ford DFR V8

8. MODENA 1'17"341
Brabham BT59-Judd V8

18. DALMAS 1'17"621
AGS JH24-Ford DFR V8

7. BRABHAM 1'17"715
Brabham BT59-Judd V8

Failed to pre-qualify: 33. MORENO (EuroBrun ER189B-Judd V8) 1'21"118
34. LANGES (EuroBrun ER189B-Judd V8) 1'23"447
39. GIACOMELLI (Life-Judd V8) —

Did not qualify: 31. GACHOT (Coloni C3-Ford DFR V8) 1'20"516
17. TARQUINI (AGS JH24-Ford DFR V8) 1'18"815
24. BARILLA (Minardi M190-Ford DFR V8) 1'18"280
14. GROUILLARD (Osella FA1M90-Ford DFR V8) 1'17"775

* Withdrawn (driver ill).
All grid times except NAKAJIMA's set in second qualifying session.

274

RESULT

	Driver	Car	Laps	Time	Fastest lap
1	MANSELL	Ferrari	61*	1.22'11"014	1'18"577
2	SENNA	McLaren	61	+ 2"808	1'18"936
3	PROST	Ferrari	61	+ 4"189	1'18"396
4	BERGER	McLaren	61	+ 5"896	1'18"438
5	PIQUET	Benetton	61	+ 57"418	1'19"713
6	NANNINI	Benetton	61	+ 58"249	1'18"355
7	PATRESE	Williams	60		1'18"306
8	ALESI	Tyrrell	60		
9	ALBORETO	Arrows	60		1'20"792
10	LARINI	Ligier	59		1'20"958
11	MARTINI	Minardi	59		1'21"180
12	GUGELMIN	Leyton House	59		1'21"894
13	CAFFI**	Arrows	57		1'21"843
14	SUZUKI**	Lola	57		1'20"349
15	PIRRO	Dallara	57		1'22"231

* Shortened race (accident to Caffi).
** Classified, not running at end.

Winner's speed: 193.725 kmh/120.374 mph.

Fastest lap: PATRESE, Williams, 1'18"306 = 199.985 kmh/124.264 mph (record).

RETIREMENTS

Driver	Laps	Reason	Fastest lap
DE CESARIS	0	spun off	
DALMAS	3	driveshaft	1'24"879
WARWICK	5	throttle linkage	1'23"510
DONNELLY	14	alternator	1'22"625
MODENA	21	gearbox	1'23"232
BERNARD	24	gearbox	1'22"434
BOUTSEN	30	gearbox	1'20"575
CAPELLI	51	engine	1'21"623
ALLIOT	52	accident	1'20"914
BRABHAM	52	gearbox	1'22"275
SUZUKI	58	accident	1'20"349
CAFFI	58	accident	1'21"843

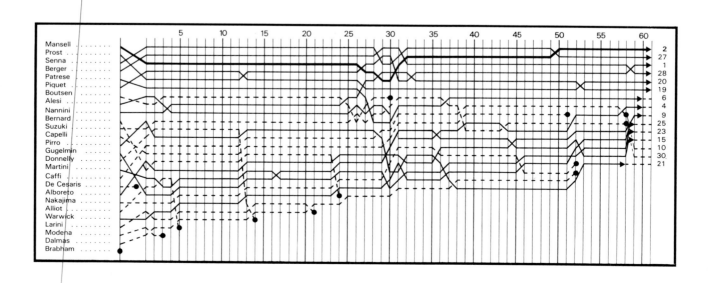

Gran Premio de España

Date:	30 September 1990
Venue and distance:	Jerez. 73 laps of the 4.218 km/2.621 mile circuit, 307.914 km/191.333 miles
Weather:	hot, some cloud
Attendance:	approx. 35 000 spectators
Previous winner:	Ayrton Senna, McLaren MP4/5, at 171.374 kmh/106.486 mph (1989)
Existing lap record:	Ayrton Senna, McLaren MP4/5, 1'25"779 = 177.022 kmh/110.000 mph (1989)

CIRCUITO DE JEREZ

STARTING GRID

27. SENNA 1'18"387
McLaren MP4/5B-Honda V10

1. PROST 1'18"824
Ferrari 641/2-Ferrari V12

2. MANSELL 1'19"106
Ferrari 641/2-Ferrari V12

4. ALESI 1'19"604
Tyrrell 019-Ford DFR V8

28. BERGER 1'19"618
McLaren MP4/5B-Honda V10

6. PATRESE 1'19"647
Williams FW13/B-Renault V10

5. BOUTSEN 1'19"689
Williams FW13/B-Renault V10

20. PIQUET 1'19"700
Benetton B190-Ford F1 V8

19. NANNINI 1'20"367
Benetton B190-Ford F1 V8

11. WARWICK 1'20"610
Lotus 102-Lamborghini V12

23. MARTINI 1'21"060
Minardi M190-Ford DFR V8

15. GUGELMIN 1'21"167
Leyton House CG901-Judd V8

26. ALLIOT 1'21"170
Ligier JS33/B-Ford DFR V8

3. NAKAJIMA 1'21"215
Tyrrell 019-Ford DFR V8

30. SUZUKI 1'21"244
Lola L90-Lamborghini V12

21. PIRRO 1'21"277
Dallara BMS 190-Ford DFR V8

22. DE CESARIS 1'21"467
Dallara BMS 190-Ford DFR V8

29. BERNARD 1'21"551
Lola L90-Lamborghini V12

16. CAPELLI 1'21"910
Leyton House CG901-Judd V8

25. LARINI 1'21"996
Ligier JS33/B-Ford DFR V8

14. GROUILLARD 1'22"288
Osella FA1M90-Ford DFR V8

17. TARQUINI 1'22"466
AGS JH24-Ford DFR V8

18. DALMAS 1'22"716
AGS JH24-Ford DFR V8

8. MODENA 1"23"133
Brabham BT59-Judd V8

9. ALBORETO 1'23"161
Arrows A11/B-Ford DFR V8

Failed to pre-qualify: 33. MORENO (EuroBrun ER189B-Judd V8) 1'24"621
34. LANGES (EuroBrun ER189B-Judd V8) 1'25"736
39. GIACOMELLI (Life-Judd V8) 1'42"699

Did not qualify: 7. BRABHAM (Brabham BT59-Judd V8) 1'23"163
24. BARILLA (Minardi M190-Ford DFR V8) 1'23"274
12. SCHNEIDER (Arrows A11/B-Ford DFR V8) 1'23"924
31. GACHOT (Coloni C3-Ford Cosworth V8) 1'25"114

All grid times set in second qualifying session (Martin Donnelly lapped in 1'22"659 before crashing very heavily near the end of the first qualifying session).

RESULT

	Driver	Car	Laps	Time	Fastest lap
1	PROST	Ferrari	73	1.48'01"461	1'25"177
2	MANSELL	Ferrari	73	+ 22"064	1'26"957
3	NANNINI	Benetton	73	+ 34"874	1'26"599
4	BOUTSEN	Williams	73	+ 43"296	1'27"206
5	PATRESE	Williams	73	+ 57"530	1'24"513
6	SUZUKI	Lola	73	+ 1'03"728	1'27"158
7	LARINI	Ligier	72		1'26"104
8	GUGELMIN	Leyton House	72		1'26"773
9	DALMAS	AGS	72		1'27"710
10	ALBORETO	Arrows	71		1'28"712

Winner's speed: 171.025 kmh/106.269 mph.

Fastest lap: PATRESE, Williams, 1'24"513 = 179.674 kmh/111.644 mph (record).

RETIREMENTS

Driver	Laps	Reason	Fastest lap
PIRRO	0	throttle stuck	
ALESI	0	accident	
TARQUINI	5	electrics	1'31"062
MODENA	5	accident	1'31"467
NAKAJIMA	13	accident	1'30"347
BERNARD	20	clutch	1'29"296
ALLIOT	22	accident	1'29"329
MARTINI	41	wheel nut failed	1'28"314
GROUILLARD	45	wheel bearing	1'29"692
PIQUET	47	electrics	1'25"095
DE CESARIS	47	engine	1'28"471
SENNA	53	radiator	1'27"430
BERGER	56	accident	1'26"250
CAPELLI	59	driver fatigue	1'28"471
WARWICK	63	gearbox	1'26"252

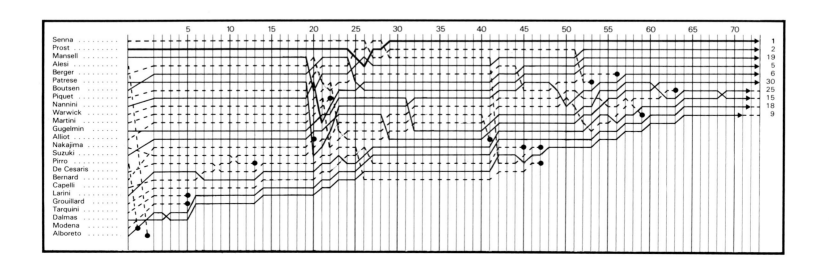

Japanese Grand Prix

Date:	21 October 1990
Venue and distance:	53 laps of the 5.859 km/3.66 mile Suzuka circuit, 310.527 km/194.079 miles
Weather:	fine
Attendance:	approx. 150 000 spectators
Previous winner:	Alessandro Nannini, Benetton, at 195.907 kmh/121.756 mph
Existing lap record:	Alain Prost, McLaren, 1'43"506 = 203.779 kmh/126.649 mph (1989)

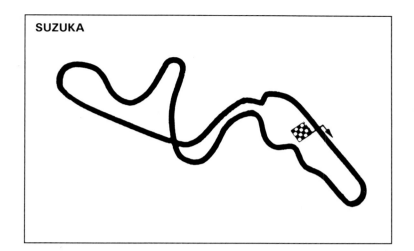

SUZUKA

STARTING GRID

1. PROST 1'37"228 [2]
Ferrari 641/2-Ferrari V12

27. SENNA 1'36"996 [2]
McLaren MP4/5B-Honda V10

28. BERGER 1'38"118 [2]
McLaren MP4/5B-Honda V10

2. MANSELL 1'37"719 [2]
Ferrari 641/2-Ferrari V12

20. PIQUET 1'40"049 [2]
Benetton B190-Ford F1 V8

5. BOUTSEN 1'39"324 [2]
Williams FW13/B-Renault V10

19. MORENO 1'40"579 [2]
Benetton B190-Ford F1 V8

6. PATRESE 1'40"355 [1]
Williams FW13/B-Renault V10

23. MARTINI 1'40"899 [1]
Minardi M190-Ford DFR V8

30. SUZUKI 1'40"888 [2]
Lola L90-Lamborghini V12

16. CAPELLI 1'41"033 [2]
Leyton House CG901-Judd V8

11. WARWICK 1'41"024 [2]
Lotus 102-Lamborghini V12

12. HERBERT 1'41"558 [2]
Lotus 102-Lamborghini V12

3. NAKAJIMA 1'41"078 [2]
Tyrrell 019-Ford DFR V8

29. BERNARD 1'41"709 [2]
Lola L90-Lamborghini V12

15. GUGELMIN 1'41"698 [2]
Leyton House CG901-Judd V8

21. PIRRO 1'42"361 [2]
Dallara BMS 190-Ford DFR V8

25. LARINI 1'42"339 [2]
Ligier JS33/B-Ford DFR V8

26. ALLIOT 1'42"593 [2]
Ligier JS33/B-Ford DFR V8

24. MORBIDELLI 1'42"364 [2]
Minardi M190-Ford DFR V8

7. BRABHAM 1'43"156 [1]
Brabham BT59-Judd V8

8. MODENA 1'42"617 [1]
Brabham BT59-Judd V8

9. ALBORETO 1'43"304 [1]
Arrows A11/B-Ford DFR V8

10. CAFFI 1'43"270 [1]
Arrows A11/B-Ford DFR V8

22. DE CESARIS 1'43"601 [1]
Dallara BMS 190-Ford DFR V8

Did not start: ALESI (Tyrrell 019-Ford DFR V8), 1'40"052 [1].

Did not qualify: 14. GROUILLARD (Osella FA1M90-Ford DFR V8) 1'43"782 [2]
17. TARQUINI (AGS JH24-Ford DFR V8) 1'44"281 [1]
18. DALMAS (AGS JH24-Ford DFR V8) 1'44"410 [1]
31. GACHOT (Coloni C3-Ford Cosworth V8) 1'45"393 [2]

[1] Time set in first qualifying session.
[2] Time set in second qualifying session.

RESULT

	Driver	Car	Laps	Time	Fastest lap
1	PIQUET	Benetton	53	1.34'36"824	1'45"114
2	MORENO	Benetton	53	+ 7"223	1'45"539
3	SUZUKI	Lola	53	+ 22"469	1'44"850
4	PATRESE	Williams	53	+ 36"258	1'44"233
5	BOUTSEN	Williams	53	+ 46"884	1'45"706
6	NAKAJIMA	Tyrrell	53	+ 1'12"350	1'45"887
7	LARINI	Ligier	52		1'46"681
8	MARTINI	Minardi	52		1'46"897
9	CAFFI	Arrows	52		1'46"849
10	ALLIOT	Ligier	52		1'46"106

Winner's speed: 196.923 kmh/123.076 mph.

Fastest lap: PATRESE, Williams, 1'44"233 = 202.358 kmh/126.473 mph.

RETIREMENTS

Driver	Laps	Reason	Fastest lap
SENNA	0	collision with Prost	
PROST	0	collision with Senna	
MODENA	0	spun off	
BERGER	1	spun off	1'49"573
BRABHAM	2	rear suspension	1'54"765
GUGELMIN	5	engine	1'49"471
DE CESARIS	13	spun off	1'49"761
CAPELLI	16	ignition	1'48"035
MORBIDELLI	18	spun off	1'48"865
BERNARD	24	oil leak	1'47"518
PIRRO	24	alternator	1'48"506
MANSELL	26	transmission	1'46"272
ALBORETO	28	engine	1'47"094
HERBERT	31	engine	1'46"463
WARWICK	38	gearbox	1'46"042

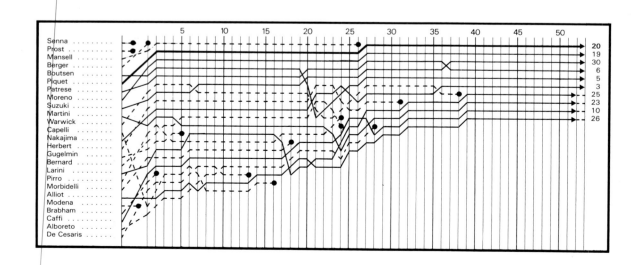

AUSTRALIAN GRAND PRIX

Date:	4 November 1990
Venue and distance:	81 laps of the 3.779 km/2.36 mile Adelaide circuit, 306.180 km/191.325 miles
Weather:	sunny, hot
Attendance:	approx. 65 000 spectators
Previous winner:	Thierry Boutsen, Williams, at 131.981 kmh/82.02 mph
Existing lap record:	Gerhard Berger, Ferrari, 1'20"416 = 169.175 kmh/105.142 mph (1987)

STARTING GRID

27. SENNA 1'15"671 [1]
McLaren MP4/5B-Honda V10

28. BERGER 1'16"244 [2]
McLaren MP4/5B-Honda V10

2. MANSELL 1'16"352 [2]
Ferrari 641/2-Ferrari V12

1. PROST 1'16"365 [1]
Ferrari 641/2-Ferrari V12

4. ALESI 1'16"837 [1]
Tyrrell 019-Ford DFR V8

6. PATRESE 1'17"156 [1]
Williams FW13/B-Renault V10

20. PIQUET 1'17"173 [2]
Benetton B190-Ford F1 V8

19. MORENO 1'17"437 [1]
Benetton B190-Ford F1 V8

5. BOUTSEN 1'17"596 [1]
Williams FW13/B-Renault V10

23. MARTINI 1'17"827 [2]
Minardi M190-Ford DFR V8

11. WARWICK 1'18"351 [2]
Lotus 102-Lamborghini V12

25. LARINI 1'18"730 [2]
Ligier JS33/B-Ford DFR V8

3. NAKAJIMA 1'18"738 [1]
Tyrrell 019-Ford DFR V8

16. CAPELLI 1'18"843 [2]
Leyton House CG901-Judd V8

22. DE CESARIS 1'18"858 [2]
Dallara BMS 190-Ford DFR V8

15. GUGELMIN 1'18"860 [2]
Leyton House CG901-Judd V8

8. MODENA 1'18"886 [2]
Brabham BT59-Judd V8

12. HERBERT 1'19"091 [1]
Lotus 102-Lamborghini V12

26. ALLIOT 1'19"202 [1]
Ligier JS33/B-Ford DFR V8

24. MORBIDELLI 1'19"347 [2]
Minardi M190-Ford DFR V8

21. PIRRO 1'19"476 [1]
Dallara BMS 190-Ford DFR V8

14. GROUILLARD 1'19"722 [2]
Osella FA1M90-Ford DFR V8

29. BERNARD 1'19"858 [2]
Lola L90-Lamborghini V12

30. SUZUKI 1'19"970 [1]
Lola L90-Lamborghini V12

7. BRABHAM 1'20"218 [2]
Brabham BT59-Judd V8

17. TARQUINI 1'20"296 [2]
AGS JH24-Ford DFR V8

Did not qualify:
9. ALBORETO (Arrows A11/B-Ford DFR V8) 1'20"545 [2]
18. DALMAS (AGS JH24-Ford DFR V8) 1'20"570 [2]
10. CAFFI (Arrows A11/B-Ford DFR V8) 1'20"609 [2]
31. GACHOT (Coloni C3-Judd V8) 1'23"135 [1]

[1] Time set in first qualifying session.
[2] Time set in second qualifying session.

ADELAIDE GRAND PRIX CIRCUIT

RESULT

	Driver	Car	Laps	Time	Fastest lap
1	PIQUET	Benetton	81	1.49'44"570	1'18"327
2	MANSELL	Ferrari	81	+ 3"129	1'18"203
3	PROST	Ferrari	81	+ 37"259	1'19"434
4	BERGER	McLaren	81	+ 46"862	1'20"025
5	BOUTSEN	Williams	81	+ 1'51"160	1'19"717
6	PATRESE	Williams	80		1'19"818
7	MORENO	Benetton	80		1'19"707
8	ALESI	Tyrrell	80		1'19"732
9	MARTINI	Minardi	79		1'21"257
10	LARINI	Ligier	79		1'21"209
11	ALLIOT	Ligier	78		1'21"921
12	MODENA	Brabham	77		1'22"693
13	GROUILLARD	Osella	74		1'25"642

Winner's speed: 167.399 kmh/104.559 mph.

Fastest lap: MANSELL, Ferrari, 1'18"203 = 174.009 kmh/108.687 mph (record).

277

RETIREMENTS

Driver	Laps	Reason	Fastest lap
SUZUKI	6	transmission	1'24"007
BRABHAM	6	spun off	1'25"703
MORBIDELLI	20	gearbox	1'24"272
BERNARD	21	gearbox	1'23"272
DE CESARIS	23	electrics	1'23"897
GUGELMIN	27	brakes, spun off	1'22"200
WARWICK	43	clutch	1'22"524
CAPELLI	46	stuck throttle	1'22"583
NAKAJIMA	53	spun off	1'21"713
HERBERT	57	clutch	1'22"142
TARQUINI	58	engine	1'23"147
SENNA	61	spun off	1'19"302
PIRRO	68	engine	1'22"505

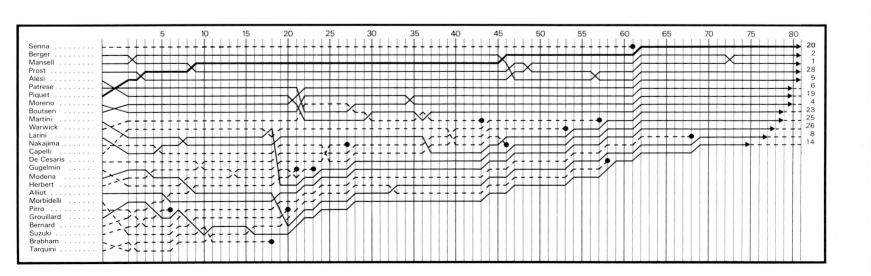

F1 Drivers World Championship

	FINAL CLASSIFICATION	USA	Brasil	San Marino	Monaco	Canada	Mexico	France	British	Deutschland	Hungarian	Belgique	Italia	Portugal	España	Japan	Australian	Total
1	A. Senna	9	4	—	9	9	—	4	4	9	6	9	9	6	—	—	—	78
2	A. Prost	—	9	3	—	2	9	9	9	3	—	6	6	4	9	—	4	71
3	N. Piquet	3	1	2	—	6	1	3	2	—	4	2	—	2	—	9	9	43
4	G. Berger	—	6	6	4	3	4	2	—	4	—	4	4	3	—	—	3	43
5	N. Mansell	—	3	—	—	4	6	—	—	—	—	—	3	9	6	—	6	37
6	T. Boutsen	4	2	—	3	—	2	—	6	1	9	—	—	—	3	2	2	34
7	R. Patrese	—	—	9	—	—	—	1	—	2	3	—	2	—	2	3	1	23
8	A. Nannini	—	—	4	—	—	3	—	—	6	—	3	—	1	4	—	—	21
9	J. Alesi	6	—	1	6	—	—	—	—	—	—	—	—	—	—	—	—	13
10	R. Moreno	—	—	—	—	—	—	—	—	—	—	—	—	—	—	6	—	6
	I. Capelli	—	—	—	—	—	—	6	—	—	—	—	—	—	—	—	—	6
	A. Suzuki	—	—	—	—	—	—	—	1	—	—	—	—	—	1	4	—	6
11	E. Bernard	—	—	—	1	—	—	—	3	—	1	—	—	—	—	—	—	5
12	D. Warwick	—	—	—	—	1	—	—	—	—	2	—	—	—	—	—	—	3
	S. Nakajima	1	—	—	—	—	—	—	—	—	—	—	1	—	—	1	—	3
13	A. Caffi	—	—	—	2	—	—	—	—	—	—	—	—	—	—	—	—	2
	S. Modena	2	—	—	—	—	—	—	—	—	—	—	—	—	—	—	—	2
14	M. Gugelmin	—	—	—	—	—	—	—	—	—	—	1	—	—	—	—	—	1

F1 Constructors World Championship

	FINAL CLASSIFICATION	USA	Brasil	San Marino	Monaco	Canada	Mexico	France	British	Deutschland	Hungarian	Belgique	Italia	Portugal	España	Japan	Australian	Total
1	McLaren-Honda	9	10	6	13	12	4	6	4	13	6	13	13	9	—	—	3	121
2	Ferrari	—	12	3	—	6	15	9	9	3	—	6	9	13	15	—	10	110
3	Benetton-Ford	3	1	6	—	6	4	3	2	6	4	5	—	3	4	15	9	71
4	Williams-Renault	4	2	9	3	—	2	1	6	3	12	—	2	—	5	5	3	57
5	Tyrrell-Ford	7	—	1	6	—	—	—	—	—	—	—	1	—	—	1	—	16
6	Larousse-Lamborghini	—	—	—	1	—	—	—	4	—	1	—	—	—	1	4	—	11
7	Leyton House-Judd	—	—	—	—	—	—	6	—	—	—	1	—	—	—	—	—	7
8	Lotus-Lamborghini	—	—	—	—	1	—	—	—	—	2	—	—	—	—	—	—	3
9	Arrows-Ford	—	—	—	2	—	—	—	—	—	—	—	—	—	—	—	—	2
	Brabham-Judd	2	—	—	—	—	—	—	—	—	—	—	—	—	—	—	—	2

EUROPEAN HILL CLIMB CHAMPIONSHIP

FINAL CLASSIFICATION Cat. 1 (Production cars)				Rechberg (A)	Rampa da Falperra (P)	Ecce Homo (CS)	Mecsek Pannon (H)	Trier (D)	Coppa Caritti, Rieti (I)	Coppa Citta di Potenza (I)	Cesana-Sestriere (I)	Le Mont Dore (F)	St. Ursanne-Les Rangiers (CH)	Turck-heim-Trois Epis (F)	Subida El Fito (E)	Total
1	F. Dosières (F)*	BMW M3	A	20	15	20	(—)	(—)	20	(—)	20	20	(15)	20	15	150
2	A. Charouz (CS)**	Ford Sierra Cos.	N	15	(—)	20	20	20	(12)	20	12	(8)	15	(6)	15	137
3	I. Ischoubrikov (BG)	Peugeot 205 T16	B	15	(—)	12	20	20	(—)	15	(—)	20	10	20	(—)	132
4	H. Böhme (D)	Porsche 944	B	20	(—)	20	(15)	15	15	10	10	(—)	20	10	(—)	120
5	R. Hahn (D)	Porsche 944	B	(—)	(—)	15	—	12	12	(—)	15	15	15	12	(—)	96
6	CJ. Cserkuti (H)	BMW M3	A	10	(—)	12	15	(—)	15	15	10	(—)	4	6	(—)	87
7	P. Moczar (H)	Ford Sierra Cos.	N	10	(—)	12	(8)	15	8	12	6	(—)	8	(—)	4	75
8	W. Böhme (D)	BMW M3 + Ford		12	(—)	15	20	(6)	10	(—)	(—)	3	10	4	—	74
9	M. Tschida (A)	Ford Sierra Cos.	N	12	(—)	15	15	(—)	6	(—)	8	1	6	4	(—)	67
10	L. Matousek (CS)	Lada 1600 VFTS	B	8	(—)	10	(—)	10	8	8	(—)	10	(—)	4	—	58
11	P. Takacs (H)	BMW M3	N	4	(—)	3	12	8	(1)	15	1	(—)	1	(—)	—	44
12	G. Borzek (D)	BMW M3	N	(—)	(—)	—	—	12	2	(—)	3	(0)	2	2	12	33
13	P. Dvorak (CS)	Lada 1600 VFTS	B	(—)	(—)	—	—	8	4	(—)	(—)	8	6	3	—	29
14	G. Poelzl (A)	Peugeot 205 GTi	A	2	(—)	6	12	1	(—)	(—)	(—)	0	0	—	4	25
15	H.-D. Meckel (D)	BMW M3	N	(—)	(—)	—	—	3	4	(—)	4	(0)	3	1	10	25
16	J. Wenc (CS)	Toyota Corolla	A	(—)	(—)	8	—	4	6	(0)	(0)	0	0	0	6	24
17	V. Liedl (CS)	Lada 1600 VFTS	B	(—)	(—)	6	—	—	—	3	(—)	4	8	0	(—)	21
18	R. di Giuseppe (I)	Lancia Delta 4WD	A	(—)	(—)	0	6	0	3	4	0	(—)	—	0	0	13
19	J. Klink (H)	Toyota Corolla	A	1	(—)	3	2	2	(—)	(—)	(—)	—	0	0	—	8
20	O. Kramsky (CS)	Skoda Favorit	A	0	(—)	(—)	4	—	0	1	0	(—)	(—)	0	0	5
21	S. Matejowsky (CS)	Suzuki SWift GTi	N	(0)	(—)	0	3	0	0	0	0	(—)	0	(—)	0	3

FINAL CLASSIFICATION Cat. II (Racing cars)				Rechberg (A)	Rampa da Falperra (P)	Ecce Homo (CS)	Mecsek Pannon (H)	Trier (D)	Coppa Caritti, Rieti (I)	Coppa Citta di Potenza (I)	Cesana-Sestriere (I)	Le Mont Dore (F)	St. Ursanne-Les Rangiers (CH)	Turck-heim-Trois Epis (F)	Subida El Fito (E)	Total
1	A. Vilarino (E)***	Lola T298	C	20	(10)	20	20	20	(—)	(—)	20	15	20	(—)	—	135
2	H. Stenger (D)	Stenger Sachs C3	C	15	(—)	15	12	(—)	—	15	10	10	(—)	15	(—)	92
3	P. Darbellay (CH)	Lucchini S289	C	(—)	(—)	—	—	—	10	(10)	12	(0)	15	10	15	62
4	W. Pedrazza (A)	PRC M89	C	(—)	(—)	—	15	15	(—)	(—)	—	—	12	12	—	54
5	J. Regosa (I)	Osella PA/90	C	(—)	(—)	—	—	—	15	(4)	(0)	8	8	8	12	51
6	R. Faustmann (D)	PRC BMW M88	C	12	(—)	12	(—)	—	—	(—)	(—)	1	6	4	—	35
7	J. Toth (H)	Osella	C	(—)	(—)	10	10	1	—	(—)	0	(—)	4	0	8	33
8	L. Bormolini (I)	Osella PA9	C	4	(—)	8	8	3	(—)	(—)	0	0	3	(—)	—	26
9	H. Steiner (CH)	Lola T298 BMW	C	(—)	(—)	—	—	10	—	(—)	2	(—)	10	3	—	25
10	H. Waldy (A)	Tiga FZR 2000	C	10	(—)	(—)	6	0	—	(—)	0	(—)	—	—	—	16
11	C. Brauer (D)	Lola T296	C	6	(—)	(—)	—	0	—	(—)	(—)	0	1	0	—	7
12	R. Köppel (D)	PRC 287 BMW	C	(—)	(—)	—	—	0	—	(—)	(—)	0	2	0	—	2

* European Hill Climb Champion, Production Cars   ** Winner of FIA Hill Climb Trophy   *** European Hill Climb Champion, Racing Cars

EUROPEAN CHAMPIONSHIP FOR RALLYCROSS DRIVERS

Division 1 — Touring (Group A) cars, restricted to 2WD			A	S	SF	IRL	F	B	NL	N	D	GB	Total
1	K. Hansen (S)	Ford Sierra RS 500 Cosworth	13	(7)	20	20	(11)	(11)	20	20	13	15	121
2	B. Skogstad (N)	Ford Sierra RS 500 Cosworth	15	13	15	(13)	20	20	(12)	17	(11)	17	117
3	B. Ekström (S)	BMW M3	20	17	(1)	12	12	15	15	(11)	20	(9)	111
4	S. Jöranli (N)	Opel Kadett GSi 16V	17	20	12	10	(6)	13	(10)	(6)	15	13	100
	E. Opland (N)	Ford Sierra RS 500 Cosworth	11	15	13	0	(10)	0	11	13	17	20	100
5	L. Hunsbedt (N)	BMW M3	—	9	11	—	9	(8)	17	15	12	12	85
6	M. Simonen (SF)	Ford Sierra RS 500 Cosworth	(1)	(4)	9	17	15	7	7	10	10	—	75
7	K. Vereeken (B)	Saab 900 Turbo 16/ Ford Sierra RS 500 Cosworth	12	—	—	—	0	10	8	—	4	8	42
8	E. Haberl (A)	VW Golf GTi 16V	10	12	0	7	0	—	—	3	5	4	41
9	T. Reeves (GB)	Ford Sierra RS 500 Cosworth	—	—	—	15	—	—	13	—	—	11	39
10	T. E. Aaserud (N)	Ford Sierra RS 500 Cosworth	—	3	6	11	—	—	—	12	6	—	38
11	K.-M. Männikkö (SF)	Ford Sierra RS 500 Cosworth	2	0	10	—	—	17	6	2	—	—	37

Division 2 — Touring (Group A) or Sports (Group B) cars			A	S	SF	IRL	F	B	NL	N	D	GB	Total
1	M. Alamäki (SF)	Peugeot 205 Turbo 16 E2	15	20	20	20	20	17	(11)	20	—	—	132
2	M. Schanche (N)	Ford RS 200 E2	(11)	13	17	15	(11)	20	20	(6)	20	20	125
3	W. Gollop (GB)	ARG MG Metro 6R4 BiTurbo	13	(1)	0	12	13	15	17	13	(12)	17	100
4	T. Schie (N)	Peugeot 205 Turbo 16 E2	(9)	15	11	(11)	15	13	13	12	(11)	12	91
5	H. Breiteneder (A)	Audi Sport Quattro S1	20	10	12	17	(7)	0	—	10	8	8	85
	P. Rantanen (SF)	Ford RS 200 E2	12	0	(7)	9	(6)	12	15	11	13	13	85
6	K. Bolsenet (N)	Ford Escort XR3 Turbo 4x4	8	17	15	0	D	10	12	(5)	15	7	84
7	T. Holm (N)	Ford RS 200 E2	3	8	6	13	0	6	(1)	17	17	0	70
8	T. Kritoffersson (S)	Audi Quattro	—	7	13	8	—	11	9	4	10	—	62
9	P. Silvennoinen (SF)	ARG MG Metro 6R4	7	0	9	—	12	9	5	0	9	10	61
10	S. Palmer (GB)	ARG MG Metro 6R4	17	12	10	0	—	—	—	—	—	15	54
11	"J. Kovanen" (SF)	ARG MG Metro 6R4 BiTurbo	—	6	8	—	9	8	10	8	—	—	49

D = Disqualified.

Photolithography by Litho Service di Zamboni Tiziano & C. S.a.S., Verona
Typesetting by TransfoTexte S.A., Lausanne
Printed and bound by Grafiche Editoriali Ambrosiane S.p.A., Milano
Printed in Italy